May St. Edith
share her love
of the Cross
with you,

Sr. Josephine Koeppel,
OCD
2/25/03

The Collected Works of Edith Stein

VI

The Collected Works of Edith Stein

Saint Teresa Benedicta of the Cross
Discalced Carmelite
1891-1942

Edited by
Dr. L. Gelber
and
Romaeus Leuven, O.C.D.

VOLUME SIX

ICS Publications
Institute of Carmelite Studies
Washington, D.C.
2002

EDITH STEIN

Saint Teresa Benedicta of the Cross
Discalced Carmelite

THE SCIENCE
OF THE CROSS

Translated by Josephine Koeppel, O.C.D.

ICS Publications
Institute of Carmelite Studies
Washington, D.C.
2002

The original of this work was published in German
by the Archivum Carmelitanum Edith Stein
under the title
Kreuzeswissenschaft, Studie über Joannes a Cruce
Band I of *Edith Steins Werke* Verlag Herder, Freiburg, Basel,
Vienna, 1983.
Translation authorized.
© Verlag Herder, Freiburg-im-Breisgau 1983.
English translation copyright
© Washington Province of Discalced Carmelites, Inc. 2003

Cover design by Rosemary Moak, O.C.D.S.
Typesetting by Stephen Tiano Page Design & Production

Library of Congress Cataloging-in-Publication Data

Stein, Edith, Saint, 1891-1942.
   [Kreuzeswissenschaft. English]
   The science of the Cross / Edith Stein (Saint Teresa Benedicta of the
Cross) ; translated by Josephine Koeppel.
      p. cm. -- (The collected works of Edith Stein ; v. 6)
   Includes bibliographical references (p.   ) and index.
   ISBN 0-935216-31-6
   1. John of the Cross, Saint, 1542-1591. I. Koeppel, Josephine. II.
Title.
   BX4700.J7 S7513 2002
   271'.7302--dc21
                                        2002007809

CONTENTS

Translator's Note vii
I.C.S. Introduction xi

THE SCIENCE OF THE CROSS

Dedication 3
Preface 5
Outline 7
Introduction 9

Chapter

1.	The Message of the Cross	15
2.	The Cross and the Night	35
3.	Taking Up One's Cross..	43
4.	Spirit and Faith..	57
5.	The Inadequacy of Knowledge	65
6.	Purgation through Hope	81
7.	Purgation through Love	89
8.	Virtues, Gifts, and Graces	99
9.	The Activity of Spirit	111
10.	Dark Contemplation	121
11.	Enkindling of Love	133
12.	The Secret Ladder	141
13.	Created Spirits...	153
14.	The Kinds of Divine Union	167
15.	Death and Resurrection	181

16.   The Triune One 195
17.   Rays of Divine Glory 203
18.   The Hidden Life of Love 213
19.   The Bridal Song 221
20.   The Bridal Symbol 245
21.   The Bridal Symbol and the Cross 259
22.   In the Image of Christ Crucified 275
23.   Spiritual Renunciation 291
24.   Conflicts Within the Order and
       Final Days 303
       Notes 315
       Bibliography 345
       Index 349

TRANSLATOR'S NOTE

The great Spanish mystic, John of the Cross, was formerly little known in Germany and German-speaking countries, and Sr. Teresa Benedicta, the Carmelite whom we also remember as Edith Stein the philosopher, wished to make her sisters better acquainted with him and his mystical writings. An excellent opportunity arose on the occasion of the celebration of the fourth centenary of St. John of the Cross's birth in 1542. Edith was asked to write a kind of *Festschrift* for the "father" of Carmel, and so *Science of the Cross—Kreuzeswissenschaft*—came into existence.

In one letter, to prepare for her task, she asked for the French biography of St. John of the Cross by Père Bruno de Jésus-Marie. It coincidentally carried a long introduction by Jacques Maritain who with his wife, Raissa, had welcomed Edith to their home in Meudon, France, September 12, 1932, on the occasion of a symposium on phenomenology and Thomism. This biography was translated into English by Fr. Benedict Zimmerman, O.C.D., of Kensington, England. I have used his translation for quotations from this work and identified them as "Bruno *St. John.*" However, this English translation (New York: Sheed and Ward, 1932) seems somewhat abridged and therefore in a number of the notes referring to Fr. Bruno's work, I have given the page numbers from the French edition and referred to it as "Bruno *St. Jean.*"

A bibliography was provided in the original *Kreuzeswissenschaft* prepared by the editors, Fr. Romaeus Leuven, O.C.D., and Dr. Lucie Gelber. The footnote to this bibliography states that it "includes all the works that Edith Stein in the course of her presentation either quotes or refers to." The Spanish works of St. John of the Cross edited by Padre Silverio, O.C.D., and another set edited by Padre Gerardo are listed. There is no mention of a German edition of St. John's works, and in this English translation I began with the assumption that the quotations from St. John were the work of Sr. Teresa Benedicta. To insure that I would not run into problems for which there were no solutions, Sr. Christina Middendorf, during my stay in the Carmel of Cologne in 1994-95, devoted many hours of her time to go over the volume sentence by sentence to clarify any doubtful passages. After about fifty pages were cleared, I remarked what a tremendous help it would be if I could double check our work with a German translation of the works of St. John and I inquired whether, as I expected, in the intervening years since Edith wrote her book, St. John's writings had been translated into German. A trip to the community library resulted in a surprising find. There was a set of five volumes of St. John of the Cross in German: the *Ascent* translated by Ambrose of St. Teresa, O.C.D., and the other four volumes translated by Aloysius of the Immaculate Conception, O.C.D. (Munich: Theatiner Verlag, 1924-29). It then became clear that Edith did not translate St. John from the Spanish because her quotations were taken from these volumes. At times, though, it was evident that she used the Spanish critical edition of Padre Gerardo to clarify some point for herself.

Another discovery was of interest. Edith was a most meticulous worker. Her paper was all of one size even when she used the blank reverse of a business letter or of a typescript of some other of her writings. Cut to uniform size, the sheets all had an inch or so at the margin, folded and creased. Opened up then, this inch served as space for Edith's notes, which gave the location of quotations from St. John. For the first thirty or forty pages of the manuscript these references were given to the German translations. Then without any explanation Edith switched to give the locations as they were to be found in Gerardo's Spanish volumes.

In the few cases where the German translation differed significantly from the English, I translated from the German and gave a reference to where the text could be found in the English translation mentioned in the notes. I have translated Edith's German versions of the Spanish poetry into English, and one can find interesting variations when comparing them with other English translations.

Edith's notes are given without identification, but to distinguish my notes from hers, I placed mine in brackets and did the same for those few notes that were made by the German editors, which I identified.

Early in 1995, a good number of the original manuscripts of Edith's writings were brought from the Netherlands to the Carmel in Cologne, and it was a grace and wonderful experience to look up some puzzling phrases in the original and so to hold in one's hands the writings of the saint. This resulted in a number of notes to explain significant differences between Edith's original manuscript and the printed version in the 1953 Archivum Carmelitanum edition. A new definitive series of St. Edith's writings is currently being published in German, and the new edition of *Kreuzeswissenschaft* will have removed most of the errors to be found in the editions published so far. The edition used for this translation was printed in Holland in 1983. It has seemed important to include in this translation notes regarding both typographical errors and misread passages because there may be students of Edith's thought who will continue to use these earlier versions of her works and not be aware of mistakes inadvertently made by a stenographer or a typesetter.

On returning to my own Carmel in 1995, I transcribed, for the most part, Edith's references to St. John's works as found in Gerardo's critical edition into a simple statement of the book or poem, chapter or stanza, and paragraph number. The list of quotations showed that Edith included every one of St. John's works in her commentary.

One bit of tedious effort remained to insure that no sentence had been inadvertently skipped over in the translation process. Kathleen Sullivan painstakingly compared the texts and found indeed that in three or four places a sentence had eluded me. Without her help I could not be as confident as I wanted to be that Edith's work was presented with the greatest possible accuracy.

A final word of deepest thanks goes to those who were my superiors over the years and to the sisters in my own Carmel for allowing me the time and giving me their support and encouragement especially when there was a dip in my energy level!

It has given me a world of satisfaction as I conclude this note to reflect that others occupied with Edith's writings see what I have been convinced of from the start. *Science of the Cross* is not an unfinished book. Perhaps Edith had some editing to add, but the essentials are all there and will reward, enrich, and delight the reader.

St. Edith reveals her spiritual greatness in this last work of hers. No wonder she could write to her prioress from the transfer camp: "So far, I have been able to pray *gloriously*." She had prayed this whole book and it was a tremendous preparation for her own way of the cross, on which she was accompanied by her sister Rosa.

Sr. Josephine Koeppel, O.C.D.
February 2, 2002
80th Anniversary of Edith's Confirmation
Carmelite Monastery, Elysburg, PA

I.C.S. INTRODUCTION

Hardly is there a need to mention this, but Edith Stein was a woman of brilliant intelligence, the first in her class as a general rule. According to one of her childhood teachers a large gap was invariably left between herself and anyone who followed next. When she arrived at the University of Göttingen, the eminent philosopher Husserl was so astonished to learn that she had accomplished the heroic feat of reading the second volume of his *Logische Untersuchungen* that he accepted her unhesitatingly into his seminar. How, then, could someone with such recognized brilliance decide to write a book called *The Science of the Cross*? Interest in the cross is not usually associated with dazzling intellectuals.

A LOVE FOR LEARNING

Edith Stein was born into a German Jewish family on 12 October 1891. Only two years later her father died, and her mother, Auguste Courant Stein, was left with the task of caring for the seven surviving children, another four having died in their infancy. Auguste took over the management of her husband's lumber business and succeeded through hard work and skill to provide the family with a certain prosperity that allowed Edith to devote her time to studies. A woman of strong faith, Auguste witnessed to her children an enduring attachment to the faith and traditions of Israel.

As a precocious child Edith continued through her early years to find herself in her element when in the midst of studies, feeling drawn particularly to literature and languages. Her love for poetry coupled with her exceptional memory prompted her to learn by heart much from the works of the great poets.

At the University of Breslau, when she was twenty years old, she had an opportunity to study philosophy, a subject that attracted very few women in those years, but which for Edith was an alluring discovery. It took scarcely two years for her to learn that a professor at the University of Göttingen named Edmund Husserl was teaching a new discipline called phenomenology. Edith considered attending his lectures for one semester, but at once recognized that she could devote a lifetime to the study of phenomenology and arranged to attend the university in Göttingen full time. Her fellow students were from all over Germany, and there were brilliant minds among them. She attended lectures by Adolph Reinach and Max Scheler, who was at the time fascinated by the Catholic faith. When Husserl received a professorship in Freiburg, he left Göttingen. Edith followed him there and in August 1916 received her doctorate under him *summa cum laude.*

Among Husserl's students just prior to Edith's time were the well known philosophers Hedwig Conrad Martius and Martin Heidegger. Although Protestant, the former became Edith's baptismal sponsor and life-long friend. Edith may have met Martin Heidegger for the first time at some of the celebrations after receiving her doctorate.

When Husserl let it be known that he needed an assistant, Edith applied and Husserl accepted her offer at once. It is to her credit that students of phenomenology can trace the development of Husserl's thought. Later, Heidegger himself did not hesitate to make use of her scholarly work on Husserl's manuscripts, but when he saw the work "Ideas" into print, he failed to give credit in any way to the massive contribution she made toward it when she transcribed thousands of Husserl's shorthand notes and arranged them into paragraphs and chapters.

Still, it seemed that her future was marked out for her, a distinguished figure in the world of German philosophy. Moreover, in the university setting and even before this, she was a formidable defender of the rights of women, with the role of women in society becoming one of her preferred subjects for reflection.

CONTACT WITH RELIGION

As a member of an ethnic and religious minority and without support in the society around her, it would have been difficult for her to practice her religion. But since she never really learned much about it in her childhood, one is not surprised that by the time she was fifteen she gave up all thought of affiliation and felt it would have been pretense to continue to pray. Her account of her attitude and convictions of the time sound very much like a typical religious crisis. At the university, however, she came into contact with religion — "a new world for me," she called it. Yet, it was not a theoretical exposition of faith that moved her to investigate further; it was her experience of the vital difference faith made in the lives of persons she liked and admired.

Adolph and Anne Reinach were especially influential. Edith found in Adolph more than a teacher; he was a model and guide. When he was killed in World War I, the news struck a devastating blow to his students. But his testimony to the strength he found in faith and his widow's subsequent demonstration of the stamina to be gained from belief in an eventual reunion with one's loved ones were decisive in showing Edith the role of faith in life. She said it was her first encounter with the cross and the first proof of its effectiveness in the life of a believer. Edith and the other students at Göttingen, then, came face to face with religion not merely as a phenomenon but also as a vital experience of some of their teachers.

Never a mere abstract intellectual, Edith was sensitive to friendship. Her letters show her as someone capable of deep, warm, and stable relationships with others. In her academic life there were the great intellectual joys under the guidance of Husserl; there were as well the many, quiet joys with her companions. But it was not the learned university world alone that brought her attention to religion. Once while Edith was visiting the cathedral of Frankfurt, a woman with a market basket entered and knelt down in one of the pews to pray briefly. This was something entirely new to her, leaving as deep an impression as the university lectures.

Philosophy, which she lived as an honest and sincere search for truth at every cost, prepared Edith for the gospel. In a letter written after Husserl's death she asserted: "All who seek truth seek God, whether this is clear to them or not" (Ltr. 259).[1] For her the pursuit of philosophy within the Husserl circle was not a game, or a going deeper into some purely theoretical knowledge. It was an existential search.

A typical aspect of phenomenology is *epoché*, the suspension of judgment, with which the phenomenologist proposes to analyze any reality that presents itself to consciousness. Europe had been experiencing a deep secularization, taking a polemical stance toward Christianity and particularly Catholicism, creating in the air a radical suspicion of religion. The new attitude of *epoché* assisted Edith in becoming totally open to religion, to Christian and even Catholic phenomena.

ILLUMINED BY FAITH

Who can resist asking how well the suspension of judgment was being practiced when Edith Stein's applications for a professorship were fruitless everywhere (Freiburg, Göttingen, Kiel, Breslau) because she was a woman? The thesis she prepared in order to qualify was not even read by at least one committee that reviewed all applications. Discrimination against women was a painful cross, one of the many that were a part of Edith's life. Yes, we can say a cross, if we accept her incisive insight that those who suffer unjustly are bearing the cross even though they may not be aware of it.

In 1921 while visiting in the summertime the home of the couple Hedwig Martius and Hans Theodore Conrad, Edith was invited to choose a book from their library to read while the two needed to be absent for a day or so. Picking up a book at random, Edith began to read. It was St. Teresa of Avila's *The Book of Her life*. Edith was so taken by this Spanish marvel of God's grace that she read through the book, it seems, without a break. On closing the volume, she had to confess to herself: "This is the truth." The following morning she bought a Catholic catechism and a missal. A short time later, on New Year's Day, 1922, she was baptized, entering a new world, in which from then on she would live entirely by faith, her conversion being the crowning point of her dedication to the pursuit of truth. What the brilliant discourses of Max Scheler on the nature of holiness were unable to accomplish, the direct, lived testimony of the full-spirited Teresa of Avila did. In the eyes of Edith, however, her conversion was not the mere natural outcome of philosophical work but the effect of a disrupting initiative taken on the part of God. In *The Science of the Cross*, Edith speaks of how God can insert his powerful hand in the destiny of souls and bring about a sanctifying rebirth under his action. She experienced her conversion as a miraculous invasion of grace, a great grace from the divine mercy. From that time on, "living at God's hand" was her only concern.

Once converted and baptized, Edith sought from the beginning a relationship with God that would bring unity into her whole life. She came to the illuminating insight that "it is possible to worship God by doing scholarly research," seeking the truth being already a kind of prayer (Ltr. 45). At first, after her conversion she thought she would have to renounce all that was secular and live totally immersed in God, but then she realized that, even in the contemplative life, you cannot sever all connection with the world, that the deeper you are drawn into God, the more you must go out of yourself to the world in order to carry the divine life into it. Thus, she spent the years before her entrance into Carmel doing teaching, writing, translating, and lecturing. Her lectures sometimes drew standing-room-only crowds, but she thought of herself merely as a tool of the Lord to whom she must lead anyone coming to her (Ltr. 76).

NO PLACE FOR A WOMAN OR A NON-ARYAN

For eight busy years Edith lived and trained young women at a teachers' college directed by Dominican nuns in Speyer. By the time she gave up that work because as she said "St. Thomas is demanding all my time" (she was translating Aquinas' *Disputed Questions* from Latin into German), she was already aware of a darkening horizon, Hitler's growing power and the ever increasing signs of the persecution of

Jews. Edith tried again for a professorship at Breslau but was not even considered because she was a woman.

When she had to admit that a career in philosophy would never become an actuality, she accepted a position to lecture at the Catholic Pedagogical Institute of Münster and began this new phase in her life on 29 February 1932. Here, she was handicapped for she had never studied the basics of pedagogy and found that "one can never catch up" if a foundation is not laid first. But she consoled herself that she was able to put stimulating questions to her colleagues at the institute when they worked together to develop an outline for Catholic education of women.

During all these months, Hitler's political career was developing and the cruel laws of his Nazi party were bent on taking away all rights from non-Aryans. Non-Aryans were excluded from public employment and had to leave all professional occupations.

Edith's services at the institute were terminated on 19 April 1933, and she was once more seemingly at an impasse. On 30 April of that year, Good Shepherd Sunday, after prolonged prayer before the Blessed Sacrament during Exposition in the Church of St. Ludger, Edith begged for assurance that her intention to enter Carmel was the will of God. She said that when the final benediction was given at the close of the day, she received "the yes of the Good Shepherd." She then obtained her spiritual director's permission to seek entry into Carmel and through a mutual friend contacted the nuns in the Carmel of Cologne.

At the same time she was increasingly aware of the oppression by Hitler's party and agonized at the way her family was affected. "Every letter from home contains more bad news" (Ltr. 139). The distress caused by her family's sufferings became and continued to be a much heavier cross for her than any of her own. At this time she heard that American newspapers were accusing Hitler of taking atrocious steps against Jews, and from that moment there was no longer any doubt in her mind about her own destiny, that it would be the same as that of God's people.

While attending a Holy Hour in the chapel of the Carmel of Cologne on the Thursday evening before Friday of Passion week that year, she was moved deeply to speak to the Lord. She told him that she knew "it was his cross that was now being laid on the Jewish people. Most of them did not understand it; but those who did understand must accept it willingly in the name of all. I wanted to do that, let him only show me how. When the service was over I had an interior conviction that I had been heard. But in what the bearing of the cross was to consist I did not yet know."[2] When her lecturing activity had been terminated, she wrote, "do not be sad about that. Something much more beautiful will be replacing it" (Ltr. 144).

IN THE CARMEL OF COLOGNE

Not surprisingly for those who knew her, Edith, on 14 October 1933, entered the Carmel of Cologne, satisfying a desire she had harbored in her heart ever since reading St. Teresa of Avila's *Life*. Now Edith could live the contemplative life in the style established by this great Spanish *madre* and writer whom she so admired and who would much later, in 1970, be proclaimed the first woman Doctor of the Church. During Edith's retreat in preparation for receiving the habit and becoming a novice, she meditated on St. John of the Cross's *Dark Night*. Along with her habit, she also received her new name in religion, Sr. Teresa Benedicta of the Cross, though the sisters in ordinary exchange usually referred to her simply as Sr. Benedicta. In preparation for her profession on Easter, 21 April 1935, she meditated once more on St. John of the Cross's *Dark Night*.

A year later on the day of the Triumph of the Cross when as was customary the entire community renewed their vows, Edith's mother, Auguste Courant Stein, died. She had never understood Edith's conversion and still less her vocation to the enclosed life of a nun. These decisions of Edith's pained her deeply, and it pained Edith deeply as well to witness her mother's grief over the matter. Shortly following her mother's death, Edith wrote: "My mother held to her faith to the very last. The faith and firm confidence she had in her God from her earliest childhood until her 87th year remained steadfast, and were the last things that stayed alive in her during the final difficult agony.

Therefore I have the firm belief that she found a merciful judge and is now my most faithful helper on my way, so that I, too, may reach my goal" (Ltr. 227).

On 24 December 1936, Edith's sister Rosa, who not wanting to add to her mother's pain had deferred her desire to become a Catholic, felt the time had come finally. Rosa came to Cologne just when it seemed most inopportune. Edith, in a fall the evening of 23 December, had broken her left foot and left hand and was being kept for observation in the hospital. Then, to everyone's relief, it was realized that now the Stein sisters were able to spend hours together without having a grille or grate between them. The time was used to prepare Rosa for baptism and as the church in Hohenlind was close to the hospital and the Carmel, it was possible for Edith on her way back to Carmel, to be present at Rosa's reception of the sacrament of baptism.

Two years later, Edith made her final profession on the Thursday of Easter week, so during her preparation retreat she had days for remembering the cross before passing on to partake in the joy of the resurrection. On 1 May 1938, she received the black veil of a Discalced Carmelite nun in exchange for the white veil worn since her days as a novice. This marked her promotion from the novitiate into the chapter, giving her a voice in the community's meetings.

The Nazi persecution of Jews, which continued mercilessly, made Sr. Benedicta anxious lest her presence in the community at Cologne bring a reprisal on her dearly loved sisters. The community thought the Carmel in Echt, Holland, which they had founded, would provide a safe haven for her. On the evening of 31 December 1938, Sister Teresa Benedicta of the Cross was driven discreetly across the border into Holland, and arrived at the Carmel in Echt at 8 P.M. on New Year's Eve.

LIVING THE MYSTERY OF THE CROSS

Soon after her entry into the novitiate, Edith's superiors had asked her to resume her writing and intellectual work, even though on entering she thought she would be renouncing all intellectual work. In fact when questioned about this, she answered that it was not human activity that could save us but only the Passion of Christ and that her aspiration was to participate in it. Nonetheless, soon after her entrance her superiors asked her to continue her intellectual work, now amid the contemplative quiet of Carmel.

In reading St. Teresa of Avila's *Life*, Edith came into the presence of Jesus Christ and as a result into the presence of the cross, the symbol of universal love. In converting to Christ, she placed herself in the shadow of the cross, and began to look upon it in a new light, the light of faith. She could then see the pains she had suffered in her life through discrimination against women as a share in the cross of Christ, and when the Third Reich began its attack on Jews and she and her family were deprived of their careers, she understood again that it was the cross of Christ and that she was being called to carry it knowingly and as a willing offering in the name of all the oppressed people of Israel.

On receiving in Carmel her new name, Teresa Benedicta of the Cross, she wrote: "I must tell you that I already brought my religious name with me into the house as a postulant. I received it exactly as I requested it. By the cross I understood the destiny of God's people which, even at that time, began to announce itself. I thought that those who recognized it as the cross of Christ had to take it upon themselves in the name of all. Certainly, today I know more of what it means to be wedded to the Lord in the sign of the cross. Of course, one can never comprehend it, for it is a mystery"(Ltr. 287).

Eventually Rosa Stein succeeded in reaching Echt, in the summer of 1940, and was made welcome at the Carmel where she lived and helped in the quarters outside the enclosure. But also in 1940 the Nazi occupation forces took over Holland. Once more, the Stein sisters were in danger. The Nazi invasion of Holland was a calamity for the Dutch, but doubly so for the Jews who had managed to find shelter there after leaving Germany. The cross once again weighed down heavily as regulations designed to harass those of Jewish birth were multiplied, and with measures to humiliate and demoralize the Germans of Jewish background who had found refuge in the Netherlands. Another search for refuge for the two Stein sisters had to begin, this time a more tedious one.

The Carmelite nuns wrote to the French-speaking Carmel of Le Pâquier in Switzerland. A separate place was sought for Rosa with a religious congregation not far from Le Pâquier. But the correspondence was slow moving. The official papers that had to be obtained in Holland, Switzerland, and Rome were so numerous that the permissions were never obtained in time. But it must be noted that had all the papers been at hand the Stein sisters would not have been permitted to leave the Netherlands, for the Nazis were determined to let no one avoid the "final solution" that was their plan. Not only was Edith worried about her sister Rosa but about the whole community in Echt. She feared that by harboring her and Rosa, all her Carmelite sisters were in a dangerous position.

In the Carmel of Echt, as in Cologne, the superiors, well aware of Sr. Benedicta's intellectual gifts and background, set her tasks that, it was hoped, might help take her mind from the threatening situation for which there seemed no remedy. And it must be added that Edith's writings in Echt are as careful, as intense, and as scholarly as anything she wrote in Germany.

A TASK TO HONOR ST. JOHN OF THE CROSS

Early in 1941, the prioress relieved Sister Benedicta of her office as turn-sister so that she might have more time free for her studies in spirituality. The fourth centenary of the birth (1542) of St. John of the Cross was approaching, and Sr. Benedicta was assigned to contribute to the literary part of the celebration.

When Edith Stein may have first read St. John of the Cross, we don't know for certain. By taking the title "of the Cross," Sr. Benedicta considered she was sharing with him a special vocation to live the mystery of the cross. The holy card to commemorate her profession carried a quotation from St. John of the Cross's *Ascent of Mt Carmel*: "To arrive at being all, desire to be nothing," and on her holy card for her final profession, she chose words from stanza 28 of the *Spiritual Canticle*: "One thing alone I do, and that is love."

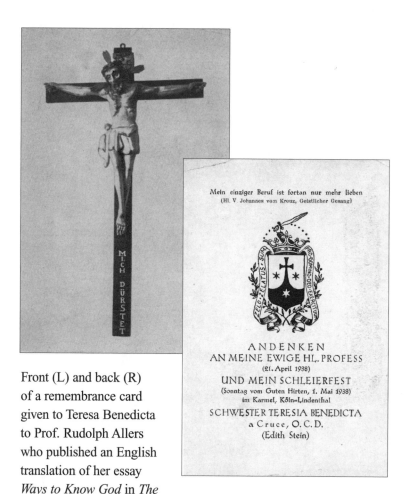

Mein einziger Beruf ist fortan nur mehr lieben
(Hl. V. Johannes vom Kreuz, Geistlicher Gesang)

ANDENKEN
AN MEINE EWIGE HL. PROFESS
(21. April 1938)
UND MEIN SCHLEIERFEST
(Sonntag vom Guten Hirten, 1. Mai 1938)
im Karmel, Köln=Lindenthal
SCHWESTER TERESIA BENEDICTA
a Cruce, O. C. D.
(Edith Stein)

Front (L) and back (R) of a remembrance card given to Teresa Benedicta to Prof. Rudolph Allers who published an English translation of her essay *Ways to Know God* in *The Thomist* (Washington, DC). Cards already bearing the cross image were purchased then printed with information about her profession of perpetual vows 21 April 1938. At the bottom of the cross the German words are those of John's Gospel (19:28) "I thirst": atop the shield of Carmel are the words "From now on my only calling is to love more" (see the *Spiritual Canticle*, st. 28, on page 227).

In answer to some questions by Sr. Agnella Stadmüller, Edith gives a remarkable little summary of St. John of the Cross's teaching, in the space of only several paragraphs, demonstrating the firm and penetrating hold she had on the material [cf. Letr. 311].

For the feast of St. John of the Cross, probably around 1934, she wrote a small essay on the mystery of suffering and the cross, showing once more as a follower of Christ the conformity of her life and thinking with the life and thinking of John the Cross.[3]

The first task confronting Edith after being asked to prepare a study for the centenary celebration was to gather more information about the life and writings of St. John of the Cross. John's doctrine itself had long been at work in her heart. From her correspondence it appears she was at this preparatory work as far back as 7 November 1940: "Just now I am gathering material for a new work, since our Reverend Mother wishes me to do some scholarly work again, as far as this will be possible in our living situation and under the present circumstances. I am very grateful to be allowed once more to do something before my brain rusts completely" (Ltr. 316).

SOURCES

What were the materials she was gathering? First, she needed a good biography of St. John of the Cross. A giant step forward in this regard was made with the critical study *Saint Jean de La Croix* by Père Bruno de Jésus-Marie (Paris, 1929), with a preface by Jacques Maritain, whom Edith knew personally. Bruno de Jésus-Marie (1892-1962), a specialist in history and psychology, directed the review "Etudes Carmélitaines" until his death, converting it into a prestigious scholarly review of religious psychology. His biography of John of the Cross was well received as a work of genuine historical scholarship, and still so popular after thirty years that a new edition was published in 1961. In this new edition some fruits of further research were taken into consideration and incorporated into the text. When Edith finally received a copy of Bruno's "big book," she was very happy as she states in a letter of 11 November 1941 (Ltr. 327).

Interest in John of the Cross as mystic and poet was growing, his personality only gradually coming into the light. He was first viewed as an ascetic, an austere and emaciated man, friend of the cross and author of the *Dark Night*. Sources, it must be remembered, were influenced by testimony given in canonization processes, thus by what was often thought at the time needed to be emphasized in the making of a saint: physical austerities, miracles, and ecstasies.

In the twentieth century John was looked on more and more as a theologian, thinker, and Doctor of the church. The image of him today is much richer, more harmonious, and illuminating, with a larger store of perspectives. Although he was sober, he was very much alive and in all his being and work, he breathed the air of a free energetic man. If his life was one of detachment, it was because things were not a hindrance to his following of Christ. Kindhearted and understanding, it pained him to see others fall into sadness, and joy was an ever-present facet of his behavior and leadership style. Actually, his own secretary thought he was too simple and kindhearted. Nonetheless, in the four monasteries he governed he had to build and do fund-raising and deal with the thousand concerns and problems such works carry in their train. His being a contemplative and mystic did not hold him back from the difficult travel of close to 17,000 miles along the rough, dusty roads of Spain for the sake of government or to give spiritual help. But always within him was the soul of an artist, a love of beauty, of nature, music, color, and poetry.[4]

Yet throughout his life the cross was there, and this is the view that Edith wished to portray: John bearing the cross as a true follower of Christ. Certainly and especially as a phenomenologist, she would have deeply appreciated the whole picture of his multifaceted personality more clearly presented in recent scholarship.

The work by Jean Baruzi (1881-1953) had arrived a few weeks before the biography by Bruno. In a letter written on 13 October 1941, Sr. Benedicta asserts: "I well know that Baruzi is an unbelieving author, but I believe one cannot easily do without him if one wishes to write about Holy Father" (Ltr. 324). In 1924 Baruzi published his dissertation defended at the Sorbonne which very quickly gave rise to decided opposition by noted Catholic intellectuals. In the scuffle, perhaps, it was not made clear what a gigantic step forward Baruzi had taken in regard to the treasures that lay hidden in the life and teaching of a Catholic saint, still very much ignored within the Catholic church. Despite his astonishing erudition, Baruzi only consulted ms. 12.738 in the Biblioteca Nacional de Madrid. Edith herself remarked: "Baruzi has astonishing gaps and needs to be supplemented. For instance, he is completely silent about the apparitions of the Mother of God" (Ltr. 327). Today scholars acknowledge Baruzi's brilliance and see him as a pioneer in the study of St. John of the Cross. Along with Edith Stein they acknowledge "that one cannot easily do without him (Ltr. 324)" in sanjuanist studies. And in a letter written several days later she gives this judgment of the Baruzi book: "It was produced with the greatest devotion, and as a serious study it probably cannot be supplanted by anything else" (Ltr. 325).

Emile Poulat in his introduction to the third edition of Baruzi's work, brought out in 1999, remarks that of all the theses published at the Sorbonne, those of Bergson, Blondel, and Baruzi are examples of the few that survive and continue to stir passions, debate, reflection, and research.[5]

Baruzi's point of departure was a question about the contribution that mystical experience brings to a solution of the metaphysical problem of the knowledge of God and relationship to the Absolute. In a letter to a German friend of his who became a Catholic, he wrote: "The demands of my thinking being what they are, I do not see myself as having the right to say I am Catholic, although by this I am not declaring that I am a total stranger to the church." A second revised edition of the book appeared in 1931, which was the edition preferred by Baruzi and used by Edith Stein. Besides complaints about his sources for the biography and his claim that the second redaction of *The Spiritual Canticle* is apocryphal, the most serious criticism is of Baruzi's transcendental Platonism, in which he thinks that in John to an intense love of God, Father, Son, and Holy Spirit, there is joined a pure union with the essential divinity, the 'deity,' or the One, as if the goal were the metaphysical *One*.

Another essential step forward in the early twentieth century was the publication of a critical edition of St. John of the Cross's works by Padre Gerardo de San Juan de la Cruz.[6] The German translation used by Edith was done by Frs. Ambrose and Aloysius, both Discalced Carmelites.

St. John of the Cross's writings were previously available only in a text containing many interpolations and omissions. None of the autographs of his major works have been preserved. After a serious effort to search out the most reliable copies of John's writings, Padre Diego de Jesús Salablanca published the works of St. John of the Cross in Alcalá de Henares in 1618. A noted philosopher and theologian, he was especially talented in sniffing out anything that carried the odor of the Alumbrados. He felt little scrupulosity over fidelity to a text, and with debatable literary taste produced a final text weighed down with glosses, disfigured by omissions, and made ugly by other alterations. Despite its unfaithfulness to the original, this text became the *textus receptus* for the *Ascent, Night, and Flame* until the critical edition of Padre Gerardo.

Gerardo's goal was to publish the works of St. John of the Cross exactly as they came from his pen, so he purged the existing text from every alien change. But he worked in haste and was better suited for searching out important manuscripts and documents than he was for judging their value. In the third volume he published two works that had been attributed to St. John the Cross, even though one of them from a critical point of view, not a historical one, he judged to be inauthentic. The other one, "The Dark Knowledge of God," he thought was probably authentic. Edith from her study rejected the authenticity of both, as do all sanjuanist scholars today. Despite the much-needed improvement, a sound critical edition of John of the Cross's writings was still required; this was prepared by Padre Silverio de Santa Teresa and published twenty years later.[7]

CHOOSING AN APPROACH

In a letter written on 29 October 1939, Edith states that her publisher lost courage over the project to publish her "big opus" (*Finite and*

Eternal Being) (Ltr. 306). At that time then she asked for more work in the house since help was needed. After a couple of years, when she was again freed from such obligations early in 1941 so as to work on her study of St. John of the Cross, she was happy to be in her element once more.

With the passing of time it became increasingly evident that in Holland as in Germany, the Nazis were determined to eliminate the Jews. In the midst of such tragedy and threat to her life and that of others, it was a great relief for Edith to be able to live her life of prayer and worship in greater solitude and in the study of someone like St. John of the Cross. "A *scientia crucis* (science of the cross) can be gained only when one comes to feel the cross radically" (Ltr. 330). On 18 November she writes "I live almost constantly immersed in thoughts about our Holy Father John. That is a great grace." The task was not always easy for her and she asked for "prayers that I can produce something appropriate for his Jubilee" (Ltr. 328). In another letter she mentions how she wanted the book to be finished "this year—for the 400th birthday of our Holy Father [St.] John of the Cross" (Ltr. 334). Two days later, on 9 April 1941, she wrote: "I have to produce everything with a great deal of effort. To be sure, the building plan is another gift bestowed on me, i.e., it unfolds little by little, but I have to quarry the stones by myself, and prepare them and drag them into place. Besides, while working on this task it often happened when I was greatly exhausted that I had the feeling I could not penetrate to what I wished to say and to grasp. I already thought that it would always remain so. But now I feel I have renewed vigor for creative effort. Holy Father John gave me renewed impetus for some remarks concerning symbols"(Ltr. 336).

It comes as no surprise in view of her whole life and her circumstances at the time that Edith would choose the subject of the cross for the topic of her study. She did not set out as others might have suspected to present a general evaluative study of John's doctrine. Nor was it her intention to offer a well-rounded biography of John, an attractive portrait of his multifaceted personality.

A SCIENCE OF THE CROSS

Turning her attention to her Holy Father John of the Cross, Sr. Teresa Benedicta of the Cross saw in his title the essential distinguishing mark of his life: to follow Christ on the way of the cross. But what did Edith mean by speaking of a "science" of the cross? The word "science" changed its meaning with the passage from antiquity and the Middle Ages to modern times. The ancients saw it as the certain intellectual knowledge of something through its causes. Science in this sense referred to a universal, demonstrated, organized knowledge of facts and truths and the reasons or causes of these. Today science means the observational or investigative sciences, sometimes called the empirical and experimental sciences. What then could Edith be thinking of when she uses the term "science of the cross"? She did not see a "science of the cross" as a theory, a structured correlation of propositions about the cross. She has in mind living, real, and effective truth, planted deep like an acorn within a person, taking root and growing. It is effective truth because it influences what one then does or omits, the cross first showing itself in the doing and the omitting. From the interior depths where the truth of the cross makes its impression, one's view of life arises, including an image of God and the world. All of this can be expressed in a mode of thinking, in a theory.

Where through a lively faith the doctrine of faith and the "tremendous deeds" of God are the content of life, a "holy realism," as Edith calls it, exists. Out of this realism comes an openness, in uninhibited simplicity, to the truths of faith, from which springs *the science of the saints*. If the mystery of the cross becomes the *inner form* of this science, a living energy that allows the soul to be molded by what is received from this mystery, it turns into a *science of the cross*. On the contrary, excessive interior preoccupation with one's own personal concerns can develop in the course of life into a general indifference to things religious.

THE CROSS IN JOHN'S LIFE AND WRITINGS

After explaining her understanding of the term science of the cross, it remained for Edith to show how this science took root and grew in

John of the Cross's soul. She needed to grasp John's unity of being, as expressed in his life and works, and the cross was the viewpoint in which she observed this unity. She first takes us through John's life describing how the seed of the cross's message was implanted in him in his childhood and youth. She shows us how he found this message in sacred Scripture, in the sacrifice of the Mass, in his visions of the cross, and in the burden of his sufferings, especially in the prison of Toledo. Then, in the form of a summary, Edith gives us in John's own words a brief description of the content of his message concerning the cross.

THE SYMBOLS OF CROSS AND NIGHT

Her attention then turns to John's writings themselves, and she presents a brief precise account of their origin and destination. This leads her to the fact that the prevailing symbol for John of the Cross is not the cross but the night, and at this point Sr. Benedicta uses her skill as a philosopher to enter into an illuminating reflection on the difference between the two symbols. Her training in phenomenology surfaces particularly in her discussion of night as a symbol, where she helps the reader toward a grasp of the difference in the symbolic character of cross and night and why the night-symbol prevails in John.

As she approaches John's teaching, she clarifies that detachment is designated by John as a night through which the soul must pass to reach union with God. It must do this in regard to the point of departure, the path, and the goal. Pointing out how entering the night is synonymous with carrying the cross, she then in her own words gives a condensed presentation of John of the Cross's thought on the night of the senses both active and passive.

IN JOHN'S OWN WORDS

As Edith moves into this presentation, she gradually begins to express the thought in John's own words, not intending to write a commentary on his doctrine but simply to put it before us. Obviously, this also required that she boil down the voluminous material into something manageable, which she did but without veering far from John's words, placing in quotation marks with great care whatever comes directly from him. At the same time, though, she by necessity weaves her own words into the text so as to condense the material. Some readers having expected from Edith Stein a different kind of study than the one she intended may at first be disappointed, thinking that all she has done is paraphrase St. John of the Cross. But since she always distinguishes between her own words and those of John, we have an interesting result in which by condensing the material and through her own remarks she often brings further clarity or deeper penetration into *sanjuanist* thought. Here is but one example where the words belong to Edith not John: "Self-satisfied joy in one's own works is an injustice and a denial of God who initiates every single good work. Souls like these make no progress in perfection" (p. 148). Yet, often enough her words serve no other purpose than to tie sections together, summing up or filling in for large amounts of omitted text.

Only at times does she break into John's exposition to give further interpretation of his doctrine, expanding on it with the use of modern philosophy and in the light of her own lifelong effort to grasp the laws of spiritual being and life. She does her own reflecting on how the spirit assimilates the content of faith, the various aspects of faith, how meditation grows into contemplation. She discusses how in contemplation one is pure spirit, freed from all images and concepts, and therefore in darkness, where faith, liberated from the grasp of the senses, directs the spirit toward God.

But to disentangle oneself from the natural world is not possible without the help of divine support and special communications. Even with the latter one can become attached to the gifts rather than to the giver. So another reality is necessary, Edith insists, a mightier reality, an intervention by God, a dark mystical contemplation. She then takes us with John through the passive night of the spirit effected by dark contemplation.

AN UNDERSTANDING OF WHAT SPIRIT IS

After leading us through John's work on the dark night of the spirit, Edith enters again into some reflections on her own, drawing from her philosophical background. She reminds us in her preface that "what is said about the *I, freedom,* and *person*, does not spring from the teaching of our Holy Father John of the Cross." From the viewpoint of her own philosophical thought—of course now illumined by faith—this is the most important part of the study. She writes: "God is pure spirit and the archetype of all spiritual being. So, really, it is only by beginning with God that it is possible to understand what spirit is; however, that means that spirit is a mystery that constantly attracts us because it is the mystery of our own being. We can approach it, in a certain way, since our own being is spiritual. We can also approach it by way of all being to the extent that all being, which has meaning and which can be comprehended intellectually, has something of spiritual being about it. But it reveals itself to a greater depth in proportion to our knowledge of God, though it is never totally unveiled, that is, it never ceases to be a mystery" (pp. 153-54).

Then in line with all her philosophical work from her first study of empathy to *Finite and Eternal Being* she seeks to clarify as much as possible, without imagery, what spiritual writers and the mystics mean when speaking of within and without, the inmost depths, or the center of the soul, and so on.

QUESTIONS ABOUT THE KINDS OF UNION

This section ends with a person in the inmost region completely committed to God and no longer wanting anything but what God wills. Then Edith asks the question whether there is a higher union, the mystical marriage, and whether there is a boundary line between it and the other union, and she finds it very difficult to draw one and to know whether John draws one. Leaving John aside, she turns to her "Holy Mother Saint Teresa" for help to explain that there is a difference not only of degree but also of kind. This had become a classic question in the history of spiritual theology, and there was little agreement on the issue. Sanjuanist scholars today usually hold that the summit of the mount toward which one journeys in the spiritual life coincides with the reality that John variously terms "union," or "divine union," "transformation in God," "perfection," or "union with God." Everything that he explains is subordinated to this supreme goal: to lead souls to the spiritual perfection of this mysterious union. This supreme finality is what confers unity to his plan. To the essential union in the natural order in which God is present sustaining creatures in existence, there is added then this union in the supernatural order, or order of grace. It is found when the two wills—of God and the soul—are in such conformity that nothing in the one is repugnant to the other. When the soul is completely rid of what is repugnant and unconformed to the divine will, it rests transformed in God through love. This union John calls the "union of the likeness of love."[8]

Once the soul has arrived at this union, through the active and passive purifications, the divine communication is converted into a rhythm of life in which the more perceptible manifestations are the touches of union, the concrete manifestations of the presence and action of God in the soul. But these are also given before this to prepare the soul for the union's ultimate demands. In the *Spiritual Canticle* the union of the likeness of love, or transformation in God through love, is presented under the image of an espousal or marriage. This marriage accomplished on the cross is bestowed by God on each one immediately at baptism, but it then develops and is achieved only gradually and by stages. "For though it is all one espousal, there is a difference in that one is attained at the soul's pace, and thus little by little, and the other at God's pace, and thus immediately."[9] This does not mean that there is not great variety in spiritual lives: John explains that he is describing the most that God communicates "to some souls he gives more and to others less, to some in one way and to others in another, although all alike may be in this same state of spiritual betrothal."[10] "The Spiritual Marriage," of the *Canticle* is the same union as that found at the summit of the mount, the goal of the *Ascent of Mount Carmel*, but described from different perspectives.

Edith agreed that the union of love, the goal of the *Ascent,* is a higher degree of the union of grace, not a union different in kind. But in turning to St. Teresa to demonstrate that the spiritual marriage is a union different in kind from the union found at the summit of the mount in the *Ascent,* she uses Teresa to explain John. What might be said of her interpretation of Teresa would lie beyond the scope of this introduction. But these problems about differences in the kinds of union are perhaps not so important in the light of Edith's whole study and ought not distract one from her fascinating discussion of how an inmost region, the heart or fountainhead of personal life, is present both in God and the soul and of how in the spiritual marriage this inmost region is surrendered by each to the other. Summing up, she states that in being seized by God in contemplation, all that is mortal in the soul is consumed in the fire of eternal love. The spirit as spirit is destined for immortal being. This consuming leads along a path through the Passion and cross of Christ to the glory of his resurrection.

THE GLORY OF RESURRECTION

After discussing the dark night of the Passion and cross wrought through contemplation, Edith goes on to speak of the glory of resurrection. The soul shares in this glory through the unitive contemplation described in *The Living Flame of Love,* which takes place in the inmost region of the soul. The object of *The Ascent* and *The Night* is the way of the cross, and so there is an inner connection between them and *The Living Flame of Love*. No other way to union exists than the way that leads through the cross, Edith insists. Here again in presenting the material she weaves together John's words and her own. The fire that was dark, consuming, and painful is now brilliant, loving, and gentle.

Presenting with John his commentary on the four stanzas of the poem, making some brief comments on the work, and comparing it with the *Ascent* and *Night*, Edith suggests that it was love for souls that opened John's lips to speak contrary to his strong compulsion toward silence about his experience of an earthly paradise at the threshold of the heavenly one. He wanted to encourage others on the hard way of the cross.

THE BRIDAL IMAGERY

Traditionally in publications of the works of John of the Cross, *The Spiritual Canticle* appears before *The Living Flame*, but Edith turns to this work last. Her doing so makes sense when she compares this work with the others. While John lived cramped in the darkness of his prison cell in Toledo, the ancient bridal song, *The Song of Songs*, came to birth anew in his heart. Sr. Benedicta explains how the *Spiritual Canticle* differs essentially from *The Dark Night* and *The Living Flame of Love*. The *Night* and *Flame* give a cross-section of the mystical life at a determined moment of the process. *The Spiritual Canticle* gives the whole mysterious process again and is written by a soul most intensely gripped by the visible charms of creation.

Two versions of the poem have reached us. In the second version or draft, John rearranged the stanzas of his poem leading Baruzi and others in his path to deny the authenticity of the second redaction and its commentary. Laying out before us an overview of the progression found in the *Canticle* and of the problem about the authenticity of the second redaction, Edith concludes through her considerations, contrary to Baruzi, that the second redaction is authentic. After her death the position of Baruzi and others became a stimulant to a number of tedious studies demonstrating the authenticity of the second version of the *Canticle* and confirming Edith's view. Now it's genuineness would be difficult to deny.

In the *Canticle* Edith sees the bridal relationship as the focal point for all that lies in the work. The relationship between the soul and God as foreseen from all eternity cannot be more fittingly described than as a nuptial bond. The divine bridal relationship is recognized as the original and actual bridal relationship. All human nuptial relationships appear as imperfect copies of this archetype, the actual human relationship taking second place and having its highest reason for existence by giving expression to a divine mystery.

Sr. Benedicta proceeds to consider the abundance of splendidly colored images, how they arose and whether they contribute to the unity of the whole. She takes us through the poem and its commentary as it progresses and expresses the progress in the relationship between the bride and the Bridegroom through many images.

Arriving at the last part of the *Spiritual Canticle* and its descriptions of the mystical union, Edith to our surprise, sees it as a share in the incarnation of Christ, just as the dark night is a share in his cross and work of redemption. Once more weaving John's words with her own she brings us through the final stanzas of the *Canticle* to its end illustrating beautifully how the hidden way of the soul is braided together with the mysteries of Christ.

THE CROSS IN JOHN'S LIFE

After her profound and compact presentation of St. John of the Cross's doctrine, Edith must, in the third section, turn to his life, reminding readers that a science of the cross in her understanding of the term cannot be based merely on intellectual insight. With apparently little worry over slipping into hagiography, she sets out to show John's love for the crucified Christ. This love appears in his oral teaching, written letters, and words of spiritual direction, but is present as well in the way he lived, the events of his life, what his poetry revealed, and in what witnesses said of him. She illustrates lastly how he accepted the cross pervading his life in the conflicts that erupted among the discalced friars and nuns, and in his last illness. Sr. Benedicta's work comes to an end with John of the Cross's painful though peaceful death. She had accomplished what she had set out to do. She had prepared a study in his honor for the celebration of the fourth centenary of his birth. Her aim had been to grasp John of the Cross in a unity that expressed itself in his life and in his works. And the viewpoint from which she beheld this unity is the cross. To assist herself in reaching this unity, she sought to do some interpreting of her own adding to the simple presentation of John's life and doctrine. For this interpretation she made generous use of the treasures stored within her after brilliant years spent in the realms of study, teaching, and research.

DESTINATION OF THE WORK

For whom did Edith Stein write this work? Clearly the stimulus came from the approaching centenary and the request of her prioress. When writing she must have had in mind the friars and nuns within the Discalced Carmelite Order. Her expressions "Holy Father John" and "Holy Mother Teresa" make her appear to be speaking to her own sisters as she writes. Certainly she was keen on introducing them to St. John of the Cross. In one of her letters she tells Mother Johanna she would like to have "something by our Holy Father John himself" in Dutch to read to the postulants for meditation (Ltr. 327). There were Dutch translations of John at the time, even of Padre Silverio's critical edition. Though a good number of the sisters knew German and they would have had the German translation, one wonders how much interest there was in St. John of the Cross in the community if they didn't even have his works in Dutch. Whatever the case may be, we see here Sr. Benedicta's desire to introduce Carmelite nuns to the writings of John. In another letter to Mother Johanna she mentions how a certain meditation book is too dry for her and that she would rather present John of the Cross to the sisters (Ltr. 329). But John himself intuited that readers might find his thought dry or at least troublesome and admitted at the beginning of his *Ascent of Mount Carmel* that though the doctrine he was to expound was solid and good for everyone, not everyone would find it easy to take in. "We are not writing on moral and pleasing topics addressed to the kind of spiritual people who like to approach God along sweet and satisfying paths" (A. Prol. 8). Yet John advises perseverance and that thereby one will come to understand better, and then to read the work again. As Sr. Benedicta must have discovered, John becomes clearer and more beneficial and even pleasing to read as one reads more. In *Science of the Cross* she gives readers an opportunity to read John of the Cross again but in a different pattern.

In a letter to a sister in the Cologne Carmel (Ltr. 336), she explained that when she finished she would send a German copy to the provincial in Germany to have duplicated for the monasteries, implying thereby that she envisioned translating her study into Dutch. How many Dutch speaking nuns were in the Carmel? In the Carmel in Echt there were thirteen choir sisters and four lay sisters when Edith arrived. Only three of them were Dutch. The official language was German until 1935 when the Carmel transferred from the German province of Bavaria to the Dutch province. As for the cultural level in the Dutch Carmel, it was not as high as in Cologne. Edith was asked to offer spiritual talks to the community, give classes in Latin and on the breviary to the novices, and to be spiritual director of the lay sisters. In 1941, five new Dutch sisters entered the Carmel.

In composing her work, though, Edith must have seen it, as well, as an opportunity to clarify and develop her own thinking about spirituality, its meaning, and development. She must have surmised that others, too, though outside the walls of Carmel, would eventually want to read what she had to say. For as Baruzi had shown, St. John of the Cross was a thinker to be dealt with, and Catholics could no longer ignore him. This gave her an opportunity to weave into her study an elaboration of a philosophy of the person, the leitmotiv of her research and creativity.

THE MANUSCRIPT

On 2 August 1942, shortly after the evening meditation period had begun, the SS men pounded at the door of the Carmel and almost before the nuns realized it, Sister Benedicta and Rosa Stein were taken away. Sr. Benedicta's manuscript *Science of the Cross* had not been returned to its place leading one to presume that she had it out and had been working on it that day. The nuns at Echt possessed a large amount of written work done by Sr. Benedicta, which they kept until the threat of bombing increased. They were in the path of the British and US planes that passed on their way to bomb Germany. When the nuns had to evacuate the monastery and flee for safety to another location, they did not keep the thousands of sheets of her writings in Echt but took them to the Carmel of Herkenbosch, where they were stored in the attic. But when that building was destroyed by a bomber attack at the end of 1944, the Dutch provincial, Fr. Avertanus, managed to salvage the majority of Edith's writings from the attic where they were scattered all over the place. A monumental task of sorting out thousands of papers remained to be done. The writings were entrusted to the noted Franciscan philosopher, Fr. Herman Leo van Breda, who had urged Fr. Avertanus to collect them. Fr. van Breda put one of his workers, Dr. Lucie Gelber in charge of the collected papers, who in turn worked on them and prepared them for publication over many years.

The first volume to appear of the works of Edith Stein was *Science of the Cross*. Though originally planned for publication in 1942, the book was not actually published until 1950, relatively soon when compared to her other works.

The cover of the manuscript has a sketch prepared by Edith herself. The initial page contains a title and dedication also by Edith: *The Science of the Cross. To the Mystical Doctor of the Church and Father of Carmelites on the 400th Anniversary of His Birth.* The official edition has for its title: *The Science of the Cross: A Study on John of the Cross.* Beneath the dedication Edith wrote "by one of his daughters in the Carmel of Echt." Though other writings appeared during her life with her religious name Teresa Benedicta of the Cross, she was here following a tradition that when a work by a Carmelite nun was published while the nun was still alive, it was generally presented anonymously.

After the title page comes the preface followed by Edith's outline. The contents are divided into three main sections with Roman numerals marking each one. Each section has a number of subdivisions except the third, which appears only with its Roman numeral, without titles or divisions, a narrative account continuing through to the end of the book.

To facilitate reading and handling of the study, the editors of this English translation have divided it into chapters and added a chapter heading that is not Edith's. To be sure, the headings and divisions as they

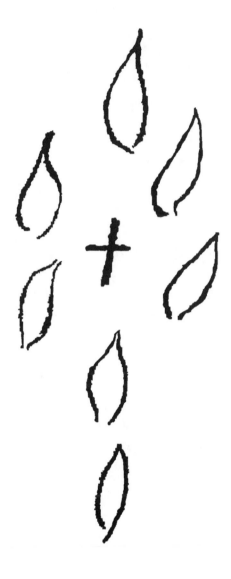

Edith Stein drew this sketch on the cover of her manuscript of *The Science of the Cross*.

appear in the outline of contents prepared by Edith have been maintained throughout.

A COMPLETED WORK

Some dramatic scenes have been invented about how the SS troops interrupted Edith Stein's work, causing it to be left incomplete on her desk. All the evidence, nonetheless, points to the fact that the work is complete. Concluding her study with the death of St. John of the Cross, Edith wrote the preface, which was for her the normal thing to do: write the preface after finishing the work.

As she was approaching the end of her manuscript, the shade of the ink begins to grow lighter, probably having been mixed with water on account of a scarcity of ink. The preface has the same shade lighter than that found in the rest of the text. Furthermore, the part that represents her own most creative and personal thought about the "I," freedom, and person, and which she admitted in the preface did not arise from the teaching of St. John of the Cross, must also have been added after she completed the third section. Page numbers are crossed out and rearranged so as to fit this part into the manuscript, and also the shade of the ink is the same as both the last part of section III and the preface. Sr. Benedicta could still have wanted to make some small revisions, or close the book with a brief conclusion, but only in that very limited way could the manuscript ever be called incomplete.[11]

Kieran Kavanaugh, O.C.D.
Institute of Carmelite Studies
Washington, D.C.

THE SCIENCE
OF THE CROSS

THE SCIENCE OF THE CROSS

TO

THE MYSTICAL DOCTOR OF THE CHURCH

AND

FATHER OF CARMELITES

JOHN OF THE CROSS

ON THE 400th ANNIVERSARY OF HIS BIRTH

by

one of his daughters

in the Carmel of Echt

1542 — 1942

PREFACE

In the following pages, an attempt will be made to grasp John of the Cross in the unity of his being as it expresses itself in his life and in his works—from a viewpoint that will enable us to see this unity.

This is, therefore, not a biography nor a general evaluative presentation of his doctrine. But the facts of his life and the content of his writings have to be taken into account in order to reach that unity through them. The witnesses will speak in detail, but after they have spoken an attempt will be made to interpret them and this interpretation will be validated by what the author believes she has gained from a lifelong effort to grasp the laws of spiritual being and life.

This holds above all for the expositions on *spirit, faith*, and *contemplation*, which are inserted at various points, particularly in the chapter: *The Soul in the Realm of the Spirit and of Created Spirits*. What is said there about the *I, freedom*, and *person*, does not derive from the teaching of our Holy Father John of the Cross.

Of course there are certain points of departure to be found in him. Expositions on them, however, were far from his main intention and his thinking processes. Constructing a philosophy of the person, such as is indicated at the passages named, has, after all, been made a task only in modern philosophy.

For summoning witnesses, our Père Bruno of Jesus and Mary's *Saint Jean de la Croix* (Paris, 1929) and *Vie d'Amour de Saint Jean de la Croix* (Paris, 1936), as well as Jean Baruzi's *Saint Jean de la Croix et le Problème de l'Expérience Mystique* (Paris, 1931), have served as excellent guides.

Baruzi has offered rich stimuli. Proportionally, little is given of him since it is impossible to base oneself on his conclusions without a critical

5

analysis of them. Such an analysis was far beyond the scope of the assigned task. Whoever knows Baruzi will discover traces of his influence as well as the points of critique. It is incontestably to his merit that he uncovers the sources and sets himself to give them their just evaluation with untiring zeal.

Questionable is his opinion that of the two existing manuscript versions of the *Spiritual Canticle* and the *Living Flame of Love*—possibly for the *Living Flame*, most probably for the *Canticle*—the later ones are to be considered apocryphal and that the unbroken transmission we have of the *Ascent* and of the *Dark Night* is presumably only an apocryphal and mutilated version.

See in this context in the work referred to, the I. Book, *Les Textes*, 3, and following, and the Introductions to the single works in the latest Spanish edition of the writings: *Obras de San Juan de la Cruz Doctor de la Iglesia, editadas y anotadas por el P[adre] Silverio de Santa Teresa, O.C.D., Burgos 1929ff.*[1]

INTRODUCTION: Meaning of the Science of the Cross and the Essentials of its Origin

I. THE MESSAGE OF THE CROSS

1. Early Encounters with the Cross
2. The Message of Sacred Scripture
3. The Sacrifice of the Mass
4. Visions of the Cross
5. The Message of the Cross
6. Content of the Message of the Cross

II. THE DOCTRINE OF THE CROSS

Introduction: John of the Cross as Author

1. CROSS AND NIGHT (Night of the Senses)
    A. Difference in Character of the Symbol: "Emblem" and "Cosmic Expression"
    B. The Song of the Dark Night
    C. The Dark Night of the Senses
        1) Introduction to the Meaning of Night
        2) Active Entrance into the Night as a Following of the Cross
        3) Passive Night as Crucifixion

2. SPIRIT AND FAITH. DEATH AND RESURRECTION (Night of the Spirit)

    Introduction: Development of the Questions

    A. Divesting the Spiritual Faculties in the Active Night
        1) The Night of Faith as the Way to Union
        2) Divesting the Spiritual Faculties as the Way of the Cross and Death on the Cross
        3) Uselessness of all Created Things as Means to Union Inadequacy of Natural and Supernatural Knowledge
        4) Purgation of the Memory
        5) Purgation of the Will
    B. Reciprocal Illumination of Spirit and Faith
        1) Retrospect and Prospect
        2) Natural Spiritual Activity: The Soul; The Soul's Parts and Faculties

3) Supernatural Elevation of the Spirit. Faith and Its Life

4) Extraordinary Graces Imparted and Detachment from Them

C. Death and Resurrection

    1) Passive Night of the Spirit

        a. Faith, Dark Contemplation, Detachment

        b. Enkindling in Love and Transformation

        c. The Secret Ladder

        d. The Soul's Tricolored Garment

        e. In Darkness and Concealed in Deep Repose

    2) The Soul in the Realm of the Spirit and of Created Spirits

        a. Construction of the Soul; God's Spirit and Created Spirits

        b. The Soul's Dealings with God and with Created Spirits

        c. The Interior of the Soul and the Thoughts of the Heart

        d. The Soul, The *"I,"* and Freedom

        e. The Different Kinds of Union with God

        f. Faith and Contemplation. Death and Resurrection

3. THE GLORY OF THE RESURRECTION

A. In the Flames of Divine Love

    1) On the Threshold of Eternal Life

    2) United with the Triune One

    3) In the Reflected Rays of Divine Glory

    4) The Hidden Life of Love

    5) Originality of *The Living Flame of Love* in Comparison with the Older Writings

B. The Soul's Bridal Song

    1) The *Spiritual Canticle* as it Relates to the Other Writings

    2) The Principal Progression of Thought in the Saint's Interpretation

    3) The Dominant Image and its Meaning for the Value of the Song

    4) The Bridal Symbol and the Specific Images

    5) The Bridal Symbol and the Cross (Mystical Marriage— Creation, Incarnation, and Redemption)

III. [UNTITLED]

INTRODUCTION

MEANING OF THE SCIENCE OF THE CROSS
AND THE ESSENTIALS OF ITS ORIGIN

In September or October of 1568 the young Carmelite *Juan de Yepez*, whose name in religion until then had been John of St. Matthias, took up his abode in the poor hovel of Duruelo, where he was to be the foundation and cornerstone of the Teresian reform. On November 28, with two companions, he bound himself by vow to observe the primitive Rule and took the title *of the Cross*. This was a symbol of what he sought when he left his home monastery and thereby publicly broke with its mitigated observance. It also symbolized what he had already practiced there, in that he had personal permission to live according to the primitive Rule. At the same time, the change of title expressed an essential distinguishing mark of the Reform: to follow Christ on the Way of the Cross. Participation in Christ's cross was to be the life of the Discalced Carmelites.

As just mentioned, John was not at that time a neophyte in the science of the cross. In the order, the title incorporated in one's name indicates that God wishes to bind the soul to himself under the sign of a particular mystery of faith. By changing his name, John showed that the cross was superimposed on his life as an emblem.

When we speak of a *science of the cross,* this is not to be understood in the usual meaning of *science;* we are not dealing merely with a theory, that is, with a body of—really or presumably—true propositions. Neither are we dealing with a structure built of ideas laid out in reasoned steps. We are dealing with a well-recognized truth—a theology of the cross—but a living, real, and effective truth. It is buried in the soul like a seed that takes root there and grows, making a distinct impression on the soul, determining what it does and omits, and by shining outwardly is recognized in this very doing and omitting. In this sense one speaks of a science of the saints and we speak of a science of the cross. From this living form and strength in one's innermost depths, a perspective of life arises, the image one has of God and of the world, and therefore one can find expression for it in a mode of thinking, in a theory. We have such a crystallization in the doctrine of our Holy Father, St. John. We will seek in his writings and in his life those elements that determine their unity and character. But first we will ask how it is possible, generally, for a science to develop in the manner just specified. There are naturally recognizable signs which indicate that human nature, as it actually is, exists in a state of degeneration. From this stems the inability to perceive and respond to facts interiorly in a way that corresponds to their authentic value. This inability may be grounded in an inborn dull-mindedness (in the literal sense), or in a general indifference developed in the course of a lifetime, or finally, in an insensitivity to certain impressions as a result of repeatedly ignoring them.

What we have often heard and long-known "leaves us cold." Added to this, frequently, is an excessive interior preoccupation with one's own personal concerns that refuses to attend to anything else. We know our interior rigidity is inappropriate and it pains us. Knowing that it arises from a psychological law does not help us to overcome it. On the other hand, we rejoice when we can convince ourselves through experience that we are still able to feel deep, genuine joy; and deep, genuine pain also seems to us a grace when compared to our rigid insensitivity.

This numbness of feeling is particularly painful for us in the religious sphere. Many believers are depressed because the facts of salvation history do not at all (or no longer) impress them as they ought, and lack the strong influence on their lives that they should exert. The example of the saints demonstrates to them how things should actually be: where there is genuine, lively faith, there the doctrine of faith and the "tremendous deeds" of God are the content of life. All else steps aside for it and is determined by it. This is *holy realism*: the original inner receptivity of the soul reborn in the Holy Spirit. Whatever the soul encounters is received in an appropriate manner and with corresponding depth, and finds in the soul a living, mobile, docile energy that allows itself to be easily and joyfully led and molded by that which it has received, unhampered by any mistaken inhibitions and rigidity. Such realism, when it leads a holy soul to accept the truths of faith, becomes *the science of the saints*. If the mystery of the cross becomes its *inner form,* it turns into a *science of the cross*.

Holy realism has a certain affinity with the realism of the child who receives and responds to impressions with unimpaired vigor and vitality, and with uninhibited simplicity. Indeed, the response naturally will in no way always be reasonable. There is insufficient maturity of insight. Besides, as soon as knowledge becomes active, there is no lack of interior as well as exterior sources of illusion and error which lead into wrong ways.

Appropriate environmental influences can prevent mistakes. The soul of a child is soft and impressionable. Whatever influence enters there can easily form it for a lifetime. When the facts of salvation history are introduced in early childhood and in an appropriate form, this may easily lay a foundation for a saintly life. Occasionally, one also meets a case of an early extraordinary election by grace, so that childlike and holy realism are blended. It is said, for example, that when St. Bridget of Sweden was ten years old, she heard for the first time about the passion and death of Jesus; that night she had an apparition of the Lord on the cross. From that time on, she was unable to meditate on the sufferings of the Lord without shedding tears.

In John's case, a third factor must be taken into consideration: he had an artistic nature. Among the various crafts and arts in which the boy tested himself were those of carver and painter. We still have drawings he made later in his life. (His sketch of the Ascent of Mount Carmel is generally known.) When he was the prior in Granada he drew up the blueprints for a contemplative monastery. He was a poet as well as a visual artist. He had a need to express in songs that which transpired in his soul. His mystical writings are merely additional explanations of all he expressed directly in his poetry. And so, in his case, we must reckon also with the characteristic realism of an artist. In the confident strength of his impressionability the artist is akin to the child and the saint.

But—in contrast to a *holy realism*—the artist's receptivity to impressions is one that the world views in the light of a particular domain of values too readily at the expense of other values. This results in a particular sort of responsive behaviors. It is characteristic of the artist to transform into image anything that causes an interior stirring and demands to be expressed exteriorly. Image here is not to be restricted to the visual arts; it must be understood to refer to any artistic expression including the poetic and musical. It is simultaneously *image* (Bild) in which something is presented and *structure* (Gebilde) as something formed into a complete and all-encompassing little world of its own. Every genuine work of art is in addition a *symbol* (Sinnbild) whether or not this is its creator's intention, be he naturalist or symbolist.

It is a symbol: that is, it comes from that infinite fullness of *meaning* (Sinn) into which every bit of human knowledge is projected to grasp something positive and speak of it. It does so in such a manner, in fact, that it mysteriously suggests the whole fullness of meaning, which for all human knowledge is inexhaustible. Understood this way, all genuine art is revelation and all artistic creation is sacred service.

Despite this, it is clear that there is a danger in an artistic inclination, and not only when the artist lacks an understanding of the sacredness of his task. The danger lies in the possibility that in constructing the image, the artist proceeds as though there were no further responsibility than producing it. What is meant here can be demonstrated most clearly by the example of images of the cross. There will scarcely be a believing artist who has not felt compelled to portray Christ on the cross or carrying the cross.

But the Crucified One demands from the artist more than a mere portrayal of the image. He demands that the artist, just as every other person, follow him: that he both make himself and allow himself to be made into an image of the one who carries the cross and is crucified.

Expressing the image externally can be a hindrance to doing so internally, but by no means must this be so; actually, it can serve the process of interior transformation because only with the production of the external expression will the inner image be fully formed and interiorly adopted. In this manner, when no obstacle is placed in its path, it becomes an interior representation that urges the artist to effectively reproduce it in action, that is, by way of imitation, externally.

And yes, the external image, one's own artistic creation, can always serve to spur one on to transform oneself interiorly according to its meaning. We have every reason to suppose that this applies to John: childlike, artistic and holy realism were combined in him and supplied for the message of the cross the most favorable soil in which it could grow into the science of the cross.

It has already been said that his artistic nature became evident even in childhood. Nor are witnesses lacking that speak of an early election to sanctity. His mother later told the Discalced Carmelite Nuns of Medina del Campo that, as a child, her son had behaved like an angel. This pious mother had endowed him with an intimate love of the Mother of God, and we have it from two reliable sources that the boy was twice rescued from death by drowning through Mary's personal intervention.

Beyond that, everything we know of his childhood and youth testifies to his being a child of grace from infancy.

1
The Message of the Cross

I. THE MESSAGE OF THE CROSS

1. Early Encounters with the Cross

Now we inquire how the seed of the cross's message was implanted in this fertile soil. We have no evidence to tell us when and how John interiorly accepted the image of the Crucified for the first time. Probably while he was a small child, his faith-filled mother already took him along to the parish church in his hometown, Fontiveros. There one could see the Savior on the cross, his face disfigured by pain, real hair hanging down over his cheeks to the scourged shoulders.[1]

And when the young widow who bore such want and suffering spoke to her children about their Mother in heaven she surely also led them to know Mary as the Mother of Sorrows beside the cross. And in all reverence for the mysteries regarding the guiding influence of grace, we may surely suppose that Mary herself would have taught her protégé the science of the cross in good time. Who could be as well instructed in it and as well penetrated by its value as this wisest of virgins?

At all events, John also encountered the image of the cross in the shops where he was employed. Perhaps even then he had already ventured to carve crosses, as he liked to do later. Though all this is based on supposition, we find real support for accepting the idea of an early encounter with the cross in the authenticated fact of a love of penance and mortification manifested so soon in John's life.

When he was only nine years old, he scorned his bed and prepared a mat of brushwood. A few years later he limited his rest on this hard couch to only a few hours, since he spent part of his nights in study. As a young pupil he begged alms for his even poorer comrades, and later for the poor in the hospitals. After many an unfortunate attempt at other occupations, he gave himself to the care of the sick and persevered in this with total dedication.

According to the testimony of his brother Francisco, he worked in a smallpox hospital (*al hospital de las bubas*).[2] It has been surmised that persons suffering from syphilis were treated in this institution.[3] Whether accurate or not—surely the boy did learn from his patients not only about physical illness but about spiritual and moral misery as well.

The faithful performance of his duties must have demanded many a painful self-conquest from this pure, deep, and most sensitive heart. What gave him the strength for this? Surely nothing other than love for the Crucified One whom he wished to follow on the difficult, steep, and narrow way. The desire to know him more closely and to conform himself all the more to his image may well have caused John to choose, besides serving the sick, to begin studies at the Jesuit college as preparation for the priesthood. In order the better to hear the message of the cross, he refused the offer of a profitable chaplaincy at his hospital and chose instead the poverty of the Carmelite Order.[4] The same desire prevented him from being content with the mitigated observance of the Carmelites of that time and led him toward the Reform.

2. The Message of Sacred Scripture

Perhaps the Jesuit pupil was already led to occupy himself with sacred Scripture. And in sermons, instruction, and liturgy the words of the Lord—among them the words from the cross—had already come his way. Daily instruction in sacred Scripture was on the horarium of the Carmelites. When, then, the young religious was sent to Salamanca to study, delving in the sacred texts under the guidance of skilled exegetes formed an essential part of the required work.

We know from later times that he lived entirely in and with the sacred Scriptures. They belonged to the few books he always kept in his cell. One cannot imagine his writings without quotations from Scripture. They had become for him the natural expression of his inner experience and when he was writing they came to his pen instinctively. His secretary and confidant during his last years, Padre Juan Evangelista, tells us that John of the Cross had scarcely any need to refer to the sacred Scriptures, because he knew them almost by heart.[5]

We can count on it, then, that the message of the cross contained in the divine Word had an ever new effect on his heart throughout his life. It is utterly impossible to treat this perhaps most important source of his science of the cross exhaustively. For we must assert from the start that the *entire* sacred Scripture—the Old as well as the New Testament—was his daily bread.

Quotations from Scripture are so numerous in his works that one cannot set about discussing all of them. On the other hand, it would be foolish to restrict oneself to these and to assume that other words that are never found among his quotations had a less lively effect on him. Nothing remains for us but to show, in various groups of examples, how we might conceive of him being influenced by the message of the cross.

The Savior himself spoke of the cross on various occasions and in varying senses. When he foretold his Passion and his death,[6] he had before his eyes in the literal sense the shameful wood of the cross-upon which he was to end his life. But when he said: "whoever does-not take up his cross and follow me, is not worthy of me,"[7] or "if any-one wishes to follow me, let him deny himself, take up his cross and follow me,"[8] then is the cross the symbol (Sinnbild) of all that is difficult and oppressive and so against human nature that taking it upon oneself is like a journey to death. And the disciple of Jesus is to take up this burden daily.[9]

The announcement of his death set the image of the Crucified One before his disciples, and even today sets it before one who reads or hears the gospel. Therein lies a silent challenge to respond appropriately. The appeals to follow on the way of the cross of life present that appropriate response and at the same time give an insight into the meaning of death on the cross. For upon the words of invitation there follows immediately the admonition: "Whoever wishes to save his life will lose it; but whoever loses his life for my sake, will save it."[10] Christ gives up his life in order to open the way to eternal life for humanity. However, to win eternal life, they too must give up their earthly life. They must die with Christ in order to rise with him: the lifelong death of suffering and of daily self-denial, and even, if necessary, the bloody death of a martyr for the gospel of Christ.

The passion narratives of the gospel paint in broad and ample fashion the image of the suffering and crucified Christ as foretold in the words of the Lord. One cannot but think that these images were indelibly etched on the child's pure and tender heart and in the artist's imagination.

We must also take into consideration that the youth attended the divine services in Holy Week, even participated in them as an altar boy. For every year on Palm Sunday and in the Sacred Triduum the liturgy of the church presents the final days in Jesus' life, his death, and his resting in the tomb to the faithful with dramatic vigor, in moving words, melodies, and ceremonies that inexorably compel one to share the experience. If even cold-hearted and unbelieving persons entangled in worldly pursuits cannot remain indifferent to it, what must its effect have been on the youthful saint, who, we know from later on could hardly speak of spiritual matters without going into ecstasy—who went into a rapture upon hearing a sacred song!

As he studied sacred Scripture, the prophecies in the Old Testament supplemented the gospel accounts, principally, no doubt, the portrayal of the suffering servant of God in Isaiah, which must already have come to the attention of the young religious in the readings of the breviary for Holy Week. Not only were new descriptions of the Passion in relentless realism to be found there, but also the great background of both world and salvation history for Golgotha's drama was presented. God, the almighty Creator and Lord of earth, who shatters peoples like vessels of clay is at the same time the Father who surrounds his chosen people with the most faithful care. He is the tender and jealous lover who woos "his bride Israel" throughout the centuries and who is repeatedly disdained and turned away—as St. John of the Cross sings in his stanzas about the lone young shepherd.[11]

Between them, the prophets and the gospels put the finishing touches to the portrait of the Messiah who comes out of obedience to the Father to win back the bride by taking upon himself her yoke, thus freeing her. Indeed, he does not shy away from death in order to win life for her. This is heard again in the *Romances*.[12] If in them the bridal relationship of Israel is expanded to the whole of humanity, doing so corresponds to the proclamations of the kingdom of God that the prophets as well as the gospels make.

Something else must have been meaningful for John in the prophetic books: the relation of the prophet himself to his Lord and God, the vocation and isolation of a man on whom the Almighty has laid his hand. It is a relationship that makes of this one a friend and confidant of God, one who is made cognizant of and who announces the eternal decrees. This relationship on the other hand demands of him complete dedication and unlimited readiness and removes him from the community of people who think only in natural terms and makes him a sign of contradiction. This was indicated not only in a direct manner by sacred Scripture but also by the importance traditionally given Scripture by the order.

In Carmel—under the mitigated Rule as well—the remembrance of the Prophet Elijah, the "Leader and Father of Carmelites"[13] lived on. The *Institutio Primorum Monachorum*[14] set the prophet before the eyes of the young religious as a model of the contemplative life. This prophet whom God commanded to go forth into the desert, to conceal himself by the brook *Carith* across from the Jordan, to drink the water of the brook and to be nourished by the food which God would send him,[15] is to be the model of all who withdraw into solitude renouncing sin and all sensory pleasures, indeed all earthly things.

Thus is "opposite the Jordan" to be understood: to conceal themselves in the love of God (*Carith* is interpreted as *caritas* or *charity*). They will drink from the stream of divine grace with delight. And the doctrine of the Fathers will offer them solid food for their souls: the bread of sorrowful contrition and penance, and the meat of true humility. Did not John find here the key to what God was working in his own soul?

Well may God's plan of salvation be directed toward all of humanity, and on their account toward his chosen people. But his purpose is to reach every single soul. With the most tender love will he seek to win every single one as a bride, caring for it with paternal fidelity. In the *Song of Songs*, sacred Scripture also perfectly expresses how this divine courtship becomes a spur that no longer allows the soul to find repose. This is echoed in the *Spiritual Canticle*. How the motif of the cross is struck again and again in the *Canticle* must be shown in detail later on.

If the poet found ample stimulus in the glowingly colorful pictures of the Old Testament singer, the theologian was able to dip into another productive source. The soul united with Christ lives out of his life — however, only in surrender to the Crucified when she has traveled the entire way of the cross with him. Nowhere is this expressed more clearly and more urgently than in the message of St. Paul who already had a well-developed *science of the cross, a theology of the cross* derived *from inner experience*.

"Christ sent me to preach the gospel, and not with eloquent wisdom, lest the cross of Christ be emptied of its power. ... For the word of the cross is folly to those who are perishing, but to us who are being saved it is the power of God." "Jews demand signs and Greeks seek wisdom, but we preach Christ crucified, a stumbling block to Jews and folly to Gentiles, but to those who are called, both Jews and Greeks, Christ the power of God and the wisdom of God. For the foolishness of God is wiser than men, and the weakness of God is stronger than men."[16]

The *word from the cross* is the gospel of Paul — the message he announced to Jews and pagans. It is a plain witness, without a trace of grandiloquence, without any effort to convince on the grounds of reason. It derives its entire force from that *which* it proclaims. And that is the cross of Christ, that is, the death of Christ on the cross, and the crucified Christ himself. Christ is God's power and God's wisdom not only as one sent by God, as God's Son who is himself God, but as the Crucified One. For the death on the cross is the salvific solution invented by God's unfathomable wisdom. In order to show that human power and human wisdom are incapable of achieving salvation, he gives salvific power to what appears to human estimation to be weak and foolish, to him who wishes to be nothing on his own, but allows the power of God alone to work in him, who has "emptied himself" and "become obedient to death on the cross."[17]

The saving power: this is the power that awakens to life those in whom divine life had died through sin. This saving power had entered the *Word from the cross* and through this word passes over into all who receive it, who open themselves to it, without demanding miraculous signs or human wisdom's reasons. In them it becomes the life-giving and life-forming power that we have named the science of the cross.

Paul brought it to fulfillment in himself: "Through the law, I died to the law, that I might live to God. I have been crucified with Christ; it is no longer I who live but Christ who lives in me; and the life that I now live in the flesh I live by faith in the Son of God who loved me and gave himself for me."[18] In those days when all turned into night about him but light filled his soul, the zealot for the Law realized that the Law was but the tutor on the way to Christ.

It could prepare one to receive life, but of itself it could not give life. Christ took the yoke of the Law upon himself in that he fulfilled it perfectly and died for and through the Law. Just so did he free from the Law those who wished to receive life from him. But they can receive it only if they relinquish their own life. For those who are baptized in Christ are baptized in his death.[19] They are submerged in his life in order to become members of his body and as such to suffer and to die with him but also to arise with him to eternal, divine life. This life will be ours in its fullness only on the day of glory.

But even now we have—"in the flesh"—a share therein insofar as we *believe*: believe that Christ died for us in order to give us life. It is this faith that unites us to him as the members are joined to the head and opens for us the stream of his life. And so faith in the Crucified— a living faith joined to loving surrender—is for us entrance into life and the beginning of future glory. The cross, therefore, is our only claim to glory: "Far be it from me to glory except in the cross of our Lord Jesus Christ, by which the world has been crucified to me, and I to the world."[20] He who has decided for Christ is dead to the world and the world to him. He carries in his body the marks of the Lord's wounds,[21] is weak and despised by the people but is precisely therefore strong because the power of God is mighty in the weak.[22]

Knowing this, Jesus' disciple not only takes up the cross that is laid upon him, but also crucifies himself: "Those who belong to Christ Jesus have crucified the flesh with its passions and desires."[23] They have waged an unrelenting battle against their nature, that the life of sin might die in them and room be made for the life of the spirit. That last is what is important. The cross has no purpose of itself. It rises on high and points above. But it is not merely a sign—it is Christ's powerful weapon; the shepherd's staff with which the divine David moves against the hellish Goliath; with it he strikes mightily against heaven's gate and throws it wide open. Then streams of divine light flow forth and enfold all who are followers of the Crucified.

3. The Sacrifice of the Mass

To die on the cross with Christ in order to be resurrected with him becomes a reality for every Christian and especially for every priest in the Holy Sacrifice of the Mass. Faith teaches that it is the renewal of the sacrifice on the cross. For those who, with living faith, offer or participate in the Mass the same thing happens in and for them that happened on Golgotha.

Even as a child, John of the Cross was an acolyte, and no doubt also served as such in the order until his ordination. We know from the accounts of his life that the mere sight of a picture of the Crucified could carry him into an ecstasy. So how must the actual offering of the sacrifice have seized him—even when he participated merely by serving, all the more so later when he himself celebrated it!

We have been instructed about his first Mass. He celebrated it in the Monastery of Santa Ana in Medina del Campo, in September, 1567, perhaps during the octave of Our Lady's birthday, September 8, in the presence of his mother and of his older brother Francisco and the latter's family. A holy dread had made him shrink away from priestly dignity, and only obedience to the directives of his superiors enabled him to overcome his hesitation.

Now, as the holy celebration began, the thought of his unworthiness was probably especially vivid. It awakened in him the burning desire to be totally pure in order to touch the Most Holy with immaculate hands. So a petition arose from his heart that the Lord preserve him from ever offending God mortally. He wanted, without the guilt of committing them, to feel compunction for all the faults into which he could fall were God not to help him. At the consecration he hears the words: "I grant you what you ask of Me." From then on, he is confirmed in grace and has a two-year-old child's purity of heart.[24]

To be free of guilt and yet to feel compunction—is that not true union with the immaculate Lamb that took upon itself the sin of the word; is it not Gethsemane and Golgotha?

Surely receptivity for the greatness of the sacrifice of the Mass never diminished for John. We know that in Baeza he once went away from the altar in an ecstasy without finishing the Mass. One of the women attending called out that angels would need to come to finish this holy Mass since the saintly priest did not remember that he had not concluded it.

During a Mass in Caravaca he was seen surrounded by rays emanating from the sacred Host. He himself admitted that sometimes he abstained from offering Mass for days because his nature was too weak to support the extremes of heavenly consolation he received.[25] It was his particular delight to celebrate the Mass of the Blessed Trinity. There is, of course, the closest connection between this exalted mystery and the Holy Sacrifice that has been instituted by the decree of the three divine Persons, which is offered in their honor, and which gives access to the eternal spring of their life. We cannot imagine what a fullness of illumination was granted to the saint in the course of his priestly life at the altar.

At all events, his growth in the science of the cross, his continual mysterious transformation into the Crucified, happened for the most part in the service of the altar.

4. Visions of the Cross

By word and image and through liturgical celebration, the message of the cross knocks at the door of every human heart that lives in a Christian cultural circle, but particularly at the heart of the priest. It is only that not all of them are capable and ready to accept it so appropriately and to respond to it as was John of the Cross. Moreover, even prescinding from the particular graces received during Mass, that message was given him in an extraordinary form. The Crucified appeared to him repeatedly in visions.

We have exact information about two such visions. In his teaching, John treats visions, locutions, and revelations as unessential byproducts of the mystical life. He constantly warns against them because in their regard one is exposed to the danger of delusion, and is, in any case, delayed on the way to union if one places any value on such things. Moreover, he was very reticent about communicating events in his own life, external ones as much as interior ones.

That he spoke about these two visions gives them, in any case, special significance. Both of them were followed, in his life, by a storm of persecution and suffering. It is thus clear that we should regard them as harbingers.

The first apparition was given him in Avila, in the Monastery of the Incarnation to which holy Mother Teresa had called him as confessor for the nuns. One day, as John was immersed in contemplation of the Passion on the cross, the Crucified showed himself to John, visible to the bodily eyes, covered with wounds and bedecked with blood.

So clear was the apparition that he was able to sketch it in ink as soon as he came to. The small yellowed sheet of paper has been preserved down to our own time in the Monastery of the Incarnation.[26] The sketch makes a very *modern* impression. The cross and the body are highly foreshortened in the depiction, as though viewed from the side; the body is in strong motion, separated far from the cross, suspended from the hands. The hands, pierced by very large and prominent nails, are particularly expressive. The head is thrown forward and down, so that the features are indiscernible, and one sees instead the neck and upper part of the back, both covered with welts.

The saint gave the small paper to Sr. Ana María de Jesús and shared his secret with her. This is easy to understand since the Lord himself had imparted to her some of his most interior secrets: for instance, the grace that had been given John at his first Mass.

It is not known whether the Savior spoke any words when he leaned down so far from the cross. But surely a heart-to-heart exchange took place. It was during the time before the battle of the Calced against the Reform began, of which John was to become a victim more than anyone else.

The second apparition, toward the end of his life, took place in Segovia. He had called his beloved brother Francisco to come there. We owe the account to Francisco: "When I had been there two or three days, I begged him to let me depart. He told me to stay a few days longer for he did not know when we would see each other again. And this was the last time I saw him. One evening after supper he took me by the hand and led me into the garden and when we were alone, he said to me: 'I want to confide in you what happened to me with Our Lord. We had in the monastery a crucifix,[27] and one day, as I stood before it, it occurred to me that it would be more suitable to have it in the church. It was my wish that not only the friars but those outside could also venerate it. And I did what I had thought of doing.

"After I had put it up in the church as fittingly as I was able to do, I was standing before it one day in prayer—and then he spoke to me: Brother John, ask of me whatever I should grant you for the favor you have done me here! And on my part I said to him: Lord, what I wish from you is suffering which I may bear for you, and that I may be despised and disdained.'"[28]

The circumstances in which John was living when he expressed this desire were such that its fulfillment could easily be the result of natural conditions. The man who headed the reformed Carmel, the provincial Nicholas Doria, was a firebrand and zealot who wished to transform Teresa of Avila's work according to his own ideas. John decisively defended the holy Mother's legacy and the victims of Doria's fanaticism: Padre Jerónimo Gracián and the Carmelite nuns. On May 30, 1591, the General Chapter of the Discalced Carmelites opened in Madrid. Before departing to go there, the saint took leave of the Carmelite nuns in Segovia. The prioress, María de la Encarnación, excitedly cried out: "Father, who knows but that Your Reverence will leave the chapter as provincial of this province." "They will throw me into a corner as one does an old rag, like an old dishcloth," was his reply. And that is what actually happened. He was not given any office anymore, and was sent into the solitude of La Peñuela.

Reports of the afflictions of the Carmelite nuns followed him there. They were being interrogated in an attempt to collect material against John. Grounds were being sought to expel him from the Order. Not long thereafter, his final illness compelled him to leave La Peñuela where it was impossible to get medical assistance. Thus he reached the final station of his Way of the Cross: Ubeda.

Covered with festering wounds, he encountered in the prior, Padre Francisco Crisóstomo, an embittered opponent who fully satisfied his desire for demeaning treatment. The summit of Golgotha was reached.

5. The Message of the Cross

There is a third testimony showing that images of the cross had an unusual effect on John.[29] And it probably happened even more frequently than we have been told. We take all these effects as messages of encouragement to carry the cross and a preparation for doing so. But all of what we symbolically combine under the name *cross*, all the burden and suffering in life, must also be reckoned as belonging to the message of the cross because from it we gain the most profound science of the cross.

The saint was acquainted with pain and envy from his first years as a child. His father's early death, his mother's struggle to earn her children's daily bread, his own constantly unsuccessful efforts to contribute something to support the family—all this must have made a very deep impression on the child's tender heart, but nothing has been recorded about it. We know just as little about the spiritual effects of the crises of his first years in the Order.

Concerning the later years, there are reports that give a somewhat deeper insight into his inner life. One evening in Avila, as the Angelus was being rung, John came out of the monastery church after hearing confessions and turned into the small path that led to the little house where he was living with his companion, Padre Germán. Suddenly, a man seized him and beat him so severely with a cudgel that he fell to the ground. (It was the revenge of a lover whose prey he had snatched away.)

As John recounted this adventure, he further stated that at no other time in his entire life had he experienced such sweet consolation: he had been treated like the Savior himself and had tasted the sweetness of the cross.

The time of his imprisonment in Toledo provided him with superabundant opportunity for such experience. The saint had begun the Reform in Duruelo, had moved with the growing monastic community to Mancera, then had been active in the novitiate in Pastrana, and finally had run the first college of the Order in Alcalá.

In 1572, Holy Mother St. Teresa called him to Avila to assist her in a very difficult task. She had been assigned to return as prioress to the monastery of the Incarnation that she had left. While preserving the mitigated Rule, she was to remedy the abuses that had crept in there and bring the large community to lead a truly spiritual life. To do so, she considered it essential to provide good confessors. She could find none better suited than John, with whose great experience in the spiritual life she was well acquainted. From 1572 to 1577 his labors there brought the richest yield for souls. While he was active there in all quiet, the work of the Reform made great progress elsewhere.

Holy Mother journeyed from one foundation to another. New monasteries of the Reform had also come into being for men. Illustrious personalities had entered the Order and had assumed positions of leadership, principal among them Padre Jerónimo Gracián and Padre Ambrosio Mariano.

Not without guilt on their part, the Calced, the fathers of the mitigated Rule, felt themselves wronged and organized a strong defensive combat. This is not the place to study why the persecution should be directed, and indeed with particular violence, against John, whose activity was a purely spiritual one. On the night of December 3, 1577, several of the Calced with their accomplices broke into the living quarters of the nuns' two confessors and took them away as captives. From then on, John was missing. True, Holy Mother learned that the prior, Maldonado, had taken him away. But where he had been taken was not revealed until nine months later when he was freed.

Blindfolded, he had been brought through a lonely suburb to the monastery of Our Lady in Toledo, the most important Carmelite monastery of the mitigated Rule in Castile. He was interrogated, and because he refused to abandon the Reform he was treated as a rebel. His prison was a narrow room, about 10 feet long and 6 feet wide. Teresa later wrote: "small though he was in stature, he could hardly stand erect in it."[30]

This cell had neither window nor air vent other than a slit high up on the wall. The prisoner had to "stand on the poor-sinner-stool and wait until the sun's rays were reflected on the wall in order to be able to pray the breviary."[31] The door was secured by a bolt. When news arrived in March, 1578, that Padre Germán had escaped, the hall leading to the prison cell was also locked.

At first every evening, later three times a week, and finally, only sometimes on Fridays, the prisoner was brought to the refectory where, seated on the floor, he ate his meal—bread and water. He was also given the discipline in the refectory. He knelt, naked to the waist, with bowed head; all the friars passed by him and struck him with the switch. And since he bore everything "with patience and love" he was dubbed "the coward."[32] Throughout, he was "immovable as a rock" when they commanded him to abandon the Reform, attempting to bribe him by offering to make him a prior. Then he would open his silent lips and assure them that he refused to turn back "no matter if it cost him his life."

The youthful novices who were witness to the humiliations and mistreatment wept out of compassion and said "This is a saint"[33] when they saw his silent patience. His tunic was drenched with blood at the scourgings; he had to put it back on as it was and it was not changed during the nine months he was a prisoner. One can imagine what suffering it caused him in the glowing heat of those summer months. The food brought to him caused him such complaints that he thought it was intended to kill him. He made an act of love at each bite in order to escape the temptation to calumny.

We know how close were the ties to his nearest relatives. He was also devoted wholeheartedly to the work of the reform and to Holy Mother and the others who were united with him in this great task, who had, like him—for the most part under his personal direction—dedicated their whole lives to the ideal of the primitive Carmel. Later, when duty forced him to remain in Andalusia for years, he openly expressed his homesickness for Castile and the circle of trusted friends. "After that whale swallowed me up and vomited me out on this alien port, I have never merited to see her (St. Teresa) again or the saints up there."[34]

Now he was so separated from all of them that for all those months he was unable to send them any news. "I was at times saddened by the thought that people would say I had turned back on what I had begun, and I felt how the Holy Mother would be grieved."[35]

But there were even more painful deprivations. On August 14, 1578, Prior Maldonado came to John's prison cell accompanied by two religious. The prisoner was so weak that he could hardly move. Thinking his jailer had entered, he did not look up. The prior poked him with his foot and asked why he did not stand up in his presence. As John begged pardon, saying he had not known who was there, Padre Maldonado asked, "What were you thinking about since you were so absorbed?"

"I was thinking that tomorrow is the feast of Our Lady and that it would be a great consolation for me if I could say Mass."[36] How he must have missed celebrating the holy sacrifice in the nine long months when he was never allowed to do so! He had to spend the Feast of Corpus Christi, on which he was accustomed to kneel for hours in adoration before the Blessed Sacrament, without Mass and Communion.

To be helplessly delivered to the malice of bitter enemies, tormented in body and soul, cut off from all human consolation and also from the strengthening sources of ecclesial-sacramental life—can there be a harder school of the cross? Yet this was not the most intense suffering. All this was incapable of separating him from the triune source of which his faith gave him certainty.[37] His spirit was not confined in the prison, it could raise itself to that ever-flowing spring, immerse itself in this unfathomable depth, in the torrent which filled everything created, including his own heart. No human power could separate him from his God—but God himself could withdraw from him. And the prisoner experienced this darkest night here in his jail.

¿Adónde te escondiste	Where have you hidden,
Amado, y me dejaste con	Beloved, and left me behind in
gemido?	tears?

This cry of a soul in pain arose in the prison of Toledo.[38]

We have no testimony to show when John first learned to know the sweetness of God's nearness. But everything indicates that he had a very early initiation into the mystical prayer life. In order to be free for God, he had separated himself from his loved ones, then he had given up the course of his studies and departed from his home monastery. To make other souls free for God and to lead them on the way of union, this was the task in Avila to which he completely applied all his effectiveness in the order. He bore all the suffering of his imprisonment for this ideal of the Reform. Joyfully he accepted all the insults and mistreatment for the sake of his beloved Lord. And now this sweet light seemed to be extinguished in his heart—God left him alone. That was the most intense suffering with which no earthly suffering could be compared. But nevertheless it was proof for him of God's preferential love. It seemed to lead to death and yet was the way to life. No human heart ever entered as dark a night as did the God-man's in Gethsemane and on Golgotha. No searching human spirit can penetrate the unfathomable mystery of the dying God-man's abandonment by God. But Jesus can give to chosen souls some taste of this extreme bitterness. They are his most faithful friends from whom he exacts this final test of their love. If they do not shrink back from it but allow themselves to be drawn willingly into the dark night, it will become their leader:

> O Night that was a guide!
> O night more lovely than the rosy dawn!
> O night, you that united
> The most beloved with her Lover.
> Transforming the belov'd into her Lover.[39]

This is the great experience of the cross that took place in Toledo: extreme abandonment, and precisely in this abandonment, union with the Crucified. Therefore it is perhaps understandable that the statements about the imprisonment sound contradictory.[40] On the one hand, it is stated that John seldom or never had consolations, had suffered both in body and soul; and on the other, that many years in prison could not pay for a single one of those graces that God granted him there. Later, it will be necessary to show in detail how the soul comes to true self-knowledge and to enlightenment about God's immeasurable greatness and holiness precisely through the experience of her own nothingness and impotence in the dark night; how she is thereby purified, adorned with virtues, and prepared for union. These certainly are precious graces— never can their purchase cost too much. So considering them only, we can understand why, after his escape from prison, John spoke to the Carmelite nuns of Toledo of his tormentors as though they were great benefactors. But when, on this occasion, he asserted he had never enjoyed as great a fullness of supernatural light and consolation as during his imprisonment, we must still assume that he arrived at something beyond the graces of suffering. The stanzas of the *Dark Night* and *The Spiritual Canticle*, which were composed in prison,[41] give testimony to a rapturous union. Cross and night are the way to heavenly light: that is the joyful message of the cross.

6. Content of the Message of the Cross

We have considered by what ways John penetrated the message of the cross. The following sections wish to show how this message was incorporated into the doctrine and life of the saint. To do so, it is necessary to set the content of the message before our eyes—for the time being, in a brief outline.

We set it down here exactly as we find it expressed by the master of the science of the cross: "'How narrow is the gate and constricting the way that leads to life! And few there are who find it' (Mt 7:14). We should particularly note the exaggeration and hyperbole conveyed by the word *how* in this passage. This is like saying: Indeed the gate is very narrow, narrower than you think. . . . This path on the high mount of perfection is narrow and steep, it can only be trodden by wanderers who carry no burden that could drag them downwards. . . .[42] Since in this, God alone is the goal that one should seek and gain, then only God ought to be sought and gained. . . . Our Lord, for our instruction and guidance along this road, imparted to us that wonderful teaching—I think it is possible to affirm that the more necessary the doctrine the less it is practiced by spiritual persons—. . . . 'If anyone wishes to be my disciple let him deny himself, take up his cross and follow me. For whoever would save his life, will lose it but whoever loses it for my sake, will save it' [Mk 8:34f]. Oh, who can make this counsel of our Savior on self-denial understandable, practicable, and attractive! . . . Annihilation of all sweetness in God . . . dryness, distaste, and trial. . . . the pure spiritual cross and the nakedness of Christ's poverty of spirit. . . . A genuine spirit seeks rather the distasteful in God than the delectable, leans more toward suffering than toward consolation, more toward going without everything for God than toward possession, and toward dryness and affliction than toward sweet consolation, for it knows that in this consists the following of Christ and self-denial, while the other is nothing further than seeking oneself in God . . . Seeking God in God [*sic*] means[43] . . . for love of Christ, to choose all that is distasteful whether in God or in the world."[44]

The renunciation according to the will of the Savior "must be the dying off and annihilation of all that the will holds in high esteem, whether temporal, natural, or spiritual."[45] But whoever carries the cross in this manner will experience that it is "a sweet yoke" and "a light burden" (Mt 11:30), for they will "discover in all things great relief and sweetness."[46] "Only when the soul is reduced to nothing, the highest degree of humility, will the spiritual union . . . with God be an accomplished fact. The journey then consists in the living death of the cross, sensory and spiritual, exterior and interior."[47] It can be nothing else, because according to God's wonderful plan of salvation, Christ "redeems and espouses the soul through the very means by which human nature was corrupted and ruined. As human nature was ruined . . . and corrupted by means of the forbidden tree in the garden of Paradise, so on the tree of the cross it was redeemed and restored" by him.[48] If the soul wishes to share his life, she must pass through the death on the cross with him: like him she must crucify her own nature through a life of mortification and self-denial, and surrender herself to be crucified in suffering and death, as God may ordain or permit it. The more perfect this active and passive crucifixion may be, the more intimate will be the union with the crucified and therefore the richer the participation in the divine life.

With this, the principal chords of the *Science of the Cross* have been struck. We will hear them reverberate if we listen to the saint's teaching and follow his path in life. It will be demonstrated that they are the deepest moving forces shaping his life and work.

2

The Cross and the Night

II. THE DOCTRINE OF THE CROSS

Introduction: John of the Cross as Author

If one seeks to understand the doctrine of St. John of the Cross from the perspective of its spiritual roots, one must take into account the specific character, indeed the uniqueness, of his writings, their origin, and their destiny.

Since the church has raised the saint to be a Doctor of the Church, anyone who wishes to gain information in the sphere of Catholic doctrine on questions of mysticism may look to him. And far beyond the boundaries of the Catholic Church, he is also recognized as one of the leading spirits, a reliable signpost, which no one who earnestly wishes to advance in the mysterious realm of the interior life may bypass. And yet John of the Cross has not given a systematic delineation of mysticism. His purpose in writing was not theoretical, although he was enough of a theoretician to allow himself sometimes to be drawn farther afield through purely objective connections than had been his original intention. What he actually wanted to do was "to lead people by the hand" (as the *Areopagite* says of himself),[1] completing his work as director of souls through his writings.

In no way has everything he ever wrote been preserved. Everything that originated before his arrest was destroyed either by himself or by others. The second persecution (within the Reform) also robbed us of much, for example, the valuable notes that the Carmelite nuns had made of his oral teachings. Likewise only a small fraction of his

35

letters have been preserved. And of the four great treatises that remain ours—*The Ascent of Mount Carmel, The Dark Night, The Spiritual Canticle,* and *The Living Flame of Love*—the *Ascent* and *Night* have come down to us in incomplete form.[2] Despite these gaps and many insoluble questions that result, those writings that remain to us as an invaluable legacy from our holy Father contain the dominant thoughts so clearly that we may well hope to find an answer to our question.

The actual origin of the existing writings is to be sought in the time of the imprisonment in Toledo. The source from which they spring is John's most intimate experience. The bliss and torment of a heart afflicted and wounded by God find their first expression in lyrical confession: the first 30 stanzas of *The Spiritual Canticle* originated in prison. So, perhaps, did the poem of the *Dark Night* that serves as the basis for the treatise bearing the same name, as well as for the *Ascent.*[3] John brought them with him from the prison (whether preserved only in memory or written down in a notebook—for this there are differing testimonies) and made them known to trusted souls.

We must thank the pleas of spiritual sons and daughters for the explanatory treatises. In them the experience is translated from the language of the poet into that of the philosophically and theologically schooled thinker, who, however, uses technical terminology from scholasticism sparingly and imagery from life abundantly. Furthermore, the experiential basis is broadened: what he experienced himself is completed through what is known to the master director of souls from his deep insight into other persons' interior life. This preserves him from one-sidedness, from making false generalizations. He always considers the manifold variations of possible ways and the tender and pliable adaptation of grace as it leads the individual soul according to its particular conditions.

Finally, sacred Scripture is for him an ever-flowing source of teaching regarding the laws of the inner life. In it he finds sure confirmation of what he knows from the most interior experience. On the other hand, his personal experience opens his eyes to the mystical meaning of the sacred books. The keen pictorial language of the psalms, of the Lord's parables, even the historical narratives of the Old Testament—

all becomes transparent for him and always gives him an ever more abundant and deeper insight into the one subject which counts for him: *the soul's way to God and God's activity in the soul.*

God has created human souls for himself. He desires to unite them to himself and to give them the immeasurable fullness and incomprehensible bliss of his own divine life, already in this life. That is the *goal* to which he directs them and toward which they themselves should strive with all their might. But the way to it is narrow, steep, and difficult. Most people remain en route. A few manage to get beyond the first beginnings—a dwindling small number arrive at the goal. That is due to the dangers on the way—worldly dangers, the evil enemy, and one's own nature—but also due to ignorance and lack of qualified guidance. Souls do not understand what is happening within them, and seldom is someone to be found who could open their eyes to what is going on. To these, John offers himself as a competent guide. He pities the errant, and he is saddened to see God's handiwork fail because of such obstacles. He is willing and able to help for he knows every highway and byway in the mysterious realm of the inner life. He is not at all able to say all he knows about it; he is constantly forced to apply the reins in order not to go beyond what the task requires.

The saint did not write his works for everyone. Of course, he does not wish to exclude anyone. But he knows that for understanding he can count only on a determinate circle of persons, those who have a certain amount of experience of the inner life. He thinks, first of all, of the Carmelite friars and nuns who are particularly called to interior prayer. But he knows that God's grace is not tied to a religious habit or to cloister walls. After all, we owe the treatise on *The Living Flame of Love* to one of his spiritual daughters "in the world." So he writes for contemplative souls, and at a very particular point along their way he wants to take them by the hand, at a crossroad where most halt, perplexed, not knowing how to proceed. Impassable barriers confront them on the way they have been traveling. But the new path that opens up before them leads through impenetrable darkness. Who has the courage to venture on it?

The crossroad in question here is that between *meditation* and *contemplation*. Previously, perhaps using an Ignatian method, one has exercised the spiritual powers in the hours of meditation—the senses, imagination, understanding, the will. But now they won't work. All efforts are in vain. The spiritual practices that up to now have been a source of inner joy become a torment, intolerably dull and fruitless. But there is no tendency to occupy oneself with worldly things. The soul desires more than all else to remain still, without bestirring itself, allowing all its faculties to rest. But this seems to them to be sloth and a waste of time. That is more or less the state of the soul when God wishes to lead it into the *Dark Night.* In usual Christian parlance such a condition will be called "a cross."

Even in earlier times there was talk that *cross* and *night* had something to do with one another. But it is of no help to us to reach the indeterminate conclusion that the meanings are similar. At some points in the writings of holy Father John there is mention of the significance of the cross in so determined a manner that it no doubt justifies our viewing his life and his doctrine as a science of the cross. But these are relatively few points. The *prevailing symbol* in his poems as in the treatises is *not the cross,* but *night*. In the *Ascent* and *Night* it is the centerpoint throughout; there remains an echo of it in the *Canticle* and the *Living Flame* (which mainly treat of the condition beyond the *Night*).[4] That is why it is necessary to give an exact account about the relationship between cross and night if one wishes to gain access to the cross's significance for John of the Cross.

1. Cross and Night (Night of the Senses)

A. Difference in the Character of the Symbol: "Emblem" and "Cosmic Expression"

First of all, it must be asked whether cross and night are *symbols* in the same sense. The word symbol, after all, is given many meanings. Sometimes it is taken in a very broad sense, so that one understands it as everything sensory by which something spiritual is signified, or everything familiar through natural experience signifying something unfamiliar, perhaps even something the natural perception cannot experience. In this broad sense cross as well as night may be called symbols. But a contrast becomes apparent as soon as we take into account the difference between *sign* and *image*. Understood as a *likeness*—the image points to what is imaged through an inner similarity; whoever sees it will immediately be directed through it to the original that he recognizes therein or that he learns to know through it.

Between a sign and what is signified there need be no such substantial agreement. Their relation is founded on an arbitrary positing about which one must be informed in order to understand the sign. The cross is obviously not an image in the strict sense. (If one calls it a symbol, that says little more than symbol in the broad sense described above: something perceivable that points to a meaning beyond that which is perceived.)

There is no immediately perceptible similarity between the cross and suffering, but neither is there a purely arbitrarily established relationship of signs. The cross has acquired its meaning through its history. It is not merely a *natural object* but rather a *tool* finished and used by human hands for a very specific purpose. As a tool it has played an incomparably important role in history. Everyone who lives in a Christian cultural sphere knows something about this role. Therefore the cross in its visible form leads immediately to the fullness of meaning which is entwined with it. It is thus a sign, but one that has not artificially gained meaning; rather it has genuinely earned it by reason of its effectiveness and its history. Its visible form indicates the meaning connected with it. Therefore we can rightly call it an *emblem [Wahrzeichen]*.

Night on the contrary is something *natural*: the counterpart of light, wrapping itself around us and all things. It is not an object[5] in the actual, literal sense: night does not stand opposite us, nor does it stand by itself. Nor is it an *image* insofar as one understands that to mean having a visible form. Night is invisible and formless. But still we perceive it, indeed it is nearer to us than all things and forms; it is more closely bound to our being. Just as light allows things to step forward with their visible qualities, so night *devours* them and threatens to devour us also. Whatever sinks into it is not simply nothing; it continues to exist but as indeterminate, invisible, and formless as night itself or shadowy, ghost-like, and therefore threatening.

Moreover, not only is our own being threatened through external dangers hidden by the night, but it is shocked interiorly by night itself. It robs us of the use of our senses, limits our movements, makes lame our strengths, banishes us in loneliness, makes us shadowy and ghostly ourselves. It is like a foretaste of death. And all this has not merely a vital, but a psychic-spiritual[6] significance as well. The cosmic night affects us similarly to what in a figurative sense is called *night*. Or, turned around, whatever brings forth in us effects similar to those of the cosmic night is, in a figurative sense, called *night*.

Before we try to identify this "whatever," we must be clear that the cosmic night already has a double face. The dark and uncanny night is other than the moonlit magic night, which is flooded by a mild, soft light. This softly lit night does not devour things but, instead, gives them a glowing nocturnal visage. Everything harsh, sharp, and glaring is muted and soothed, and characteristic traits are revealed that never appear in bright daylight. Voices can also be heard that are drowned out by daytime noises. And not only does the light-filled night have its own values, but so does the dark one. The latter puts an end to the haste and noise of the day, it brings rest and peace. All of this pertains as well to what is referred to as psychic-spiritual. There is a night-like, gentle lucidity of the spirit, in which, freed from the drudgery of the day's duties, relaxed and recollected at the same time, it is absorbed in the profound relationships of its own being and life, of the world, and the world beyond. And there is a deep, grateful repose in the peace of night.

One must think of all of this if one is to understand St. John of the Cross's night symbolism. We know from testimonies about his life and from his poems that he was extremely sensitive to the cosmic night with all its tonalities. He spent entire nights gazing over the wide landscape from a window or out in the open. And he found words for the night which no other bard of the night has surpassed (*Spiritual Canticle*, Stanza 15[7]). The soul compares her beloved to:

| La noche sosegada, | The tranquil night, the lovely one, |
| En par de los levantes de la aurora, | Already pierced by new morn's light, |

La música callada	Music of softest tones
La soledad sonora,	And solitude that rings,
La cena, que recrea,	The supper that refreshes and
y enamora.	Lends love wings.

When John the thinker speaks of the night in his treatises, all the plenitude of meaning that the word has for the poet and the human being lies behind it. Insofar as it is a symbolic expression, we have sought to interpret it in a few lines without exhausting its meaning. Now we must make an effort to grasp what is to be expressed symbolically in such ways. John's treatment is detailed and we will have to return to it.

For the time being, it is important to gain an insight that will make apparent the specific character of the symbolic relationship in question. The *mystical night* is not to be understood in a cosmic sense. It does not impose itself on us from without but rather has its origin in the interior of the soul and affects only this single soul in whom it arises. The effects it produces, however, in the interior can be compared to those of the cosmic night: it entails a submersion of the exterior world even though outside it is bathed in bright daylight. It casts the soul into loneliness, desolation, and emptiness, stops the activity of all her faculties, frightens her by threatening horrors it conceals within itself. However, here there is also a *nocturnal light* that reveals a new world deep in the interior and at the same time illumines the outer world from within so that this outer is given back to us as entirely transformed.

We will now attempt to gain clarity about the *relation between the mystic and the cosmic night* insofar as possible on the basis of this first introductory consideration. Obviously it is not a matter of a relation of signs here, nothing stipulated arbitrarily from beyond, nor are we dealing with a causal and historically produced connection as with an emblem. There is an extensive *agreement in content* that permits the use, here and there, of the same name. When one speaks of the *image* of night one surely wishes to say that the name, first of all, belongs to the cosmic night and from there is transferred to the mystic night, in order to become acquainted with something unknown and inaccessible through something commonly known and familiar that it resembles.

But one cannot speak of a *relationship of likeness*; one is not a copy of the other. Rather one must think of it as a relationship of *symbolic expression* such as commonly exists between the *sensory* and the *spiritual*. So facial features and expressions can express spiritual character and spiritual life, just as the spiritual and even the divine can reveal itself in nature. There exists an original mutuality and an objective correspondence that enables the sensory to reveal knowledge of the spiritual. Of the relationship of the image, only the similarity remains—a similarity, however, in which what is mutually "alike" is not actually comprehensible but can only be indicated through certain corresponding features. What distinguishes this similarity from the image-relationship is not only that there is a lack of replication but also that we are not dealing with the structures that have definite outlines. Here there is also a contrast to mimicry: a very decided facial alteration that an artist can copy with pencil or brush corresponds to an equally decided spiritual happening. Night, however, the cosmic as well as the mystic, is something shapeless and something comprehensive whose fullness of meaning can only be indicated but not exhausted. An entire world-view and grasp of existence is resolved therein. And precisely here what they have in common is to be found: the fact of and the character of this worldview and grasp of existence. Something intangible here and something intangible there and yet clearly one overlays the other and can be used to access the other, not by arbitrary choice and systematic comparison but in *symbolic experience* that strikes upon *primitive connections* and thus finds a necessary figuration for what is conceptually unutterable.

We are now in a position to summarize briefly the difference in the symbolic character of *cross* and *night*. The *cross* is the *emblem* of all that has causal and historical connection with the cross of Christ. *Night* is the necessary *cosmic expression* of St. John of the Cross's mystical world-view. That the night-symbol prevails is a sign that the poet and mystic is spokesman in the writings of the holy Doctor of the Church rather than the theologian, even though the theologian conscientiously supervises thought and expression.

3

Taking Up One's Cross

B. The Song of the Dark Night

It is now necessary to examine the mystic night in order to perceive within it the echo of the message from the cross. The best way to do this will be to use the *Song of the Dark Night* as the point of departure. It is, after all, the basis for the two large tracts that deal with the mystical night.[1]

DUNKLE NACHT	THE DARK NIGHT
1. In einer dunklen Nacht Da Liebessehnen zehrend mich entflammte, O glückliches Geschick! Entwich ich unbemerkt, Als schon mein Haus in tiefer Ruhe lag.	1. One dark night, As love's yearning [tugging sinews] did enflame me I escaped unnoticed O happy fate [skill]![2] I escaped unnoticed When my house lay at rest so still.
2. Im Dunkel wohl geborgen Vermummt und auf geheimer Leiter, O glückliches Geschick! Im Dunkel und verborgen, Da schon mein Haus in tiefer Ruhe lag.	2. Quite safe within the dark, Disguised and on a secret ladder, O happy fate! In darkness and concealed, Since my house lay at rest so still
3. In dieser Nacht voll Glück, in Heimlichkeit, da niemand mich erblickte,	3. In this night so full of chance In secrecy, since none caught sight of me,

43

Da ich auch nichts
   gewahrte,
Und ohne Licht noch
   Führer
Als jenes, das in meinem
   Herzen brannte.

4. Und dieses führte mich
   Weit sichrer als das Licht
     des hellen Tages
   Dahin, wo meiner harrte
   Er, der mir wohlbekannt,
   Abseits, da, wo uns
     niemand scheiden
     konnte.

5. O Nacht, die Führer war!
   O Nacht, viel liebenswerter
     als die Morgenröte!
   O Nacht, die du verbunden
   Die Liebste dem Geliebten,
   In den Geliebten die
     Geliebte umgewandelt!

6. An meiner blüh'nden Brust
   Die sich für ihn allein
     bewahrte,
   Entschlief er sanft,
   Ich streichelte ihn sacht,
   Und Kühlung gab des
     Zedernfächers Wehen.

7. Als leicht der Morgenwind
   Die Haare spielend ihm
     begann zu lüften,
   Mit seiner linden Hand
   Umfing er meinen Nacken,
   Und alle meine Sinne mir
     entschwanden.

Since, too, I was aware of
   naught
and without light or guide
Save that which in my heart
   was burning.

4. And this conducted me
   Far surer than the light of
     brightest day
   Thence, where for me eagerly
     was waiting
   He whom I know so well,
   Aside, there where no one
     could part us.

5. O night that was a guide!
   O night, more lovely than the
     rosy dawn!
   O night, you that united
   The most beloved with her
     Lover
   Transforming the belov'd into
     her Lover.

6. At my blossoming breast
   Which has reserved herself
     for him alone,
   He gently fell asleep.
   Softly I caressed him
   The stir of waving cedars
     brought coolness.

7. As morn's wind with
     lightest touch
   Playfully began to lift his hair
   With his gentle hand
   He encircled my neck
   And all my senses vanished.

8. In Stille und Vergessen	8. In silence and forgetfulness
Das Haupt auf den Geliebten hin ich lehnte	I leaned my head on the Beloved,
Entsunken alles mir,	All things had drained away from me
Verschwunden war die Angst,	Vanished was the fear
Begraben unter Lilien im Vergessen.	Buried neath lilies into oblivion.

C. The Dark Night of the Senses

1) Introduction to the Meaning of Night

The poetic image is carried through perfectly, not one didactic word intrudes. Instead, the two explanatory treatises, *The Ascent* and *The Dark Night,* give the key for understanding the poem.

The soul that sings the song has passed through the night; she has arrived at the goal, has entered union with the divine Beloved. Therefore it is a song in praise of the night that has become a way to blessed happiness. The jubilant cry—oh, happy fate!—is repeated. But darkness and fear are not forgotten. It is still possible to bring them in retrospectively.

The house from which the Bride has departed is the sensory part of the soul.[3] It is at rest because all its appetites have been stilled. The soul was able to detach herself from, them because God himself freed her. She would not have had the strength [*Kraft*] to do it herself. In this brief explanation the significant difference between the *active* and the *passive* night is already characterized, their mutual relationship noted; the distinction between them will be treated in detail later. To be freed from the confinement imposed by her sensory nature, the soul must strain with all her might, but God must come to her assistance with his efficacy, indeed he must act first. God's action incites hers and perfects it.

Detachment is designated as a *night* through which the soul must pass. It is this in a threefold sense: in regard to the *point of departure,* the *path*, and the *goal*. The point of departure is the desire for the things of this world, which the soul must renounce. But this renunciation transplants her into darkness and as though into nothingness. That is why it is called *night*. The world that we perceive with the senses is, after all, naturally the firm foundation that supports us, the house in which we feel at home, that nourishes us and provides us with everything necessary, the source of all our joys and gratifications. If this world is taken from us or if we are forced to withdraw ourselves from it, it is truly as though the ground were swept away from under our feet and as though it became night all around us; as though we ourselves must sink and vanish.

But this is not so. In fact, we are set upon a surer *way,* albeit a dark way, one engulfed by night, the way of *faith*. It is a *way,* for it leads to the goal of union. But it is a *nocturnal way*, since in comparison to the clear insight of the natural understanding, faith is a *dark knowledge*: it acquaints us with something but we do not get to see it.

That is why it must be said that the *goal* we reach on the way of faith is also night. *God* remains hidden from us on earth, even in the bliss of union. The eyes of the spirit are not adapted to the excessive radiance of his light, and gaze as it were into the darkness of night. But just as the cosmic night is not equally dark for its entire duration, the mystic night has its divisions of time and corresponding intensities. The submersion of the world of the senses is like the oncoming of night, when a mere *twilight* remains of the day's brightness. Faith, on the contrary, is the *midnight darkness* because here not only are the senses inactive but the knowledge from natural understanding is eliminated. The *dawn* of the new day of eternity, however, breaks into her night when the soul finds God.

One might already discern a certain harmony between night and cross on the basis of this brief general view; the relationship will become even clearer if we now consider the phases of the night individually.

2) Active Entrance into the Night as a Following of the Cross

The saint calls the point of departure or the first segment the *dark night of the senses*.[4] What is actually entailed here is the *mortification of joy in the desire for all things*. It can, after all, not be a matter of no longer perceiving with the senses. They are the windows through which the light of knowledge falls into the darkness of the prison of our bodily life, and we cannot dispense with them as long as we live. But we must learn to see and to hear, and so on, as though we neither saw nor heard. Our basic attitude toward the world we perceive by the senses must change. This basic attitude in a natural person is usually not solely a question of pure perception—much more, he is in the world as one who craves things and as a man of action. He is bound up with the world in a thousand ways because it satisfies his demands, goads him into action, and is the material of his deeds. Commonly, he is led in his actions and his aspirations by drives and appetites, concerning nourishment and clothing, labor and rest, play and recreation, in interaction with others. He feels happy and content when he does not meet with any extraordinary obstacles. No extraordinary ones—for from his youth he has taken for granted that it is impossible to live without ordinary hindrances; this has become second nature.

He knows as a result of his education and experience that unbridled satisfaction of desire is ruinous for one's own nature, and healthy common sense leads him to practice a certain voluntary restriction and regulation. Consideration of others, which is irrefutably demanded when living a common life, has a similar effect, enjoined as a natural right and a natural moral law. All of this, however, does not impinge on the natural right of the human drives, it is only brought into balance with other rights.

On the other hand, something entirely new is begun when the *Dark Night* starts. The entirely comfortable being-at-home in the world, the satiety of pleasures that it offers, the demand for these pleasures and the matter-of-course consent to these demands—all of this that human nature considers bright daily life—all of this is *darkness*[5] in God's eyes and incompatible with the divine light. It has to be totally uprooted if room for God is to be made in the soul. Meeting this demand means engaging in battle with one's own nature all along the line, *taking up one's cross and delivering oneself up to be crucified.* Holy Father St. John here invokes the Lord's saying in this connection: "Whoever does not renounce all that the will possesses cannot be my disciple" [Lk. 14:33].[6]

That the domination of desires is truly darkness in the soul is demonstrated in full: the appetites weary and torment the soul, darken, besmirch and weaken her, rob her of the Spirit of God because she turns away from him by her surrender to the animal spirit. To take up the battle against it, or to take one's cross upon oneself, means *entering into the dark night actively.* The saint gives several concise directions of which he himself says: "A person who sincerely wants to practice them will need no others since all the others are included in these."[7] These directions are:

"1) Sustain always the desire to imitate Christ in all things and to bring your life into conformity with his. You must therefore study his life in order to imitate it and behave always as he would.

"2) In order to do this well, you must deny yourself every pleasure that presents itself to your senses, keep it far from you if it is not solely directed to the honor and glory of God.

"And in fact you should do this out of love for Jesus who knew no other joy and had no desire in his life other than to fulfill the will of his Father. He called this his food and nourishment [Jn 4:34]. If, for instance, some amusement offers itself to you in hearing of things that do not contribute to the service of God, then you should neither have pleasure in them nor wish to hear them. . . . Likewise, practice renunciation in regard to all your senses, for as much as you are able to refuse their impressions readily.[8] Insofar as you are unable to ward them off, it is sufficient that you take no enjoyment when these things approach you. Take care how you mortify your senses and preserve them from being touched by any inordinate desire. Then they will remain alike in darkness and in a short time you will make great progress.

"The following maxims will serve as a thoroughly effective means of mortification and of harmoniously ordering the four natural passions: joy, hope, fear, and sorrow. For where these passions are calmed and well ordered, the above named good things plus many others can flourish. That is why these maxims are of great value and are the root of great virtues. Take care that your inclination is ever directed:

not toward the easier, but toward the more difficult;
not toward the pleasant, but toward the unpleasant;
not toward the restful, but toward the troublesome;

not toward the more, but toward the less;

not toward what brings you more joy, but what brings displeasure

not toward what prepares consolation for you, but toward what makes you disconsolate;

not toward the higher and more valuable, but toward the lowly and insignificant;

not toward what wants to be something, but toward what wants to be nothing.

"Seek not what is the better in things, but what is worse. Demand for the sake of Christ to enter into total denudation and freedom and poverty from all there is in the world. You should embrace these works from your heart and take care that your will rises to the task. . . . If what is said here is truly carried out, it will suffice to give entry into the night of the senses."[9]

No further explanation is necessary to see that this active entry into the dark night of the senses is synonymous with ready willingness to take up the cross, and with persistence in carrying the cross. But one does not die from carrying the cross. And in order to pass completely through the night, a person must die to sin. One can deliver oneself up to crucifixion, but one cannot crucify oneself. Therefore that which the active night has begun must be completed by the *passive* night, that is, through God himself.

"No matter how much individuals do through their own efforts, they cannot actively purify themselves enough to be disposed in the least degree for the divine union of the perfection of love. God must take over and purge them in that fire that is dark for them."[10]

3) Passive Night as Crucifixion

It was mentioned earlier that the active entrance of the soul into the dark night is only possible for her because God's grace anticipates her, draws her, and supports her along the entire way. But for beginners this anticipatory and enabling grace does not as yet have the character of the *dark night*. Rather, God treats them the way a tender mother treats her tiny children—carrying them in her arms and feeding them with sweet milk: in all their spiritual exercises—in prayer, meditation, and mortifications—they receive abundant joy and consolation. This joy then motivates them to devote themselves to spiritual exercises. They are unaware of the imperfections that lie therein and how many faults they commit in their practice of virtue. The saint demonstrates by living examples that all seven capital sins, carried into the spiritual sphere, are to be found in beginners: *spiritual pride* that compliments itself on its graces and virtues, looks down on others, and prefers to instruct rather than accept instruction; *spiritual avarice* that cannot have enough of books, crucifixes, rosaries, and so on.[11]

In order to be freed from all these defects we must be weaned from the milk of consolations and be fed with strengthening nourishment. . . . "After beginners have exercised themselves for a time in the way of virtue and have persevered in meditation and prayer and through the delight and satisfaction they experience in this have become detached from worldly things and have gained some spiritual strength in God, which helps them to restrain their appetites for creatures, and for God's sake are able to suffer a little oppression and dryness without yearning to return to those better times when they experienced more pleasurable satisfaction and gratification . . . then . . . God darkens all this light and closes the door and the spring of sweet spiritual water they were tasting as often and as long as they desired . . . . Now he leaves them in such darkness that they do not know which way to turn in their discursive imaginings."[12]

Now all pious exercises appear distasteful, even repugnant. That this is not the result of sins and imperfections but is rather a case of *purgative dryness* of the dark night can be discerned by three signs:

1) that the soul finds no delight in creatures;[13]

2) that "the soul turns to God solicitously and with painful care, and thinks it is not serving God but turning back because it is aware of this distaste for the things of God."[14] Now, if the dryness were the result of lukewarmness, the soul would not be worried about it. In

purgative dryness on the other hand, there is always the desire to serve God. And the spirit grows stronger while the sensory part feels weakened and powerless because of its lack of satisfaction. "God transfers his goods and strength from sense to spirit. Since the sensory part of the soul and its natural powers are incapable of receiving the goods of the spirit, they remain deprived, dry and empty. Thus while the spirit is tasting refreshment, the flesh feels aversion and becomes weak in its work. But the spirit grows much stronger and more alert through this nourishment, and becomes more solicitous than before about not failing God."[15] However, since it is not yet accustomed to spiritual sweetness, at first it feels none of it but only dryness and distaste;

3) one recognizes purgative dryness in that "the soul is powerless in spite of all its efforts to meditate and make use of the imagination, the interior sense, . . . God no longer communicates himself through the senses as he did before, by means of the discursive analysis and synthesis of ideas, but has now begun to communicate himself through pure spirit by an act of simple contemplation for which neither the exterior nor the interior senses of the sensory human being have any capacity."[16]

This dark and, for the senses, dry contemplation is "something secret and hidden and even for the one who possesses it, mysterious." Ordinarily it imparts to the soul an inclination and a demand to remain alone and at rest. She is unable to dwell on any particular thought, nor does she have any desire to do so.[17] If those in whom this occurs knew how to remain quiet, "they would soon experience in that unconcern and idleness a precious interior nourishment. This refection is namely so delicate that the soul cannot usually feel it if it desires it excessively or tries to experience it specifically. . . . It is like air that escapes when one tries to grasp it in one's hand . . . God deals with the soul in this state in such a manner and leads it along such a special way that, if it desires to work with its own faculties and strength, it would rather hinder than help the work of God." The peace God produces in the spirit through the dryness of the sensory being is "spiritual and most precious" and its "fruit is quiet, delicate, solitary, satisfying, and peaceful, and far removed from all the earlier gratifications which were more palpable and sensory."[18] So one understands that only the dying of the sensory being is felt and nothing is experienced of the beginning of the new life that is concealed beneath it.

It is no exaggeration when we call the suffering of the souls in this state a crucifixion. In their inability to make use of their own faculties they are as though nailed fast. And to the dryness is added the torment of fear that they are on the wrong path. "They live in the belief that they will have no more spiritual blessings and that God has abandoned them." Then they strive to act in the former manner, but are unable to achieve anything and only disturb the peace that God is working in them.

They should do absolutely nothing other than "persevere patiently in prayer without any activity whatsoever; all that is required of them here is freedom of soul, that they liberate themselves from the impediment and fatigue of ideas and thoughts, and care not about thinking and meditating. They must be content simply with a loving and peaceful attentiveness to God, and live without the concern, without the effort, and without the desire to taste or feel him." Instead of doing this, because they lack competent guidance, they strive in vain, and possibly plague themselves with the thought that they are only wasting time with their prayer and ought to give it up.

Were they to remain peacefully surrendered to this dark contemplation they would soon experience what the second line of the song of the *Night* calls the *inflaming love*. "For contemplation is nothing else than a secret and peaceful and loving inflow of God, which, if not hampered, fires the soul in the spirit of love."[19]

In the beginning this being inflamed in love is not commonly perceived. The soul feels rather only dryness and emptiness, sorrowful fear and concern. And if she does feel any of the love, it is as a painful yearning for God, a smarting wound of love. Only later will she recognize that God has purified her through the night of the senses and wished to make the senses subject to the spirit. Then she will exclaim: "Oh, happy fate!" And she will clearly see what gain the "unnoticed escape" means for her: it has freed her from the servitude in which the senses had kept her, and little by little she is detached from all creatures and attracted to eternal goods. The *night of the senses* was for her *the narrow gate* (Mt 7:14) that leads to life.

Now she is to travel on the constricted road, which is the night of the spirit. Of course, few will come so far, yet the advantages of the first night are very great: the soul is granted *self-knowledge;* she gains insight into her own misery, no longer finds anything good in herself and learns therefore to approach God with greater reverence. Yes, only now is she aware of the *grandeur and majesty* of God. Precisely this being freed from all sensory supports enables her to receive illumination and become receptive for the truth. That is why we find in the psalm: "In a desert land, without water, dry and without a way, I appeared before you to be able to see your power and your glory" (Ps 63:1-2). The psalmist gives us to understand that "the means to the knowledge of the glory of God were not the many spiritual delights and gratifications he had received, but the aridities and the detachments of the sensory be- ing [*Mensch*]."[20] By "a land without a way" John understands one's inability to grasp an idea of God through discursive thought or to at- tempt to investigate with the help of imaginative powers.

In dryness and emptiness the soul becomes *humble.* The earlier arro- gance disappears when one no longer finds in oneself anything that would give reason to look down on others; instead, others now appear to one to be more perfect; love and esteem for them awakens in the heart. One is too occupied with one's own misery to be concerned about others. Through her helplessness the soul also becomes *subservient* and *obedi- ent;* she longs for instruction in order to reach the right way. Spiritual avarice is thoroughly healed; when one no longer finds any practice to one's taste, one becomes very moderate and does whatever one does purely for the sake of God without seeking any satisfaction for the self. And so it goes with all imperfections. All the confusion and unrest dis- appear with them. Instead, a deep *peace* and a *constant remembrance* of God are established. The only care that remains is the concern not to displease God.

The dark night becomes the school of all *virtues:* it exercises one in *surrender* and *patience* if one remains faithful in the spiritual life without seeking consolation or refreshment. The soul attains a pure love of God so that all is done now only for God's sake. Perseverance despite all unpleasantness gives the soul strength and *courage*. Being completely purged of all sensory inclinations and appetites leads to a *freedom of the spirit* in which the twelve fruits of the spirit ripen. It gives security against the three enemies: the devil, the world, and the flesh. These can do nothing against the soul: she has "escaped unnoticed" from them. And now that the passions have been calmed, and the natural sensory appetites have been lulled to sleep, her "house lies" now "at rest so still."

The soul has escaped and has found the way of the spirit, the way of the proficients, the illuminative way on which God now wishes to instruct her without any activity on her part. She is now in a state of transition. Contemplation affords her purely spiritual joys in which the purified senses also share. But from time to time she returns to meditation. And the joys alternate with painful visitations. Before the night of the spirit is entered, severe and burdensome trials through painful temptations are joined to the dryness and emptiness: the spirit of fornication and of blasphemy overpowers her imagination and a *spirit of confusion* casts her into a thousand scruples, in entanglement and perplexity. These storms are intended to try and to steel souls. But all are not tested to the same degree. Many do not even get beyond this state of transition. However, those who are to arrive at the goal must undergo a great deal. The higher the degree of union of love to which God desires to lead them, the more intense and prolonged will the purification be. For even proficients still have many habitual imperfections from which the night of the spirit must free them. And the senses are only fully purified along with the spirit. It is in the spirit, after all, that the imperfections are rooted.[21]

The exposition of the way of purification shows plainly that this night is not without light even though the eyes of the soul are not accustomed to it and cannot perceive it. In the relatively brief explanations in which John addresses the night of the senses, the valuable fruits of the night are stressed emphatically. But in this there is no contradiction to the message of the cross. For mention had already been made that the Savior united to the announcement of his Passion and death on the cross the good news of the resurrection. According to the liturgy of the church the progression is "*per passionem et crucem ad resurrectionis gloriam.*" ["Through the Passion and cross to the glory of the resurrection."] The death of the sensory human being keeps in step with the rise of the spiritual human being. But this marvelous new birth has so far only been hinted at. John has been brief in the explanation of the first night because he is in haste to arrive at the *night of the spirit.* It is his main objective. Therefore it is better to examine the relationship between death and resurrection only after treating the dark night of the spirit.

4

Spirit and Faith

2. Spirit and Faith. Death and Resurrection (Night of the Spirit)

Introduction: Development of the Questions

John marked the *night of the spirit* as the *narrow way*. But earlier it was called the *way of faith* and its darkness was termed that of *midnight*. Accordingly, faith must have a dominant role in the night of the spirit. In order to understand clearly, it will be necessary to establish what the saint understands when he speaks of *spirit* and of *faith*. This is not an easy task. Beneath all he writes there lies an *ontology of the spirit*. But there is no treatise on it, and perhaps he never even took the trouble to develop a theory about the habitual knowledge living in him that determined his occasional disclosures. Even less does he appear to have asked himself from what sources his knowledge arose. His goal did not require clarity on this point.

And were we to pursue this question, significant in the history of spirituality, we would be led too far astray. However, we may not pass over the *applicable* questions: what does John understand when he speaks of *spirit* [*Geist*], and of *faith*? But they must be answered in the light of what we are told about the night of the spirit. A certain amount of difficulty arises from the fact that the dark night is given a double treatment—in *The Ascent* and in *The Night*—and both parts are incomplete.

A. Divesting the Spiritual Faculties in the Active Night

1) The Night of Faith as the Way to Union

The second night is the darker because the first affects the lower, sensory part of the human being and is, consequently, more external. The night of faith, on the other hand, involves the higher, sensible part and is therefore interior and robs the soul of the light of reason or makes her blind.

"Theologians call faith a sure but obscure habit (*habitus*) of the soul;" obscure, because "it brings us to believe divinely revealed truths that transcend every natural light and infinitely exceed all human understanding. As a result, the excessive light of faith bestowed on a soul is darkness for it; a brighter light will eclipse and suppress a dimmer one." "So the light of faith suppresses and overwhelms that of the intellect through its abundance. For the intellect, by its own power, extends only to natural knowledge."[1] It can meanwhile become capable of receiving supernatural knowledge when God wishes to raise it to do so. On its own the intellect can only gain knowledge in the natural way, that is, by means of the senses which present an object to it. "To know in this way one will need to have the phantasms and species of objects present either in themselves or in their likenesses."[2]

If one speaks to others about something they have never seen, and if they know of nothing similar which could give them a clue, they may perhaps be able to accept the name, but will never be able to form an image of the thing, as for example a person born blind will have no idea of color. Such is faith to the soul. It informs us of things we have never seen nor heard nor do we know anything that might be similar to them. We can only accept what we are told by turning off the light of our natural knowledge. We have to agree with what we hear without having any of the senses elucidate it for us. Therefore faith is a totally dark night for the soul. But it is precisely by these means that it brings her light: a knowledge of perfect certainty that exceeds all other knowledge and science so that one can arrive in perfect contemplation at a correct conception of faith. That is why it is said: *Si non credideritis, non intelligetis* ("If you do not believe, you will not understand," Is 7:9).[3]

From what was last said, it has not only been made clear that faith is a dark night, but also that it is a *way*: the way to the goal toward which the soul strives, to union with God. For it alone gives knowledge of God. And how is one to arrive at union with God without knowing him? However, in order to be led by faith to the goal, the soul must conduct itself in the right manner. She must enter into the night of faith of her own choice and by her own power. After having renounced all desire for creatures in the night of the senses, in order to reach God, she must now die to her natural faculties, her senses, and to her intellect also. For in order to reach the supernatural transformation, she must leave behind everything natural. Yes, she must divest herself, as well, of all supernatural goods when God grants her any of these. She must let go of everything that falls into the realm of her power of comprehension. "And she must remain in the dark like a blind man, leaning upon dark faith and choosing it as light and guide and not supporting herself by anything she understands or enjoys or feels or imagines. For all this is darkness that will lead her into error or delay. Faith, on the other hand, is above all such understanding, enjoyment, feeling, or imagining."[4]

The soul must become totally blind to all of this and remain so in order to reach what faith teaches. For those who are not yet totally blind are reluctant to allow a guide to lead them; instead they still depend on that which they can see themselves. "So it is with the soul. If she relies on that which she herself knows about God, or enjoys or feels. . . . she can easily go astray or stand still, because she does not yet blindly surrender herself to faith which is after all her true guide." In order to arrive at union with God, one must "simply believe in the existence of God which is not matter for the intellect or will, or imagination or any other of the senses; for in this life we cannot grasp what God is. One may have the loftiest impressions of God, or know him or enjoy him, and yet all this is infinitely removed from what God really is and from the pure possession of God."

If the soul desires to "become perfectly united through grace with him to whom she will be united through glory in the next, which according to St. Paul no eye has seen, no ear heard, nor anyone's heart conceived

(1 Cor 2:9; Is 64:4)," then she must "as far as possible become totally unreceptive to everything that may enter through the eye, be perceived through the ear, imagined by the fantasy, or grasped by the heart, the heart here meaning the soul."[5] Should she support herself by her own faculties, the soul prepares only difficulties and obstacles for herself. To reach her goal, leaving her own path is synonymous with entering on the right path. Indeed, "to strive toward the goal and renounce her own mode is already to arrive *at that goal* which has no mode: that is, God. For the soul that reaches this state knows no mode and method anymore, nor does she hold fast to anything; indeed, she is unable to hold on to anything," cannot understand any particular mode, or taste, or feeling, "she now possesses all modes alike, like one who has nothing and yet has everything."[6] Through going beyond her natural boundaries, interiorly and exteriorly, "she enters into supernatural bounds— bounds that have no mode, yet *in substance* possess all modes."

She must elevate herself above all that is naturally and spiritually intelligible, above all she is able to understand and know in a natural way, as well as above all that is spiritual which one can taste and feel with the senses in this life. The more she still esteems all this the more she distances herself from the highest good. But if she considers all as slight in comparison to the highest good, she "will approach union swiftly by means of faith, which is also dark."[7]

To be more clear, the saint inserts a brief explanation here of what he means when he speaks of *union* in all of these expositions. It is not God's substantial union with all things by which he conserves their being, which union always exists, but rather "the soul's union with and transformation in God through love." This union does not always exist; rather, its existence is possible only "when the soul arrives at a likeness of love."[8] The other substantial union is natural, this one is supernatural. The supernatural union exists when God's will and the soul's are in *conformity,* so that nothing in the one is repugnant to the other. When the soul "rids herself completely of what is repugnant and unconformed to the divine will, she rests transformed in God through love . . . Not only must actual voluntary imperfections cease, but habitual imperfections must be annihilated too. No creature, none of its actions and abilities, can reach or encompass God's nature. Consequently, a soul must strip herself of everything pertaining to creatures and of her actions and abilities. . . . Only thus will she be transformed in God."

The divine light, then, already dwells in the soul by nature. But only when for God's sake she divests herself of all that is not God—that is what is called love!—will the soul be illumined by and transformed in God. "God will so communicate his supernatural being to the soul that she will appear to be God himself and will possess what God himself possesses." So great a union is caused "that all the things of both God and the soul become one in participant transformation, and the soul appears to be God more than a soul. Indeed, she is God by participation. Yet, truly, her being (even though transformed) is naturally as distinct from God's as it was before."[9]

2) Divesting the Spiritual Faculties as the Way of the Cross and Death on the Cross

The denudation of the faculties that is demanded for this transforming union is effected in the *intellect* through *faith,* in the *memory* through *hope*, and in the *will* through *love*. It has already been shown how faith gives the intellect a sure but dark knowledge. It shows God as inaccessible light, as the incomprehensibly Infinite One in face of whom all natural faculties fail totally. The intellect is brought back to its total nothingness in precisely this manner: it recognizes its own powerlessness and God's greatness. Hope puts the memory into emptiness since it occupies it with something that one does not possess. "For how does one hope for what is already seen?" (Rom 8:24). It teaches us to hope for everything from God and not from ourselves or any other creature; to expect to receive from him the bliss that will have no end and therefore to renounce in this life every pleasure and possession. Love finally frees the will from all things since it obliges the will to love God above all. This becomes possible only when the desire for everything created is given up.

This way of perfect renunciation has already been called the *narrow way* that only a few find (Mt 7:14). The way that leads to the high mountain of perfection can only be traveled by those who are not weighed down by any burden. It is the Way of the Cross to which the Lord invites his disciple: "If anyone wishes to follow my way, let him deny himself, take up his cross, and follow me. For whoever would save his soul will lose it, but whoever loses it for me will gain it" (Mk 8:34f). What is demanded here is not merely a small degree of withdrawal from the world, a certain improvement in this or that circumstance, praying a little longer, or practicing a little renunciation while at the same time enjoying consolations and spiritual feelings.

Those who wish to satisfy themselves with this much will "run as from death itself" "as soon as they encounter something of this solid perfection that consists of the annihilation of all sweetness in God, in dryness, distaste, and trial. This is the purely spiritual cross and nakedness of poverty in the spirit of Christ." The other is "nothing other than the seeking of oneself in God—something entirely contrary to love. Seeking oneself in God means looking only for God's caresses and consolations. Seeking God in himself[10] [that is, oneself] . . . entails not only the desire to do without these consolations for God's sake, but also the inclination to choose for love of Christ all that is most distasteful whether in God or in the world; and this is what loving God means."[11] To hate one's soul—and thereby to save it—means for Christ's sake to renounce all that the "the will can ever desire or taste, and to keep for oneself only that which bears a closer resemblance to the cross."

To drink the chalice with the Lord (Mt 20:21) means dying to one's natural self—both in the sensitive and in the spiritual part. Only in this way can one enter the narrow way. "For on this road there is room only for self-denial and the cross. The cross is the staff upon which one leans and through which one greatly facilitates moving forward. That is why the Lord says in St. Matthew, 'My yoke is sweet and my burden light' (Mt 11:30); the burden here is the cross. If individuals resolutely submit to carrying the cross, that is . . . seeking in all things for God's sake only trials and joyfully enduring them, they will discover in all of them great relief and sweetness, and will travel on this road in total denudation, no longer desiring anything. If they self-seekingly aim after the possession of anything, whether from God or from the world, they are no longer detached and divested of all things. Then they are unable to gain a foothold on this narrow path and make progress."

Spiritual souls ought to recognize "that this path to God does not consist in having a multitude of meditations or particular practices, nor in having ecstasies . . . but rather in the one thing necessary . . . earnestly to deny oneself interiorly as well as exteriorly, and for Christ's sake to be ready to suffer and die to self in every respect. Whoever . . . schools himself in this will achieve and find all and more than that. But, if one fails to practice this, then, no matter how exalted one's contemplation or how much one's communication with God resembles that of the angels, all other practice of virtue will be nothing more than a water sprout, which is totally unproductive."[12]

Christ is our way. Everything depends on understanding how we are to model our journey on that of Christ. "First, incontestably, he died: in a spiritual sense, during his entire life to all that is of the senses; and in the natural sense, at his death. He had in life, as he himself said, nowhere to lay his head (Mt 8:20). In death, he had even less. Second, at the moment of his death he was certainly annihilated in his soul, since the Father had left him without any consolation or relief, in utmost aridity. He was thereby compelled to cry out, 'My God, my God, why have you forsaken me?' (Mt 27:46). This was the most extreme abandonment, sensitively, that he had suffered in his whole life. But precisely by this, he accomplished a greater work than any he had wrought in his entire life with all its signs and wonders: . . . he brought about the reconciliation and union of the human race with God through grace.

"This was achieved in the moment in which the Lord was most annihilated in all things . . . in his reputation before people, since as they watched him die they mocked him; in his human nature which was totally destroyed through death; in the help and consolation from the Father, for at that time he was left completely without help, so that, totally stripped and annihilated, as though dissolved into nothingness, he should purge all guilt and unite humanity to God . . . From this, truly spiritual souls may come to understand the mystery of Christ as the door and the way to union with God, and so realize that their union with God will be the more intimate, and the work they accomplish the greater, the more they annihilate themselves in their sensory as well as their spiritual parts for the sake of God. When they are reduced to nothingness in the highest degree of humility, then the spiritual union of the soul with God takes place, the most noble and sublime state attainable in this life. It does not, therefore, consist in spiritual refreshment, delights, and feelings, but in the living death on the cross, in what is sensory as well as in what is spiritual, and exteriorly as well as interiorly."[13]

5

The Inadequacy of Knowledge

3) Uselessness of all Created Things as Means to Union Inadequacy of Natural and Supernatural Knowledge

Here one feels the heartbeat of our Holy Father. He speaks of the great truth that he has recognized; it is his mission to proclaim it: our goal is union with God, our way that of the crucified Christ, our becoming one with him takes place when we are crucified. The only proportionate means to arrive at this union is faith. This will now be demonstrated by showing that no other real or imagined thing is capable of effecting it. Every means must be proportionate to its goal. Only "that which brings about union with God and which has the greatest similarity to God" can serve as a means to union with God. This cannot be applied to any created being. Certainly all have some kind of connection with God and bear a certain trace of God in themselves. "Yet God has no relation or essential likeness to creatures. For the disparity between his divine Being and theirs is infinite. Therefore it is also impossible that the intellect can comprehend God perfectly through the means of anything created, be it heavenly or earthly."[1]

Even the angels and saints are so far removed from the divine Being that the intellect cannot attain to God through them. This is true of everything concerning "that which can be imagined or received and understood by the intellect in this life."[2]

In the natural world, the intellect grasps objects through the forms and images that the senses perceive. These cannot serve to lead forward on the way to God. As well, whatever of the supernatural world is accessible to the intellect here cannot help it attain any certain knowledge of God. The intellect, therefore, in its own insights cannot construct an adequate concept of God. The memory out of all its fantasy cannot create a form or picture that could portray God; the will cannot taste any joy or delight that is at all similar to God himself. Therefore, in order to attain to God, one must "rather strive . . . not to understand as to understand . . . rather to be blind and transport oneself into darkness . . . than to open the eyes." This is why the Areopagite calls contemplation *mystical theology,* that is, secret knowledge of God and a *ray of darkness.*[3]

The darkness that leads to God is, as we already know, *faith.* It is the only means that leads to union because it sets God before our eyes as he is: as infinite, as triune. Faith resembles God in that both blind the intellect and appear to it as darkness. "The greater one's faith the closer is one's union with God."[4] Its darkness is indicated in sacred Scripture by the image of the *cloud*, in which God concealed himself in the Old Testament revelations: to Moses on the mount,[5] in Solomon's temple.[6] The light of truth is concealed in this darkness. It will "at once appear when faith reaches its end .... by the ending of this mortal life."[7]

Temporarily, though, we are totally dependent on faith. What it gives us—*contemplation*—is a *dark* and *general knowledge*; it stands in contrast not only to natural cognition but also to the various ways in which the intellect receives distinct and particular *supernatural knowledge: visions, revelations, locutions,* and *spiritual feelings.* The bodily eyes may be shown images and persons from the other world: angels or saints, or unusual shining lights. One can hear extraordinary words, smell the sweetest fragrances, savor exquisite tastes, or feel extreme delight through the sense of touch. A person should refuse to attend to this, without seeking to examine whether it is good or bad. To be sure, these things may come from God but there is no certainty about that. "God's self-communication is more appropriately given to the spirit than to the senses, and the soul finds greater security and makes greater progress for through what is received by the senses, as a rule, great danger of deception exists. For the senses then believe they can arbitrate and judge spiritual matters, whereas they are as ignorant of them as a beast of burden is of rational matters."

The devil can easily practice his arts in this quarter because he has influence on the bodily senses. And even when the images come from God, they are the less conducive to good for the spirit the more exterior these forms and objects are. They motivate the spirit of prayer less and give the impression that they are more worthwhile and a better guide than faith. They mislead the soul to have a specially high opinion of herself. For this reason, the devil likes to make use of them in order to harm souls. For all these reasons it is best to reject all such representations. If they come from God, the soul will lose nothing thereby; this for the reason that every communication from God "produces its effect in the spirit at the very moment of its perception, without allowing any deliberation about wanting or not wanting it." And contrary to diabolical communications, which "arouse only the first movements without being able to move the will any further if it is unwilling to be moved," direct communications from God "penetrate deeply into the soul, move the will to love, and leave their effect that the soul cannot resist even should she wish to do so."[8]

Despite their remedial effect the soul should never dare to desire such sensory apprehensions because: 1) they will diminish faith, which transcends all sensory perceptions, and in doing so will lead the soul away from the only means to union with God; 2) they will detain the soul and prevent the spirit from soaring to the invisible; 3) they will not allow the soul to attain to genuine renunciation and nakedness of spirit; 4) through her attachment to the sensory she becomes less receptive of the spirit of devotion; 5) she will lose the graces which God wishes to give her because she selfishly strains after such visions; and 6) the desire to accept the communications opens the door to the devil to deceive her with feigned communications. If the soul lives in renunciation and "opposes such representations, the devil will desist because he sees he is unable to harm her. God, on the other hand, will pour his graces into such a humble and dispossessed soul with surpassing love, and will set her over many things, as in the case of the servant who was faithful in a few things [Mt 25:21].

"If individuals remain both faithful and retiring in the midst of these favors, the Lord will not cease raising them degree by degree until they reach divine union and transformation." [9]

Like the perceptions of the exterior senses, the *apprehensions* of the *interior senses—imagination* and *phantasy*—are to be rejected. One of these seeks to present pictures, the other gives form to what is presented. Both are significant for meditation, which is a reflection connected with such pictures.(For instance, one can imagine Christ on the cross or at the pillar of the scourging, or God on the throne of glory.) All such images are of as little use as proximate means to union with God as are the objects presented by the external senses, because "the power of imagination cannot fashion or imagine anything beyond what it has experienced through the external senses. . . . At the most it can compose resemblances of these objects that are seen, heard, or felt;" but these do not belong to a higher category of being than what was perceived by the senses. "Since created things. . . have no proportion to God's being," nothing that has been fashioned from the likenesses of creatures can serve as a proximate means toward union with God. It may be necessary for beginners to imagine God as an immense fire or brightness or something similar in order to move the soul by sensory means toward love or to inflame it. These images are but a remote means; souls must "ordinarily use them to attain their goal and the abode of spiritual repose." Yet these means must not be so used that one always employs them and never passes beyond them, for then one would never reach the goal."[10]

The proper time to abandon the stage of meditation has arrived when those three signs we already know from the *Dark Night of the Senses* occur together:[11] when the soul no longer finds delight and refreshment in discursive meditation; when she is equally disinclined to occupy herself with other things; when she desires most of all to rest totally in God in a general, loving knowledge of God. This loving knowledge is, as a rule, the fruit of many preceding meditations evolving from strenuous reflection on isolated perceptions that coalesce into a habitual condition through long practice. However, God effects this habit in many souls who have little practice "in that he suddenly places them in contemplation and love." This general loving knowledge is no longer either distinct or particular. "Now, the moment prayer begins, the soul, as one with a store of water, drinks peaceably without the labor and the need to fetch the water through the channels of past considerations, forms, and figures. The moment she recollects herself in the presence of God she enters into an act of general,[12] loving, peaceful, and tranquil knowledge, drinking wisdom and love and delight." All unrest and pain comes from misunderstanding this condition and from a return to reflection that has become fruitless.

In contemplation, the spiritual faculties, memory, intellect, and will act together. On the contrary, John of the Cross considers meditation and reflection as activities dependent on the sensory faculties. The purer, simpler, more perfect, spiritual, and interior the general knowledge is— and that is how it is when it inundates an entirely clear soul that is free from any other impressions or specific knowledge—the freer and more delicate it is and therefore more apt to evade being perceived. The soul finds herself as though in deep forgetfulness and simultaneously un-aware of time. Her prayer seems to be very brief, even when it has lasted for hours. This brief prayer "pierces the heavens, because such a soul is united with heavenly knowledge."[13]

The prayer leaves as after-effect an elevation of the mind to heav-enly knowledge and a withdrawal and abstraction from all objects, forms, and figures. Usually the will is also seized in this prayer: immersed in the delight of loving without particular knowledge of what is being loved. The activity of the soul in this condition consists purely in the reception of that "which God bestows on her in illuminations, revela-tions and inspirations." It is a clear and pellucid light that is poured into her. There is nothing that can be compared to it and every attention given to particular objects or considerations "would hinder the perception of this general, limpid and simple light of the spirit as though a cloud were shoved in between. . . . This light is never lacking to the soul, but because of creature forms and veils that weigh on her and cover her, the light is never infused. If the soul would eliminate these impedi-ments and veils and live in pure nakedness and poverty of spirit in her simplicity and purity she would then be immediately transformed into simple and pure Wisdom, the Son of God." Infused into her, will be "the calm and peace of God . . . with wondrous . . . knowledge of God, enveloped in love."[14] In this high state of union of love, God no longer communicates himself to the soul "through the disguise of any imaginative vision, likeness, or figure . . . but rather . . . mouth to mouth . . . that is, the pure and naked essence of God, which is like the mouth of God, imparts itself to the pure and naked essence of the soul through the will as the mouth of the soul in her love for God."[15]

But a long way has to be covered before arriving there. God leads the soul to this lofty pinnacle by stages. At first he accommodates himself to her nature, imparting to her in the beginning "spirituality under more exterior, palpable things," instructing her "through forms, images, and sensible means; now naturally, then supernaturally, and also according to the soul's own manner of coming to understand, he brings her to his supreme spirit." Imaginative visions are also included in this divine plan of education. But regarding these, one who receives them must pay attention only to "what God wants one to take from such apprehensions, that is, the spirit of devotion, since God gives these sense experiences for no other principal reason. A soul thus favored is to reject the sensory element, which would not have been imparted had she possessed the capacity to receive spirituality without the apprehensions and exercises of the senses."[16]

Under the Old Testament it was permissible, indeed it corresponded to the divine plan, to seek visions and revelations, and to be led by them because it was in this way that God revealed the mysteries of faith and made his will known. However, "that which God formerly spoke to our fathers through the prophets in many ways and manners, now, finally, in these days he has spoken to us all at once in his Son," [Heb 1:1-2] and has told us to " hear him" [Mt 17:5]. To demand revelations now, then, would be to lack faith since "in him are hidden all the treasure of the wisdom and knowledge of God" [Col 2:3]. "Thus we must be guided humanly and visibly in all by the law of Christ, who is human, and that of his Church and of his ministers. This is the way to remedy our spiritual ignorances and weaknesses. . . . One should not believe anything coming in a supernatural way, but believe only the teaching of Christ who is human, and of his ministers who are human. . . . All else is good for nothing, and one may only accept it in faith when it corresponds to the teaching of Christ."[17] We see also that in the Old Testament "it was not lawful for just anyone to question God; nor did God give answer to just anyone, but only to the priests and prophets."

"God has a very special predilection that . . . direction of humans be through other humans and that a person be governed by natural reason. Therefore, he definitely does not want us to bestow entire credence on his supernatural communications . . . until they pass to us through . . . the mouth of another human being. As often, then, as he reveals something to a soul" he bestows on her "a certain inclination to manifest it to the appropriate person who has a right to know about it." "For wherever several persons gather in an endeavor to know the truth, God draws near to them and enlightens them and confirms them in truth."[18]

In addition to that which reason perceives with the aid of the exterior or the interior senses there are further *purely spiritual communications*: they present themselves to the intellect without the mediation of an external or inner sense and without the individual's own contribution. "They are clearly, distinctly, and supernaturally imparted . . . passively, that is, without the soul's positing any act, at least through its own effort." John distinguishes *spiritual visions, revelations, locutions,* and *feelings* but joins all four together under the name of *intellectual visions* because in them all a *spiritual visibility* is present.

In a strict sense, a *vision* is anything the intellect perceives spiritually in a manner resembling sight; consequently, one can call a revelation anything the intellect understands in a new way, as the ear [19] does when a sound never previously heard is perceived; what the intellect receives in manner of hearing is called a *locution*. And what it receives after the manner of other sensory perceptions are called *spiritual feelings*. In all of them no form, image, or figure plays any kind of role. It is a communication bestowed immediately upon the soul by *supernatural intervention* and by supernatural means. Although these apprehensions are nobler, safer, and more advantageous than those received through the bodily senses or the imagination, one should not encumber oneself with them. For through them, also, "the intellect loses keenness and of itself impedes . . . the way of solitude and denudation."

These visions can place corporeal as well as incorporeal substances before the spiritual eye. In a certain supernatural light the soul can see all the corporeal objects there are in heaven or on earth. The incorporeal beings (God, angels, souls)[20] can only be seen in the light of glory and therefore not in this life. "If God should desire to let the soul see these substances essentially, she would immediately depart from the body and be loosed from this mortal life." In exceptional cases, such visions are granted to someone only "when God either dispenses from the natural law or preserves the nature and life of the individual, or abstracts the spirit entirely from nature. Paul, for example, was transported above the ways of our natural life (2 Cor 12:2) when he saw the third heaven. But such visions occur only in rare cases and only to such persons who, like Moses, Elijah and Paul, are "sources of the spirit of the Church and of God's law."

In the ordinary run of things in this life, spiritual substances cannot be "seen unclothed and clearly by the intellect, but they can be felt in the substance of the soul by the most delightful touches and conjunctions." This "dark loving knowledge which is faith serves as a means for divine union in this life, as does the light of glory for the clear vision of God in the next."[21]

Mention has been made of something that will be developed later. Temporarily, it suffices to strive for clarity about the spiritual visions of corporeal substances. They are perceived interiorly by the intellect through supernatural light, as the eyes see things through natural light. But spiritual vision is much sharper and far clearer than corporeal vision. It is like the sudden illumination by a bolt of lightning, that in a dark night allows things to stand out clear and distinct for a moment. Under the influence of the spiritual light, the objects seen are impressed so deeply on the soul that every time she adverts to them by the grace of God, she beholds them as she did the first time. They engender peace and clarity, heavenly joy, pure love, humility and an elevation and inclination toward God in the soul. Through these effects they are distinguished from the apings the devil is able to produce. Nonetheless, one should reject them.

Were the soul to desire to hoard them within as treasures, these impressions, images, and persons would absorb her interior and become an obstacle on the path to God which consists of the renunciation of all created things. The remembrance of such visions may well engender a certain degree of the love of God. But *pure faith* can do this to a much higher degree. When faith is rooted in the soul through denudation, darkness, and spiritual poverty, *hope and love* are poured into her—of course, a love that does not make itself felt through a particular tenderness, but rather reveals itself in the soul through strength and greater courage and a hitherto unknown bravery. "It behooves us to go by the way of total renunciation to the God who is incomprehensible and transcendent."[22]

Under the name of *revelations* John includes two different types of spiritual disclosures: *intellectual knowledge* in which *hidden truths* are manifested—these can refer to material as well as spiritual things—and *revelations in the strict and actual sense*, through which *secrets* and *mysteries* are revealed. The knowledge gained of naked truths is vastly different from the previously discussed visions of corporeal objects. This knowledge has for its object truths about the Creator or creatures. It is accompanied by an incomparable and inexpressible delight. "The knowledge having God for its object is given directly in that one of his attributes . . . is sublimely experienced . . . Each of these experiences is permanently impressed on the soul. Since this is pure contemplation, the soul clearly understands that it is ineffable. . . . it is totally impossible to express anything about it in words, except perhaps in general terms. . . . which however are totally incapable of explaining what the soul has tasted and felt." When the knowledge is about God himself, it never deals with particular things. "This sublime knowledge can be received only by a person who has arrived at union with God, for it is itself that very union," consisting "in a certain touch between the Divinity and the soul" that "penetrates the substance of the soul."

Some of "these divine touches produced in the substance of the soul are so enriching that one of them would be sufficient not only to remove definitively all the imperfections that the soul would have been unable to eradicate throughout its entire life but also to fill it with virtues and blessings from God." And they are so full of intimate delight that "one of them would more than compensate for all the trials suffered in life, even though these were innumerable. "It is impossible for the soul to arrive at such elevated knowledge through her own efforts. God alone effects it in her without any of her own doing, often when she is least thinking of it or desiring it. And because it is imparted to the soul so suddenly and without her doing anything, she may "neither seek nor refuse it; she should only accept it in humility and surrender, then God will do his work, as and when it pleases Him."[23] The saint, then, does not advise us to reject these discoveries as he did all those mentioned earlier. After all, they are a part of the union to which God desires to lead the soul. For their sake one should renounce all else and "take upon oneself" all suffering "in humility and surrender, without considering a likely recompense but purely for the love of God. For these graces. . . . are a token of a very special love God has for the recipient, because she too loves with great detachment. . . . God manifests himself to the soul who abandons herself to him and truly loves him."[24]

The other kind of knowledge differs greatly from the foregoing, in that it deals with things in themselves, human deeds and events. This *class* of knowledge belongs to the spirit of prophets [sic][25] and to what St. Paul calls the discernment of spirits (1 Cor 12:10). It is so embedded in the soul that it awakens an unshakable conviction that it is true. Even so, she must submit her judgment to the spiritual director because the way of believing leads more surely to union with God than that of understanding. So, many persons arrive at a knowledge of nature and its powers by supernatural means. Occasionally these are only single and transitory illuminations, but for those who are far advanced, they can now and then impart general and lasting knowledge.

On the strength of supernatural enlightenment, spiritual persons can perceive what is going on in the interior of other persons, through exterior indications, even though often these are extremely slight.

Furthermore they may also be given knowledge of the deeds and of events involving persons who are absent. This knowledge is attained by the soul without her doing anything on her own. It can happen that, without thinking about it in the least, a very clear understanding is gained of something read or heard, indeed far more clear than the wording is capable of communicating. It may even happen that one hears words in an unknown language and can still understand the meaning perfectly. In this domain (compared to the foregoing one) the devil has far more room to cause harm. But even without considering that, these enlightenments are of little value in attaining the goal of union with God and they are accompanied by many dangers. Therefore it is best to reject them, give an account of them to one's spiritual guide and follow the director's advice. These things are, after all, given the soul passively and "the effect God desires to produce through them will be fixed in the soul without need for efforts of her own."[26]

Revelations in the strict sense concern *articles of faith*: about *God's own Being*—the Trinity and unity of God—as well as *the divine works in creation*. To this second group belong the promises and threats of God through the mouths of prophets as well as "many other particular facts revealed ordinarily by God about the universe in general and, in particular, about kingdoms, provinces, states, families, and individuals." When the mysteries of faith are revealed to the spirit, they are not revelations, properly speaking, since they are already revealed, but would be instead a new manifestation or declaration of the already revealed mysteries. Since all of this is imparted through words or figures, it is easy for the devil to ape it.

Therefore, were anything to be revealed that is at variance with revealed truths of faith, one may by no means assent to it. And even when a new revelation about an already revealed truth is offered, the soul "should not believe . . . because they are again revealed, but because they were already sufficiently revealed to the Church." For "it greatly behooves the soul not to want to understand the truths of faith so clearly, that she may thereby conserve the merit of faith pure and entire; only in this manner will she pass through this night of the intellect to the divine light of union." The soul is wise to be cautious regarding such communications "so that through the night of faith she may journey to union purely and without error."[27]

As a third group of purely spiritual communications, John names *locutions* that are perceived by the intellect without the mediation of any corporeal sense. He classifies them as *successive, formal,* and *substantial.* The first are words and reasonings that the recollected spirit itself constructs. This occurs when it "is entirely recollected and at the same time attentively absorbed in some consideration." The spirit "proceeds from thought to thought, forming precise words and judgments, which correspond exactly to the subject matter and, indeed, with great ease and certitude and about things that were previously entirely unknown to it." It appears to the spirit as though someone in its interior were giving it answers and teaching it.

Actually it is speaking with itself, posing questions and replying to them, but in doing so it is the tool of the Holy Spirit under whose inspiration it is thinking. "The intellect is recollected and united with the truth that is the subject of its thought, and just so the Holy Spirit is united to it in that truth. As a result, during the time the intellect is thus communing with the divine Spirit by means of that truth, it simultaneously forms interiorly and successively other truths about its subject while the Holy Spirit, the Teacher, leads the way and gives light." Despite this enlightenment, one is not thereby totally secure against deception. The reason is, first of all, that the light is so delicate and spiritual that the intellect does not succeed in completely finding its way about in it.

Besides that, the intellect itself forms the statements of its own power and so it can err. At first, "so to say, it has the thread of truth firmly in its hands, then afterward it joins with it something of its own: the dexterity or the clumsiness of its scanty insight."[28] It can even be that an intellect that is very lively and subtle by nature will arrive at similar spiritual activity and will then believe it has been enlightened by God.

Added to this danger is another: the soul thinks that in these presumably divine locutions she has experienced something great and will allow herself to be drawn away from the abyss of faith. So one should guard against making much of them even when the intellect is indebted to the Holy Spirit for these illuminations. Of course, the intellect will be illumined by the Holy Spirit according to the degree in which it is recollected. But the Holy Spirit will not illumine it in any other recollection more than in faith. "The purer and more refined a soul is in faith, the more infused charity she has. And the more charity she has, the more the Holy Spirit illumines her and communicates his gifts to her." The light she receives in faith is qualitatively as different from that received through the latter illumination regarding a particular truth as is the purest gold from the basest metal, and, quantitatively as is the sea from a drop of water. "For through the intellect you receive wisdom concerning one, two or three truths; however, in the light of faith, the soul receives, at once, all of God's wisdom, that is, the Son of God, who communicates himself to her in faith." This fullness of illumination is impaired if one focuses one's attention on such supernatural communications. One should rather in all sincerity and simplicity of heart "center the will on God," establish the will in humble love and practice true virtue, that is, "imitate the son of God in his life and suffering and mortify herself in all things. For this is the road to the attainment of every spiritual good, and not that other road of profuse interior discourse."[29]

These latter discourses can proceed from the activity of a person's own natural light, as well as through the suggestions of the devil. Indeed, they do leave behind in the soul varying consequences depending upon their origin, but only a person with a great deal of experience in the spiritual life will be able to discern the differences with certainty. Therefore it is best to attribute no value to any of them. We should be "content with knowing the mysteries and truths of faith in the simplicity and verity with which the Church proposes them. Such an attitude will suffice to vigorously enkindle our will."[30]

Formal locutions differ from the successive ones in that the spirit receives them without any independent cooperation of its own, also without being recollected and without having thought about that which it hears. Often they are very explicit; often they are only like thoughts through which something has been communicated. Sometimes, it is only a single word; other times, more. It may even be a longer instruction. They do not leave much of an impression behind, for as a rule

they merely have the object of teaching or clarifying a single point for
a soul. Most often, they also impart the readiness to comply with the
command. But it can also happen that there is repugnance in the soul
to doing what is ordered. God more frequently allows this repugnance
when it is a matter of important works which may bring honor to the
soul. For ordinary or humbling matters, he imparts more facility and
easy readiness.[31]

The opposite is true when the locutions come from the devil. Then
the soul is full of zeal for great and extraordinary things and feels a
resistance to ordinary ones. However, here, too, it is difficult to distinguish what comes from a good or an evil spirit. That is why "the soul
should pay no more attention to the formal locutions than to the successive ones." Neither should one do at once what these words tell
them, rather one should discuss them with an experienced confessor
and follow his advice. If one is unable to find a person with enough
experience, it is best to restrict oneself to the certain and essential
points the locutions contain, then one ought not concern oneself with
them any further, nor tell anyone about them.[32]

Substantial locutions have this in common with formal locutions:
they are impressed very clearly on the soul. Nevertheless, substantial
locutions differ in that their effect is vital and substantial. They bring
about in the soul what they express. Should the Lord say to her: "Love
me!" she would possess and feel true love of God at once if they are
substantial words. The words "Fear not!" would, in a moment, awaken
great fortitude and tranquillity in an anxious soul. Such locutions are
for the soul "life, virtue, and incomparable blessing. One locution of
this sort does more good for a person than a whole lifetime of deeds."
Therefore the soul has nothing to do, to desire, or to fear. It also makes
no difference at all whether the soul wants the locutions or resists
them. Nor need she take care to translate what she has heard into deed,
since God himself will achieve it. The locutions are given her without
her desiring them. "She should be resigned and humble about them. The
person need not resist these locutions because their effect is essentially in the soul and replete with God's blessings. Since the soul receives this passively, her own activity would be entirely superfluous."

Nor are deceptions through the intellect or the devil to be feared, here, since neither of them are capable of producing such substantial effects. Only if a soul were to have entered into a voluntary pact with the devil would he be able to impress on her his thoughts and words; but these would be evil effects; it is impossible for him to produce anything resembling divine works.

"Consequently these substantial locutions are a great aid to union with God. And the more interior and substantial they are, the more advantageous for the soul."[33]

Spiritual feelings are the fourth and last kind of intellectual apprehension mentioned. They may be of two kinds: spiritual feelings rooted in the affection of the will; and spiritual feelings that have their seat in the substance of the soul. The first kind are already very lofty when their source is in God. The second kind totally "surpass all others and are exceptionally rich in blessings and usefulness." Both the soul and her spiritual director find it unfathomable why and how God grants it such graces that are not dependent on the soul's works or reflections. These exercises may dispose it well to receive such gifts, but God grants them "to whom he wills,[34] how he wills and for the reason he wills." To some who have done many works these touches will not be granted; others who can show far fewer good works receive an abundance of the most sublime touches. Some of these touches are distinct but of short duration; others may be less distinct but, instead, last longer. From all these spiritual feelings—those of the will and those in the substance of the soul—a certain kind of knowledge and insight overflows into the intellect. These are usually exceptionally sublime and delightful experiences of God in the intellect. They cannot be given a name, nor can the feeling which engenders them be described. The knowledge imparted is sometimes more sublime and clear than at other times, depending on the property of the touches produced by God from which the feelings and consequent knowledge proceed. This knowledge and the feelings are produced passively in the soul. "If all error is to be avoided and if there is to be no impediment to the profit derived from them, the intellect must refrain from meddling through the use of its natural capacity. . . . For by its own activity, the intellect could easily disturb and undo the delicate knowledge, for it consists of a delightful, supernatural knowing that is totally unattainable through one's natural capacity. . . . A person should not . . . want it, lest the intellect begin to form other knowledge of its own, or the devil find an entrance for his varied and false knowledge."[35]

The soul "should merely be resigned, humble, and passive with respect to it." God will "grant this knowledge to it when he finds the soul humble and unpossessive."[36]

6

Purgation through Hope

4) Purgation of the Memory

The saint has occupied himself in the expositions given so far with the relationship of knowledge and faith to the goal of union with God. A broad plane of the spirit has opened up before us. A great multiplicity of spiritual occurrences, about which ordinary experience has no notion, have been unveiled with a masterly touch and described; their significance in connection with the spiritual phenomena has been investigated. Within our scope it will be impossible even to indicate the fullness of questions and viewpoints that open before us here. We shall choose what is of greatest importance for our inquiry. But before that, we must continue following the saint's thoughts. In the preceding expositions he has stressed the fact that the way of faith leads through a dark night and is a Way of the Cross. However, there has also been so much talk about light and bliss that, often, it might have appeared as though the theme of darkness and of the cross had been set aside. But as far as it has not been a matter involving anticipatory representations of the goal—which one must know in order to understand the way—this entire realm of enlightenment and graces has been unfolded only to show that one must renounce it. Only one who has possessed this realm can properly estimate how very painful it is to have to give it up voluntarily: how dark it becomes when in the midst of bright light one closes one's eyes. How like a crucifixion it is to call a halt in the life of the spirit and to deprive that spirit of all that is life-giving. As has been said, the intellect is not the only faculty affected by this divestment, but the other two spiritual faculties, the memory and the will, are also involved. The last book of *The Ascent* is devoted to recounting their preparation for divine union.

Because "the soul must know God more by what he is not than by what he is, she must . . . journey to him by way of the denial and rejection of natural and supernatural apprehensions, rather than by admitting them."

In the case of the memory we must draw it away from all its natural props and boundaries and raise it above itself to "supreme hope in the incomprehensible God." First of all, then, it must be divested of all the knowledge and images that it has gained through the corporeal senses. "Since there is no form and no image by which the memory could grasp God" it must be freed from all forms other than God. "For as long as it is united to God" it is "without form or figure, its faculty of imagining is no longer active, the memory is totally absorbed in the supreme good in total forgetfulness without the least remembrance of anything at all." This perfect emptying out that takes place in divine union—like the union itself—is not the fruit of one's own activity. "Something entirely extraordinary" is happening here. "When God on occasion produces these touches of union in the memory, it sometimes happens that, suddenly, . . . a jolt is experienced in the brain. This is so strong that it seems the whole head swoons and consciousness and sensibility are lost. And then . . . the memory is emptied and purged of all knowledge. The suspension of the imagination and the forgetfulness of the memory is sometimes so great . . . that a long time passes before it comes to itself and is aware of what has taken place during this time." [1] But such suspension of the faculties occurs only in the beginnings of union, no longer when its perfection has been attained. Then all is directed by the Holy Spirit; he reminds the soul at the proper time of whatever she has to do, and so she is preserved from the errors in exterior behavior that are characteristic of the transitional stage.

The perfect purgation of the soul is received passively from God. All the soul has to do is prepare herself to receive it: whatever the senses present "must not be stored in the memory...but she must leave them immediately and forget them, and put as much effort into this as one would to remember other things. No image of remembrance should remain in the memory, as though these things had never existed. The memory should be left completely free and unhindered, and one must not seek to engage it in any meditation on heavenly or terrestrial things. . . . One should leave . . . these things and remain forgetful of them, counting them but a hindrance on the way."[2]

A spiritual person, on the contrary, who "still wishes to make use of natural knowledge and discursive reflection of the memory in the journey to God" will experience three kinds of harm. She will suffer from manifold miseries concerning things of the world, "for instance, falsehoods, imperfections, appetites, inclination to criticize, waste of time, etc. . . . " If one allows the memory to occupy itself with what has been perceived through the senses, one falls "into imperfections step by step. For some emotion will cling to these sensory objects, now of sorrow and fear, soon of hate and vain hopes or vainglory, which will remain in the soul. . . . all things that hinder the perfect purity of the soul and perfect union with God. . . . These imperfections are better overcome all at once through complete denial of the memory."[3] It is best "to learn to silence and quiet the faculties of the soul so that God may speak to her." Then "a river of peace will descend on her . . . and . . . in this peace, God will remove all the misgivings, suspicions, disturbances, and darknesses which awakened in her the fear that she is already lost or is near to being lost."[4]

Further harm comes from the intervention of the devil. He "can add to the soul's knowledge new impressions, ideas, and reasonings, and by means of them move her to pride, avarice, anger, envy, and so on, and thus seduce her to unjust hatred and vain love . . . By far, most of the great delusions and evils that the devil causes in the soul spring from the knowledge and thought processes of the memory. When therefore, this faculty is shrouded in the complete darkness of forgetfulness and its activity is halted, the gates remain locked against the diabolical influence . . . and this leads to great blessings for the soul."[5]

The third kind of harm to the soul consists in this: the natural content of the memory can be "an impediment to moral good and deprive one of spiritual good." The moral good "consists in bridling the passions and curbing the inordinate appetites, and then in the soul's resulting tranquillity and peace, as well as in the moral virtues engendered in her."

All confusion and disturbance in the soul is caused by the contents of the memory. The soul that lives in restlessness, and that gets no support from moral good, is "incapable of receiving any spiritual good, for this spiritual good can abide only in an even-tempered and peaceful soul." Should the soul value the contents of the memory and turn to them, "it is impossible for her to be free to receive the Incomprehensible, Who is God." If she wishes to go to God, she must "replace the mutable and comprehensible by the Immutable and Incomprehensible."[6]

Then in place of the harm so far described, the soul will gain the opposite advantages: rest and peace of the spirit, purity of conscience and of soul, and therewith the best preparation "for the reception of human and divine wisdom and virtues." She is preserved from many suggestions, temptations, and disturbances caused by the evil enemy, for whom those thoughts provided a handhold. The soul becomes receptive for the motivation by and inspirations of the Holy Spirit."[7]

Similar to the effect of the perceptions of the natural senses, the supernatural visions, revelations, locutions, and feelings leave impressions in the memory or the phantasy, most vivid ones at times. For these, as well, the basic principle holds that the soul should never reflect on clear and distinct matters in order to remember them. "The more importance given to any clear and distinct apprehension, natural or supernatural, the less capacity and preparedness the soul has for entering the abyss of faith, where all else is absorbed. For . . . none of these forms or ideas . . . is God, nor have they any relation to God and therefore they cannot serve as a proximate means for union with God." The memory must be freed from them all "in order to be able to be united with God in perfect mystical hope. For every possession is against hope. . . . The more, therefore, that the memory practices detachment, the more hope it wins, and the more hope grows the more intimately the soul is united with God. When the memory has reached perfect dispossession, it will remain with perfect possession of God in divine union."[8]

Preoccupation with supernatural apprehensions will bring the soul five kinds of harm: first, she will often be deluded into taking what is merely the play of phantasy to be a divine revelation, or she may consider divine things to be a deception of the devil, etc. Therefore the soul should "be unwilling to make judgments about the nature of her experiences and should, by herself, banish the desire to recognize what is happening to her. . . . No matter how great the value of such apprehensions may be, they are not as great a help toward increasing love as is the least act of living faith and hope made in perfect emptiness and renunciation of all things."[9]

The second kind of harm is the danger of falling into presumption or vanity. One gets the idea that one is now pretty advanced since one receives supernatural communications, and so one looks down with pharisaic arrogance on others who do not experience such proofs of favor. To avoid this, the soul must keep two things in mind:

"1) Virtue consists neither in apprehensions and feelings of God, no matter how sublime they may be, nor in anything similar one can experience; rather, virtue consists much more in what one does not experience . . . . It consists in deep humility and contempt of oneself and of all one possesses . . . as well as in the desire that others might have the same opinion of one . . . ;

2) One must be convinced that all visions, revelations and supernatural feelings . . . are far less valuable than the slightest act of humility: humility includes within itself the effects of a love that does not esteem itself and seeks to think evil only of oneself, and no good of oneself, but indeed so of others."[10]

The third kind of harm comes from the evil enemy. "He has the power to present to the memory and imagination . . . false knowledge and images, which appear to be true and good. . . ." He appears to the soul as an angel of light. With regard to the communications that really do come from God, he is able so to arouse disorderly sensual and spiritual feelings as to deceive the soul and cast her into spiritual gluttony. She becomes blinded by savoring the delight and pays more attention to sensory satisfactions than to love. She is no longer available for the renunciation and love that the theological virtues demand from her. The cause of all this evil is to be found in the fact that "the soul failed from the very beginning to deny the pleasure taken in such supernatural apprehensions."[11]

The fourth kind of harm has been mentioned repeatedly: that all possessions of the memory are a hindrance to the union with God through hope.

Finally, the imagination's preconceptions and images that the memory preserves may lead to "approaching God's essence and sublimity in terms of lesser worth than befits his incomprehensibility," and not "as sublime as the faith teaches which is that God is incomparable and incomprehensible." In this life the soul is able to perceive clearly and distinctly only what falls into classifications of genus and species. But God does not come into any such classification and therefore cannot be compared with any creature on earth, nor with any image or knowledge that can be grasped by the soul's faculties. "Therefore anyone encumbering the memory and the other faculties of the soul with what is comprehensible cannot have a proper esteem or opinion of God."[12]

When there is perfect renunciation, these kinds of harm are countered by the respective advantages. In addition to the tranquillity and freedom already experienced through the renunciation of natural apprehensions, there is freedom from the care of discerning whether the supernatural communications are good or bad. Nor need one "waste the time and effort to consult spiritual persons in an attempt to gain certainty about these matters . . . since one no longer places any value on such things. So the soul's time and effort can be put to much better use . . . to the subjection of the will to the divine will, to carefully striving for self-denial and spiritual and corporeal poverty," that is, that one truly strives, interiorly as well as exteriorly, to get along without the support of any consolation or perception.

Such a renunciation of divine communications is in no way "an extinguishing of the Spirit." By her own power, the soul is capable only of natural activity. On her own, she cannot move herself to supernatural works; God alone moves the soul to such activity. Therefore, "if the soul were to desire to make use of her own efforts, she would necessarily impede the passive communication of God which is the spirit. The soul would be absorbed in her own activity, which is of another and lower kind than that which God is communicating to her, for the work of God is passive and supernatural, that of the soul is active and natural. This natural activity is what would extinguish the spirit."[13]

"The faculties of the soul, by their own nature, can only reflect and work when they make use of some form, figure, or image, which would be only the rind of the exterior appearance (*corteza y accidente*) beneath which the substance and spirit (*sustancia y espiritu*) are concealed. This substance and spirit will only unite with the faculties of the soul in true understanding and love when the faculties discontinue operating. For the aim of this operation is the reception of substantial understanding and love through these forms. The same difference exists between active and passive activity . . . as between that which we wish to do and that which one has already done; as between that which one wishes to reach and to possess and that which one already has reached and now possesses." So, to make active use of the faculties with regard to these supernatural apprehensions would be "to abandon what has been completed in order to do it again."[14]

The soul must direct all her care to "pay no attention in all the apprehensions that come to it from above . . . to the letter and rind, that is, to what is signified, represented, or made known. She may only fix her eye on and preserve the feelings of love of God that are caused within her. Only for this one purpose may one recall a certain image or apprehension that called forth love: in order to move the spirit to love anew. Although the effect of recollecting may not be as strong as it was at the first perception, it will still engender love anew . . . each time and elevate the mind to God especially when the soul remembers some supernatural figures, images, or feelings that are usually imprinted in the soul like a seal so that they last for a long time and sometimes are never erased from the soul." Such recollections "produce, almost as often as remembered, divine effects of love, sweetness, light, and so on, . . . because God imprinted them on the soul for this reason. This is consequently a great grace since the recollection is an inexhaustible source of blessings for her." These images "are vividly impressed upon the soul's spiritual memory and are unlike the other forms and images that are preserved in the phantasy." The soul therefore has no need of the phantasy in order to recall them, but rather "sees these images within itself as one sees images in a mirror." When the soul recalls them in order to reawaken love they no longer constitute a hindrance to "the union of love in faith. However, the soul must not allow herself to be completely absorbed with the figure, but turn away from it as soon as she is moved to love."

These formal apprehensions, however, are rare and for one who has had no experience of them, they are difficult to distinguish from those that are represented by the phantasy. " Of whatever kind they may be, it is good for the soul to have no desire to comprehend anything through them other than God through faith and in hope."[15]

The memory preserves not only images but pure *spiritual knowledge* as well. "Once the soul has received knowledge of this sort, she can freely call it to memory as often as she pleases," for the knowledge leaves behind a figure in the soul, an image or an idea in a spiritual form. We are concerned here with that knowledge of uncreated perfections or created things that was discussed earlier.

Knowledge of the second kind may be recalled in order to renew love. "But if this recollection of the knowledge of creatures produces no good effect it should be banned from the memory. If, however, it is about the uncreated things, one may direct one's thoughts to them as often as possible. . . . For these are touches and feelings of the union with God to which we wish to lead the soul." One does not remind oneself of them through any form or figure, since they possess nothing of this sort, but by recalling their effects of light, love, delight, and spiritual renewal. And as often as one recalls them "one of these effects is renewed."

Summarizing, the saint once more reminds us that he is only intent on leading the memory to union with God. Because one can only hope for what one does not possess, hope will be the more perfect the less one possesses. "So, the more the soul keeps the memory free of forms and things that are not God, the deeper she will fix the memory in God, the better she will be able to hope that God will take the memory perfectly into his possession." As often as distinct images or knowledge offer themselves, one should go beyond them and turn to God. The soul may occupy herself with recalling them only insofar as the fulfillment of her duties demands. And at such times she should do so without becoming attached to or taking pleasure in them so that they will not totally absorb the soul.[16]

7
Purgation through Love

5) Purgation of the Will

"We would achieve nothing by purifying the intellect in order to base it in faith, and the memory for the sake of hope, if we did not purify the will for the sake of the third virtue, love." All that is needed in order to form this faculty through the love of God is perfectly expressed in the words of *Deuteronomy*: "You shall love the Lord your God with all your heart, and with all your soul, and with all your strength" [Dt 6:5]. "The strength of the soul comprises: the faculties; passively experienced states (the passions); and appetites (*potencias, pasiones y apetitos*). But all of this is ruled by the will. When the will therefore directs all these faculties, passions, and appetites to God and turns them away from all that is not God, then the will preserves the strength of the soul for God, and she can then love God with all her strength."

As principal deterrents, the four *passions* of the soul, *joy, hope, sorrow* and *fear*, obstruct the way to loving God with all one's strength. "If one orders these *passions* so toward God that the soul finds joy only in whatever serves the honor and glory of God our Lord, that her hope has no other goal, that nothing causes her sorrow but that which concerns God, and she fears nothing but God, then clearly, all the soul's strength and faculties have been kept for God. The more the soul rejoices over something other [than God], the less intense will be her joy in God." If she purges her will of its desires, "the human and coarse will become divine, that is, one with the will of God." When they are unbridled, the passions beget all the imperfections in the soul, but as soon as they are well-ordered and brought into subjection they will give rise to all the virtues. All four are so closely connected that the subjection of one makes the others docile as well. The reverse is also true: where the will rejoices in something, it also bears the seeds of hope, sorrow, and fear with respect to the same matter. A single one of the passions when stirred makes captives of the others, the will, and the whole soul, and prevents her flight "to the freedom and rest of sweet contemplation and union."[1]

In the discussion of *joy* that follows, the fundamental rule is set forth: "The will may only rejoice in that which serves the honor and glory of God; and we can show God no greater honor than when we serve him in evangelical perfection. Whatever falls outside the bounds of this perfection has neither value nor use for human beings."[2] Later, a supplementary explanation is given: "Every particular thing in which the will can rejoice is sweet and delightful for it, and no particular thing that is sweet and delightful is God. Because God is not apprehensible to any of the faculties, neither is he apprehensible to the appetites and inclinations of the will. Since the soul cannot enjoy God essentially in this life, all the sweetness and delight she tastes, however sublime, cannot be God. Likewise, any particular satisfaction and desire of the will derives from its knowledge of such and such an object. The will has never tasted God as he is, or known him through some gratification of the appetite. Consequently it does not know what God is or what it means to enjoy God. . . . So it is obvious that none of all those particular things in which the will rejoices is God." Thus in order to reach union with God, it is necessary to renounce the desire to find joy in natural or supernatural things.

This union is possible only through love. "And since the delight, sweetness, and satisfaction that can come to the will are not love, none of the delightful feelings can be an adequate means for union of the will with God. What is needed is the act of the will itself, and this act differs totally from the will's feelings. It is through its act, or activity, that the will unites itself with God and he is the goal of the will's love. The will does not attain union by the feeling and gratification of its appetitive powers, which have their seat, their end, and their goal in the soul. Feelings can only serve as motivation for love . . . and no more."[3]

They do not lead the soul "out of herself toward God, rather they want her to find satisfaction in herself.

The activity of the will, on the other hand, consists of loving God, directs the soul to him, raises itself above all things and loves God above all. When, therefore, someone is moved toward God by a feeling of sweetness, they are to go beyond this sweet feeling and turn their love to God who cannot be grasped by means of any feeling." Turning to the feeling would mean for the soul that she "turn her love to something created, confusing the motivation with the goal. Doing this would be to misuse the will's activity. The soul loves securely and truly in the spirit of faith only when she is in darkness and in emptiness of all that the will can feel and the intellect can understand."[4] Therefore, it would "be very foolish to think that God is failing one because of the lack of spiritual sweetness and delight, or to rejoice, thinking one possesses God because of the presence of this sweetness. It would be even more foolish were one to seek this sweetness in God and delight in it, for this would mean one is seeking God with a will no longer grounded in the emptiness of faith but with a will looking for spiritual satisfaction, which is a creature . . . thus God would no longer be loved above all else, for this [love] means centering all the strength of one's will on him alone. . . . Therefore it is impossible for the will to reach the sweetness and delight of divine union if its appetite is not empty of every particular satisfaction. That is what the Psalm says: *Dilata os tuum et implebo illud* ("Open wide your mouth and I will fill it")[Ps 81:10]. The appetite is the mouth of the will; and this mouth is opened when it is not encumbered by any mouthful of desire, so that God may fill it with the sweetness of his love."[5]

This is now proved with regard to the various kinds of objects in which the desires seek satisfaction: riches, honor, descendants, and the like. They need not necessarily tempt one to sin, although, as a rule, they do lead to infidelity toward God. One may only take delight in them if one is better able to serve God by means of them, or if they make the attainment of everlasting life more certain. However, since one cannot "know with certitude that one is serving God, it would be vanity to rejoice over these goods."[6]

The *principal harm* brought about by this inclination of the will toward these goods is *withdrawal from God*. This privative harm is fulfilled in *four degrees* which are summed up in the words of Scripture: "The darling (Jacob) grew fat and frisky; he was surfeited, grew fat, and spread out; he forsook God his Maker, and departed from God his Savior" (Dt 32:15). Becoming fat signifies *blunting the mind in relation to God*. As soon as "the spiritual soul seeks delight in frivolous things, her relationship with God is darkened and the formerly unclouded intellect becomes obscured. . . . Neither the soul's sanctity nor her keen judgment can prevent this injury if she gives way to concupiscence for temporal goods or takes joy in them."[7] "He grew fat and spread out"—this is the second degree: an *"enlargement of the will* which now gives itself to temporal things with greater freedom." Because one did not bridle joy in the beginning, the will becomes estranged from divine things and sacred practices and no longer finds a taste for them. These persons finally omit "their usual daily spiritual practices and fix all their mind and covetousness on the secular." Now, not only are their understanding and judgment darkened "so that they no longer recognize what is true and just, but also, in extreme tepidity and laziness, they no longer place any value in knowing and practicing true judgment."[8]

The third degree consists in the complete *abandoning of God:* "He forsook God his Maker" [Dt 32:15]. Those who have come so far no longer have an eye for that to which God's law compels them. "They forget and are sluggish about matters pertaining to their salvation, and turn their whole attention to worldly matters. These are the "children of this world" about whom the Lord says "they are more prudent and keen in their affairs than the children of light are in theirs" (Lk 16:8). They are the truly greedy who "cannot be satisfied. Rather their appetite and thirst increase more as they regress further from God, the fount that alone can satisfy them." They fall into "thousands of kinds of sin out of love for temporal goods and suffer indeterminable harm."

And so they arrive at the fourth degree where the soul forgets God as though he did not even exist. This entire *forgetfulness of God* is a consequence of "deliberately turning the heart that ought to be centered on God to center on money as though they had no other God."[9]

Such persons make an idol of temporal goods and sacrifice their lives to this idol when this god of theirs undergoes some temporal loss. Their idol gives them what he has: "despair and death. And those he does not pursue right up to death, the ultimate injury, he permits to perish in constantly painful mortal fear . . . But even those to whom . . . less harm comes should be pitied greatly . . . for they fall far back on the way to God."[10]

Whoever, on the other hand, frees himself of all attachment to temporal goods attains to magnanimity, liberty of spirit, clarity of reason, deep rest, peaceful confidence in God, true homage of God, and genuine submission of his will to the will of God. One even obtains more joy in creatures through detachment from them, a joy the greedy will never taste because in their unrest the necessary freedom of spirit is lacking. The one who is free of them recognizes in temporal goods their true natural and supernatural values. "He delights in their truth, what is best in them, and their substance . . . whereas the one who perceives them only with the senses delights in what is false, worst, and has no substance."

"Whoever keeps his heart free will not be disturbed by cares either in prayer or outside of prayer. Without losing any time, such persons easily store up an abundance of spiritual good, while those whose heart is bound to creatures spend their time going to and fro in the snare in which they are caught. . . . At the first movement of joy at something created, therefore, the spiritual person should strive to curb it." In this way one keeps the heart "free for God and that is the essential prerequisite for receiving all the graces that God wishes to grant." God rewards a hundredfold already in this life "the renunciation of a single—even though transitory—joy, out of love for God and for evangelical perfection."[11] On the other hand, "we must fear, that as often as we allow ourselves to rejoice vainly, God imposes on us a severe chastisement corresponding to our fault."[12]

John designates a second group as *natural goods*: the advantages provided by the body and soul, for example, beauty, a graceful body, intelligence, and sound judgment. For one who possesses them and for others, they are a temptation to attachment and vain joy. To counter them, one should "consider that beauty and all other natural gifts are but earth, arising from the earth to which they will return; grace and elegance are but the smoke and fog of this earth. . . . " One ought to "keep one's heart directed to God in joy and gladness that God himself is all this beauty and grace—eminently and infinitely so, above all creatures."[13]

The special kinds of harm ensuing from joy in natural goods are "vainglory, presumption, pride, and disregard of neighbor;" arousal of sensuality and self-indulgence; a mania for flattery and vain praise that exercises a harmful influence on others; an even stronger blunting of the reason and judgment than occurs when taking joy in temporal goods; spiritual tepidity and weakness even to the extent of abhorring the things of God. The saint emphasizes especially the danger that comes from giving in to the temptation to sensual lust: "No pen can describe and no word can express it. It ever remains a dark and hidden secret how far one can err in this respect and what harm is wrought by joy in natural beauty and charm. There would be few even among the saintly who would not have been ravished and confused after drinking of the joy and satisfaction in natural beauty and graces." The wine of sensual gratification clouds reason. If one does not immediately take an antidote "the life of the soul will be in danger." "As soon as the heart feels drawn by vain joy in natural goods it should recall how vain it is to rejoice in anything other than the service of God, and how dangerous and pernicious every other joy is . . . what misery the angels ran into because they looked with joy and satisfaction on their own beauty and natural gifts. For this joy was the cause of their fall into the terrible abyss."[14]

If the soul renounces all such joys, she "prepares a home for herself in humility and in general charity toward her neighbor." If she "in no way allows herself to be taken in by the seductive natural goods that strike the eye, the soul preserves her freedom and clarity to be able to love all in a rational and spiritual manner as God requires . . . the more love increases, the more the love of God increases and likewise, as the love of God increases, so does the love of neighbor." Renunciation also "begets deep tranquillity, empties one of distractions, and brings recollection to the senses, especially to the eyes." When one has arrived at some proficiency in it, obscene objects no longer make any impression at all. One wins "purity in soul and body, that is, in spirit and in the senses, and reaches an angelic harmony with God so that the soul and body become a worthy temple of the Holy Spirit." Thus one arrives at "freedom of the spirit, an excellent good for the soul, so necessary for the service of God. With it, the soul easily conquers temptations, endures trials with patience, and grows ever stronger in the virtues."[15]

John considers as *sensory goods* everything that is apprehensible through the exterior senses or achieved by the discursive imagination. Since God cannot be reached by any of the senses it would be "at the least, a useless undertaking" to seek one's delight in sensory apprehensions; the will could then "no longer occupy itself with God nor seek all its joy in Him alone." However, if one does not dwell on them, but if rather, one directs one's joy to God as soon as one is aware of finding delight in any such thing, then one need not refuse such impressions "for there are souls who are greatly moved toward God by sensible objects." However, in many people the attention merely *seems* to be directed to God, while in truth "the effect is sensory gratification which calls forth weaknesses and imperfections instead of quickening the will and directing it toward God." Whoever, on the contrary, is directed toward God at the first movement does not take "the trouble to seek sensory gratifications; and when they approach him, the will immediately disengages itself of them, rejects, and turns to God."[16]

Surrender to sensory goods brings with it many other *kinds of harm* besides the common ones which it shares with all joy in created things. Joy in *visible objects* calls forth "vanity of spirit, mental distraction, inordinate covetousness, indecency, inner and outer lack of composure, impure thoughts, and envy.

Joy at *hearing useless things* gives direct rise to distraction of the imagination, gossip, envy, rash judgment, wandering thoughts, and many other very destructive disadvantages.

Joy in sweet *fragrances* arouses disgust for poor persons, which is contrary to the spirit of Christ, also a reluctance to perform acts of service,[17] an aversion of the heart to humble matters, and a spiritual insensitivity, at least in relation to avidity.

Joy in *delicious foods* leads directly to overindulgence in eating, to anger, conflict, a cooling off of love of neighbor and of the poor. . . . Bodily disorders arise, illnesses, and impure movements from increasing lustful incentives. It begets directly a great dullness of the spirit and spoils the taste for spiritual things. . . . Finally, there arises from this joy the distraction of the remaining senses and of the heart and dissatisfaction with many things."

"Enjoyment in the *touch of pleasant things* brings the senses and the spirit completely into disorder and destroys its strength and vigor. It develops into that abominable vice of effeminacy . . . it nourishes lustful excess, makes the soul timid and fearful, and the senses . . . are always ready to sin and to cause harm. It fills the heart with vain lightheartedness and leads to licentiousness of the tongue and uncontrolled use of the eyes. It inhibits the power of judgment and seduces the spirit to silliness and spiritual stupidity; it morally engenders cowardice and inconstancy. It darkens the soul, weakens the heart and makes it fearful where there is nothing to fear. All too often this same enjoyment engenders a spirit of confusion and insensitivity to the promptings of conscience or of the spirit. This greatly weakens the understanding, which is reduced to such a state that it can no longer receive or give good counsel and becomes unreceptive for other spiritual and moral blessings and is as useless as a broken jar."[18] All of these kinds of harm cause more or less damage depending on the passionate intensity of the joy and the susceptibility of the varying natures.

"The benefits the soul wins from denial of these joys are amazing: . . . she is strengthened in the battle against distractions . . . and recollects herself again in God. The spirit preserves itself carefully and the virtues gained are increased and blossom anew." Then a *sublime transformation* takes place: "We can truthfully say that what was sensory becomes spiritual; what was animal, rational; the human nature becomes similar to the angelic; from being worldly and human, it becomes heavenly and divine." Even in this life the will is granted the hundredfold reward that the Savior promised (Mt 19:29). For sensory joys, the will exchanges spiritual ones and remains ever joined to God. As was the case with our first parents in paradise, all sensory impressions now serve to increase contemplation. Finally, in the life of glory, in reward for the renunciation, "the corporeal gifts, such as agility and clarity, will be far more exalted than in those who did not deny themselves sensory joys; and besides this, for every momentary and perishable joy the soul has denied itself, there will be worked in it an immeasurable, eternal weight of glory" (2 Cor 4:17).[19]

8

Virtues, Gifts, and Graces

In contrast to the exterior, natural, and sensory goods, the *moral* ones give joy because they have *value in and of themselves*; beyond that, because they are a *means* and instrument to goods that they procure for the person. *Virtues* in themselves merit love and esteem; moreover, they bring temporal benefits. Therefore "a person—-humanly speaking—can well rejoice in their practice and possession because of what they are in themselves, as well as because of the good they humanly and temporally effect." Rulers and wise men of ancient times did so. They valued and practiced the virtues and God rewarded them with temporal blessings "since, because of their unbelief they were incapable of eternal reward."

The Christian, although he may rejoice in the moral goods and works temporally performed, and do so for the primary reason that they cause the temporal benefits spoken of, may not stop there. . . . Because, in possession of the light of faith, he hopes to attain eternal life and because aside from this, nothing from above or below has any value, he ought to rejoice that he possesses and exercises these moral goods only and chiefly for the second reason, namely, that he performs his works out of love for God and thereby wins eternal life. Therefore, he should always fix his eyes only on this, and rejoice in serving and honoring God by leading a good life and practicing the virtues. Without this intention, virtue has no worth in God's sight, as we see in the case of the ten virgins in the Gospel [Mt 25:1ff.]." "Christians should not rejoice that they accomplish good works and lead a good life, but rather that they do this only out of love for God, excluding every other motive."[1]

Through this misguided joy in one's own good works there can occur an awakening of pharisaic pride and boasting; a custom of comparing oneself with others and finding them of inferior worth; a desire for human praise, thereby casting aside all chance of an eternal reward. Self-satisfied joy in one's own works is an injustice and a denial of God who initiates every single good work. Souls like these make no progress in perfection. When they no longer find satisfaction in their practices because God is offering them the dry bread of the strong, they become discouraged and are not capable of eating it. They "lose the perseverance that would give them spiritual sweetness and interior consolation." Usually they also fall into the delusion that exercises and works that please them are better than those that displease them. However, God is most pleased, especially in advanced souls, by those works that demand more self-denial. Finally, misguided joy in their own works "makes them incapable of taking counsel and of receiving reasonable instructions" about what they ought to do. "Such souls become very slack in charity toward God and neighbor for the self-love contained in their works makes them grow cold in charity."[2]

By denying this vain joy, one is preserved from "many temptations and deceits of the evil enemy which are concealed in the joy of these good works." The vain joy alone is already a deception in itself. To this is added the second benefit of a "more diligent and precise accomplishment of one's works." For passionate joy inhibits the reason and makes the soul inconstant in her resolves and dealings. She then orders her activity according to her changeable tastes and leaves the most important works unfinished when pleasure in doing them is gone. If, on the other hand, the will denies itself natural satisfaction then it can persevere and reach its goal. By this means one also arrives at poverty of spirit which the Savior calls blessed. One becomes meek, humble, and prudent in all of one's work, does not act impetuously or hastily, nor is one presumptuous. Thus, denial of vain joy makes one "become pleasing to God and to other human beings; free of avarice, of spiritual gluttony and sloth, of spiritual envy, and countless other evils."[3]

As the fifth group of goods in which the will can rejoice John treats the *supernatural goods*, that is, "all the gifts and graces of God that exceed our natural faculties and powers. They are called *dona gratis data*,[4] for example, the wisdom and knowledge given to Solomon, and the graces of which Paul speaks: . . . 'faith, the gift of healing the sick, working of miracles, the gift of prophecy, the gift of knowledge and discernment of spirits, interpretation of words, and also the gift of tongues' (1 Cor 12:9-10)." Their effectiveness concerns the "benefit of persons . . . and this is the purpose for which God grants them." (The *spiritual goods* flow only between God and the soul, as will be said later.)

The supernatural gifts have as *temporal benefits*: healing the sick, restoring sight to the blind, and raising the dead to life, and the like; and as *spiritual benefits,* the knowledge and praise of God caused in the one who performs the works or in the witnesses before whose eyes they are accomplished. One ought not take any pleasure in the temporal effects of the supernatural gifts since of themselves they are not a means for uniting the soul to God. One can "accomplish them without possessing sanctifying grace and love." God can bestow them thus (as happened with Balaam and Solomon); they can also be the result of the cooperation of the devil, or by means of other secret, natural powers. Paul taught that all these gifts of grace are nothing without love (1 Cor 13:1-2). Therefore Christ will answer many who demand an eternal reward for working wonders: "Depart from me, workers of iniquity!" (Mt 7:23). So one should take pleasure only in the spiritual gain from these gifts, i.e. "that one serves God truly out of love, for in charity lies the fruit of eternal life."

Vain joy in supernatural goods leads the soul "to deceive others and to be deceived herself," to fall back in one's life of faith and fall prey to a vain search for fame or another form of vanity. These errors are caused because only through a high degree of insight and divine enlightenment can one recognize whether such works "are genuine or false, and how and when one ought to perform them." Having a high esteem of the works impedes this kind of knowledge. Taking satisfaction in the works clouds the judgment, and a passionate urge to have this satisfaction as soon as possible keeps one from awaiting the right time. God does indeed give with such gifts and graces the necessary enlightenment and disposition to recognize how and when one is to make use of them. Because of their imperfection, however, persons pay no attention to the divine will and do not keep to the time and the manner in which the Lord wants the works performed. In this way an unjust and a perverse use of God-given graces becomes possible. Even beyond this, a vain joy at working wonders may lead to their being performed with powers that do not come from God. "When the devil observes the attachment that people have to these wonders, he opens a wide field for them, provides ample material for their endeavors and meddles extensively." [5] "Whoever, then, receives such a gift or supernatural grace should suppress the passionate desire and the joy of using it. . . . For God, who grants them supernaturally for the usefulness of the Church and her children will also move the gifted supernaturally as to the manner and time in which they should use their gift . . . for he wishes . . . that the soul pay attention to the divine inspiration and the divine activity of God in her heart, since every work must be performed by the power of God."

The retrogression in faith that results from such unwarranted works affects the neighbor. Whoever wishes to work a wonder when neither the time nor the circumstances call for it, commits a grave sin because he tempts God. If the attempt fails, faith in the hearts of others may weaken and be brought into contempt. But one can damage one's own soul by a loss of faith. "For . . . the more signs and external proofs there are for something, the less merit there is in faith." All indications show that God is not inclined to reveal himself through miracles. When he works them, it is in order "to lead someone to faith, or for other purposes that redound to his glory or the praise of his saints." "Those then who love to rejoice in these supernatural works suffer a great loss in faith."[6]

The soul that renounces such joys gives glory to God and raises herself above the self. God is exalted in the soul when "the heart . . . withdraws itself from all that is not God. . . ." At the same time, the soul is exalted when she turns to God and concentrates on him alone. God manifests his excellence and grandeur to the soul and gives her testimony of who he is. "If God is already extolled when joy is withdrawn from all things and centered on him, he receives even more glory when these more marvelous things are ignored. . . . " God is exalted even more, the more the soul believes in and serves God without signs and wonders. "For then she believes more of God than signs and miracles can teach." Instead, the soul attains to a faith that is far more pure. God infuses this in great abundance, and also increases hope and charity as well. "As a result the soul enjoys "divine and lofty knowledge by means of the dark and naked habit of faith; the greatest delight of love through divine charity by which she rejoices in nothing except in the living God; satisfaction in the will [sic][7] through hope. All of this is a remarkable benefit which leads essentially and directly to the perfect union of the soul with God.[8]

More than all others, the *spiritual goods* lead to union with God. These are "those that are an aid and motivating force in turning the soul to divine things and communion with God, as well as a help in God's communications to the soul." They may be either *delightful* or *painful* goods, and they may be goods that are *clearly and distinctly* understood or about goods that are *unclear and obscure*. Here the saint wishes to treat only the delightful ones that have clear and distinct things as objects. (He leaves discussion of the others for later.)[9] The same rules of behavior that hold for the intellect and the memory are valid for the will, since these can neither accept nor reject anything without the will's intervention. Whatever these faculties must be purified of may not give the will any pleasure.[10]

The goods that can give *clear distinct joy* to the will may be *motivating, provocative, directive* or *perfective*. To the motivating goods belong statues and paintings of the saints, oratories, and ceremonies. "Pictures and statues may occasion a great deal of vain joy and vanity" if persons "pay more attention to the workmanship and artistic value of the image than to the object represented." For then only the senses are "taken in and delighted, while love and the satisfaction of the will do not receive their due." They go so far as to clothe "the statues of the saints with garments that accord to present worldly fashions—a practice that was and still is abhorrent to the saints." One's devotion is directed to the "doll's adornments" to which one is attached as to an idol. Many persons "are unable to obtain enough pictures and these must have this or that form, . . . in order to satisfy the senses, while there is very little devotion of the heart. . . . " When rightly used, pictures "have great meaning in the liturgy and are needed to stimulate the will to devotion." For this purpose and to venerate the saints, the Church has sanctioned their use. "Therefore one should give preference to those that represent a faithful and living image and move the will the more to devotion." "The truly devout direct their devotion above all to the invisible; they are satisfied with a small number of pictures," and prefer "those that express the divine traits more than the human ones. They conform in ornamenting the pictures to divine traits in accord with the fashion and condition of the saints of bygone times and not according to present-day fashions." Such a person "is not attached to the pictures of which she makes use, nor is she saddened when these are taken away from her. She seeks the living image, Christ the Crucified, in herself . . . and bears it gladly if all others are taken from her . . . even when they have been a help in raising her attention to God with greater ease. The deprivation of them does not trouble her peace."

One must look beyond that which serves the spirit in raising the heart to God, . . . must look away, and not let it act as a charm to the senses; for if I give in to the pleasure that the means afford, then that which should serve as a prop for my imperfection will become a hindrance . . . "in just such a way as is the case of attachment and attraction to any other thing."

Even worse than the misuse of pictures is the imperfection with which "one is accustomed to use a rosary. One rarely meets someone who does not show some weakness in this regard. They want the rosary to be made in one style rather than another, or that it be of this color or that metal rather than another. . . . Will God hear the prayer more readily if it is prayed with this or that rosary? It is after all only important that one prays with a simple and pure heart, that one aims only to please God ."[11]

Great is the ignorance of persons "who trust more in one image than another and think that God will answer them more readily through it, even when both represent the same subject. . . . After all, God looks only at the praying person's faith and purity of heart. If God sometimes bestows more favors through one image rather than another, he does so because the one enkindles the devotion of the faithful more than the other. Were their devotion to one image as great as to the other

(as also without one or the other) God would grant the same favors."
If dormant devotion is awakened through a certain image's miraculous
effects, if the faithful are stirred and moved to pray with perseverance—
"these are the means by which God hears and grants one's petitions—
then, moved by the prayer and love of the faithful, God continues to
make use of this same image to grant his graces and to work miracles."
"Experience shows us that God attaches some graces and miracles through
some statues that are not very well carved . . . so that the faithful will
not . . . attribute the results to the artistic form of the image. Frequently,
our Lord bestows favor by means of images situated in remote and
solitary places, because the effort required in journeying to these places
makes love grow . . . or, again, because a person may withdraw from
people and noise in order to pray, as our Lord did" (Mt 14:23; Lk 6:12).
"Therefore one does well to make pilgrimages without a lot of company. If one goes with a crowd, one usually comes back more distracted than one was before going."

"Where devotion and faith are found, any image will suffice; where
they are lacking, none will be sufficient. Was there ever an image so
alive as our Savior while he was on earth, still those who did not
believe in him drew no benefit from going about with him and seeing
his wondrous works."[12] However, even where devotion is present, the
use of images may present some dangers. The devil likes to use them
to bring unwary souls into his power, for example, through supernatural apparitions by which he deceives them (images begin to move or
to give signs, etc.). In order to escape all damage, one should look "to
the images only for a stimulus to love and joy in that living object
which they represent." If an image is able to "awaken sensory or spiritual devotion, or give supernatural signs of itself," the soul "should pay
no attention to these peripheral matters . . . and give the image only
that honor which is in accord with the intention of the Church. Then
she should raise her mind to that which it represents and direct all her
strength and joy of the will to God in devout, interior prayer."[13]

Attachment to images or to beautifully adorned oratories is perhaps
more dangerous than that to worldly things, because one feels safe about
the former, and does not fear being at fault. There are persons who spend

all their time on decorating their prayer rooms "which are to bring them to prayer to God and to interior recollection. . . . Satisfying their wishes in this way . . . however, serves to unsettle them at every moment, especially if one wishes to take these things from them." [14] For beginners it is probably "useful and salutary to find a certain sensory joy and satisfaction in pictures, oratories, and other visible devotional things." It helps to detach them from the taste for worldly things. On the other hand, the pure spirit knows "only interior recollection and spiritual contact with God." True, one should pray in a place that is fitting. Churches and quiet places possess the correct dedication to prayer; still, in order to "praise God in spirit and in truth" (Jn 4:23-24) one should not choose a place that flatters the senses. Much more, "a solitary, austere location seems to be most apt to enable the spirit to ascend to God with its full strength and in the most direct way and it is neither impeded nor detained by visible things. . . . Therefore (to give us an example) the Savior usually chose solitary places for prayer and such places that gave the senses little nourishment but raised the soul to God, as for example, the mountains that rise from the earth, are usually bare, and offer the senses no stimulus." [15]

God made use of three kinds of locations to move the will to devotion: *impressive landscapes*, which naturally awaken sentiments of devotion by their arrangement of land and trees and their solitariness. But at such sites one ought "to behave as though one were not there if one wishes to be with God interiorly." There are localities, then, at which God grants to some individuals some very delightful spiritual favors, whether these places are solitary or not. This awakens in these individuals an attachment to the place and the yearning to return to it. There is nothing reprehensible in this, if it is not a self-seeking desire. Indeed, God is not bound to any particular place, and it does appear that he wishes to receive praise from this particular person on whom he bestowed his favor at this precise location. Here the soul is more intensely aware of its obligation to be grateful and the memory gives a powerful stimulus to devotion. Finally, there are "places that God chooses in a special manner in order that he be served there through the invocation of his name. Such was Mount Sinai, where he gave the law to Moses (Ex 22:2 [sic]);[16] in the same way, Mount Horeb, to which God

sent Elijah in order to reveal himself to him there (1Kgs 19:8). . . .
God himself knows why he chose these places in preference to others
in which to receive praise. As far as we are concerned, it is enough to
know that everything happens for our spiritual progress and that God
listens to us there and everywhere when we invoke him with perfect
faith. And if we call on him at places that are especially dedicated to
his service, we have a greater expectation of being heard since the
Church has particularly marked and dedicated them for this purpose."[17]

The errors mentioned so far "are perhaps somewhat tolerable and
may be ascribed to an innocent enthusiasm." But the boundless confidence many place "in all kinds of ceremonies thought up by persons
who are insufficiently instructed and who lack simplicity of faith is
entirely insufferable." They attribute so much efficacy to certain practices that they believe "all is useless and God will not hear them if only
a small point is omitted or if a certain limit has been exceeded. They
place more confidence in these practices than in the living spirit of
prayer: this is greatly disrespectful and offensive to God! For example,
they demand that a Mass be said with so many candles, no more nor
less; a very particular priest is to say it, exactly at such an hour, neither earlier nor later. . . . And should any of this be lacking, all is for
nothing. . . . What is worse and intolerable, is that some desire to experience or to achieve an effect in themselves: either the granting of their
petition or to have an assurance that it is being granted as an immediate consequence of their superstitious prayer."[18]

"Such persons should know, then, that their trust in God is so much
the less, the more they ascribe to the vain external formalities. Therefore
they do not obtain from God what they ask from him. Too many desire
the fulfillment of their wishes far more than they wish to honor God."

"It would be much more important were they to direct their strength
to more important things, such as, for example, the perfect purification of their conscience, or understanding that which leads to their
salvation. For this is the command of the Lord in the Gospel: 'Seek ye
first the kingdom of God and his justice, and all the rest will be added
unto you' (Mt 6:33). This petition for eternal salvation pleases God
the most, and there is no better means of attaining the fulfillment of

the desires of our hearts than to direct the entire force of our prayer to whatever pleases God the most. For then he will give us not only that for which we ask him, eternal salvation, but also everything he deems good and fit for us. 'The Lord is near to those who call upon him in truth' (Ps 145:18). Those call upon him in truth who beg of him the highest, genuine goods that pertain to salvation. . . . So one must direct the energies of the will and its joy in prayer to God and may not rely on practices one invents oneself. One should not initiate new practices as though one understood matters better than the Holy Spirit and his Church. If God does not hear their prayer when they offered it in simplicity let them be convinced that he would not answer them, no matter how many ceremonies they might invent." We shall receive from God all we ask for "if we live in harmony with him. If, however, we pursue our personal interests, then it is useless to turn to him."[19]

"When his disciples asked the Lord: 'Lord, teach us to pray', he surely instructed them about everything that was necessary to be heard by the Eternal Father . . . .He taught them only the seven petitions of the *Our Father* in which all our spiritual and temporal needs are contained, and said nothing further about numerous other kinds of prayers and ceremonies. On the contrary, he urged them not to use many words in their prayers, since our Father in heaven surely knows what we need. (Mt 6:7-8). Only one thing did he stress with special emphasis: that we should persevere in prayer."

He gave only two instructions concerning external conditions when we pray: "When you pray, go into your room, close the door, and pray to your Father in secret (Mt 6:6)." Or, otherwise, "withdraw, as he did, to a solitary place, at the best and most quiet of times, at night." He said nothing at all about particular times and days, ceremonies, and turns of speech.[20]

In conclusion, John speaks about *sermons* which can move us to serve the Lord. In order to be of use to the people and not to fall prey to vain self-complacency, the preacher must "keep in mind that preaching is more a spiritual practice than a vocal one." For the efficacy of the sermon a certain receptivity on the part of the listener is a prerequisite, but most important is the proper attitude of the preacher. If he is not penetrated by the true spirit, then the loftiest doctrine or a perfect style of presentation will be of no use. The more exemplary his life, the more effective will he be, even if his style is inferior, his rhetoric poor, and his doctrine plain. A good style, sublime doctrine, and well-chosen words are immensely moving when the spirit of piety permeates them. "But without this spirit, only the senses and the intellect find delight and satisfaction in the sermon, and the will, on the other hand, is but slightly or not at all warmed and enlivened. . . . Resonant words alone have no power to raise a dead man from his grave."

The saint has no intention of belittling good style, lofty rhetoric, and effective delivery. All of this "is of as great significance to the preacher as to every businessman, for the right words and a good style can please and restore even things that have fallen or been spoiled, whereas poorly chosen expressions can ruin and destroy the very best things."[21]

9
The Activity of Spirit

B. Reciprocal Illumination of Spirit and Faith

1) Retrospect and Prospect

Here the *Ascent of Mount Carmel* comes to an abrupt end.[1] We do not know whether the work was ever completed or whether a completed manuscript was not preserved. The treatise on joy was never finished, and the other passions are not treated at all. The aforementioned sections on the passive purification are expounded in the *Dark Night*. Furthermore, it is remarkable that there are direct interpretations of the indicated poem only at the outset, then the exposition moves further and further away from the poem ever broaching new questions. Here, too, the *Dark Night* offers a completion. In the last sections the verses actually serve as guides. In any case, at the third strophe of Verse 1, the explanation breaks off as suddenly as does the *Ascent* in the very midst of the treatise on joy. One can probably understand the fragmentary and, when viewed at times in hindsight, rather discordant aspects of these writings when considering the circumstances and the manner in which they came into being. John did not write them as an artist who wishes to form a fully conceived and well-rounded whole. Nor did he want to construct, as a theologian, a system of mysticism[2] nor, as philosopher and psychologist, a complete, extended doctrine on the passions. He wrote as a father and teacher for his spiritual sons and daughters. He wished to comply with their request that he explain his spiritual songs. He meditated on the inner experience that had found expression in this manner and wanted to translate the images into the language of intelligible thought. Probably he noticed only while at work what preparatory considerations were necessary, what had to be brought forward, step by step, in order to make it understandable. Thus he could be led farther along some side-tracks that he had not had in mind originally. However, he never lost the trend of his thought. With a firm hand on the reins, he held the lively movement of the spirit in check and repelled the onset of a plenitude of thoughts. It must also be noted that he wrote these treatises precisely in the years in which he was most overburdened with holding offices and dealing with external affairs. Certainly he had not the leisure to compose in peace and, subsequently, to proofread and to make comparisons. It could very well be that after a lengthier interruption he did not pick up the thread where it had slipped from his grasp, but rather set the second discourse beside the first. All of this needs to be recalled in order to assess the saint's preceding explanations correctly.

We have repeated what John said in the *Ascent* about entrance into the night of the spirit in order to see clearly what he understands as *spirit* and *faith*. For faith leads the way through the night to the goal of union with God. In faith the spirit is painfully reborn; it is remodeled from the natural to the supernatural. The explanations of spirit and faith mutually elucidate each other. Faith demands the renunciation of the natural activity of the spirit. This renunciation constitutes the active night of faith, one's own active following of the cross. To comprehend this renunciation and, thereby, faith, the natural activity of the spirit must be discussed. On the other hand, the very presence of faith reveals the possibility of a spiritual being and activity surpassing the natural, thus an explanation of faith can cast a new light on the spirit. Consequently, it will be understood that the spirit may be spoken of in different ways, in different instances. Viewed superficially, this may seem to be contradictory and disproportionate. In truth it is a pertinent necessity. For insofar as spiritual being is life and change, it cannot be captured in static definitions, but must rather be a continual movement seeking fluid expression. This is true also of faith. After all, it is of itself a spiritual being and therefore movement: an ascent to ever less conceivable heights and a descent into ever more immeasurable depths.

Therefore the understanding must seek to lay hold on it by means of manifold expressions, insofar as this is at all achievable.

2) Natural Spiritual Activity: The Soul; The Soul's Parts and Faculties

In the first place then, the natural activity of the soul must be made clear. It is the result of the way that being itself is constructed of psyche and intellect. John seeks to grasp this through the concepts imparted by scholastic psychology that were surely familiar to him from his student days in Salamanca. The soul is a reality that has many faculties: inferior and superior, or sensual and spiritual. In both the inferior and the superior *parts* the faculties are divided into functions of knowing and of striving. (John does not express this but it is prerequisite for his descriptions.) The *senses* are bodily organs but at the same time, they are the *windows* of the soul through which it gains knowledge of the external world. *Sensuality* therefore is common to the body and soul, but John hardly considers the bodily aspect, relatively speaking. Sensuality includes, in addition to the impressions that mediate a knowledge of the sense world, the enjoyments and the desires called forth in the soul through sensory perceptions. As has already been said, the *night of the senses* is primarily concerned with sensuality in that second aspect. In the first night, the soul is to free herself, or as the case may be, to be purified from, craving or desiring sensory gratification. Such limitation is entirely justified because enjoyment and desire are already possible on the level of a purely sensory life of the soul (therefore, in animals as well). Knowledge, on the other hand, even in the inferior form of sensory perception, is impossible without intellectual activity. Furthermore, it is desire and enjoyment which actually captivate the soul.

Sensory knowledge is impossible without intellectual activity. This states the close connection between the *superior* and the *inferior* spiritual being. They are not constructed as one story over another. Talk of superior and inferior parts is but a spatial image for a being which has nothing spatial about it at all. John says expressly, that of "the soul, insofar as it is a spirit, one cannot speak of high or low . . . as one can regarding quantitative bodies."[3] In the natural sphere sensory and intellectual activities are closely intertwined. Just as the *windows of the senses* do not provide any knowledge of the sensory world if the spirit does not peer through them, so, on the other hand, it has to make use of them in order to look out into the world. Expressed in another way: the senses deliver the matter with which the spirit occupies itself. In agreement with Augustine[4] and deviating from St. Thomas, John places the memory as the third spiritual faculty beside the intellect and the will. This is not to be seen as a seriously contrary technicality since it is not a matter of an actual partitioning of the soul, rather of varying operations and of the preparation of the *single* spiritual faculty to proceed in this or that direction. Good reasons can be adduced for both divisions. Without the original achievement of the memory—the *keeping in mind*—there would be no possibility of a sensory impression or of any spiritual activity.

This is because both have a temporally successive structure and therefore it is necessary that the respective momentary contents (roughly stated) not be annihilated but preserved instead. For the actual functioning of the intellect (comparing, generalizing, making conclusions, and so on), it can be demonstrated that the other exercises of the memory (recollections and free associations by the imagination) are also necessary. But it is impossible to pursue this further here. It was merely indicated to let it be understood that one can perceive sensory and spiritual activity in the memory and consider it in relation to the other faculties.[5] On the other hand, the memory's achievements are not really acts of knowledge, but merely assist the intellect. (The same may be demonstrated respectively for the relation between the memory and the will.) All of this entitles us to see the memory as a separate faculty. For Augustine, in any case, the consideration of the trinitarian structure of the spirit was decisive for the tripartite division. For John it was the reciprocal relationship between the three spiritual faculties and the three theological virtues. Here we touch on the decisive point of his spiritual doctrine.

3) Supernatural Elevation of the Spirit. Faith and Its Life

The spirit is dependent on the senses for its natural activity. It accepts what they offer, keeps what it perceives to be true, recalls it to view on occasion, connects it to other things, changes it, and arrives at judgments and conclusions, through making comparisons, generalizations, deductions, etc. with its conceptual knowledge. This process constitutes the actual function of the intellect.

Likewise, the will naturally occupies itself with what is provided through the senses, finds in this its joy, seeks to take possession of it, feels pain over its loss, hopes for possession, and fears loss. But it is not the spirit's calling to recognize created things and to enjoy them. To be thus involved is a perversion of the spirit's original and actual purpose for existence. It must be liberated from this captivity and elevated to the true being for which it was created. Its gaze must be directed to its Creator. It must surrender itself to him with all its faculties. This will be achieved progressively, step by step, through *a work of education and detachment*. God gives the stimulus for this and completes it, but demands the person's own spiritual effort in collaboration. Everything with which the spirit naturally occupies itself must be *taken from it*.

It must be *educated*[6] to know God and to rejoice only in him. First of all, this is achieved by offering to the natural faculties something that attracts them more powerfully and satisfies them more than what they naturally know and enjoy. *Faith* points the intellect toward the Creator who has called every last thing into being and who is, himself, infinitely greater, more exalted, and worthier of love than all of them. Faith teaches the intellect about God's qualities and about all he has done for humankind and what the human being owes to him.

What does faith signify in this connection? Apparently, *that which* is proffered to our faith, the entirety of revealed truths proclaimed by the Church: *fides, quae creditur*. When the intellect accepts what is offered to it, what it could not know through its own capability, then it takes the first step into the dark night of faith. But this is nothing but the *fides, qua creditur*, a vital activity of the spirit and, correspondingly, a *durable attitude*, (*habitus* or *virtue of faith*), the conviction that God exists (*credere Deum*), and the convinced acceptance of that which God teaches through the Church (*credere Deo*).[7] By means of this life-in-faith the spirit raises itself above its natural activity, but in no way detaches itself from it.

Rather, in the new world that faith reveals to them, the natural spiritual faculties receive plenty of new material with which to occupy themselves.

This occupation, in which the spirit interiorly assimilates the content of faith is *meditation.* Here the imagination presents itself with images of events in salvation history, seeks to plumb their depths with all the senses, weighs with the intellect their general meaning and the demands they place on one. In this way the will is inspired to love and to resolve to form a lifestyle in the spirit of faith.

John knows an even higher form of meditation:[8] a spirit that is richly endowed and vibrant by nature penetrates by means of the intellect deep into the truths of faith. It carries on a dialogue with itself, investigating all sides, proceeding thought by thought and discovering their intrinsic connections. This activity becomes even livelier, easier, and more fruitful when the Holy Spirit gives the human spirit wings and bears it aloft. The spirit feels itself so thoroughly in the hand of a superior power and enlightened by this power, that it appears to itself to have ceased all activity of its own and to be, instead, receiving instruction through divine revelation.

Whatever the spirit has elaborated through this or the other manner of operating will be its permanent possession. And this is more than a treasure of stored truths that may be recalled from the memory on demand. The spirit—and this, if one understands it in a broad and objective way, means not only the intellect but also the *heart*—has gained confidence in God through continual engagement and has come to know and love him. This knowledge and love have become a very part of the spirit's being, somewhat resembling the relationship to a person with whom one has lived a long time and whom one trusts intimately. Such persons no longer need to gather information or to think about each other to arrive at mutual comprehension and love each other. There is scarcely any need for words between them.

Of course, every time they are together again there is both a new awakening and an increase of love, perhaps also a learning of new individual traits, but this happens almost of itself, one need not trouble oneself about it. This applies to the relationship of a soul with God after a lengthy practice in the spiritual life. She no longer needs to meditate in order to love and to come to know God. The path lies far in the past, she has arrived at her goal. As soon as she sets herself to pray she is with God and, in loving surrender, remains in his presence. Her silence is more precious to him than many words. This is known today as *acquired contemplation.* (John of the Cross does not use that term but it was well known to him.)[9] It is the fruit of one's own activity but, of course, is inspired and supported by the help of many graces. It is a grace when the message of faith, God's revealed truth, reaches us. It is grace that enables us to accept this message of faith and to become *believers*—even though we must actually do so by our own free decision. Without the support of grace, prayer and contemplation are impossible. Yet, all of this is achieved by our freedom and is completed under our own power. It also depends on us whether we give ourselves to prayer, whether and how long we remain in this *acquired contemplation.* If we examine this *contemplation* itself, the peaceful, loving surrender to God, we can also claim it as a *form of faith*, the *fides qua creditur*, not as *credere Deum* (although faith in God's existence is a prerequisite and is included in it), nor as *credere Deo* (although it is the result of all God's revealed truths we have accepted with faith). Rather it is *credere in Deum*: belief "into" God, venturing into him by faith.

This is the pinnacle of what can be attained in the life of faith by dint of one's own activity, even if, as an appropriate consequence, one's own will is surrendered to the divine and all one's doing and leaving-undone is regulated according to the divine will. Also, it already raises the spirit far above its natural conditions of being. To be sure, at first, the truths of faith bring God near to us through images and parables and concepts that derive from created things. But more than that, they teach us that God far surpasses everything created and is beyond all that can be grasped and understood. Therefore we must leave all creatures behind as well as all those faculties by which we comprehend and understand creatures in order to raise ourselves in faith to God, the inconceivable and incomprehensible one. But neither the senses nor the intellect are capable of raising us to God if we understand that capability as thinking in tangible concepts.

When we surrender to the incomprehensible God in faith we are pure spirit, freed from all images and concepts—therefore in darkness, because the world we see by day is constructed of images and concepts—*detached* also from the mechanism composed of manifold powers, and *unified* and *simple* in a life that is at once knowledge, remembrance, and love. Herewith we are only at the threshold of the mystical life, at the entrance to the transformation that is to be reached through the night of the spirit. But we have reached something that was not touched when the faculties were suspended. For, after all, something must remain if union with God and transformation in God is still possible after a suspension of the faculties. And this something, beyond being beyond affectivity and the intellect dependent on the sense must only then be what is, *in the proper sense, the spirit.* John also speaks of the *substance of the soul* in this connection.

In its substance, the soul is spirit and receptive in her inmost being for all that is spiritual, for God, the pure Spirit, and for all creatures that are also spiritual according to their inner essence. But she is buried in corporeality and has senses which are bound to the body as receptive organs for whatever is material. As a consequence of the Fall, these servile organs have become ruling ones. In order to regain strength for a purely spiritual life and activity and to have mastery over the senses, the spirit must first be freed from their grasp. We have followed the action of faith in this liberating process to a certain point: how it directs the spirit toward God and finally raises it to a purely spiritual relationship with God. Something else must be added that will render our attitude to God more perfect: a turn away from all that is not God. This is the principal task achieved in the active night of the spirit.

4) Extraordinary Graces Imparted and Detachment from Them

It has been said that faith attracts the spiritual faculties and inspires them to be occupied with God and with divine things. But by no means does this signify that detachment from the created world has been achieved. Even persons who have seriously resolved to lead a spiritual life and who persevere in the effort, devote only a lesser or greater part of the day to prayer and meditation. For the rest, they have both feet firmly planted on the ground of the created world. They take pains to penetrate this world intellectually and to gain mastery over it, to acquire temporal goods and to enjoy them. They still succumb to the captivating magic of natural goods and do not yet reject that which satisfies the senses even though, perhaps influenced by their prayer life, they already set up extensive barriers in this direction.

So their intellect is occupied, to the point of exhausting its energy, with the things of this world, their imagination filled with these things, their will's efforts directed toward them, and their passions set on them. All of this inhibits the prayer life within and would, finally, completely annihilate it if God did not come to the help of the soul with the particular support of his grace. However, this happens, and indeed, not only through the message of faith but through extraordinary communications that are able to surpass the attractions of the natural world and to make them ineffective. Images are offered to the senses and to the imagination that excel all things terrestrial. The intellect is raised through supernatural enlightenment to insights it could never attain through its own intellectual endeavors. The heart is filled with heavenly consolation before which all earthly joys and satisfactions pale. In this way, the soul is readied to turn with all her might from earthly goods and to raise herself toward what is heavenly.

But this is only half the task. One would never reach the goal, union with God, if one were to stand still before these supernatural communications and wish to rest in their enjoyment. For visions, revelations and sweet sensations are not God himself nor do they lead to him—with the exception of those most sublime, purely spiritual *touches*, in which God imparts himself to the substance of the soul and precisely in this way accomplishes that union. Therefore the soul must detach herself again, from all that is supernatural, from God's gifts, in order to win the giver, not the gifts. But what can induce her voluntarily to renounce such great goods? Here faith once more is active, teaching her that God is not anything that she is capable of grasping and understanding, and invites her to that dark way that alone leads to the goal. [10] But faith would achieve little were it only to turn to the intellect with instructive words. The powerful reality of the natural world and the supernatural gifts of grace must be upset by an even mightier reality. This takes place in the passive night.

Without this passive night—as John repeatedly insists—one would never arrive at the goal. The strong hand of the living God must intervene to free the soul from all the bonds of created things and draw her to himself. This intervention is the *dark, mystical contemplation*, joined to *detachment* from all that which so far has given light, support, and consolation.

10
Dark Contemplation

C. Death and Resurrection

1) Passive Night of the Spirit

a. Faith, Dark Contemplation, Detachment.

We already know from the *Night of the Senses* that a time arrives at which all taste for spiritual exercises as well as for all terrestrial things is taken away from the soul. She is put into total darkness and emptiness. Absolutely nothing that might give her a hold is left to her anymore except faith. Faith sets Christ before her eyes: the poor, humiliated, crucified one, who is abandoned on the cross even by his heavenly Father. In his poverty and abandonment she rediscovers herself. Dryness, distaste, and affliction are the "purely spiritual cross" that is handed to her. If she accepts it she experiences that it is an easy yoke and a light burden. It becomes a staff for her that will quickly lead her up the mountain.

When she realizes that Christ, in his extreme humiliation and annihilation on the cross, achieved the greatest result, the reconciliation and union of mankind with God, there awakens in her the understanding that for her, also, annihilation, the "living death by crucifixion of all that is sensory as well as spiritual" leads to union with God.[1] Just as Jesus in the extreme abandonment at his death surrendered himself into the hands of the invisible and incomprehensible God, so will the soul yield herself to the midnight darkness of faith which is the only way to the incomprehensible God. Then she will be granted mystical contemplation, the "ray of darkness,"[2] the mysterious wisdom of God, the dark and general knowledge that alone corresponds to the unfathomable

God who blinds the understanding and appears to it as darkness. It floods the soul and does this all the more easily the more the soul is free from all other impressions. This wisdom is something much purer, more tender, spiritual, and interior than all that is familiar to the intellect from the natural life of the spirit. Also raised above temporality, it is a true beginning of eternal life in us. It is not a mere acceptance of the message of faith that has been heard, nor a mere turning of oneself to God, who is known only from hearsay, rather it is an interior *being touched* and an *experience* of God that has the power to detach the soul from all created things, and to raise her, simultaneously plunging her into a love that does not know its object.

We will not attempt to determine here whether this dark, loving knowledge, in which the soul is touched in her innermost depth by God—from "mouth to mouth," from substance to substance—can still be reckoned as faith.[3] This dark, loving knowledge is the surrender of the soul through the will (as her mouth) to the loving approach of the still-concealed God: love, which is not feeling, but rather a readiness for action and sacrifice, an insertion of one's own will into the divine will in order to be led by it alone. Now, if the soul again receives particular illuminations, revelations, and consolations—which are often received during the usually very long time of the spiritual night— the soul will be prepared not to linger over them. She will leave it to God to achieve in her what he intends with these supernatural communications, but will herself remain in the darkness of faith. She has not only *learned*, but also *experienced*, that all of this is not God nor does it give God to her, but that she has everything she needs in faith: Christ himself, who is eternal wisdom, and in him, the incomprehensible God. She will be the more ready to make this renunciation, and to wait in faith, the more profoundly she has already been purified through the dark night.

After all, it has been repeated frequently that the soul, even after being exercised a long time in the spiritual life, is still full of imperfections and requires a thorough purification in order to be fit for divine union. It has also been shown that these imperfections can exist compatibly at the same time as supernatural communications of all kinds;

indeed, that in a soul not yet fully purified the divine gifts of grace can become, themselves, an occasion for imperfections, especially of pride, arrogance, and spiritual gluttony. All these weaknesses are healed by God through the *denudation* that takes place in the dark night "in that he delivers the intellect into darkness, the will into aridity, bitterness, and anguish."[4] Here the spirit and senses together experience the final purification. They do so after the senses have been strengthened enough in the first night, through transformation and curbing of the appetites and through relationship with God to bear the hardship of this intense second purification. This purification is also the work of the dark contemplation.

Hitherto we have looked at contemplation principally with regard to the gain it brings the soul in that it directs the spiritual faculties toward God and leads toward detachment from all created things. This gain was already clearly shown in the discussion of the *Ascent* of the active night of the spirit. It is once more summed up in the new explanation the saint gives to the introductory strophe of the Canticle on the *Dark Night of the Spirit*: "Poor, abandoned, and unsupported by any of the apprehensions of my soul, (in the darkness of my intellect, the distress of my will, and the affliction and anguish of my memory), left to darkness in pure faith, which is a dark night for these natural faculties, and with my will touched only by sorrows, afflictions, and longings of love of God, I went out from myself. That is, I departed from my low manner of understanding, and my feeble way of loving, and my poor and limited method of finding satisfaction in God. I did this unhindered by either the flesh or the devil. This was great happiness . . . because through the annihilation and calming of my faculties, passions, appetites, and affection, by which my experience and satisfaction in God had been base . . . my intellect departed from itself, changing from human and natural to divine. . . . It no longer understands by means of its natural vigor and light, but by means of the divine wisdom to which it was united. And my will departed from itself and became divine. United with the divine love, it no longer loves . . . with its natural strength, but with the strength and purity of the Holy Spirit. . . . The memory, too, was changed into presentiments of eternal glory. . . . All the strength and affections of the soul, by means of this night and purgation of the old self, are renewed with divine qualities and delight in divine harmony and joys."[5]

The *purification*, however, is not only *night* but also *affliction and torment* and this for two reasons: "first, because divine wisdom is so sublime that it exceeds the abilities of the soul and on this account the wisdom is dark for the soul; second, because the soul is base and impure and on this account the wisdom is painful, afflictive, and also dark for the soul."[6] Through the extraordinary, supernatural light "the natural understanding is overwhelmed and extinguished." So it happens that God "when he communicates this bright ray of his secret wisdom to the soul not yet transformed, causes thick darkness in the intellect." The soul's pain and affliction stem from the fact that the "divine infused contemplation is replete with extremely lofty perfection; the still unpurged soul that receives it is plunged into a sea of extreme misery, and because two contraries cannot coexist in one subject. . . . " Therefore, in this very bright light, she feels herself to be "so impure and wretched that it seems God is against her and she against God. It seems to her that God has rejected her." She is tormented by the fear that she will never be worthy of God and that she has lost all her blessings. This divine and dark light brings all her miseries into relief so the soul "sees clearly that of herself she will never possess anything else."[7]

The soul also suffers affliction on account of her natural, moral, and spiritual weakness. When the "divine contemplation assails them forcibly in order to subdue and strengthen their souls, they suffer so much in their weakness that they almost despair. Especially at times when the contemplation absorbs them with extraordinary force, the senses and the spirit undergo such agony and pain that they seem to have been cast to the ground under an immense and dark load;" they wish that death would come to relieve them as a favor.

It is amazing that "the soul be so utterly weak and impure that as a result she feels the hand of God as very heavy and hostile, which of itself is so light and gentle, and which has no intention of weighing on the soul and laying a burden upon her, but rather touches her mercifully . . . not in order to chastise but to grant her favors."[8] When the two extremes, the contemplation coming from God and the soul herself, come together, "God so disentangles and dissolves the spiritual substance of the soul—absorbing her in a profound darkness—that she feels she is melting away and being undone by a cruel spiritual death."

"But what the sorrowing soul feels most is the conviction that God has rejected her, and cast her into darkness with abhorrence. . . . The soul feels . . . the shadow of death, the sighs of death, and the sorrows of hell. . . . It is a feeling of God's absence, of being chastised and rejected by him as the object of his anger, . . . and even more, it seems that this affliction will last forever." Finally, the majesty and grandeur of this dark contemplation causes the soul to feel within herself her own intimate poverty and extreme misery. The soul experiences an emptiness and poverty in temporal, natural, and spiritual goods and is conscious of being placed in the midst of the contrary evils, "the miseries of imperfections, aridities, and the total incapability of her spiritual faculties to imagine anything at all, and of an abandonment of her spirit in darkness. . . . The soul feels as though she has been hung up, suspended in midair, unable to breathe.

But God also purges the soul in that he annihilates, empties, and consumes all her affections and imperfect habits . . . just as fire burns away rust and mold on metal. Since these are rooted deep within the substance of the soul, besides the natural and spiritual poverty and emptiness, she must usually suffer great afflictions, annihilation, and inner torments. . . . " In order to rid herself of this rust of her inclinations and to uproot them, the soul must, in a certain sense, first "annihilate and consume herself, since these passions and imperfections have become like a second nature to her." "And she feels this terrible undoing in her very substance . . . as though she were approaching her end." "Here God humbles the soul greatly in order to exalt her greatly afterward."

Were this condition to last, "the person would die in a very few days. Fortunately these feelings force themselves upon her in all their intensity only for short intervals. But sometimes this experience is so intense that the soul seems to see her abject unworthiness so vividly that she sees hell . . . open before her. These are the souls who go down into hell alive [Ps 55:15] since their purgation on earth is similar to what takes place there. The soul that endures it here on earth either does not enter that place or is detained there for only a short while since she accomplishes more in one hour here on earth by this purgation than she would in many there."[9]

The suffering is even more acute because of her former happy condition since usually such souls, "before they enter this night had previously had many consolations in God and rendered him many services." Now they are far from such good and can in no way reach it in any way. The solitude and desolation caused by this night is so great "that she cannot find consolation or support in any doctrine or in a spiritual master.

When one lays before her eyes the manifold reasons for being consoled . . . she feels the others just do not see what she sees and feels, or only speak as though they do while not knowing what they are saying. And she is filled with new pain instead of consolation, since according to her view there is absolutely no help for all of this. And this is actually true. For indeed, until the Lord finishes purging her in the way he desires, no remedy is effective, no medication can reduce her suffering." They remain in this condition until their spirit is humbled, softened, and purified, until it becomes so delicate, simple, and refined that it can be one with the Spirit of God, according to the degree of union of love that God, in his mercy, desires to grant.

The intensity and duration of the purgation are determined by that degree. Usually, it will last for some years although there are intervals in which, "by God's dispensation, the dark contemplation affects the soul not in a purgative but in an illuminative and loving way. Then the soul, like one who has been unshackled and released from a dungeon, breathes freely and unrestrainedly, feels and enjoys the highest delight of peace and loving friendship with God in a ready abundance of spiritual communication." Then one thinks that all trials are over forever, just as one believed earlier that the suffering would never end. This is all because two contraries cannot be present at the same time in the same spirit.

This conflict does not occur in the sensory part of the soul because of the weakness of her apprehensive power. "But since the spirit is not yet completely purged and cleansed of affections contracted from the lower part, it can, insofar as it is affected by them, be changed and suffer affliction, although insofar as it is spirit, it does not change." However, the impression that all troubles are now passed is very rare. "Until the spiritual purification is completed, the tranquil communication is seldom so abundant as to conceal the roots that still remain. The soul does not cease to feel that something is lacking. . . . This feeling keeps her from fully enjoying the alleviation. She feels as though an enemy is within her who, although pacified and put to sleep, will awaken and cause trouble. And this is true, for when a person feels safest and least expects it, the purgation returns to engulf the soul in another degree more severe, dark, and piteous than the former."

Such persons then believe again that their blessings are gone forever because the "present apprehension of the spirit annihilates within itself everything contrary to its conviction." For this reason the souls in purgatory suffer great doubts about whether their afflictions will ever end. They are, of course, in possession of the three theological virtues, faith, hope, and charity, and are aware that they love God, yet this gives them no consolation "because they cannot believe that God loves them or that they are worthy of that love. . . . And when the soul in the midst of this purification perceives that she loves God and would give a thousand lives for him, she finds no relief, instead she experiences deeper affliction. For she loves God so intensely that nothing else gives her concern. Yet, aware of her own misery, she is unable to believe that God loves her. She is convinced, much more, that it is with every reason that she is abhorred not only by God but by all creatures, and, full of pain, she sees in herself grounds for meriting rejection by him whom she loves so much and for whom she experiences such deep longings."[10]

The faculties are impeded in this painful condition, and this leads to the soul's inability to raise her mind and heart to God in prayer as she was formerly able to do. If she does pray, "it happens in such dryness, without strength or savor, that she cannot avoid the impression that God does not listen to her or bother about her prayer. . . . And actually, this is not the time to speak with God, rather . . . to press one's mouth in the dust . . . and endure this purification with patience. For it is God who here accomplishes the work in the soul and therefore she can do nothing. She can neither pray vocally nor be attentive at liturgical observances, nor still less attend to temporal affairs and business. Not only that, but she suffers at times from such great absorption and profound forgetfulness that many hours pass without her knowing what she did or thought during them, nor what she is doing now or wishes to do."

This is so because the memory, too, must be purged of all thoughts and discursive knowledge. The spiritual abstraction and oblivion is caused by the deep interior recollection in which contemplation immerses the soul and all her faculties as well, and withdraws her from all creature affections and apprehensions. The duration of this absorption is proportionate to the intensity of the contemplation. The more simply and purely the divine light strikes the soul, the more it darkens and empties and annihilates her. "And when the soul has been emptied and is in darkness, she is purified and enlightened" by the divine ray of light while the soul does not notice receiving the divine light. She remains rather in darkness, like the ray of sunlight "which when it is pure and finds nothing to obstruct it" remains invisible, even when it traverses the room.

"Yet when this spiritual light finds an object on which to shine, when something is to be understood spiritually concerning perfection . . . or a judgment concerning the truth or falsity of some matter, persons will understand more clearly than they did before they were in this darkness. And the spiritual soul will perceive the light just as clearly in order to recognize an imperfection when it presents itself." "Because . . . this spiritual light is so simple, pure, and so general, and unaffected and unrestricted by any particular intelligible object, it happens that the soul penetrates all that is presented to her, be it high or low . . . 'The Spirit penetrates all things, even the depths of the Godhead' (1 Cor 2:10) and 'Wisdom . . . touches everywhere because of its purity' (Wis 7:24), that is, because it is not particularized by any distinct object of affection. This is characteristic of the spirit, purged and annihilated of all particular knowledge and affection: not finding satisfaction in anything or understanding anything in particular, rather remaining in its emptiness and darkness, it embraces all things with great readiness."[11]

So this auspicious night, by darkening the spirit, aims to "impart light to it concerning all things." The night "humbles the soul, revealing her misery, only in order to raise and exalt her . . . impoverishing and emptying her of all possessions and natural affection, only that she may reach out divinely to the enjoyment of all earthly and heavenly things with a general freedom of spirit in them all." Because the intellect is unable to grasp this divine light by its nature alone it must be led into darkness by contemplation. This "darkness must last as long as is necessary to expel and annihilate the habit the intellect acquired over a long period of time of understanding in its own way."[12]

The destruction of the natural way of understanding is profound, frightful, and extremely painful. "One feels it in the deep substance of the soul and so it seems to be a substantial darkness that attacks one's very being." The will, too, must be purified and annihilated in order, through the union of love, to experience that very pure, divine, spiritual, and sublime affection and delight which exceeds every natural affection, feeling, and appetite of the will. "It must remain in dryness and distress for a length of time proportionate to its habitual natural affections (whether for divine or human things)." In this manner, "the will must remain in the fire of dark contemplation . . . until it is debilitated, dried up, and perfectly freed regarding all evil influences, so that it becomes pure and simple, its palate purged, healthy, and ready to experience the sublime and marvelous touches of divine love. . . . The soul must also . . . be furnished with all she needs to commune with God in a certain glorious splendor, for this contains innumerable treasures and delights, surpassing all the abundance the soul can possess naturally, for nature, so weak and impure, cannot receive these delights. Therefore the soul must first be set in emptiness and poverty of spirit . . . in order then, stripped of the old self, to be able to live the new life which is the state of union with God.

The soul must receive a very sublime understanding and a delightful sense and knowledge of all divine and human things. She sees things with entirely different eyes than before; the difference is as great as between the light and grace of the Holy Spirit and ordinary sensory perceptions or between divine and human things." For this, the memory must also be freed, its ability to perceive must become much more interior and more attuned toward abandoning all things; so that it seems all is unfamiliar and other than it was before.

So this night draws the spirit out of its customary and lowly manner of experience and fills it with divine insight—this seems so foreign and so different from every human way of experience[13] that the soul feels carried out of herself. Sometimes she wonders if she is not being bewitched or is in ecstasy, for she is amazed by the things she sees and hears; they seem to her to be entirely foreign and unusual, although they are the same ones she usually had to deal with.

"The soul must endure all these troubles and purifications . . . in order to be reborn into the life of the spirit. And it is with these sufferings that she gives birth to the spirit of salvation. . . . Besides this the soul prepares herself by means of this night of contemplation for that rest and that peace which is so deep and so delightful that it . . . surpasses all understanding (Phil 4:7). For this reason that former peace must be completely banished from the soul because it is still full of imperfections" and therefore was "no peace, even though to the soul . . . it appeared to be a twofold peace." That is to say, she had already attained to a sensory and spiritual understanding and beheld within herself a spiritual abundance. But first a purgation of this peace must be undergone in the soul. "This peace must be disturbed and taken away from her and she must experience the fulfillment of the Word: 'My soul is withdrawn and removed from peace' [Lam. 3:17]. This causes souls many fears, struggles, and false perceptions. On account of the feeling that they have been lost forever, there arises in their spirit so deep a sorrow and moaning that it causes a vehement spiritual outcry and clamor; sometimes this is expressed in words and streams of tears if they have the strength and power for this. This relief however is granted to a soul less frequently."[14] As happens with overflowing waters, "this outcry and sorrowful feeling of the soul becomes so intense that she is completely flooded and immersed and all her deep affections and energies are filled with indescribable spiritual anguish and suffering.

These are the effects produced in the soul by this night, which casts a shroud over the hopes she has for the light of day." The will is pierced through, at the same time, by sufferings, doubts, and fears which are never inclined to end. "This war and combat is profound because the peace awaiting the soul must be exceedingly profound, and the spiritual suffering is intimate and penetrating because the love to be possessed by the soul will also be intimate and refined. The more intimate and highly finished the work must be, so the more intimate, careful, and pure must the labor be. . . . Because in the state of perfection toward which she journeys by means of this purgative night, the soul must reach the possession and enjoyment of innumerable blessings of gifts and virtues," she must first be stripped "empty and impoverished of these blessings . . . indeed, she must be brought to think she is far removed from them, and become so convinced that no one can persuade her otherwise or make her believe she will ever be able to possess them."[15]

11
Enkindling of Love

b. Enkindling in Love and Transformation

In the agonies of the night of the spirit the imperfections of the soul are set aglow just as wood is freed from all moisture, in order then for itself to be enkindled in the radiance of the fire. The fire that first made the soul glow and then set her aflame is love. So what was announced by the second line of the first stanza of the poem *The Dark Night* is fulfilled: she is "inflamed by love's tugging sinews." An impassioned love sets it aflame, but it is an enkindling in the spirit and is as different from that which occurs in the sensory part as is the spiritual from the sensory part. It is an infused love and expresses itself more in endurance than in action. She "is now beginning to possess something of union with God and thereby shares to a certain extent in the properties of this union": that is, what occurs in the soul now "are actions of God more than of the soul and they reside in her passively, the soul merely giving her consent. But the heat, strength, temper, and passion of love, or fire . . . is caused only by the love of God that is being united to the soul."

Through this dark purgation, the soul is being prepared marvelously for union. In this state "the soul must love God with all her strength and all her sensory and spiritual appetites." It is a powerful enkindling of love since "God shackles all the strength, faculties, and appetites of the soul, spiritual and sensory alike, so that the energy and power of this whole harmonious composite may be employed in this love. Consequently, the soul arrives at the true fulfillment of the first commandment (Dt 6:5).[1] When the soul becomes aware of the fire and wound of this love but remains in darkness and doubt, not getting any satisfaction from it,

133

there awakens in her an urgent desire that makes her pine for God with all eagerness." "In all her thoughts and in all her business and in all events, the soul loves in many ways and desires, and also suffers in her desire . . . at all times and in many places and finds rest in nothing."

"Everything becomes narrow for this soul. She cannot bear to be by herself and cannot find room for herself in heaven or on earth. She is filled with sorrows unto darkness . . . that is, she suffers without the comfort of certain hope for some light or spiritual good. Her anxiety and affliction grow steadily, on the one hand through the spiritual darkness in which she sees herself engulfed and on the other, through the love of God that inflames her. Nonetheless, in the midst of these afflictions she feels a certain interior strength that decreases as soon as the burden of darkness is lifted from her. This is because this strength of the soul that was bestowed on her passively to support her in the assault of darkness is now dissipated by the dark fire of love that assails her. So when the inflammation of love comes to an end, the darkness, strength and warmth of love also diminish."[2]

The purgation of the soul by this loving, dark, spiritual fire corresponds to the purgation of the spirit in the next life by a dark material fire. In this way she attains to purity of heart, nothing other than divine grace and love. It is divine wisdom that purifies and illumines the soul in dark contemplation. It is the same wisdom that illumines the angels on matters of which they are ignorant. This wisdom descends from God through the first hierarchies unto the last and from these last finally passes over to humans. But humans must receive this loving contemplation "in a mode corresponding to their state, in a very limited and painful way. For God's light, which illumines the angels by clarifying and giving them the sweetness of love—for they are pure spirits prepared for this inflow—illumines humans, as we said, by darkening them and giving them pain and anguish, since naturally they are impure and feeble. The communication affects them as sunlight affects a sick eye, irritating it and filling it with pain. This lasts until it spiritualizes and refines the soul and she becomes capable, as are all the angels, of receiving this inpouring of loving influence in tranquillity."

The inflaming, anxious longing does not always fill the soul and usually not at the beginning of the purification, but only when the divine fire has been warming her for some time. Occasionally, then, the intellect, "is enlightened so blissfully and divinely by this mystical and loving knowledge of God . . . that the will, supported thereby, is marvelously enkindled in fervor, and while the will remains passive, this divine fire of love sets it aflame so that it seems to be receiving a live fire of living knowledge. . . . This enkindling of love in the two faculties that have been united is something immensely rich and delightful for the soul because certainly it is already a touch of the divinity, a beginning of the perfect union of love for which the soul hopes." But when these graces are being bestowed, it can also be "that the will loves without the intellect understanding, just as the intellect can know without the will loving. That is to say, since this dark night of contemplation consists of divine light and divine love, as fire consists of light and warmth, it may happen that this love-filled light acts more upon the will, inflaming it with love, while it leaves the intellect in darkness. . . . At another time the intellect is filled with love . . . while the will remains in dryness. The Lord does this, for he communicates himself as he wills."[3]

God is not bound by the laws of the natural life of the soul. According to these, indeed, "it is impossible to love an object that one has not hitherto known. But in a supernatural way, God can easily infuse and increase love without giving or increasing particular knowledge. This is the experience of many spiritual persons."[4] Some "whose understanding of God is not very advanced have made all the more progress according to their wills. Instead of the science of the intellect, faith suffices for them, and through it God infuses love and increases it without increasing the person's knowledge." This last, of course, may not be understood to say that faith *generally* awakens only love, without imparting knowledge. On the contrary: of itself it is primarily directed toward the intellect and divulges divine truth to it. But at times it does so in a veiled form, not in the manner of natural knowledge. Then, too, it does not always have to set definite, single truths before its eyes.

To believe can also mean to turn toward the reality about whom all articles of faith speak: God. This turning toward him is in such a way that one does not look at him in the light of any single article of faith, rather one is surrendered to him, the incomprehensible one, who is himself the embodiment of all the articles of faith and yet surpasses them all in his incomprehensibility, in darkness, and indistinction. If the soul *experiences* in this surrender that she is seized by the dark and incomprehensible God, then this is the dark contemplation that God himself gives to the soul as light and love together. It is "dark and indistinct for the intellect. . . . And as this knowledge that God infuses is common and dark in the intellect, the will also loves in a common way, without distinguishing any one recognized object."

Sometimes, though, "God, in this tender communication . . . acts more upon one faculty than the other . . . often only the understanding is noticeable and not the love, another time only the love and not the understanding. . . . For God can act on one faculty of the soul without affecting the others; thus he can inflame the will with a touch of his warm love while the intellect has no awareness, just as someone can be warmed by a fire without seeing it."⁵

When, however, some mystical knowledge is communicated to the intellect, the soul is "filled with light in the midst of these darknesses, 'and the light shines in the darkness' (Jn 1:5). . . . The serenity is so delicate and delightful to the senses of the soul that it is ineffable. This experience of God is felt now in one way and now in another."

Even though the two faculties are being purged equally, purgative contemplation is experienced as an inflaming of love in the will before it is valued in the intellect as knowledge. This can be explained by noting the contrast between love that is felt as ardor (*passion*) and a free act of the will. The "burning love is more the passion of love than a free act of the will." It "wounds the substance of the soul and thus moves the affections passively. As a result the enkindling of love is called the passion of love rather than a free act of the will. An act of the will is such only insofar as it is free. Yet, since these passions and affections bear a relation to the will, it is said that if the soul is impassioned with some affection, the will is. This is true, because the will thus becomes captive and loses its freedom, carried away by the impetus and force of the passion. As a result we say that this enkindling of love takes place in the will; that is, the appetites of the will are enkindled.

This enkindling is called the passion of love rather than the free exercise of the will. Since the receptive capacity of the intellect can only take in the naked and passive knowledge, and since the intellect, unless purged, cannot receive this knowledge, the soul, prior to the purgation of the intellect, experiences the touch of knowledge less frequently than the passion of love. For to feel the passion of love it is unnecessary that the will be so purged in relation to the passions; the passions even help it experience impassioned love.

Since this inflammation and yearning of love already come from the Holy Spirit they are entirely different from that which we discussed in the night of the senses." They are felt in the spirit even though the senses have a share in them. What is perceived and that which one does without, are felt in such a way that in comparison with this all the suffering of the senses is as nothing—even though it is incomparably greater than in the first, sensory night. "For the soul is conscious deeply within herself of the lack of an immense and inestimable good which cannot be healed by any means."

Even at the beginning of this spiritual night "when the fire of love has not begun to catch. . . . God gives . . . the soul an esteeming love by which he is held in such high favor that the soul's greatest suffering in the trials of this night is the anguish of thinking she has lost God and been abandoned by him. . . . If she could be assured that all is not over and lost, that what she suffers is for the better . . . and that God is not angry with her, she would be unconcerned about all these sufferings, rather she would rejoice in the knowledge that by them she is able to serve God. For her love of esteem for God is so intense . . . that she would with the greatest joy die many times if that were to please him. Once the fire of love has inflamed the soul and joined itself to the esteem of God she already possessed, she usually acquires such strength, courage, and longing relative to God, that with singular boldness and without consideration or concern for anything, in the strength and in-ebriation[6] of her love and desire, she would perform even unusual and extreme things in order to find him whom her soul loves."

Through the sufferings of the night of the spirit the soul's "youth is renewed like the eagle's" (Ps. 103:5).[7] The human intellect, united with the divine through supernatural illumination, becomes divine. In like manner, the will is united with the divine will and divine love, and the memory, affections, and appetites are converted and changed according to God. "Thus this soul will be a soul of heaven, heavenly, and more divine than human." Therefore, in retrospect of the night, she can cry out: "Ah, the sheer grace!"[8] She has now "escaped, unnoticed, since her house lay at rest, so still." Her house is the soul's customary way of acting, her wishes and desires, all her spiritual faculties. These are the members of her household who must be at rest in order not to impede the way to union with the Beloved. Now she recognizes that "in the darkness she was secure." All the soul's straying is caused "through her appetites or her gratifications, her discursive meditation or through knowledge. . . . Once these operations and movements are impeded, the soul will obviously be freed from error in them. In this way she frees herself not only from herself but also from . . . the world and the devil. These enemies have no other means of warring against the soul when her affections and operations are deadened." Now her appetites and faculties are no longer distracted by useless and harmful things; she feels secure from "vainglory and from false joy, and from many other evils," and also "by walking in darkness, she is no longer in any way in danger of getting lost but thereby . . . gains . . . the virtues."

The dark night of the soul also deprives the soul of satisfaction in good things, yes, even in supernatural and divine things. This is so because the soul's impure, lowly, and very natural faculties can receive supernatural things only according to a human and lowly mode. Through "being weaned, purged, and annihilated ... they will lose that lowly and human mode of working and receiving, and thus all these faculties and appetites of the soul are tempered and prepared for the sublime reception, experience, and savoring of the divine and supernatural that cannot be received until the old self dies.

Consequently, if these spiritual communications are not bestowed from above, from the Father of lights, to the human will and appetite, no soul can taste them divinely and spiritually no matter how much . . . her faculties are employed in God and no matter how great the satisfaction she seems to find in God. She will be able to taste God only in human and natural ways as she does other things. For the goods of grace do not go from humans to God, but they come from God to humans."⁹ Thus many persons have great satisfaction in God and spiritual things and "think these are something supernatural and spiritual, while it is, after all, but purely natural and human activity and desire."

For this reason the soul may take dryness and darkness as fortunate symptoms: symptoms that God is freeing her from herself. He is disentangling her from the activity of her faculties. Probably she would have been able to acquire much through this, her own activity, but never as completely, perfectly, and securely as she does now since God takes her by the hand. He leads her in the darkness as though she were blind, without her knowing by what way and to which place—however, by ways that she herself, in the happiest of wanderings while using her own eyes and feet, would never have succeeded in finding. She makes great progress without herself suspecting this; indeed, she thinks she has gotten lost. For she does not know this new condition yet and sees only "that she suffers loss in all that is familiar to her and which used to give her satisfaction." It is also a more secure way because it is a way of suffering. "For the way of suffering is a surer and more advantageous road than that of joy and action. In suffering one receives strength from God, whereas in our activity and in gratification the soul's weaknesses and imperfections come to light. Then again . . . in suffering, virtues are practiced and acquired and the soul is purified and made wiser and more cautious."

But more than all else, obscure wisdom lies at the root of the perceived security. "The dark night of contemplation engulfs and absorbs the soul and brings her so near to God that he himself takes her under his protection and frees her from all that is not God. Since the soul is here undergoing a cure to regain her health, which is God himself, she allows His Majesty to restrict her to a diet, to abstinence from all things, and he causes her to lose her appetite for all else." "So she is hidden in the face of God from the disturbance of people" (Ps 31:20), that is, through dark contemplation she is "fortified against all the occasions that may arise unexpectedly in her path because of others." She also gains security in "the fortitude this obscure, painful, and dark water of God bestows on the soul from the beginning. Even though it is dark, it is water, and thereby refreshes and fortifies the soul in what most suits it . . . Then the soul soon becomes conscious of a true determination and power to do nothing that she perceives would be an offense against God and to omit nothing that seems to be for his service. That dark love enkindles in the soul a remarkably vigilant care and interior solicitude about what to do or omit in order to please God. Now all her appetites, strength, and faculties, having been withdrawn from all other things, aim to serve God with all their power and might." And so the soul departs from herself and all created things and goes forward, "quite safe within the dark," toward the sweet and delightful union with God through love, "by the secret ladder, disguised."[10]

12
The Secret Ladder

c. The Secret Ladder

Dark contemplation is the secret ladder: secret as is mystical theology that is communicated and infused into the soul through love. How this happens, the soul neither "knows herself nor does anyone else, not even the devil has knowledge of it. The master who teaches the soul dwells within it substantially where neither the devil nor the natural senses nor the intellect can reach." Secret or hidden is this wisdom in its workings, also, in the darkness and straits of the soul's purgation as well as in the illumination that follows. The soul can "neither recognize it, nor describe it, nor give it a name." She has "no inclination at all to give it a name, and finds . . . no means of giving adequate expression for so sublime an understanding and so delicate a spiritual feeling. The interior wisdom is so simple, general, and spiritual that it cannot be grasped since it did not enter the intellect in any concept, nor was it portrayed in any sensory image." "The knowledge would resemble that of those who see an object they had never seen before, nor have they seen anything at all like it. . . . They would be unable, despite all the effort possible, to name it or to say what it is, even though the senses accurately perceived it. And so, how much more difficult will it be for them to express what has not entered through the senses."[1] Since God speaks to the soul in a completely interior and purely spiritual way, his language transcends all the ability of the exterior and interior senses and so silences them. The senses do not understand this language, are unable to repeat it in words, nor do they even desire to hear it.

The mystical wisdom is therefore also called secret because it has the characteristic of hiding the soul within itself. . . . Occasionally, it so engulfs the soul in its secret abyss that she has the keen awareness of being brought into a place far removed from every creature. She accordingly feels that she has been led into a remarkably deep and vast wilderness unattainable by any human being, into an immense, unbounded desert. And this, for her, is the more delightful, pleasant, and lovely, the deeper, vaster, and more solitary it is. She is conscious of being so much more hidden, the more she is raised above every created being. This abyss of wisdom elevates and enriches the soul to a high degree: it engulfs her in the veins of the science of love and lets her know in this way how base are creatures in comparison with the lofty, divine knowledge and feelings, and gives her an insight into how lowly, inadequate, and entirely incapable all images and words are with which one speaks of divine things in this life.

She also takes note how impossible it is to know or experience them through any natural means; only through the mystical wisdom of God can one be illumined regarding these matters. Because "these things are, humanly speaking, beyond our ability to understand, one must attain them by humanly not knowing and divinely by ignorance, for speaking mystically . . . the divine things and perfections are not known as they are in themselves while they are being sought and acquired, but when they are already found and practiced." "The footsteps of God and the paths he follows in souls to draw them to himself and unite them with his wisdom are unrecognizable." [2]

The poem of the *Night* calls this dark contemplation a *ladder* since "as one ascends a ladder to pillage the fortresses containing goods and treasures, so too, by this secret contemplation, the soul ascends in order to plunder, know, and possess the goods and treasures of heaven." Furthermore "as the same steps of a ladder are used for both ascent and descent, so this secret contemplation humbles the soul by means of the same favors by which . . . it has been exalted in God. For all favors that truly come from God have this trait: they simultaneously humble and exalt the soul." She is subjected to this way of continual ups and downs. "Immediately after prosperity some tempest or trial follows, so much so that the calm was seemingly given to forewarn and strengthen it against the future misery. So, abundance and welfare follow upon that misery and torment. It seems to the soul, then, that in her case, for the celebration of every feast, a vigil of fasting has been prescribed. This is the ordinary procedure . . . in the state of contemplation . . . until one arrives at the quiet state.

"The soul never remains in one state, but everything is ascent and descent. The reason is that since the state of perfection, that consists in perfect love of God and contempt of self, cannot exist without knowledge of God and of self, the soul necessarily must first be exercised in both. She is now given the one, in which she finds satisfaction and exaltation, and now made to experience the other, humbled until the ascent and descent cease through the acquisition of the perfect habits. For the soul will then have reached God and been united with him. He is at the top of the ladder and it is in him that the ladder rests."[3]

Principally, contemplation is called a ladder because it "is a science of love, an infused loving knowledge of God, that both illumines and inflames the soul with love, elevating her step by step to God, her creator. For it is love alone that unifies the soul and unites it to God." We distinguish the *rungs* of the ladder (as do St. Bernard and St. Thomas) according to their effects, "since this ladder of love . . . is so secret, that God alone can measure and weigh it, and so it is impossible to know these steps in themselves, by natural ways."[4]

"The first rung makes the soul sick, for her good. . . . But this sickness is not unto death, rather for the glory of God. For in this sickness, through God himself, the soul dies to sin and to all that is not God. . . . The second rung causes a person to seek God unceasingly. . . . On this rung the soul goes about so solicitously that she seeks her Beloved in all things, and in all that forces her to keep busy she speaks about and acts for the Beloved. . . . The third rung of the ladder of love prompts the soul to action and awakens her to fervor so that she does not tire. . . . On this rung the soul considers the heroic works she performs for the Beloved's sake insignificant, the many as few, the long time in which she serves God as short as a consequence of the fire of love that has set her aflame. . . . Because of her intense love for God the soul here considers the greatest sorrow and pain that she bears for God's sake as little, and it would be her sole consolation if she were allowed to annihilate herself a thousandfold for him. Therefore she considers herself useless in all she does, and thinks she is living in vain. Another wonderful effect is produced here, namely the firm conviction that she is far worse than all other souls. . . . Because love always brings her to see how much she owes God and . . . because she knows that the many works she performs for God in this state are faulty and imperfect, they all become for her an occasion of shame and pain since she recognizes in what a lowly way she works for so great a Lord.

The fourth rung causes in the soul a persisting suffering for the sake of the Beloved.[5] Love lets her see "all that is great and difficult and burdensome as nothing. . . . The spirit possesses so much energy here that it brings the flesh under complete control and takes as little account of it as would a tree of one of its leaves. The soul in no way seeks consolation or satisfaction either in God or in anything else; neither does she desire or ask favors of God, for she is clearly aware that she has already received many from him. All her care is directed toward how she might give some pleasure to God and render him some service because of what he deserves and the favors he has bestowed, even though this too will be at his expense. . . . This degree of love is very elevated. For as the soul at this stage through so genuine a love pursues God in the spirit of suffering for his sake, His Majesty frequently gives her joy by paying her visits of spiritual delight. For the immense love of the Word, Jesus Christ, cannot allow the soul that loves him to suffer long without coming to her assistance. . . . The fifth rung . . . causes an impatient striving and yearning for God. At this stage the desire of the loving soul for the possession of the Beloved and for union with him is so vehement that she deems the least delay as extremely long, burdensome, and annoying and she lives only in the thought of how she might find the Beloved. . . . On this rung the loving soul must either gain possession of the Beloved or die."[6]

"The sixth rung causes the soul to hurry quickly toward God and she frequently perceives his nearness by the senses. Without tiring, she hurries toward him in hope, for love empowers her to fly swiftly." The

agility granted to the soul here comes from the fact that she has expanded
a great deal and that her purification from all things is almost complete.
Therefore she soon attains the seventh rung. Here the "soul is extremely
emboldened. At this stage love no longer allows the understanding to
determine her to wait; nor does she accept advice to hold herself back,
nor can she be restrained through being shamed[7]. . . . Such souls receive from God what they beg for in the great joy of their hearts. . . .
From the freedom and boldness God gives the soul on this seventh
rung, so that she may be daring in his presence and fearlessly deal with
him with the full power of love, the soul attains the eighth rung which
gives her possession of the Beloved and union with him. . . . 'I have
found him whom my soul loves; I hold him fast and will not let him go
anymore'" [Sg.3:4]. The soul's desire is satisfied at this stage of union,
but with interruptions. Some souls indeed do attain to union for a short
time, but are withdrawn again soon; for . . . could they remain in this
stage longer they would already arrive at a certain kind of glory in this
life. . . . The ninth rung . . . is . . . the state of those who are perfect, who
already burn in the sweet love of God. The Holy Spirit produces this
gentle and delightful ardor by reason of the union which unites the soul
to God. "The riches of grace and treasures of God that the soul receives
on this rung cannot be expressed in words. Were one to write many
books on the subject, the greater part would still remain unsaid."

The tenth and last rung of the hidden ladder of love no longer
belongs to this life. "It makes the soul perfectly like God because of
the vision of God that the soul attains at once upon leaving the body
when she arrives at the ninth rung in this life. These souls, whose number is small, are spared purgatory since they have been perfectly purified by love. Therefore it is written in Matthew: "Blessed are the pure
of heart for they shall see God" [Mt 5:8]. This vision is . . . the reason
for the perfect likeness to God. . . . Not because the soul will have as
much capacity as God, for that is impossible, but because all that the
soul is, will be like God."

Therefore one will call her divine through participation and she will
be. In this topmost stage of clear vision, the last rung of the ladder,
"nothing is any longer hidden from the soul because of her likeness to

God. But, until that day, however high the soul may ascend, there will still be much hidden in proportion to her lack of total assimilation to God. Thus, by means of this mystical theology and secret love, the soul departs from herself and all things and ascends to God. For love is like a fire that always rises upward in the longing to be immersed in the center of its sphere."[8]

d. The Soul's Tricolored Garment

The soul has said that she escaped *disguised* or *camouflaged*. To disguise oneself, that is, to hide one's own clothing and one's own form under another form, is what one does "in order to give someone whom one loves through this other form and clothing an outward manifestation of one's love and attraction and thereby to win the Beloved's favor and good pleasure. Or it is done to hide from one's antagonists in order the better to carry out one's plans. . . . The soul, therefore, . . . who is burning with love for Christ, her Bridegroom . . . conceals herself while she is escaping in that clothing which most clearly shows the inclinations of her spirit and in which she best eludes her antagonists . . . the devil, the world, and the flesh."

Her clothing, therefore, has three principal colors: white, green, and red as symbols of the three theological virtues. Through them the soul wins the good pleasure of her Beloved, and at the same time, enjoys complete protection against her three enemies. "For faith is a white undergarment of such blinding brilliance that it destroys every intellect's ability to see. If the soul walks in the garment of faith, the devil neither sees her nor dares to attack her." Nor is there any better garment than the dazzlingly white one of faith, the foundation of all the other virtues, to win the good pleasure of the Beloved and to attain to union with him. "The soul wears this dazzling white radiance of faith at her escape" when she walks in the darkness and interior afflictions of the dark night. She no longer finds satisfaction in any kind of natural knowledge, nor is she refreshed by any supernatural enlightenment, since heaven seems shut to her. "However, she suffers steadfastly, and perseveres, and walks through the trials without growing weak or leaving the Beloved." In these trials and afflictions he puts her faith to the test.

Over the white undergarment of faith the soul wears the green coat of mail of hope. In the strength of this virtue "the soul frees herself from the second enemy, the world, and shields herself against it. For this fresh green of living hope in God procures such a life-giving strength and intrepidity for the soul and elevates her so mightily to the goods of eternal life that in comparison to that which she hopes for, all things of this world appear to be dry, withered, dead, and worthless, as indeed they are. Here the soul divests and releases herself of all worldly costumes and clothing, nor does she set her heart on anything anymore. Not hoping for anything that is in or will be in the world, she lives clothed only in the hope of eternal life. Having her heart so lifted up above the things of the world, she is not only unable to touch or take hold of worldly things, but she cannot even see them. And so the soul walks in this green livery and disguise, well protected against the second enemy, the world. It is "the actual task of hope to allow the soul to raise her eyes only to look at God" so that she expects no good from anywhere else. In this garment she is so pleasing to the Beloved that she receives from him all she hopes for. Without this green livery she would "attain nothing, since God is only moved and conquered by persevering hope."

"Over the white and the green garment, the soul wears the third color, a precious bright-red toga," the symbol of love, similar to a crowning and completion of the whole outfit. Through this "the soul is protected and hidden from the third enemy, the flesh. (For where love of God reigns, there love of self and one's belongings can no longer enter.) That love . . . moreover, strengthens the other virtues, gives them life and power to protect the soul, bestows loveliness and charm on her with which she can please the Beloved. For without this holy love, no virtue is pleasing to God."

This, then, is the disguise in which the soul ascends to God in the night of faith. Faith, hope, and love give her the preparation most suitable for union: "Faith empties and darkens the intellect in regard to all its natural knowledge and prepares it thus for union with divine wisdom.

Hope empties and separates the memory from all possession of created things . . . and puts it in possession of that for which it hopes. . . . In the same manner, love empties the will of its affections and tendencies toward all that is not God and directs them to him alone. . . . Since . . . these virtues have the task of separating the soul from all that is less than God, they have also as a consequence the task of uniting her with God." So it is that without the garment of these three virtues "it is impossible for the soul to attain to perfect love of God. . . . Therefore it is a "happy fate" for the soul when she has put on such clothing and worn it perseveringly until she has reached the goal she longs and strives for, the union of love."[9]

Now it is clear that it was a happy fortune for the soul to complete such a difficult task: she has freed herself from the devil, from the world, and her own sensuality, has won the precious freedom of the spirit, has been transformed from an earthly to a heavenly soul and has arrived at having her conversation in heaven [Phil 3:20].[10]

e. In Darkness and Concealed in Deep Repose

It was also fortunate that the soul could escape "in darkness and concealed": in darkness she is safe from all the malicious plans and wiles of the devil. For infused contemplation is given her passively and secretly; all the faculties of the sensory part of the soul remain in the dark throughout. And only with the help of the sensory powers can the devil be aware of and understand "what is in the soul and what is transpiring in her. The more spiritual and interior the communication, and the more removed it is from the senses, the less the devil understands it. Therefore, for the soul's security, such an inner communion with God is very important so that the weakness of its sensory part will not hinder her freedom of spirit and an abundant spiritual communication will be made possible." In that case the soul is safe from the evil enemy. Of that which happens in the superior part of the soul, the lower portion should know nothing: "this is to remain a secret between God and the soul."

Indeed, the devil concludes that the soul is receiving interior and spiritual communications "because of the great quietude and silence some of them cause in the senses and faculties of the soul. . . . When he now sees that he cannot impede these proofs of grace in the depths of the soul, he does everything possible to excite and disturb the sensory part, which he can affect with suffering, horrors, and fears. He intends by this agitation to disquiet the superior and spiritual part of the soul in its reception and enjoyment of that good. Yet often, when the communication of such contemplation is poured into the spirit in total purity and produces strength there, all the devil's exertion to disturb the soul is in vain, and, on the contrary, the soul receives new gains, new love, and a deep-seated peace. For as soon as she perceives the disturbing presence of the evil enemy, she withdraws—and this is wholly remarkable—without knowing how she does so, and without any effort of her own, all the deeper into the interior of the soul's inner depths where she is well aware of being placed in a sure refuge, removed from the evil enemy, and concealed from him.

All her fears remain outside; she exults in being clearly conscious of how she can enjoy that quiet peace in such perfect security and that sweetness of the Bridegroom in concealment, the peace that the world and the devil can neither give nor take away.

But sometimes, when the spiritual communications do not penetrate far enough into the spirit, and instead touch the sensory part also, the evil enemy can more easily disturb and agitate the spirit with horrors he presents by way of sensuality. Then the torment and pain he causes is immense, indeed occasionally inexpressibly immense. Since here it is a case of an unconcealed encounter of spirit and spirit, the horrors that the evil spirit occasions in the good spirit, that is, in the soul, are unbearable when he succeeds in entangling her. At other times it happens that the devil detects some of the favors granted to the soul through a good angel; for God usually allows the antagonist to . . . recognize the reception of such favors . . . above all, that he may do what he can to hinder them, in accord with justice . . . and that he cannot claim that he was not given the opportunity to conquer the soul. And he could do that if God did not allow a certain parity between the two warriors (the good angel and the bad) in their struggle for the soul. So the victory will be more estimable, and the soul, victorious and faithful in temptation, will receive a more abundant reward.

For this reason . . . God permits the devil to deal with the soul in the same measure and mode in which he himself conducts and deals with it." "If God allows her to receive a true vision from the good angel ... then the evil spirit may represent to her false visions that are deceptively like the true ones. He is also able to simulate spiritual communications that come through the mediation of good angels. But he cannot ape[11] purely spiritual communications for these are without form and figure. In order then to attack the soul in the same way in which she is graced by God, he represents his frightful spirit to the soul so as to assail and destroy the spiritual with the spiritual. If this happens at a time when the good angel is raising the soul into the state of spiritual contemplation, the soul cannot enter the hiding place of this contemplation quickly enough to go unnoticed by the devil . . . and the consequence is a horror and disturbance that is most painful for the soul.

Sometimes, however, the soul can withdraw instantaneously, so that the evil spirit is unable to make any impression on her or to frighten her. Strengthened by the effective grace given her by the good angel, she hides herself in her interior. Sometimes the devil prevails and disturbance and terror seize upon the soul that are far more painful for her than any other suffering in life. Namely, since these frightful intrusions take place purely and simply between spirit and spirit without any admixture of the corporeal, the torment exceeds everything imaginable. In any case, the torment does not last long in the soul, for if it did, the frightful invasion of the other spirit would force her to separate from the body. . . . All this . . . takes place in the soul without any participation by her, nor can she put up any resistance."

It happens, however, only "that she may be purified and, be prepared for some great feast and spiritual gift of grace through this spiritual vigil; according to the degree of the dark and terrible purification . . . the soul will enjoy a wondrous and delightful spiritual communication, and in fact, in so sublime a manner that she cannot find expression for it." The preceding terrors made her receptive to this delight to a great degree "since these spiritual visions belong more to the other than to this life, and each is a preparation for the one following." This, however, holds only for graces received through the mediation of angels.

When God himself visits the soul, she remains totally "in darkness and concealed" because "His Majesty dwells substantially in the part of the soul, where neither an angel nor a devil can gain access in order to learn what is happening. And neither can they gain knowledge about the intimate and secret communications between God and the soul; in a single one of these touches, which constitute the highest degree of prayer, the soul receives more graces than in all else. Therefore she covets such a divine touch and esteems it higher than all other graces that God bestows on her."

When these favors are bestowed in concealment, that is, only in the spirit, the soul sees herself, without knowing how, withdrawn in her superior and spiritual part and alienated from the lower and sensory part, perceiving within herself two parts so distinct from one another that, it seems to her, they have nothing in common anymore. And, in a certain sense, this is really so, for everything she does here is totally spiritual and she no longer has anything in common with the sensory part. Thus the soul becomes wholly spiritual and in this concealment of unitive contemplation, the spiritual movements and appetites give up almost all their activity." Therefore the soul sings, when she speaks of the superior part . . . "my house lay at rest so still."[12]

"Here she means to say: 'Since the superior part of my soul as well as the lower part with its appetites and faculties were already at rest, I escaped to divine union in love with God.' " The sensory part as well as the spiritual one were attacked in the dark night. Both had "to be brought to rest and to peace with all their faculties and appetites." For this reason, the phrase is repeated a second time. "This quietude and this peace of her spiritual house must become the soul's habitual and perfect possession, as far as this is possible in this present life. This is achieved by means of the acts of substantial touches of divine union." Through them the soul is purified, quieted, and strengthened to withstand attacks, so that she may enter into this union: "the divine espousal between the soul and the Son of God.

As soon, then, as the two dwellings of the soul, together will all the members of the household, the soul's faculties and desires, attain to perfect rest and are strengthened, as soon as they lie in sleep and silence with regard to earthly and heavenly things, Divine Wisdom unites itself directly with the soul and takes possession of her through a new bond of love. . . . One cannot attain to this union without thorough purification. . . . Therefore, whoever refuses to enter the night in order to find the Beloved, to deny her self-will, and to die to self, whoever wishes to seek him only in the bed of the comfortable . . . will never find him."[13]

In this glad night the soul was blessed with an undisturbed and hidden contemplation, which is so foreign and incomprehensible to the senses that no creature can touch it and turn her away from the way of love's union. All the powers of the superior part of the soul were placed in darkness through the spiritual obscurity of this night. Therefore, she cannot discern anything anymore nor, in order to reach him, does she give her attention to anything other than God. She is free of all forms, figures, and apprehensions which are an obstacle to a lasting union with God. She can no longer lean on any illumination of the intellect nor on an exterior guide in order to find comfort and satisfaction in them. "For the dense darkness has robbed her of all these. So love, which now burns in her and turns her heart toward the Beloved, is the only motivating strength and guide for the soul and, without her knowing how or in what way, this love raises her aloft in solitary flight to God."[14]

The *Treatise on the Dark Night* breaks off here. Of the eight stanzas of the poem, only six[15] have been explained. This explanation has a double significance for us: it gives us further information about the *spirit's being*, and shows us that dark contemplation is simultaneously *death and resurrection* to a new life. An actual representation and clarification of this new life is as absent here as in the *Ascent*.

13

Created Spirits

2) The Soul in the Realm of the Spirit
and of Created Spirits

a. Construction of the Soul; God's Spirit and Created Spirits

The soul as a spirit is positioned in a realm of the Spirit and of spirits. She, however, possesses her own structure. She is more than a simple form that animates the body, more than the *interior* of an *exterior*. Rather, within her there lies an opposition between internal and external.[1] The soul can be said to be at home at her most interior point, at her essence or the deepest ground of the soul. She goes out through the activity of her senses to a domain inferior to her realm. It influences the soul in what she does and does not do and limits her freedom in a certain sense. It is unable to penetrate to the soul's innermost center, but it can distance the soul from that center within.

In her ascent to God, the soul raises herself above herself or is raised above herself. But at the same time, by this more than by anything else she actually attains her innermost center. That sounds contradictory, but corresponds with the facts and is grounded in the realm of the spirit's relationship to God.

God is pure spirit and the archetype of all spiritual being.[2] So, really, it is only by beginning with God that it is possible to understand what spirit is; however, that means it is a mystery that constantly attracts us because it is the mystery of our own being. We can approach it, in a certain way, since our own being is spiritual. We can also approach it by way of all being to the extent that all being, which has meaning and which can be comprehended intellectually, has something of spiritual being about it. But it reveals itself to a greater depth in proportion to our knowledge of God, though it is never totally unveiled, that is, it never ceases to be a mystery.

God's spirit is totally transparent to himself; is totally free to dispose of itself (in that unrestrictedness that is intrinsic to being-through-itself). It freely goes out of itself, yet always remains within itself. The Spirit sets up all other being out of itself, envelops it, penetrates, and rules it. Created spirit is a limited image of God (in all the forenamed features): as an image [*Abbild*] it is similar to God; as *limited* it is God's opposite. It is more or less extensively capable of receiving God, in the highest degree; it has the possibility of being united to God in mutual, free, personal surrender.

We speak of a *realm* of the Spirit and of spirits, inasmuch as all spiritual beings have at least a possible connection among themselves and form part of a whole. We call it the realm *of the Spirit* because *Spirit* includes more than all spirits, namely all that is spiritual and that, in a certain sense, is everything that has being. But we say further: realm *of the spirits* because in this realm *spirits*, that is personal-spiritual beings, play a prominent role.

God is at the peak of this realm, infinitely surpassing all that is spiritual and all spirits. A created spirit can only ascend to him by transcending itself. However, since he bestows being on all that has being, and preserves it in being, God is the sustaining ground of everything. Whatever ascends to him descends at the same time, by that very act, into its own center or resting place.

b. The Soul's Dealings with God and with Created Spirits

Using a spatial image borrowed from the natural science of his time, the saint calls God the soul's *resting point* her *deepest center*.[3] According to that scientific view, bodies are pulled most forcefully toward the center of the earth since that is the point with the strongest power of attraction. A stone within the earth would already be at a certain point of rest, but not yet at the deepest center because it would have the capability, power, and inclination to fall farther, as long as it is not at the center point. Thus the soul has found its final and deepest resting point in God, "when, with all her might, she knows, loves, and enjoys God." That is never completely the case in this life. When, therefore, through the grace of God she is at her resting place, it is not yet the deepest center because she can always penetrate more deeply into God. For the power that draws her to God is love, and here love can always reach a higher degree. The higher the degree, the deeper love's anchor plumbs the soul, the more profoundly is she seized by God. On the rungs of the ladder the soul rises to God, i.e. to union with him. The higher she ascends to God, the deeper she descends within herself: the union is consummated in the innermost soul, in the deepest ground of the soul. If all of this seems contradictory, it is to be remembered that these are only different spatial images that—by reciprocally complementing themselves—wish to indicate something that is totally alien to space and for which natural experience cannot supply any adequate delineation.

God is in the inmost depth of the soul and nothing that is in her is hidden from him. But no created spirit is capable by itself of entering this enclosed garden or of getting even a glimpse of it. The created spirits comprise both good and bad spirits (which are also called *pure spirits* because they have no body) and human souls. Little is to be found in John about the mutual interaction of human souls. Actually, there is only *one* human relationship that he frequently refers to: that of the spiritual soul to her director. But he is not interested in the manner in which they come to understand one another. He remarks a single time that persons to whom the grace of discernment of spirits is given can recognize the inner state of another by slight external signs.[4] This points out the normal way of acquiring knowledge about the life of a stranger's soul: it is by way of sensory expressions of the spiritual life and leads as far within as that interior reveals itself.

For all external going-out-of-oneself perceptible in physical expressions, in sentient utterances, and words, in deeds and works, has, as a prerequisite, an internal going-out-of-oneself—whether this be voluntary or involuntary, conscious or unconscious. If it comes from the interior then something of the interior will illumine it. But this will not have sharp outlines; not be something securely and distinctly grasped, as long as one is dependent on a purely natural way and is not led through extraordinary divine illumination. Rather, it will remain something mysterious. And when the interior is closed, no human glance, by its own power, will penetrate it.

The soul has connections not only to others of her own kind, but also to created *pure spirits,* good and evil. Along with the *Areopagite,* John assumes that human beings receive divine illumination through the mediation of angels; to be sure, he does not hold that grace's being handed down along the descending steps of the *heavenly hierarchy* is the only possible way for it to be received. He knows about a direct union of God with the soul and this is what actually matters to him. He considers the snares of the devil to be more powerful than the influence of the good angel. He sees the devil continually sneaking around souls in order to divert them on their way to God.

What possible connections exist between human souls and pure— that is, incorporeal—spirits? One feasible way of knowing leads here also via bodily expression and other sensory manifestations. This is possible for human beings since, in order to make themselves understood, pure spirits have the power to appear in visible form or to be heard through audible words. But this is a highly dangerous way, for one is exposed on it to manifold deceptions and errors: one can regard as spiritual visions what are only sensory deceptions or illusions of the imagination. The devil can appear in the luminous guise of a good angel in order to lead souls astray more easily. The soul can, for fear of such deceptions, reject genuine heavenly apparitions as deceit of the senses or of the devil.

On the other hand, can one take into consideration that the pure spirits find access to the soul's interior via the sense-oriented exterior? One can hardly interpret the stories in the Books of *Job* and *Tobit* in any way other than that the devil and angels keenly observe and supervise the external behavior of human beings. That the angels have knowledge of the world as it is accessible to the senses, and so also of the human exterior, is a concept consonant with the doctrines of faith, since it is a requisite for the service angels give to human beings.[5] If this can be done without requiring bodily senses, it indicates that there are still other possibilities of perceiving corporeal nature: "a knowledge of the sensory, without senses"[6].

It is not our task to examine these possibilities now. In any case, for pure spirits what is external is not the only entrance into the interior life; they can also perceive the interior, spiritual words and expressions. The guardian angel "hears" the prayer that, without sound, rises to him from the heart. The evil enemy observes certain of the soul's movements, which can give him a handhold for his whispered suggestions.

And the spirits, for their part, have the possibility of making themselves heard in spiritual ways: through soundless words that, without any mediation of the external senses, are spoken in the interior and perceived there interiorly; or through effects that one feels in oneself, but which are occasioned from outside, for example, mood changes or impulses of the will that are incomprehensible in connection with one's own experience. What has not entered the outer senses is not, on that account alone, generally free from all sensuality and therefore is not *purely* spiritual in the sense in which John of the Cross speaks of pure spirituality. True, he does call memory, intellect, and will spiritual faculties but their natural activity is still conditioned by the senses and shares therefore in *sensory life*. Only that is purely spiritual that takes place in the inmost heart, the life of the soul from and in God.[7] Here, created spirits have no entry. The *thoughts of the heart* are concealed from them in natural ways—we say in natural ways because God can reveal these thoughts to them.

c. The Interior of the Soul and the Thoughts of the Heart

The thoughts of the heart are the original life of the soul at the ground of her being, at a depth that precedes all splitting into different faculties and their activity. There the soul lives precisely as she is in herself, beyond all that will be called forth in her through created beings. Although this most interior region is the dwelling of God and the place where the soul is united to God, her own life flows out of here before the life of union begins; and this is so, even in cases where such a union never occurs. For every soul has an inmost region and its being is life.

But this primary life is not only hidden from other spirits but from the soul herself. This is so for various reasons. Primary life is formless. The *thoughts of the heart* are absolutely not *thoughts* in the usual sense of the word; they are not clearly outlined, arranged, and comprehensible constructions of the thinking intellect. They must pass through various formulations before they become such constructions. First, they must rise out of the ground of the heart. Then they arrive at a first threshold, where they become noticeable. This *noticing* is a far more original manner of being conscious than is perception by the intellect. It too lies before the splitting into faculties and activities. It lacks the clarity of purely sensible perception; on the other hand, it is richer than a bare grasping by the intellect. That which arises is perceived as bearing a stamp of value on the basis of which a decision is made: whether to allow what is rising to come up or not. It must be mentioned here that, already, what rises in purely natural ways and becomes noticed, is no longer the purely interior life of the soul, but is rather already an answer to something that she has brought into motion. But this leads in a direction in which we cannot follow further here.

At the threshold where the rising movements are perceived, types of recognizable spiritual faculties begin to split off and conceivable structures are formed: to these belong thoughts elaborated by the intellect with their reasonable arrangement (these are *interior words* for which, then, *exterior words* can be found) movements of the mind and impulses of the will that, as active energies, enter all that is connected with the spiritual life.

Spiritual life is now no longer the primal life in the depth, rather it is something that can be grasped by *interior perception*. And interior perception is a totally different art of comprehending than is that first noticing of what arises out of the depth. So, too, this emergence out of the depth is different from the surfacing of an already formed image that was stored in the memory and now has become alive again.

By no means is all that rises and becomes perceptible actually perceived. Much rises up, becomes interior and exterior word, turns into wish and will and deed "before one is aware of it." Only those who live completely recollected in their inmost region keep faithful watch over these *first movements*.

With this we arrive at the second reason why people keep their inmost region hidden. It has been said that the soul is really at home here. But — as odd as this may sound — she is as a rule *not* at home. There are very few souls who live *in* their inmost self and *out of* their inmost region; and still fewer who constantly live *from* and *out of* their deepest interior. According to their nature—that is, their *fallen* nature— these persons keep themselves in the *outer rooms* of the *castle* which is their soul. What approaches them from outside draws them to the outside. It is necessary that God call and draw them insistently so as to move them to "enter into themselves".[8]

d. The Soul, the "I," and Freedom

It is important to clarify as much as possible, spiritually and without imagery, what these spatial images express. These images are indispens- able. But they are ambiguous and easily misunderstood. What approaches the soul from without belongs to the *outer world* and by this is meant whatever does not belong to the soul herself; as a rule, it also includes whatever does not belong to her body. For even though the body is called her exterior, it is *her* exterior, at one with her in the unity of one being and not as external as that which confronts her as totally strange and separate.[9] Among these strange and separate ones, there is the difference between things which have a clearly *exterior* being, i.e. are spatially extended, and such as have an *interior* like the soul herself.

On the other hand we had to speak, in the soul herself, of an exte- rior and an interior. For when she is drawn outside, she does not leave herself, she is only farther away from her inmost region and with that, at the same time, devotes herself to the outer world. What approaches from outside has a certain right to claim her attention, and, depending on its *weight,* the value, and meaning it has in itself and for the soul, it deserves to be admitted to an appropriate depth of the soul. So it is objectively reasonable that she accepts it from there. But to do so, she is not required to sacrifice her position at a deeper level; because she is a spirit and her *castle* is a spiritual realm, there are totally different rules valid here than in the external sphere.

When she is in the deepest and inmost region of this, her inner realm, then she rules over it completely and has the freedom to go to what- ever *place* in it she pleases, without having to leave *her place,* the place of her rest. The possibility to move within oneself is based on the soul's being formed as an "I." The "I" is that in the soul by which she possesses herself and that which moves within her as in its own *space*. The deepest point is at the same time the place of her freedom: the place at which she can collect her entire being and make decisions about it. Free decisions of lesser importance can, in a certain sense, also be made at a point located farther toward the outside. However, these are superficial decisions: it is a *coincidence* when such a decision proves to be appropriate, for only at the deepest point can one possibly measure everything against one's ultimate standards. Nor is it an *irrefutably* free decision, for anyone who does not have herself completely in hand can not decide in true freedom but rather, allows herself to be determined by outside factors.

Human beings[10] are called upon to live in their inmost region and to have themselves as much in hand as is possible only from that center-point; only from there can they rightly come to terms with the world. Only from there can they find the place in the world that has been intended for them. In all of this, they can never *see through* this inmost region completely. It is God's mystery, which God alone can reveal to the degree that pleases him. This inmost region, however, has been laid in the hand of human beings; they can make use of it in complete freedom but they also have the duty to guard it as a precious good entrusted to them. In the realm of spirits, it must be given great value. The angels have the task of protecting it. Evil spirits seek to gain control of it. God himself has chosen it as his dwelling. The good and evil spirits do not have free entrance into the inmost region. The good spirits are no more able, in natural ways, to read the "thoughts of the heart" than are the evil spirits, but they receive illumination from God about all they must know of the heart's secrets. Furthermore, there are spiritual ways in which the soul can make contact with the other created spirits. She can address herself to another spirit with whatever has become an *interior word* in her. This is how St. Thomas imagines the *language* of the angels with which they mutually communicate: as a purely spiritual self-offering with the intention of sharing with another what one has in oneself.[11] In this wise, also, is the soundless cry to the guardian angel to be imagined, or an interior summoning of evil spirits.

But even without our intention to share, the created spirits have a certain access to what occurs within us: not to that which is concealed in our inmost region, but probably about whatever has entered the interior regions of the soul in a perceptible form. From that point, they are also able to draw conclusions about that which may be concealed from their sight. We must assume that the angels protect the locked sanctuary with reverent awe. They desire only to bring the soul there in order for her to surrender it to God. But Satan strives to wrest into his possession that which is God's kingdom. He cannot do this by his own power, but the soul can surrender herself to him. She will not do this if she herself has entered her inmost region and come to know it as happens in divine union. For then she is so immersed in God and so secure that no temptation can approach her anymore. But how is it possible that she can hand herself over to the devil when she has not yet fully taken herself into possession as can happen only upon entrance to the inmost region? One can only think she does it by blindly grabbing hold, as it were, while she is still outside. She gives herself away without knowing what she surrenders by that. And neither can the devil break the seal on that which, still closed, has been handed to him. He can only destroy what remains forever hidden from him.

The soul has the right to make decisions that concern herself. It is the great mystery of personal freedom, before which God himself comes to a halt. He wants his sovereign authority over created spirits only as a free gift of their love. He knows the thoughts of the heart. He sees through the deepest foundations and abysses of the soul, where her own glance cannot penetrate unless God specifically grants her light to do so. But he does not want to take possession of her without her wanting it herself. Yet he does everything to achieve the free surrender of her will to his as a gift of her love in order, then, to be able to lead her to the bliss of union. That is the gospel John of the Cross has to announce and for which all his writings serve. What was said last about the structure of the soul's being, especially about the relation of freedom to her inmost region, does not come from the expositions of our holy Father St. John. It is therefore necessary to prove whether it is in harmony with his teaching, and may, in fact, even serve to clarify his doctrine. (Only if this proves to be the case can this interjection be justified in this context.) At first glance, some of what has been said may well appear incompatible with certain of the saint's expositions.

Every human being is free and is confronted with decisions on a daily and hourly basis. But the inmost region of the soul is the place where God lives "all alone" as long as the soul has not reached the perfect union of love.[12] Holy Mother Teresa calls it the seventh dwelling place that opens for the soul only when the mystical marriage takes place.[13] So then, is it only the soul that has arrived at the highest degree of perfection that decides in perfect freedom? Here it must be considered that the autonomous action of the soul apparently diminishes the more she nears her inmost self. And when she arrives there, God does everything in her, she no longer has anything more to do than to receive.[14] However, it is precisely this act of receiving that expresses her free participation. But beyond that, freedom comes into play at a far more decisive moment. God does everything here only because the soul has totally surrendered herself to him. And this surrender is the highest act of her freedom. John himself depicts the mystical marriage as voluntary surrender of God and the soul to each other and ascribes so great a power to the soul that has arrived at this step of perfection that she has not only herself but even God at her service.[15] For this highest stage of the personal life there is perfect agreement between the mystical doctrine of our holy parents and the view that the inmost region of the soul is the place of the most perfect freedom.

But how do matters stand with the large mass of humans who do not arrive at mystical marriage? Can they enter the inmost region and make decisions from there, or are they only capable of more or less superficial decisions? The answer is not a simple yes or no.

The structure of the soul's being—her greater and lesser depths as well as the inmost region—are hers by nature. The movement of the "I" within this space similarly exists as a possibility resulting from the soul's essence. This "I" sets itself up now here, now there, according to the *motivations* that appeal to it. But it undertakes its movements from a position it prefers to occupy. This position, now, is not the same in everyone; rather, it is distinguished according to the various types of persons. The one who desires sensory delights is mostly engrossed in a sensual satisfaction or preoccupied about gaining such satisfaction; his position is located very far from his inmost region. One who seeks truth lives principally at the heart of an actively searching intellect. If he is really concerned about *the* truth (not merely collecting single bits of knowledge) then he is perhaps nearer to the God who is Truth, and therefore to his own inmost region than he himself knows.

To these two examples we wish to add only a third which seems to have particular meaning: the "I-human being," that is, the one for whom his own "I" stands as the central point. Considered superficially, one might think such a human being to be particularly close to his inmost region. Yet, perhaps for no other type is the way there as obstructed as for this one. (Every human being has something of this in himself as long as he has not suffered through to the end of the *Dark Night*.) We must examine for all these types the possibilities for the mobility of the "I," the possibilities of free decision-making, and the possibility of reaching the inmost region.

When the sensual human being, who is engrossed in some satisfaction, is presented with the possibility of procuring something even more satisfying, he will perhaps, without further consideration or choice, move from satisfaction into action. When the *drives* lie on the same level, a movement takes place but not an actually free decision; nor a breakthrough to a greater depth. But it is possible for the sensual human being to be approached by something that belongs to a completely different area of values. No type is exclusively restricted to one area. At a given time one area simply has the ascendancy over the others. He may, for example, be asked to deny himself some pleasure in order to help another human being. Here, the solution will hardly be reached without a free decision. At all events, the sensual person will not make a sacrifice as a matter of course, rather he will have to pull himself together to do so. If he declines—whether after some evaluation or with an immediate "that's out of the question"—that, too, is a decision of the will. In an extreme case one can even think of him continuing in his enjoyment without dismissing the perspective of sacrifice. In this case, the spirit is so suffocated in sensuality that the challenge cannot even reach him. The words are heard, and perhaps their immediate meaning may be understood, but the area where the real sense of the call would be received is buried in rubble. In this extreme, not only does a single free decision fail to materialize but freedom itself was already abandoned previously. Where one declines, the meaning is probably grasped, even though, apparently, it is not evaluated at full range.

In such a refusal to take the full range into consideration lies both the superficiality of the decision and a bridled freedom. One does not allow certain motives to appeal with their full import and takes good care not to return to that depth where these motives could instigate involvement. In this case, one surrenders oneself to a single area of decision-making. One never takes oneself, that is, all the deeper levels of one's own being, into one's hands and so deprives oneself of the possibility of taking a stand after evaluating the true circumstances, that is, what is truly reasonable and truly free. Besides this superficial rejection, one can think of course of something that would be more appropriate: having allowed the call for help to be weighed fully by the soul, with full consideration of all the aspects, one could feel obliged to refuse when evaluation of all the pros and cons establishes it as unjustified. Such a refusal is on the same level as compliance after objectively weighing the pros and cons. Both are possible only when the sensual human being has abandoned his attitude *as* a sensual person and has gone over to an *ethical* attitude, that is, the attitude of one who wants to recognize and do what is morally right. To do this he must take up a position deep within himself: so deep, that the crossover resembles a formal transformation of the human being. And this may not even be possible in a natural way, but only on the basis of an extraordinary *awakening*. Yes, we may well say: an *ultimately* appropriate decision can be made only at the extreme depth of the soul. For no human being is by nature in a position to scan *all* the pros and cons that have a say about a decision. The decision can only be made according to one's own best knowledge and conscience, within the circumference of one's own vision. However, a person with faith knows that there is one whose view is not circumscribed but truly comprises and perceives every-thing. The conscience of the one who lives in this certainty of faith can no longer quiet itself by following its own best knowledge. It must strive to recognize what is right in God's eyes. (For this reason only a religious position is the truly ethical one. There is in all likeli-hood a natural seeking and longing for the right and good, as well as finding this in some cases, but only in seeking for the divine will can human beings truly reach their goal.)

The question is answered once and for all by the one who is drawn by God himself into the soul's own inmost region and has surrendered there in the union of love. Nothing further is necessary than to allow God's Spirit to direct and lead, for the Spirit will distinctly urge him on, and he will always and everywhere be certain he is doing the right thing. In that one great decision, made with the utmost freedom, all future ones are included and can then, almost as a matter of course, be made accordingly. But, instead of simply searching for the right deci-sion in a particular case, to arrive at this height there is a long way to go—if indeed there is a way to it. A person who, only here and now, seeks what is right and accordingly decides by what he believes he knows, is on the way to God and on the way to himself even when he does not know this. But he does not yet have such a hold on himself as that which is given in the ultimate depth; therefore he cannot fully make disposition of himself nor can he make perfectly free decisions about *things*.

Whoever *fundamentally* seeks to do what is right, that is, whoever is determined to do it always and everywhere, has made a decision about himself and has set his will within the divine will, even when it is not yet clear to him that the good action corresponds to what God wills. But if this is not clear to him, the sure way of discerning what is right is still wanting; and he has made disposition of himself as though he had himself completely in hand, although the ultimate depth of his inmost region has not yet opened to him. The final decision only be-comes possible eye to eye with God. But when a person has arrived so far in the life of faith that he has committed himself to God com-pletely and no longer wants anything but what God wills, has he not then arrived at his inmost region, and is his state still different from that of the highest union in love? It is very difficult to draw a boundary line here, and difficult, also, to know how our holy Father St. John draws it. Still I believe—objectively and as he teaches—it is necessary to acknowledge a boundary and to bring it into relief. Whoever truly wants, in blind faith, nothing more but what God wills, has, with God's grace, reached the highest state a human being can reach. His will is totally purified and free of all constraint through earthly desires; he is united to the divine will through free surrender. And still, for the highest union of love, the mystical marriage, something decisive is lacking.

14

The Kinds of Divine Union

e. The Different Kinds of Union with God

We must remember here that John has distinguished three kinds of union with God.[1] By means of the first God dwells substantially in all created things and sustains their existence. By the second, we are to understand the indwelling of God in the soul through grace; by the third, the transforming union through perfect love that divinizes the soul. As John states at the quoted source, between the second and third kinds, there is only a difference in degree. If we look at other passages and evaluate the matter as a whole, there seems to be a difference in kind, and within each of the kinds, a series of steps. In the *Spiritual Canticle*, for instance, the saint mentions the same three categories, without speaking of only a degree of difference between God's presence by grace and that by love. Rather, he emphasizes the perceptible feeling of the presence of the highest good in the union of love and what it effects: the ardent longing for the unveiled beatific vision of God.[2]

Our holy Mother, St. Teresa has also been greatly occupied with this question. In the *Interior Castle*,[3] she says that through the prayer of union she came to know the article of faith that God is in everything through his essence, his presence, and his power. She had only known, before that, of the indwelling through grace. Now she consulted various theologians in order to gain clarity about her discovery. A "half-learned man" also knew only of the indwelling through grace. But others were able to confirm for her that the enlightenment she received through her experience of union was an article of faith. Perhaps if we attempt a comparison of our order's founders' presentations,

167

which differ so much from each other it will help us gain greater objective clarity.

They agree on the article of faith, which was familiar to John, the theologian, while Teresa had to discover it at first: God the Creator is present in each thing and sustains it in existence. He has foreseen each, and knows it through and through with all its changes and destinies. By the might of his omnipotence he can do with each, at every moment, whatever he pleases. He can leave it to its own laws and the normal flow of events. He can also intervene with extraordinary measures. God dwells in this manner in every human soul, also. He knows each one from all eternity, with all the mysteries of her being and every wave that breaks over her life. She is in his power. It is up to him whether he leaves her to herself and the course of worldly events or whether, with his strong hand, he will interfere in her destiny. Such a marvel of his power is every rebirth of a soul through sanctifying grace.

John and Teresa again agree that God's indwelling through grace is different from the presence common to all creatures by which he maintains their existence. With "essence, presence, and power" God can be in the soul without her knowing or willing it even when she lives hardened in sin at the utmost distance from God. It is possible that she does not perceive the slightest effect of his presence. The indwelling by grace is possible only in personal-spiritual beings, for it requires the free acceptance of sanctifying grace by the recipient. (At the baptism of infants, this free acceptance is made by adults as proxy and is later personally ratified through the baptized person's whole life of faith, and expressly in words at the renewal of the baptismal vows.) Herein lies the implication that, in this second mode, God cannot dwell in a sinful soul who has turned away from him. *Sanctifying grace*, after all, is called that because it wipes out sin.

By reason of its own nature, the indwelling through sanctifying grace is impossible in non-personal, that is, subhuman beings. It denotes that divine being and life continually flow into the graced soul. Divine Being, however, is personal life and can only flow in where one personally admits him. For that precise reason, it is impossible to receive grace without its being freely accepted. It results in a being-within-each-other such as is possible only where a genuine *interior being*, that is, a spiritual one is available. Only in that which lives spiritually can spiritual life be received. The soul in which God lives through grace is not an impersonal stage on which divine life appears, rather she is herself drawn into this life.

The divine life is tri-personal life. It is the overflowing love with which the Father begets the Son and surrenders to him his own being, while the Son embraces this being and surrenders it back to the Father, the love in which Father and Son are One, which they breathe out together as their Spirit. Through grace this Spirit is poured out into hearts. Thus the soul lives her life of grace through this Holy Spirit. In him she loves the Father with the love of the Son and the Son with the love of the Father. This sharing of life with the trinitarian life can take place without the soul's awareness that the divine persons dwell in her. Actually, only a small number of elect come to perceptibly experience that the triune God is in their soul. For a larger number an enlightened faith leads to a living knowledge of this indwelling and to a loving communion with the divine three in pure faith.

A person who has not yet arrived at this high level is still united to God through faith, hope, and love, even when he is not clearly aware that God lives in his inmost region and that he can find him there, that all of this life of grace and virtue is an effect of this divine life in himself and is his participation therein. Living faith is the firm conviction that God exists, the acceptance-as-truth of all that has been revealed by God, and a loving readiness to be led by the divine will. As supernatural knowledge infused by God, living faith is the "beginning of the eternal life in us"[4]— but it is only a *beginning*. Through sanctifying grace it is laid within us as a seed; under our careful custody it is to burgeon into a great tree bearing glorious fruits. For it is the way that is to lead us to union with God even in this life, though the highest fulfillment belongs to the next life.

Now we face the hard task of determining how the union of love differs from the indwelling by grace. At this point there is a divergence between our holy Mother St. Teresa's delineation and holy Father St. John's. Our holy Mother believes she has discerned the *first* mode of the indwelling in the prayer of union, which differs from the indwelling by grace, while in the *Ascent* the union through love is to be considered a higher degree of the union of grace. Besides this, St. Teresa knows a union with God that can be attained purely through untiring cooperation with grace, through a mortification of nature, and perfect practice of the love of God and neighbor. She stresses this with particular emphasis as consolation for those who do not attain to that which is called the *prayer of union*.[5] However, earlier, she explained with as much emphasis and with all desirable clarity that the *prayer of union* can in no way be attained through one's own effort.[6] The soul is so captivated by God that she is bereft of all feeling for the things of the world while she is fully awake for God. She is "as though out of her senses" so that she has no power to think of anything. . . . "Here she only loves, but . . . does not even know how she loves, nor what it is that she does love. . . . The intellect would want to be wholly occupied in understanding something of what the soul is feeling; but since its powers cannot achieve this, it is so stunned that it moves neither hand nor foot."

Here, God works within the soul "without anyone—not even we—disturbing him." And what he effects in it "exceeds all joy and all delights and all the happiness on earth."[7] This condition lasts only a brief time (scarcely more than half an hour). But the manner in which God remains in the soul during that time is such "that when she comes to herself again, she cannot doubt at all that she was in God and God in her." She holds to this truth with such security that she will never forget it nor can she ever doubt it, even when God does not again grant her such a grace for years. And this happens entirely apart from the effects that remain in the soul." As long as the mysterious incident lasts, she has no perception of God. But afterward she is certain he was present.

She did not see him clearly "but for her there remains a certainty that God alone can give." There is nothing corporeal about it as there is in the invisible presence of Christ in the Blessed Sacrament. The divinity alone is present. "But how can we have such certainty about what we cannot see? That I do not know; that is God's working; but I know that I tell the truth. . . . It is enough for us to know that he who is the cause of it is almighty. Since we have no part at all to play in bringing it about no matter how much effort we put forth, but it is God who does so, let us not desire the capacity to understand this union."

Without intending it, our holy Mother attempted all the same to suggest some explanations. It was one explanation when she interpreted God's indwelling that she experienced with such unshakable certainty as that indwelling which is common to all creatures. It was also an explanation when she remarked: "I would say that whoever does not receive this certitude does not experience union of the whole soul with God, but union of some faculty or that he experiences one of the many other kinds of favors God grants souls."[8] Granted, in true union, God is united with the substance of the soul.

It is extremely valuable for us that Teresa wrote about her experience with such artlessness. She was unconcerned about the possibility that there was a theoretical explanation of the experience and unconcerned, too, about the judgment her explanation might find. Her faithful depiction can perhaps help us to recognize which kind of indwelling is described and at the same time make it possible for us to evaluate her explanation. *The soul possesses certainty that she was in God and God in her.* This certainty remains hers after the experience of union with God. It was part of the experience itself, essentially helping to construct it, even though it can only be brought into relief afterwards. The consciousness of union does not join the union from without, rather it belongs to the union itself. Where such consciousness and a subsequently prominent certainty are impossible—as would be the case with a stone or a plant—such a form of indwelling or union is also impossible. So what Teresa experienced in the prayer of union is actually a different form of indwelling than that common to all creatures. And this new form of indwelling is not always really available where it would basically be possible. Teresa expresses this when she says the soul is certain that she *was* in God and God in her. It was a temporary condition. The indwelling through "presence, essence, and power," however, does not cease for a moment as long as a thing exists. Its cessation would mean annihilation for the thing.

So we hold with John of the Cross that the indwelling of the union of love differs from that which sustains all things in existence. On the other hand, our holy Mother's explanation makes it penetratingly clear that an indwelling is meant here that differs in kind from the one by grace and not merely by degree.

She emphatically urges her daughters to endeavor with all their might to attain the highest level of the life of grace that is to be reached by faithful cooperation with grace: the perfect union of the human will with the divine through the perfect practice of the love of God and neighbor. But just as decidedly she explains that it is senseless to try to attain that union, which God alone can give. By one's own effort, even when this is supported by grace, one can never arrive at having, in living reality, a feeling of God's presence and union with him. The labor of the will undergirded by grace will never produce the wonderful effect that is brought about in the brief span of the time of union: a transformation of the soul so thorough that she can scarcely recognize herself anymore. The caterpillar is transformed into a butterfly. One's own work requires many years of hard struggle to achieve something similar.

The prayer of union is not yet *the* union John always has in sight as the goal of the *Dark Night*. It is the forerunner to that and its initial stage. It serves to prepare the soul to surrender completely to God, and to awaken in her a burning longing for the return of union and to possess it permanently. This is clearly expressed in the fifth and sixth dwelling places of the *Interior Castle* where the preparation for and the consummation of the *spiritual betrothal* are described. The corresponding explanation is to be found in the exposition on the thirteenth and fourteenth stanzas of *The Spiritual Canticle*. At the two passages, John and Teresa state in full agreement that the betrothal takes place in ecstasy. God wrests the soul to himself with such force that nature nearly succumbs. For this reason, our holy Mother emphasizes that great courage is demanded to enter this betrothal.[9] And in the *Spiritual Canticle*, the frightened bride begs her Beloved to turn his eyes away when, suddenly, after she has waited, longed, and begged for such a long time, he answers and looks at her.

It is with a certain kind of contradiction, then, that we read in another passage from John that possession by grace and the possession by union correspond to each other much as do betrothal and marriage. The one is said to mean what we can obtain through the will and grace—the perfect conformity of the human will with the divine will through the complete purification of the soul—the other, the mutual complete surrender and union.[10] This contradiction can be explained in part by reason of the terminology: the expression *betrothal* apparently is not used in the same sense in both cases. Beyond that, there is an essential difference present: what is actually mystical in one case seems to be restricted to the highest stage, while in the other explanation it begins at an earlier stage.[11] What is predominantly decisive in all these considerations is that John clearly expresses a difference between what can be attained by outward means through grace and the will and what takes place through the mystical marriage. This, apparently, supersedes the explanation from the *Ascent* that purports to see only a difference in degree between the union by grace and mystical union. Furthermore passages can be shown in all his writings that clearly show that the beginnings of what is actually mystical are to be sought at a much lower level. We but recall those *touches* in the substance of the soul of which there was talk in the *Ascent*.[12] It is said of them that they make the intellect experience God in an exceptionally sublime and delightful way that has no proportion at all to the works the soul has performed, that one can only prepare oneself to receive them but in no way can one produce them. They are produced passively in the soul and are intended to lead to union with God.

All of this indicates something that lies outside the *normal paths of grace*: a temporary union that gives a foretaste of the lasting one.

How are we to understand why John of the Cross does not express himself clearly and unequivocally in this decisive question? To answer that with certainty we would need to know more about the personal life of the silent saint than he has divulged through his writings or entrusted to his contemporaries. We can only express as possibilities what the history of his time and the latest research on the textual history of his works reveal.[13] The great religious battles of the time, the ever-widening spread of heresies, the dangers of an unhealthy mysticism had led to a strict supervision of religious literature. Everyone who wrote about questions of the interior life had to reckon that the Inquisition would lay hands on him and his work. It is conceivable that John, out of foresight, was careful to make a sharp distinction between his doctrine and that of the *Alumbrados* (as occurs obviously in some passages) and endeavored to connect the mystical process as closely as possible to the *normal path of grace.*

That such an intention determined the editions of his writings has been verified by the comparisons made between the older publications and the manuscripts, and of the manuscripts among themselves. *The Living Flame* and *The Spiritual Canticle* are available in two manuscript versions. The editing apparent in the later versions demonstrates that keen statements were softened and explanations inserted in an effort to prevent misinterpretation. Do these changes date back to the saint himself or were they undertaken by an anonymous hand? Only one manuscript version of *The Ascent* and one of *The Night* has come down to us. The difference between these manuscripts and all older printed versions down to the first critical one of P. Gerardo (as well as the difference between the old printed versions of *The Living Flame* and the first handwritten version on which they are based) is so considerable that the mutilation here by alien hands cannot be denied. *The Ascent* and *The Night* are available only in fragments. In both cases, those sections are missing in which union might be spoken of in detail and clarification found for the questions that preoccupy us now.

Were these sections never written or were they suppressed in the copies? (All four major treatises are extant only in copies; we do not have any original manuscripts; only one copy of the *Spiritual Canticle* contains corrections in the saint's own hand.) And was such suppression made at the direction of the author or did an alien will decree it? We have no answer to any of these questions.

Out of a desire to arrive at clarity, we have taken refuge in our holy Mother's unconstrained descriptions. They give us certitude where the differing formulations in John of the Cross allow doubts to arise. As totally authentic factual accounts, hers are not merely an invaluable documentation enabling one to arrive at one's own theoretical understanding. We also have a right to assume that the two saints were of one mind in their grasp of the essentials of the interior life—despite all their differences in character, in literary individuality, as well as of their types of sanctity, and their evaluation of non-essential mystical graces.

The Interior Castle and the writings of our holy Father St. John were composed after the two had lived in Avila for years exchanging their most intimate thoughts. Our holy Mother consequently called her youthful collaborator the "father of her soul,"[14] and John occasionally made reference to her writings to avoid having to write explanations that could be found there.[15] Therefore, if we find in her explanation of the different stages of mystical union something that can be unmistakably distinguished in kind from the union of grace, we may be convinced that what we have before us had John of the Cross's approbation. And so we come through the combination of the explanations of both parents of our order to a confirmation of the view that the three named modes of God's indwelling are not mere gradations but rather differences in kind. We will seek now to establish their objective differences more precisely.

It is the same one God in three persons who is present in each of the three modes, and his immutable being is the same in all three modes. Still the indwelling is different because that wherein dwells the one and same, unchanged deity changes its mode of being each time. Thus the nature of the indwelling is modified.[16] The first mode of indwelling—or better, of the divine presence, since it is not yet strictly speaking a dwelling *within*—requires from that within which God is present nothing more than subjection to God's knowledge and might, as well as its dependence on the divine being for its existence. All this is common to all creatures. Divine and created being remain totally separate; the only relation between them is the unilateral dependence for existence, which does not signify an actual "in-one-another," and so no actual *in*dwelling. For, to be an indwelling, both sides must have an inner being, that is, a being that contains itself interiorly and can receive another being within itself, so that without the accepted and the accepting beings ceasing to be independent, a unity of being comes into existence. This is only possible in spiritual being: only what is spiritual is self-contained and can take within itself another being, again only a spiritual one. This alone is authentic indwelling. The indwelling by grace is already something of this kind.

Whoever is subject to God's being, wisdom, and power, not without his own knowledge and willingness, but indeed says "Yes" to this,

takes God into himself, and his being is penetrated by the divine being. But this is not complete penetration. It only extends as far as the
recipient's capacity permits. In order to be completely penetrated by
the divine being—this constitutes the perfect union of love—the soul
must be detached from every other being: empty of all other creatures
and of itself, as our holy Father St. John has so emphatically explained.
Love's highest fulfillment is "being-one" in free mutual surrender:
this is the inter-trinitarian divine life. The *creature's aspiring, yearning love (amor, **eros**)* that strives to ascend, and God's merciful, condescending love for his creatures (*Caritas, **agape***) aim for this fulfillment.
Where these two meet, the union can progressively happen: at the
expense of whatever still stands in its way, and in the measure in which
this obstacle is destroyed. As we know, this happens both actively and
passively in the *Dark Night*. Through its own efforts to purify itself,
the human will enters more and more into the divine will, but in such
a manner that the divine will is not felt as a present reality, rather it is
accepted in blind faith. Here there is actually only a difference in degree
between the indwelling by grace and the union of love. In the purification passively experienced through the consuming fire of divine love,
on the contrary, the divine will penetrates the human will more and more
by allowing itself to be felt simultaneously as a present reality. Here,
in my opinion, there is a new mode of indwelling that differs not only
in degree from that of the indwelling by grace. The difference is made
clear in connection with the explanation that St. Augustine gives to
the words in the Gospel of John: "Many believed in his name, . . .
Jesus himself, though, did not entrust himself to them."[17]

Augustine applies this to the catechumens: they already profess
their faith in Jesus Christ, but he does not yet give himself to them in
the most Blessed Sacrament. We can also apply it to the two modes of
the indwelling whose differences we want to grasp, and at the same
time, to the difference between faith and contemplation. The indwelling by grace imparts the virtue of faith, that is, the strength to accept
as real what one cannot perceive as present and to hold as true what
one cannot strictly prove on rational grounds. It is like the case of a
person about whom you have heard many good and great things. He

has bestowed on you many benefactions and given many gifts. Therefore you are inclined to him in love and gratitude and have, increasingly, the desire to get to know him personally. But he has not yet *confided* himself to you, his protégé; not even in the very least degree of allowing a meeting. Even less has he revealed to you his inner thoughts or even made you a gift of his heart. But all of this is granted—again in an ascent by steps—to the human being by God in the third mode of indwelling, that of mystical election. God grants him a personal encounter through a *touch* in his inmost region. He opens to him his own inner being through particular enlightenment about his nature and his secret decrees. He gives him his heart—at first in a momentary transport by a personal meeting (in the prayer of union),[18] then as a permanent possession (in mystical betrothal,[19] and marriage).[20]

All of this is not a gaze from face to face—it is here that the image of the development of the attraction between human beings fails. But as far as a person-to-person encounter and therefore an experiential recognition is concerned, that already has taken place on the lowest step. God touches with his being the inmost region of the soul (which our holy Father St. John also calls her *substance*). God's essence however is nothing other than his *being* and himself. He is himself a person, his *being* is personal being; the inmost region of the soul is the heart and fountainhead of her personal life and at the same time the actual place where she meets other personal life. It is only possible for one person to touch another in their inmost region; through such a touch one person gives the other notice of his presence.[21] When one feels one has been touched interiorly in this manner, one is in lively *sentience* with another person. This is not yet a union, but merely the point of departure thereto. However, compared to the indwelling by grace it is already a breakthrough to something new. In the former the soul is given participation in divine being, but God's personal fountainhead remains hidden and does not enter into the sharing of being. Here the fountainhead of the divine life (insofar as one can speak of it) makes contact with the fountainhead of the human-spiritual life and by that touch is manifested as distinctly present. But still the divine source remains in darkness and locked away. When the divine mysteries are illuminated, the *locked inner region* of God opens up. When the soul experiences the influx of the divine being into her own in the communication of grace, then she enters into divine life. In the union (with its various stages) a becoming-one is accomplished, proceeding from [their] personal fountainhead of life through mutual personal surrender.

Here some different things must be mentioned: the indwelling by grace is not necessarily a prerequisite for a simple touch in the inmost region. It can be given to a total unbeliever to cause an awakening of faith and as preparation for the reception of sanctifying grace. It can also serve as a means of making an unbeliever capable of serving as a tool for certain purposes. Particular illuminations may be given for either of these same reasons. Union, on the contrary, as mutual surrender, cannot happen without faith and love, that is, not without sanctifying grace. Were it to start within a soul that is not in the state of grace, its beginning would have to coincide with the gift of sanctifying grace and as a prerequisite for the latter, perfect contrition. These possibilities confirm the basic difference between union by grace and mystical union, and between the corresponding ways of indwelling. It is a matter of two different ways of gradual ascent. But it does not preclude the preparation of the way to mystical union through a life of grace.

That the inmost region of the soul is fundamentally the place of personal encounter and union makes it understandable—as much as it is possible to speak of understanding where divine mysteries are concerned—that God has chosen the inmost region of the soul as his dwelling. When union is the goal for which souls are created, then the condition which makes this union possible must, after all, exist from the beginning.

It is likewise understandable that this inmost region of the soul is given into the hand of the soul along with the freedom to dispose of it, since loving surrender is only possible for a free being. Is this loving surrender in mystical marriage on the side of the soul still something other than the unconditional surrender of her will to the divine will? Apparently yes. It differs according to the degree of *knowledge*: when God gives himself to her in mystical marriage she learns to know God in a manner in which she had not known him earlier, and in which she cannot know him by any other means. Nor had she come to know, before this, her own inmost depths. So, until now, she had not at all really known, as she does now, to whom she surrenders her will, what it is that she surrenders, or what this surrender to the divine will can demand from her.

There is a difference according to the *will* also: in the *goal,* for the surrender of the will is the union of one's own will with the divine *will,* not with the heart of God, nor with the divine *persons*; in the *point of departure,* for only now is that deepest fountainhead attained, only now does the will involve itself fully because only now does it enfold the whole person from her personal center; in the *consummation,* for in the bridal surrender not only is one's own will subordinated and conformed with the divine one, but the divine surrender is also received. For this reason, in surrendering one's own person, one takes possession of God in a way so daring that it surpasses all human understanding. John of the Cross gives clear expression to this when he says that the soul can now give God *more* than she is herself: she gives to God, God himself in God.[22] So it is that there is something in *essence* that differs from the union of grace: a being drawn to the utmost limit within the divine being. This divinizes the soul herself. It is a union of persons that does not end their independence, but rather has it as a prerequisite, an interpenetration that is surpassed only by the circumincession of the divine persons upon which it is modeled.

This is the union that John unmistakably has as the goal before his eyes in all his writings, even though he often uses the word in a different sense and has not delineated its characteristics as sharply against the other modes as we have endeavored to do here. It has been said, in anticipation, that the mystical marriage is union with the triune God. As long as God touches the soul only in darkness and hiddenness, she can only feel the personal touch as just that without also perceiving whether it is *one* person who touches or whether there are more. But once she is completely drawn into the divine life in the perfect union of love, it can no longer be concealed from her that it is a tri-personal life and she must establish contact with all three divine persons.[23]

15

Death and Resurrection

f. Faith and Contemplation. Death and Resurrection.

The difference between the indwelling of God by grace and through mystical union appears to us as a fitting foundation on which to base a clear demarcation between *faith* and *contemplation*. Holy Father St. John speaks very frequently of both, but he gives no actual comparison of them in a way that would enable one to make an unequivocal determination of their mutual relationship. Many times his explanations sound as though, generally speaking, there is no distinct boundary to draw; both are marked as ways to union, both as dark and loving knowledge. The darkness of faith is treated primarily in the *Ascent of Mount Carmel*.[1] There faith is called the darkness of midnight, because we must totally renounce the light of natural knowledge in order to gain *its* light. John frequently gives contemplation the name used by the *Areopagite, mystical theology* (secret wisdom of God) and *ray of darkness*.[2] The two are very close when it is said that God wraps himself in the darkness of faith when he communicates himself to the soul.[3] On the other hand, it is precisely in these explanations in the *Ascent* that it is made clear that faith and contemplation cannot simply be synonymous since it is said that faith is the guide in the delights of pure contemplation and union. A differentiation is also prerequisite when in the prologue to the *Spiritual Canticle* it is said that *mystical wisdom* does not need to be understood distinctly since it resembles, in this, faith through which we love God without understanding him.[4] Were the two to coincide there could be no talk of similarity.

Difference and a close correlation are most clearly expressed, perhaps, in the passage that juxtaposes contemplation as a vague, dark, and general knowledge with clearly distinct and particular supernatural intellectual apprehensions: "The dark and general knowledge is of one kind only: contemplation which is imparted in faith."[5] To understand this sentence and the relation between faith and contemplation one must remember what was said in former passages about the manifold meanings necessarily covered by the word *faith*; also that *contemplation* can signify more than one thing. The content of divine revelation and the acceptance of this revelation are called faith; and so is the loving surrender to God about whom revelation speaks, and to whom we are indebted for revelation. The content of faith delivers the material for meditation. In meditation the soul occupies its faculties with that which we have accepted in faith, which we represent to ourselves in images, in intellectual reflection, and about which we have decided opinions. A habitual condition of loving knowledge is won as the fruit of meditation.[6]

The soul now remains in tranquil, peaceful, loving surrender in the presence of God whom she has come to know through faith without having meditated on any single article of truth. As the fruit of meditation, this is *acquired contemplation*. There is no difference between the content experienced here and that of faith in the third sense: the *credere in Deum*, entering into God in faith and love. But usually John of the Cross has something else in mind when he speaks of contemplation. God can grant the soul a dark, loving knowledge of himself without a preliminary practice of meditation. He can raise her suddenly into the condition of contemplation and love by *infusing* contemplation in her. This too does not happen without a connection to faith. As a rule it is imparted to souls who are prepared to receive it through lively faith and lives built on faith. But should ever an unbeliever be caught up by it, he would, all the same, be enlightened by the hitherto rejected doctrine of faith as to the identity of the one who has seized him. And the faithful, loving soul will repeatedly take refuge from the darkness of contemplation in the sure clarity of the doctrines of faith in order to understand from that viewpoint what has happened to her.[7]

What has happened to her, however, is despite all coincidences something fundamentally other than *acquired contemplation* and the surrender to God in mere faith, the experience of which is similar to that of acquired contemplation. The new form is a being seized by the God whose presence is felt or—in those experiences of the *Dark Night* when the soul is deprived of this sensible perception of his presence— the painful wound of love and the fervent longings that remain in the soul when God withdraws from her. Both are mystical experiences, based on that form of indwelling that is a person-to-person touch in the inmost region of the soul. Faith, on the contrary, and all that belongs to a life of faith rests on the indwelling by grace.

The contrast of sensibly perceived presence and sensibly perceived withdrawal of God in mystical contemplation points to something else that serves to differentiate it from faith. Faith is primarily a matter of the intellect. Though in the *acceptance* of faith, participation of the will is expressed, it is still the acceptance of knowledge. The *darkness* of faith signifies a characteristic of this knowledge. Contemplation is a matter of the heart, that is, the inmost region of the soul and therefore of all her faculties. The presence and the apparent absence of God are felt in the heart—either in bliss or in most painful desire. Here at the inmost center where she is totally by herself, the soul, however, feels herself and her condition.[8] As long as she is not completely purified, she feels it painfully as opposition to the experienced holiness of the God who is present there. Thus the *Night* of contemplation does not only designate the darkness of knowledge, but also the darkness of impurity and of purifying torment.

In faith and in contemplation the soul is taken hold of by God. The acceptance of revealed truth does not happen simply through a natural act of the will. The message of the faith comes to many who do not accept it. Natural reasons may contribute to this but there are cases in which a mysterious "cannot" is fundamental. The hour of grace has not yet come. The indwelling of faith has not yet taken place. But in contemplation the soul meets God himself, who takes possession of the soul.

God is love. Therefore, being seized by God is an enkindling in love—when the spirit is ready for it. For all that is mortal is consumed in the fire of eternal love. And that means all movements that are released in the soul through creatures. If she turns toward the creature, she withdraws herself from the divine love, although she cannot escape it. Then love becomes a fire that consumes the soul herself. The human spirit as spirit is destined for immortal being. This is shown in the immutability that he ascribes to himself in his own circumstances: he thinks that as things are ordered about him, they will forever remain.[9] That is a deception, for during his mortal existence he is subject to change. But one hears in this the consciousness that one's being is not consumed by what is temporal, but is rooted in the eternal. According to his nature, he cannot decay like material forms. But if, in free surrender, the spirit fastens on to what is temporal, it will come to feel the hand of the living God who can destroy it by his almighty power through the avenging fire of rejected divine love or can preserve it as with the fallen angels, in eternal ruin. This second and most actual death would be our common lot if Christ had not stepped between us and divine justice with his Passion and death and opened a way for mercy.

There was nothing in Christ through his nature and his free decision that resisted love. He lived every moment of his existence in the boundless surrender to divine love. But in the Incarnation he had taken upon himself the entire burden of mankind's sin, embraced it with his merciful love, and hidden it in his soul. This he did in the *Ecce venio* [*"Behold, I come."*] with which he began his earthly life, and specifically renewed in his baptism, and in the *Fiat!* [*"Let it be!"*] of Gethsemani (Lk 22:39). This is how the expiating fire burned in his inmost being, in his entire, lifelong suffering, in the most intense form in the Garden of Olives and on the cross, because here the sensible joy of the indestructible union ceased, subjecting him totally to the Passion, and allowing this Passion to become the experience of the total abandonment by God. In the *Consummatum est* [*"It is finished"* (Jn 19:30)], the end of the expiatory fire is announced as is the final return into eternal, undisturbed union of love in the *Pater, in manus tuas commendo spiritum meum* [*"Father, into your hands I commend my spirit"* (Lk 23:46).]

In the Passion and death of Christ our sins were consumed by fire. If we accept that in faith, and if we accept the whole Christ in faith-filled surrender, which means, however, that we choose and walk the path of the imitation of Christ, then he will lead us "through his Passion and cross to the glory of his Resurrection." This is exactly what is experienced in contemplation: passing through the expiatory flames to the bliss of the union of love. This explains its twofold character. It is death and Resurrection. After the *Dark Night*, the *Living Flame* shines forth.

3. The Glory of the Resurrection

A. In The Flames of Divine Love

LEBENDIGE LIEBESFLAMME[10]	LIVING FLAME OF LOVE
[Edith's translation of the Spanish]	[translation of Edith's German]

1. O Flamme lebend'ger Liebe
   Die zart Du mich verwundest
   In meiner Seele allertiefstem
   Grunde!
   Da Du nicht mehr voll
   Schmerzen
   Vollende, wenn's Dein Wille
   Zerreiß den Schleier dieses
   süßen Treffens.

2. O Feuerbrand, so lieblich!
   O Wunde voller Wonne!
   O linde Hand! O zarteste
   Berührung!
   Läßt ew'ges Leben kosten
   Und zahlest alle Schuld!
   Die tötend Du den Tod
   in Leben wandelst.

1. O flame of living love,
   Most tenderly, didst wound
   My soul in deepest center—
   Since you are no longer full
   of pain,
   Perfect, if't be your will!
   Tear through the veil of
   this sweet encounter!

2. O cautery so sweet!
   O wound full of delight!
   O soft hand! O gentle touch!
   Taste of eternal life you give
   And pay off every debt!
   By slaying, you change death
   to life.

3. O lichte Feuerlampen,
   In deren Strahlenfluten
   Des Sinnes abgrundtiefe
      Höhlen
   So blind einst und so dunkel,
   In Schönheit sondergleichen
   Wärme und Licht vereint
      weih'n dem Geliebten!

3. O luminous lamps of fire
   In whose resplendent rays
   The caves of sense—
      profound abyss—
   Which once were dark, bereft
      of sight,
   With rarest beauty unite
   In gift for the Beloved,
      warmth and light.

4. Wie sanft und voller Liebe
   In meinem Schoß erwachst Du,
   Wo Du verborgen weilest
      ganz allein;
   Mit Deinem süßen Hauche,
   Voll Glück und Herrlich-
      keiten,
   Wie zart läßt Du in Liebe
      mich entbrennen.

4. How gently, filled with love,
   You awake in my inmost
      heart
   Where secretly you dwell,
      alone:
   With your breath so delicious,
   Replete with good and glory,
   How delicately you enamor
      me!

1) On the Threshold of Eternal Life

The soul has escaped from the night. What now transpires in her is far more powerful than can be put into words. The cries of desire, "Oh" and "How", seek to express this. That is why the saint hesitated to fulfill the plea of his spiritual daughter, Ana de Peñalosa, who asked for a commentary on the four stanzas. He felt how incapable language would be to explain what was so spiritual and interior. After some time, however, it appeared to him that "the Lord seems to have uncovered some knowledge and bestowed some fervor" in him, indeed, even encouraged him to set to work.[11]

"Some fervor!" One actually has the impression that not only the four stanzas of the *Song* but the entire explanation as well, are an eruption of the *Living Flame of Love*. So we approach these divine secrets in the inmost region of a chosen soul with holy awe. But once the veil is lifted, one may not remain silent. For we have before us here what—

in the form in which they have come down to us—the *Ascent* and the *Night* owed us: a view of the soul at the goal of her long way of the cross, in blissful union.

Earlier it was said that the first writings were obviously composed by someone who had already arrived at the goal. The *Song of the Dark Night* can hardly be understood in any other way. But in the explanation of the stanzas he had placed himself back in the time of night and described it as though he were still engulfed by it. Only by foresight did he say anything about the goal. Now, however, he is bathed in the brilliant light of Resurrection morning. When he now continues to speak of the cross and night, it is only in retrospect. It is precisely this retrospection that makes the work meaningful and coherent: new life is born out of death; the glory of the Resurrection is the reward for faithful endurance through night and cross. Thus "every debt is paid."

The soul "feels that out of her heart will flow streams of living water,"[12] and it seems to her that she is "so forcefully transformed in God, so sublimely possessed by him, and arrayed with such rich gifts and virtues, that she is singularly close to beatitude—so close that only a thin veil separates her from it." When this tender flame of love, which burns within her, seizes her, she is each time "as though glorified with gentle and powerful glory" and thinks the veil of earthly life is about to be torn and only a very little is lacking before she possesses eternal happiness and eternal life. And so she is completely filled with fervent longing and begs to be freed from the veil of mortal life.[13]

The *Living Flame of Love* is the *Holy Spirit* "whom the soul feels henceforth in herself . . . as a fire, which consumes her and transforms her into blissful love," and further, as "a fire that burns and flames within her. As often as that flame flares up, it bathes the soul in glory and refreshes her with the quality of divine life." The activity of the Holy Spirit in the soul produces an inflamed love in which the will of the soul becomes one single love in union with the divine flame. The transformation in love is the *habitus*, the lasting condition into which the soul is placed, the fire that burns in her constantly. Her acts however "are the flames that blaze out of the fire of love and that burst forth the more vehemently, the more intense the fire of union burns." In this condition the soul cannot make any acts herself. All of them are initiated by the Holy Spirit and brought to completion by him, and so they are totally divine. Thus it is that it seems to the soul that every time this flame shoots up eternal life is given to her: "for she is raised up to the activity of God in God." By this transformation into a flame of love, God the Father, the Son, and the Holy Spirit are communicated to her. She comes therein so close to God that she catches a glimmer of the divine life; she has a sensation that this is eternal life.[14]

The flame of divine life *touches* the soul with the tenderness of God's life and *wounds* her so mightily in her innermost depth that she dissolves wholly in love. How can one speak of wounding here? In actuality, these wounds are "like the most tender flares of delicate love." Playfulness of eternal wisdom, these "flames of tender touches arising from the fire of love, which is never idle, quicken the soul incessantly."[15]

This happens in the *inmost region* of the soul where neither the devil nor sensuality can penetrate, therefore what occurs is the more secure, substantial, and delightful. "The more interior it is, the purer, and the greater the purity, the more abundantly, frequently, and generously God communicates himself and the more intense is the delight and joy of the soul. . . . It is God who does it all, the soul contributes nothing of her own."

The soul can only act herself with the help of the corporeal senses, and in this state she is totally free and far removed from them, and so "she limits herself to one thing which is receiving from God. He alone can move the soul and complete his work in the depths of her being . . . without the mediation of the senses." So all movements of the soul become divine, are acts of God, yet also acts of the soul. "For God works them in her and with her, insofar as she gives her consent and agreement."

When the soul says that the Holy Spirit wounds her in her deepest center, she means that there are within her some areas that are not as deep, corresponding to the degrees of the love of God. But now the substance of her being, her power and strength are touched and grasped. She does not wish to assert "that this is as essential and integral as in the beatific vision of the next life." She speaks thus only in order to "manifest the fullness and abundance of the delight and glory she feels in this communication from the Holy Spirit. The delight is so much the more intense and tender the stronger and more substantially the soul is transformed and concentrated in God." This does not happen here as perfectly as in eternal life. "The soul may perhaps possess in this life a habit of charity as perfect as in the next, yet the operation and fruition of charity in this life will not be so perfect." But the condition will be so similar to that of life in eternity that the soul, convinced of it, dares to say: I am wounded in my deepest center.

Whoever has no experience may take this as exaggeration. Still, the "Father of Lights, whose hand is never shortened . . . and who dispenses blessings in abundance . . . does not hesitate to fulfill even in this life in a soul who has been examined, purged, and tried in the fire of tribulations . . . and found faithful in love, precisely because of this fidelity, what the Son of God has promised when anyone loves him, the Most Holy Trinity will come and take up their abode in that soul (Jn 14:23).[16] This taking up their abode consists in divinely enlightening the intellect with the wisdom of the Son, and in filling the will with delight in the Holy Spirit, and absorbing the soul powerfully and mightily in the unfathomed embrace of the Father's love." In the soul in which the living flame of love burns, the Holy Spirit's activity brings about something far greater than the communication and transformation of love. "This latter resembles glowing embers, the other is similar to embers that are not merely glowing but have become so hot that they shoot forth a living flame." The *simple union* of love alone is like the "fire of God in Zion" (Is 31:9), that is, in the church militant in which the fire of charity is not enkindled to an extreme. The *loving union,* with an inflaming of love, is like the "furnace of God in Jerusalem," the vision of peace that is the church triumphant where this fire is like a furnace blazing in the perfection of love.

The soul has not yet attained the perfection of heaven, but she is like a blazing furnace in which there is a vision much more peaceful and glorious and tender. The soul feels that "this living flame of love vividly communicates to her every good." Therefore she cries out "O flame of living love that tenderly wounds my soul!" by which she means to say "O burning love, with your loving movements you pleasantly glorify me according to the greater capacity and strength of my soul! You give me divine knowledge according to the ability and capacity of my intellect. You give me a love according to the greater power of my will, and fill the substance of my soul with the torrent of your delight through the divine contact and substantial union, in harmony with the greater purity of my substance and the capacity and breadth of my memory."

When the purgation of all the faculties is complete, then "divine wisdom absorbs the soul in itself profoundly, subtly, and sublimely with its divine flame. In this immersion of the soul in wisdom, the Holy Spirit sets in motion the glorious flickering of his flame."[17] It is *the same fire, which was dark and painful for the soul during her purification.* Now, however, it is brilliant, loving, and gentle. Therefore the soul says: "Since you are no longer full of pain."[18]

Formerly the divine light had but allowed her to see her own darkness. Now that she is enlightened and transformed, she sees the light in herself. Formerly the flame was terrifying for the will that was thereby made painfully aware of its own hardness and dryness. The will was unable to feel the love and tenderness of the flame. Nor could it savor the sweetness because its taste was ruined through inordinate inclinations. The soul could not grasp the immeasurable riches and delights of the flame of love and under its influence was aware only of her own poverty and misery. Now she thinks back on all of that and with that brief acknowledgment that all trace of pain is gone, she wishes to say: "You are now no longer dark as you were before, rather you are the divine light of my intellect by which I can look at you. You not only have ceased to make me faint in my weakness, but are rather the strength of my will by which I can love and enjoy you, being wholly converted into divine love; and you are no longer heavy and constraining to the substance of my soul but rather its glory and delight and amplitude."[19] And because she knows how near she is to the goal now, she begs for the final gift: "Perfect it, if it be your will!"

It is a plea for the perfect consummation of the spiritual marriage by means of the beatific vision. In reality, the soul at this stage is so calmly collected and almost without a single wish; she would like to ask for nothing more. But since she still lives in hope and not yet in perfect possession of the adoption of the children of God, she longs for its consummation and this all the more, since she has a foretaste and appreciation of that delight as much as is possible on earth.

So sublime a state is this that the soul believes her nature must dissolve since her lower part is incapable of bearing so much of this divine fire. And indeed she would really die were God not to come to the aid of her weak nature and support her with his right hand. The brief flashes of contemplation are of the kind "that it would be a sign of weak love not to try to enter into that perfection and completion of love." She is also conscious that the Holy Spirit himself invites her to that glory, telling her as he told the bride in the *Song of Songs*: "Arise and make haste, my love, my dove, my beautiful one, and come. . . . " (Sg 2:10ff.) "Perfect it, if it be your will"; in this way the soul makes "the two requests that the Bridegroom taught us in the Gospel: 'Thy kingdom come—Thy will be done.'"[20]

In order for so perfect a union to take place every impediment between God and the soul must be removed. It can be a threefold veil: "a temporal one, comprising all creatures . . . a natural one, embodying the purely natural inclinations and operations; and a sensitive one, which in the union of soul and body combines the life of the senses and the animal life." The first and second must already have been torn in order to arrive at the union that is now almost within reach. That happened "through the painful encounters with that flame when it was still terrible." Now only the third veil of the sensate life remains to be torn, and through union with God this has been worn as thin and fragile as film. And when this is torn the soul can speak only of a *sweet encounter.* For the natural death of such a soul is wholly different from that of others, although the natural circumstances of the death may be similar. "Whether they die of an illness or because of the weakness of old age, the soul still wrests herself free with great force and in an exalted impulse of love . . . this impulse of love has . . . the power to tear the veil and to take the precious jewel of the soul with it.

Therefore the death of such souls is sweeter and gentler than was their whole spiritual life up to that time. Their death is caused by the most lofty impulses and delightful encounters of love, resembling the

swan whose *Song* is much sweeter when it is about to die. Therefore
David says: 'Precious in the eyes of God is the death of his saints'
(Ps 116:15). For here, all the riches of the soul are gathered together,
and her rivers of love flow into the ocean of love . . . so vast that they
themselves resemble oceans." The soul sees herself "at the threshold
admitting her to the fullness of joy ... on the point of possessing her
kingdom, whole and entirely. . . . She sees herself to be pure, rich, full of
virtues, and prepared for taking possession. . . . For in this condition,
God allows the soul to see her own beauty. . . . All is now transformed
into love and praises without a touch of presumption or vanity, since all
the leaven of imperfections has been removed. . . . Now the soul sees
that the only thing that remains to be done is to tear the fine veil of her
natural life. . . . And so she longs to be dissolved and to be with Christ,
and it is for her a torment to see that so poor and weak a life can hinder
her from taking possession of the other sublime and everlasting life.
Therefore she pleads: 'Tear the veil of this sweet encounter.'"[21]

Since she now "perceives the power of the other life . . . she is also
. . . conscious of the weakness of this life. It seems to her . . . as a veil
of delicate fabric, as thin as a spider's web (Ps 90:9) . . . indeed . . .
even more insignificant." For now she regards things as God does,
"they are in her eyes as nothing, and she herself is nothing, God alone
is her all."

She begs for tearing not for cutting: first, because this fits better
with the image of an encounter; furthermore, "because love is a friend
of powerful love, and of forceful, impetuous touch .... Third, because
love desires the act to be carried out in the briefest of time." For it is
the "more powerful and valuable, the shorter and more spiritual it is.
For strength united is mightier than when it is splintered." Actions
that are completed in moments in the soul are infused by God; those
that proceed from the soul herself are better called preparatory desires
than perfect acts of love, although God does occasionally, "form and
perfect them very quickly in the spirit." "In the soul that has prepared
herself, the act of love enters immediately, for at each touch the spark
catches fire in the dry tinder. Thus the enamored soul desires a swift
tearing." She does not want to delay or to wait for the natural end.

"The force of love and the preparation that she perceives in herself awaken in her . . . the longing that life may soon end through some impetus or supernatural incentive of love." She knows "that God is pleased to take to himself such souls whom he loves intimately, before their time, in order to perfect them in a short time through this love." "Therefore it is an important task of the soul to practice acts of love in this life so that without being detained here or there, she may reach the vision of God in a short time."

The soul "calls this inner assault of the Spirit an *encounter*"[22] or a *meeting*. God seizes her with this supernatural vehemence in order to raise her out of the flesh and to lead her toward the desired fulfillment. These are true encounters; the Holy Spirit pervades the substance of the soul by them, illumines and divinizes her. "Hereby the divine being absorbs the soul's being above all being." Here the soul may taste God in a living way and she calls this encounter sweeter than all other touches and encounters because this one outranks them all in eminence. Thus the Lord prepares the soul for perfect beatitude and himself inspires in her the plea that this tender veil be torn, so that thereby she can in the future love God in fullness and plenitude without any limit or end.[23]

16
The Triune One

2) United with the Triune One

> O cautery so sweet!
> O wound full of delight!
> O soft hand! O gentle touch!
> Taste of eternal life you give
> And pay off every debt.
> By slaying, you change death to life.

In the first stanza, union was considered as principally the work of the Holy Spirit. There was but a brief mention that all three divine persons take up their dwelling in the soul. Now an attempt will be made to describe how each of the three persons participates in the "divine work of union." Cautery, hand, and touch are the same as far as substance is concerned. The terms are applied to the persons of the Trinity according to the effect each produces in the soul. "The cautery is the Holy Spirit, the hand is the Father and the touch is the Son." Each bestows a particular gift on the soul. She owes the *wound full of delight* to the Holy Spirit, the *sweet cautery*. The Son gives her to taste eternal life through his *gentle touch*. With his *soft hand* the Father transforms her in God. And yet, she speaks but to the one deity "for all three work together, and accordingly, she attributes everything to one, and everything to all."[1]

We already know the Holy Spirit as a *consuming fire* (Dt 4:24) as "a fire of love that, being of infinite power, can inestimably consume and transform into itself the soul it touches. . . . And when this divine flame has entirely transformed the soul, it feels not only the cautery, but has herself completely become a cautery of blazing fire. It is a wonderful thing . . . that this vehement and consuming fire that could consume a thousand worlds more easily than the fire of this earth would burn up a straw does not consume and destroy the soul . . . but rather . . . divinizes and delights her."

She has been given "the great fortune to know all things, taste all things, and do all she wishes; she prospers, no one prevails against her and nothing touches her." It is rightly said of her "in the words of the apostle: 'The spiritual person judges all things and is judged by no one' [1 Cor 2:15] and again, 'The spirit searches out all things, even the deep things of God' [1 Cor 2:10]. This is love's trait: to scrutinize all the good things of the Beloved."[2]

The sweet cautery causes a wound full of delight; "since the fire was one of love the wound is a wound of sweet love and will refresh the soul sweetly." Just as material fire converts existing wounds into burn wounds when the fire touches them, so the cautery of love injures the wounds of misery and sin, then heals them and changes them into wounds of love. And the wounds it causes itself are healed by it—in this it differs from material fire—and they can be healed by nothing else. But the fire heals them in order to cause deeper wounds of love. "As often as the cautery of love touches the wound of love, it causes a deeper wound of love, and thus the more it wounds, the more it cures and heals. . . . The cure caused by love is to wound and inflict wound upon wound, to such an extent that the entire soul is dissolved into a wound of love. And now . . . made into one wound of love, it is completely healthy in love, for it is transformed in love." Still the cautery does not cease to work, rather like a good doctor gives the wound loving attention.

This highest form of wounding by love "is caused by a direct touch of the divinity in the soul, without any intellectual or imaginative form or figure." But there are other very sublime manners in which the soul is inflamed in which a spiritual being has an auxiliary role. St. John here gives a very detailed account of how the soul can be wounded by a seraph with a burning arrow or spear. One can hardly take this as anything but the transpiercing of the heart of our holy Mother Teresa. His description gives remarkable features that Teresa has not included in her own account.[3] That is not surprising since she had opened her whole soul to John and in doing so, in any case, expressed herself with less reservation than in her literary description. The soul, so he says, "feels the delicate wound and the herb (which serves as a keen temper to the dart) as though it were a sharp point in the substance of the spirit, in the heart of the pierced soul. And in this living point of the wound that makes its mark in the middle of the heart of the spirit—who can fittingly speak of this?—the soul feels a tiny mustard seed, very much alive and enkindled, sending into its surroundings a living and enkindled fire. She feels that the fire issuing from the substance and power of that living point, which contains the substance and power of the herb, is diffused through all the spiritual and substantial veins of the soul . . . She sees the ardor of love increase and grow to the highest degree. In this ardor her love becomes so purified that it seems to her that seas of loving fire flow within her, which are so overflowingly full that they rise and fall, imbuing all with love.

In this fire the whole universe appears like an ocean of love in which she herself is engulfed and is unable to catch sight of an end or boundary for this love. Meanwhile she perceives within herself the living point or center of love. About the soul's enjoyment here, one can only say that in it she realizes how appropriately the kingdom of heaven was compared in the gospel to a grain of mustard seed that, despite its tiny size, by reason of its intense drive to grow, becomes a large tree (Mt 13:31-32). For the soul beholds itself converted into an immense fire of love that emanates from that enkindled point at the heart of the spirit.

Few persons have reached these heights. Some have, however, especially those whose virtue and spirit were to be diffused among their children. God accords to founders the first fruits of the spirit, riches and power according to the greater or lesser number of those who will follow them and who are to inherit their doctrine and their spirit." (This comment, too, points to our holy Mother.)

In some cases the interior wounding is visible externally on the body. John here calls to mind the stigmata of St. Francis that the seraph "impressed on the body, which was wounded just as his soul was wounded with love.[4] For God usually does not grant the body a favor that he did not previously and principally bestow on the soul." The greater the delight and strength of the love that the wound produces in the soul, "so much greater is the pain perceived outwardly in the wound of the body. And when there is an increase in one there is an increase in the other." For "what is a cause of pain and torment to their corruptible flesh is sweet and delectable to these souls who are purified and established in God. . . . Nevertheless, when the wound is made only in the soul . . . the delight can be more intense and sublime, for the flesh bridles the spirit, and when it shares in the spiritual goods of grace, it pulls the reins and . . . pulls back at the mouth of this swift horse of the spirit and restrains its wild impetuosity; for were the spirit to make use of its power, the reins would have to break."[5]

The short insertion treating of varieties of wounding by love is remarkable first because it shows how carefully the saint takes the trouble to enlarge on his own inner experience by bringing in what has become accessible to him through other souls and how precisely and clearly he establishes the differences and firmly holds to what has become fundamentally clear to him. No matter how exalted the wounding by love in visionary experiences may be, nothing can come up to the purely spiritual happenings in the inmost region of the soul. To this corresponds the very distinct view of the relationship of body and soul, which is to be remarked at this point. The soul as spirit is essentially dominant, even though in her condition after the fall—and this even when elevated to the highest degree imaginable on earth—she is burdened by the body, and weighed down by the earthly shell. And the ordering of grace adapts itself to this original ordering of nature and gives gifts especially and in the first place to the soul, then only in descending order and eventually through the mediation of the soul, to the body.

The *hand* which causes the wound is the *loving* and *almighty Father*: "a hand . . . which, when it opens to distribute its favors, is as generous and bountiful as it is mighty and rich when it gives . . . costly presents to the soul." The soul feels its loving condescension and touch to be the more gentle, since this hand could cast the entire world into the abyss were it to rest upon it more perceptibly. It causes death and gives life, and no one can escape from it. "You kill, O divine life, only to give life . . . When you punish, you touch softly, but this would suffice to annihilate the whole world. But when you refresh the soul, you show yourself extremely condescending and the consolations of your sweetness are countless. You have wounded me in order to heal me, O divine hand; you have slain in me whatever held me captive under the tree of death and at a great distance from eternal life. . . . This you have accomplished with the generosity of your great-hearted love in that touch of the splendor of your glory and with the image of your substance (Heb 1:3). This is your only begotten Son; through him who is your wisdom you reach mightily from one end to the other (Wis 8:1). And this, your only begotten Son, O merciful hand of the Father, is the delicate touch by which you touched me with the force of your cautery and wounded me.

O delicate Touch, the Word, Son of God, through the delicacy of your divine being, you subtly penetrate the substance of my soul, and lightly touch it all, absorb it entirely in yourself in divine sweetness and delight, unheard of in the land of Canaan and never before seen in Teman (Bar 3:22). O exceedingly gentle touch of the Word, to me so wholly unique! By the shadow of your might and power, which preceded you, you cast down the mountains and smashed the rocks on Mount Horeb to pieces and let yourself be perceived in truth by the prophet in the whisper of a gentle breeze (1 Kg 19:11-12).

O gentle and soft breeze, tell me how you were a mild and gentle breeze and how you can touch so mildly since you are so awesome and mighty! O blessed and exceedingly happy the soul whom you, who are so terrible and strong, touch so gently and lightly! Proclaim this to the world—but no, do not tell it, for the world has no understanding for such a gentle breeze . . . O my God and my life! only those will perceive and recognize you by your gentle touch who have themselves become mild through withdrawal from the world, since the gentle will meet only the gentle; they will experience and enjoy you. . . . O repeatedly delicate touch, you are so much the stronger and mightier, the more delicate you are! For through the might of your delicacy you liberate

. . . the soul from all the touches of creatures; you unite her with your-self, and take possession of her totally for yourself. So mild an effect and feeling do you leave in the soul that every other touch of creatures . . . seems coarse and spurious. . . . Just the sight of them arouses aversion in the soul, and it is painful and a torment for her to speak of them or to come in contact with them."

With delicacy, capacity increases, and with simplicity and refinement, so does the fullness of communication. The Word is infinitely simple and delicate; the soul is a vessel of great capacity and content in this state through her sincerity and purity. And the finer and more delicate the touch is, the more delight it communicates. This divine touch is without form or figure, because the divine Word does not insert itself into any mode. It is substantial, that is, it is produced in the soul through God's most simple being and therefore it is inexpressible. It is infinite and therefore also infinitely tender.[6] For this reason, it can give "a taste of eternal life." This is not impossible when God's substance touches the soul's substance. The delight felt in this contact is inexpressible. "I would desire not to speak of it so as to avoid giving the impression that it is no more than I describe."[7]

The souls who have these experiences have for these exalted divine things their own manner of expression that only one who has experienced them can understand: he rejoices over them and keeps silent about them. This is similar to the name on a white pebble; no one knows it except the one who receives it (Rev 2:17). So it is that the divine touch gives a foretaste of eternal life even if the joy is not as perfect as it will be in eternal glory. The soul "tastes here, by participation, all the divine riches, the fortitude, wisdom, love, beauty, grace, goodness, and so on. And because God is all these things, a person enjoys them in only one touch of God, and the soul rejoices within its faculties and within its substance. From this blissful delight of the soul, sometimes the unction of the Holy Spirit overflows into the body. Then all the sensory substance, all the members and bones and marrow rejoice . . . with a feeling of great delight and glory, even in the outermost joints of the hands and feet."[8] In this foretaste of eternal life the soul feels she has been rewarded, richly and far beyond her merits for all her former efforts, troubles, difficulties and penances. Thus "every debt has been paid off."

If so few "attain to this exalted stage of perfect union with God" the reason is not to be sought in God, for he would like to see all become perfect. But he finds but few vessels that can bear the necessary "lofty and sublime belaboring." Most "refuse to take upon themselves insignificant discomforts and mortification and to work with persevering patience. . . . And so he does not lead them forward any more in order, through the labor of mortification, to purify them and raise them out of the dust of the earth. . . . O you souls who wish to advance in the spiritual life in security and consolation, if only you knew how necessary these sufferings are for you in order to attain to that security and consolation. . . . Take . . . the cross upon yourself, and fastened upon it, drink the gall and undiluted vinegar. Consider it a great happiness, for if you are thus dead to the world and to yourself, you will attain to a life in God in the delights of the Spirit." Those to whom the very special grace of interior trials is given must first show God many acts of service, demonstrate great patience and endurance, and so become very acceptable in the eyes of God by their life and works. This is why "only a few merit to be purged through suffering so as to reach such an exalted state."[9]

The soul then, in retrospect, recognizes that all has been a safeguard for her and that the light corresponds to the darknesses. Not only is she rewarded for everything; all the imperfect desires that wanted to rob her of her spiritual life have been slain, as well. So God's hand *by slaying, changed death to life.*

Life here has a double meaning: the beatific vision of God to which we can attain only through natural death; and the perfect spiritual life in the union of love with God, which one arrives at after total mortification of all the vices and lust. What the soul calls *death* here is "all that goes to make up the old self, . . . the entire engagement of the memory, the intellect, and the will in the things of the world . . . and the desires and inclinations that are directed to creatures." All of this constitutes the old life, which connotes death of the new, spiritual life.

In this new life of union all the appetites and faculties of the soul, all her inclinations and activities are changed and become divine. The soul lives "the life of God. Thus her death has been changed to life, her animal life to spiritual life." Her intellect becomes divine, her will, her memory, and her natural desires are all divinized. "The substance (*sustancia*) of the soul is not divine substance, since it cannot undergo a conversion in God substantially (*sustancialmente*), but through the union with God and through being absorbed in him, she is God by participation." Consequently the soul has every right to say: "I live, now not I, but Christ lives in me" (Gal 2:20). She is now "always, inwardly and outwardly, in a festive mood, and from the mouth of her spirit a *Song* of great jubilation frequently streams toward God, a *Song* always new, enfolded in a gladness and love, arising from the knowledge the soul has of her happy state." God, who makes all things new, renews the soul constantly. He does not permit her to relapse as formerly, but rather multiplies her merits. "Besides being conscious of the exalted grace she has received, she feels that God is carefully intent on regaling her with precious, delicate, and enhancing words, and in extolling her by various favors and so it seems to her that he has no one else in the world to favor, nor anything else to do but concern himself with her alone. With this feeling she proclaims like the bride in the *Song* of *Song*s: 'My beloved is mine, and I am his'"(Sg 2:16).[10]

17

Rays of Divine Glory

3) In the Reflected Rays of Divine Glory

> O luminous lamps of fire
> In whose resplendent rays
> The caves of sense—profound abyss—
> Which once were dark, bereft of sight,
> With rarest beauty unite
> In gift for the Belov'd, warmth and light.

The soul overflows with gratitude for the graces she has received through union with God. Her senses and faculties, once blind and in darkness, are now illuminated and inflamed through her knowledge of God which is aglow with love. Therefore she can give back to her Beloved both light and love; this fills her with delight.

In the substantial union with God the soul recognizes the grandeurs and powers of all the *divine attributes* that are consolidated in God's simple divine being: his omnipotence, wisdom, goodness, mercy, and so on. "Each of these attributes is the same being of God in one single person . . . *namely*[1] in the Father, or in the Son, or in the Holy Spirit, and each of these perfections is also God himself. And since God is an infinite divine light and an immense divine fire . . . so each of these numberless attributes and powers burns and illumines like God himself. So each of these attributes is a *lamp* that enlightens the soul and fills her with the forms of love." In one single act of union the soul receives the knowledge of these various attributes, and so "God is for her many lamps together, each of which illumines and imparts warmth to her."

In this way, each of these lamps, individually, and all of them together, inflame the soul. "For all these attributes are *one* Being . . . and so all these lamps are but *one* lamp which according to its powers and attributes shines and burns like many lamps." The splendor of this lamp of God's being, insofar as he is omnipotent, gives her light and warmth of love according to his omnipotence. He also fills her with splendor as the all-knowing, and so is a lamp of wisdom for her. It is the same with all the rest of the attributes that reveal themselves to the soul. The soul receives wonderful delight from the fire and light of these lamps, an immense fullness, since it comes from so many lamps each of which burns with love. "And the splendor of one increases that of the others, the flame of one the flames of the others and the light of one that of the others. For through every single perfection the other is known. And so all of them together are one light and one fire."

The soul is immensely absorbed in these, subtly wounded with love through each of them and more wounded by all of them together with the love that comes from life and she "perceives clearly that this love is proper to eternal life, which life is the aggregation of all goods." God communicates to the soul his love and his good deeds according to his attributes and powers. He omnipotently loves and does good to the soul, in wisdom, in goodness and holiness, in justice and mercy, purity and integrity, and so on. His esteem for her is supreme, and he wishes to make her equal with himself and shows himself therefore delighted to reveal himself to her in these ways of knowledge. He pours streams of love over her and she is made joyous in the perfect harmony of soul and body, converted completely into a paradise built perfectly by God. And so gentle is this infinite fire that it is like the waters of life that satisfy the spirit's thirst with all the impetus it desires.

This represents that wonderful event recorded in the book of the Maccabees: the holy fire that was hidden in a cistern, and which there, in the cistern, turned into water. On the altar of sacrifice it was once more turned into fire.[2] The spirit of God is like soft refreshing water as long as it remains hidden in the soul's veins; but when it serves as a sacrifice of love offered to God, it again leaps up in living flames. Since the soul is inflamed now and active in loving surrender, she now speaks of lamps rather than waters.

But all these attempts are incapable of expressing sufficiently what is really happening: "for the transformation of the soul in God is indescribable."[3]

When *resplendent rays* are spoken of, in which the soul is set aglow, what is meant is the loving knowledge the lamps of God's perfections give forth. United with these perfections, she is transformed into loving splendors, and resplendent like them. The illumination from these splendors of divine light is entirely different from that of material lamps. The latter illumine the things outside themselves with their flames; the former light up things interior to the rays. The soul is, after all, *within* these splendors, is transformed by them, and has herself become transformed into a flame. She is like the air within the flame, enkindled and transformed into flame. The movements of these flames, their flickering and flaring up proceed from the soul and the Holy Spirit at the same time. "They are not only splendors, but also glorifications of the soul, the happy festivals and games the Holy Spirit inspires in the soul," as has been said earlier.[4] It seems as though he wishes to bestow eternal life on her and transport her to [5]perfect glory. All the preceding and following graces have that as their goal. However, no matter how efficacious the movements of the Holy Spirit may be, the complete absorption of the soul in sublime glory is only possible when the soul "departs from the sphere . . . of this mortal life and enters the center of the spirit of the perfect life in Christ."

When one speaks of *movements* of the flame, these are motions not actually to be ascribed to God, but rather to the soul. God does not move; it only seems to the soul that he is moving within her.

The *fullness of the splendors* of these lamps may also be called an *overshadowing,* as was that of the angel at the Annunciation (Lk 1:35). *Overshadowing* or *casting a shadow* means "protecting, favoring, and granting graces." That is to say, as soon as the shadow of one person falls on another, it is a sign that the former is near at hand to offer protection and support.

The shadow of a thing conforms to the nature of the thing. "If it is opaque and dark, it makes a dark shadow; if it is transparent and delicate its shadow is transparent and delicate." Therefore the shadows of the divine lamps of God's splendors will be enkindled and resplendent.

The lamp of God's beauty casts another beauty as a shadow over the soul; the lamp of fortitude, another fortitude; and the shadow of God's wisdom is again a wisdom. Better said, the wisdom, beauty, and fortitude of God are in shadow, because the soul cannot comprehend God perfectly here. Since, however, the shadow corresponds totally with God's being and properties, the soul clearly recognizes in the shadow the excellence of God. God's omnipotence and wisdom, his infinite goodness, and his holiness pass by "in the clear and enkindled shadows of those clear and enkindled lamps," which the soul recognizes and partakes of as such. Thus the soul understands and enjoys all the riches that are united in the infinite, undivided and simple being of God. The knowledge of one does not infringe on the knowledge and enjoyment of the others; rather, every beauty and fortitude is a light for each of the other grandeurs. The purity of divine wisdom causes one to behold in it many things.[6]

All these splendors fill "the profound abyss of the caves of sense." These caves designate the faculties of the soul: memory, intellect, and will. "They are the deeper, the greater the boundless graces they are capable of receiving." Only the infinite can fill them. As much pain as they have endured, when they were empty, so great is the delight they taste now that they are being filled by God. They did not feel the vast emptiness of their deep capacity as long as they were not emptied, purged, and cleansed of every affection for creatures. The least trifle to which they are attached makes them insensible so that they "do not perceive the harm[7] or note the lack of their immense goods, nor do they know their own capacity. Despite their capability to receive infinite goods, any little thing can be enough to encumber the faculties, making them incapable of receiving these goods. . . . If, however, they are empty and pure, then the thirst, hunger, and yearning of the spiritual sense is intolerable. Each of these caves has a very deep stomach, and so they suffer profoundly since the food they lack is also unfathomable: it is, after all . . . God himself. This intense feeling (of hunger and thirst) commonly occurs toward the end of the illumination and purification of the soul."

When the spiritual appetite is purified of all things created and of all attachment thereto, then the soul has taken on divine qualities rather than her own natural ones and she now possesses an empty, prepared room. But since the divine is not yet communicated to her in union, the soul feels "pain that is worse than death, especially when a divine ray appears vaguely through some crevice and is not communicated to her by God. These are the souls who suffer with impatient love, for they cannot remain long in this condition; they must either receive what they long for, or die."[8]

The first cave is the *intellect*, its emptiness is a *thirst for God* and it longs for divine *wisdom*. The second cave is the *will*, which *hungers* for God and *clamors* for the perfection of love. The third cave is the *memory*. It is *consumed* with the desire for the *possession of God*. These caves are capable of grasping God. And because God is profound and infinite, so in a certain fashion, their capacity is infinite, their thirst and their hunger both infinite, their languishing and their suffering constitute a death without end. Although the suffering is not yet as deep as in the next life, it still gives a living image of it since the soul already possesses the necessary disposition to receive the fullness of eternal life. However, there is no alleviation for this affliction because it has its seat in love. "For the greater the love, so much more impatient is she for the possession of God; she hopes for it at every moment with intense longing."[9]

Yet, if the soul longs for God in truth, she already possesses the one she loves and so it seems that she is no longer capable of feeling any pain. "For the desire the angels have to see the Son of God (1 Pt 1:12) is free of pain and anxious desire, since they already possess him. But the possession of God lends delight and satisfaction. Therefore the soul must receive the more satisfaction and delight, the more intensely she desires to possess God, and she does this all the more because she lives all the more in possessing him. Therefore she, too, feels neither suffering nor pain."

Here it is well to note that there are two ways of understanding the *possession of God*: the possession *through grace*, and that *through union*. The two are related in a way somewhat similar to *betrothal's* relation to *marriage*. In the betrothal a mutual agreement is made; bride and bridegroom visit each other often and exchange gifts; but a mutual bestowal and union of persons takes place only in the marriage.[10] So, in the perfect purification of the soul, God's will and hers have become one through their own free consent; she now possesses "everything that one can attain through the will and grace, that is to say, God has placed within the soul's being his own true being and the fullness of his grace. That is the high state of spiritual betrothal of the soul with the Word of God in which the Bridegroom favors her and frequently pays her loving visits."

But the wonderful delights she is given here are not comparable to those of mystical marriage—these are but preparations for that union. For it is not only purification from all attachment to creatures that is necessary, but also a preparation through visits and gifts which purify, beautify, and refine her to make her more worthy of so lofty a union. This preparation takes more time for some, and less for others. The preparation is achieved through the anointings of the Holy Spirit. When the ointments "are more sublime . . . the urgent longings of the caves of the soul are wont to be extreme and delicate . . . since, namely, the preparations have become more closely related to God and therefore make the soul more profoundly desirous of God, and draw her to him, so also will the desire for him become more refined and profound. For the desire for God is the preparation for union with him."[11]

The anointings of the Holy Spirit are "so exalted and delicate that they pierce the innermost region of the soul's substance . . . and make the soul melt in sweetness; then the suffering and the fainting of desire in the tremendous void of these caves is immense." Still, the more delicate the preparation has been, the more exquisite will be the fruition experienced by the sense of the soul in the possession of the spiritual marriage. "By the sense of the soul" [the caves of sense] the verse refers to the power and strength the substance of the soul has for feeling and enjoying the objects of the spiritual faculties. Through these faculties she tastes the wisdom, the love, and the communication of God."

The soul calls her faculties "caves of sense—profound abyss" because in them she experiences the grandeurs of God's wisdom and perfections. And "when she feels that the deep knowledge and splendors of the lamps of fire will fit into these caves, the soul knows that its capacity and recesses correspond to the particular things she receives from the knowledge, savor, joy, delight, and so on, of God." Similar to the way in which the common sense of the phantasy becomes the receptacle and archives of images and forms collected by the outer senses, "so the common sense or feeling of the soul becomes the receptacle or archives of God's grandeurs and is illumined and enriched according to what it attains of this high and enlightened possession."[12]

Once they were dark, bereft of sight, namely, before the soul was enlightened and illumined by God. The bodily eye cannot see when it is in darkness or if it is blind. Just so, the soul, even with very excellent vision, cannot recognize anything unless God, her light, enlightens her. On the other hand, if her spiritual eye is blinded through sin or the desire for anything created, the divine light streams into it in vain. She does not recognize her own darkness, that is, her ignorance. A distinction must be made between the *darkness* of sin and the soul's *obscurity,* her inculpable ignorance concerning natural or supernatural things. So, before union, the soul's senses were doubly in the dark. "For until the Lord speaks the words, 'Let there be light!' darkness covers the abyss of the caves of the soul's sense. The more unfathomable the sense and its caves, the more profound and blacker will its darkness be concerning the supernatural things when God, its light, does not illumine it.

The sense cannot possibly lift its eyes to the divine light or even think of doing so. For it knows not what this light is, since it has never seen it. Accordingly it is unable to desire this light. It would rather desire darkness for it knows what darkness is." But when God has given the soul the light of grace, the eyes of her spirit are enlightened and open up to the divine light. And just as previously one abyss of darkness called to another (Ps 42:7, 19:2) so now, one abyss of grace calls another, that is, for the transformation of the soul in God. Then the light of God will become one with that of the soul; the natural light of the soul unites itself with the supernatural light of God and now only the supernatural light is shining.

The sense of the soul was also blind because it was enjoying something other than God. The desire lay like a cataract or cloud on the eye of the intellect; it was blind to the grandeurs of the divine riches. The smallest thing that is placed directly in front of the eye is sufficient to obstruct the sight of other, more distant, objects. So, too, a slight desire is sufficient to make the grandeurs of the divine glory impossible to see. In such a condition "the eye of reason" sees only the small cloud, now this way, and soon in another color. It mistakes the cloud for God, because the cloud covers the faculty and God cannot be grasped by the senses.

Persons who have not freed themselves of all desire and inclinations should therefore be convinced that they make fallible judgments. That which is usual and insignificant but which satisfies the senses is taken to be something highly important; what is lofty and more precious to the spirit but has little attraction for the senses is considered to be of little value. In the sensory person, that is, one who lives totally with natural appetites and gratifications, even desires that originate in the spirit are reduced to the purely natural. Even when this soul desires God this desire is not always supernatural. It is so only when God infuses it and gives it strength.

Thus the sense of the soul with its appetites and affections was obscure and blind.[13] But now it is enlightened through the supernatural union with God, and more: it has itself, together with its faculties, become a resplendent light and can *with rarest beauty unite in gift for the Belov'd, warmth and light.* The caves of the faculties of the soul are flooded with the fullness of light from the divine lamps. They themselves now burn and send the splendors they have received with loving glory in God to God, just as glass reflects the splendor of the sun shining on it. Yet the soul reflects the divine light in a more excellent way because the will cooperates. This happens in a totally unique fullness, which is foreign to every common way of thinking and defies every attempt to express it in words. In the fullness in which the intellect, which is united with God's, receives divine wisdom, it radiates it back to God. And in the perfection with which the will is united to the divine goodness, the will returns God to God in him. For the soul receives only in order to give; she gives back to him all the light and all the warmth of love that the Beloved gives to her.

Through a substantial transformation, she has become a shadow of God, and thus "she does in God through God whatever he does in her through himself, and in the same manner in which he does it. . . . Just as . . . God gives himself with a free and gracious will, so her will, too (the more generously and freely, the more intimately it is united with God), gives to God in God, God himself. . . . She perceives here that God belongs to her perfectly, that as his adopted child she has entered into her inheritance with full rights of ownership. As her possession she can . . . give him to whomever she wishes, whenever she pleases. . . . And so she gives him to her Beloved . . . God himself . . . who has given himself to her. And she feels inexpressible delight and satisfaction from the perception that she gives God her possession and that it is suited to him according to his infinite being. . . . God is perfectly satisfied with this gift from the soul—less could not possibly suffice—and he accepts it gratefully as something she gives him of her own.

In this surrender to God the soul loves him in a new fashion, and he freely gives himself anew to the soul. . . . So, between God and the soul, a reciprocal love is actually founded similar to the union and surrender of marriage, in which through mutual voluntary surrender and union they possess together the goods of both, the divine essence. The soul's deep satisfaction and happiness come from seeing that she can give God more than her own worth and capacity, since she, in such generosity, gives God to himself as her possession. In the next life this is done by means of the light of glory, in this life through a highly illumined faith. So 'the caves of sense—profound abyss—with rarest beauty unite, in gift for the Beloved, warmth and light.'" Unite—for in the soul, the communication of the Father and the Son and the Holy Spirit is combined; for her they are light and fire of love.

The love between God and the soul is of entirely extraordinary perfection, as is the enjoyment that she finds in it, and the praise and gratitude she brings to God. "The soul here loves God, not through herself but through God; through the Holy Spirit, as the Father loves the Son." Furthermore, the soul loves God *in* God: "in this ardent union the soul is absorbed in the love of God and God gives himself to the soul in great ardor." Finally, "the soul here loves God for his own sake. She does not love him only because he is so generous, good, glorious, and so on, but with greater intensity she loves him because he is all this in himself essentially."

The *enjoyment* is so exalted because it is an enjoyment of God by means of God himself. For the soul's intellect is here united with the omnipotence, wisdom, and goodness of God; and although this union is not as clear as it will be in the next life, her delight in all these distinctly understood attributes is extremely great. Furthermore the soul delights now in God alone, without any interference from any creature. And she enjoys God only on account of who he himself is, without interference from any pleasure of her own.

Her *praise* is distinguished by the fact that she praises God as her duty, because she recognizes that God created her for his own praise. She praises him, furthermore, because of the goods of grace which she receives and because of the delight she experiences when praising him. But finally, she praises God for what he is in himself. "For, even though the soul were to experience no delight, she would still praise him for who he is."[14]

18
The Hidden Life of Love

4) The Hidden Life of Love

> How gently, filled with love,
> You awake in my inmost heart
> Where secretly you dwell, alone:
> With your breath so delicious,
> Replete with good and glory,
> How delicately you enamor me!

The soul speaks of a wonderful action of God that she notices in herself occasionally. She has in mind the picture of a person who is waking from sleep and takes a deep breath, for she really has a feeling that something of this kind is happening in her.

"God awakes in many ways in the soul. If we wished to enumerate them all we should never come to an end. But this awakening of the Son of God which the soul here indicates, is elevated above all else and full of benefit for her. It is a movement that calls forth the Word in the substance of the soul, containing such grandeur, dominion, glory, and intimate sweetness that it seems to the soul that all the balsams and fragrant spices and flowers of the world have been strewn about . . . as though all the kingdoms and dominions of the world and all the powers and virtues of heaven are moved . . . as though all the virtues and substances and perfections and graces of every created thing glow and unanimously make the same movement at the same time toward the same goal. . . . So when the great emperor within the soul wishes to assert himself, he who bears on his shoulders dominion over the three worldly spheres, and who . . . bears all things through the word of his power, it seems that everything moves in unison, as at the movement of the earth all material things to be found on it move as though they did not exist. . . . This comparison, however, is most inadequate, for here all things seem not only to move but to reveal the beauty of their being, power, loveliness, and graces, as well as the root of their existence and life.

The soul here sees how all creatures of the higher and the lower orders have their life, their power and their existence in him . . . but that the being of God in himself is infinitely eminent and above all these things so that she understands them better in God's being than in themselves. In this lies the remarkable delight of this awakening. The soul knows creatures through God and no longer God through creatures. . . . How this movement takes place in the soul is a wonderful thing since God is immovable. . . . For, although God does not really move, it seems to the soul that in truth he moves. Namely, in order to perceive that supernatural sight, since she is changed through God and is moved by him, divine life and the being and harmony of every creature, with their movements in God in that life, are revealed to her with such newness that it seems to her that God moves, and the cause assumes the name of the effect it produces". . . . So it is also the soul that is moved and awakened from the sleep of natural vision to supernatural vision.

"In my opinion this awakening and view given to the soul is effected in this way: since the soul, like every creature, is in God substantially, he removes some of the many veils and curtains hanging in front of it so that it might get a glimmer of him as he is. And then that countenance of his, full of graces, becomes partially and vaguely discernible, for not all the veils are removed. Because all things are moved by his power, what he is doing is also evident, so he seems to move in them and they in him with continual movement. That is why the soul has the impression that he moves and awakens when, actually, it is she who is moved and awakened. . . . And so human beings ascribe to God what is actually to be found in them. They who are lazy and sleepy say that God raises himself and wakes up, although he never sleeps. . . . But since in truth all good comes from God and human beings of themselves can do nothing good, it is according to truth that one says that our awakening is an awakening of God and our rising is God's rising. And since the soul was sunk in sleep out of which she could never by herself have awakened, and because only God could now have opened her eyes and effected this awakening, the soul very appropriately calls this an awakening of God. . . . What the soul experiences and feels in this awakening of God's excellence is entirely beyond words."

The glory of God imparts itself to the substance of the soul (she calls it her inmost *heart*) and reveals itself in immeasurable power, with the voice "of a multitude, of thousands upon thousands of the powers of God, which are infinite beyond counting. In their midst the soul remains immovable, terribly and solidly set in array in them like an army [Sg 6:4] and at the same time gentle and charming with all the attractions of created things."

That a soul, because of the weakness of the flesh, does not faint or become afraid at such a powerful and glorious awakening is due, first of all, to her being already in a state of perfection. The lower part is perfectly purified and in conformity with the spirit, so that it no longer feels any detriment or pain when it receives spiritual communications, as it did formerly. Further, God shows himself "gentle and full of love." He takes care that the soul will not be harmed, and fortifies what is natural while he unveils his grandeur to the spirit.

That is why the soul experiences in him as much gentleness and love as she does power and dominion and grandeur. The greater her delight, the more the protection in gentleness and love that the soul can endure the strong delight. The soul, then, rather than fainting, stands powerful and strong. The king of heaven shows himself to her as her equal and brother. He steps down from his throne, bends down to her, and embraces her. He clothes her with royal garments: with the wonderful virtues of God, surrounds her with the golden glow of love and has her adorned with the precious stones of knowledge of the higher and lower substances.[1] All of this occurs in her inmost region where he "secretly dwells alone." Of course, God dwells secretly and concealed in all souls— or they could not exist. "But in some he dwells alone, and in others, not alone. In the ones, with pleasure, in the others, with aversion. In some he dwells as in his own home, where he directs and rules everything, in others like a stranger who is not allowed to give orders or to do anything. The less a soul is encumbered by her own appetites and inclinations, the more he is alone and as in his own home in her, and the more alone, the more concealed does he remain there. In a soul that is free of all desires, disrobed of all forms, images, and creaturely inclinations, he lingers totally concealed and in the most intimate embrace." Neither the devil nor any human intellect can detect what happens there.

But for the soul herself, on this step of perfection, nothing remains secret, for "within herself she has the experience of this intimate embrace." But the difference between sleep and awakening is still there. Sometimes it is as though the Beloved remains resting within the soul, so that an exchange of love and knowledge is not possible, and then again, it is as though he awakens. Happy the soul that can ever feel vitally that God rests in her and finds refreshment in her! She must remain in immense tranquillity, so that no movement nor any noise disturb the Beloved. Were he always awake within her, communicating knowledge and love, she would already be in glory. In souls who have not yet reached the union of love, he is mostly concealed. They do not experience him ordinarily, except when he grants them some delightful awakening. But such an awakening is other than that in the state of perfection. Nor is everything as hidden from the devil and from the human intellect as in the case of union, for in these souls not everything is fully spiritual; there are still stirrings of sensuality in them. But in that awakening, which the Bridegroom himself causes in the perfect soul, everything is perfect because he is the cause of it all. The awakening and drawing of breath in the soul is then like that of a person who awakes and takes a deep breath: she breathes in the Holy Spirit.[2] "Therefore she says: With your breath so delightful, replete with good and glory, how delicately you enamor me!" "I do not desire to speak of this spiration, for I am aware of being incapable of doing so; and were I to try, it might seem less than it is. It is a spiration that God produces in the soul, in which, by that awakening of lofty knowledge of the Godhead, the Holy Spirit breathes in the soul. In the same proportion in which she is absorbed most profoundly in the Holy Spirit, she is roused in love with a divine exquisite quality and delicacy according to what she beholds in him. Since this breathing is filled with grace and glory, the Holy Spirit fills her with joy and happiness, and in love she is rapt out of herself and is drawn in an indescribable and incomprehensible way into the depth of God; and that is why I break off here."[3]

5) Originality of the *Living Flame of Love* in Comparison with the Older Writings

If the saint is compelled to silence by the feeling of his inability to write the inexpressible—how shall we dare to follow his words with a technical explanation? We would only like to thank him for allowing us to have a glimpse of a wonderful land, an earthly paradise at the threshold of the heavenly one. Still we must endeavor to bring what he has here disclosed to us into connection with the already known. Love for souls opened his lips: he wishes to encourage them on the hard way of the cross, the steep and narrow way, which ends upon such a luminous, blessed height.

This, briefly, expressed the inner connection between the *Living Flame of Love* and the two works that have the Way of the Cross itself as their object: *The Ascent* and *The Night*. An actual comparison of the cognitive content would be possible only if we had the lost or never written parts of the two former writings before us. But after all, one may say this much: after that which those two works seemed to foreshadow at several places, one has the impression that a new basis of experience is presented. The fundamental setting is the same: there is no other way to union than that which leads through the cross and night, the death of the old self. Nor can one strike out in afterthought what was frequently emphasized: that the author and interpreter of the *Night Song* had arrived at union. But the union seemed to be achieved *in* the night, indeed on the Cross. Only later, it seems, did the saint have the happy experience of just how wide heaven opens itself even in this life.

The external fortune of the last writing was also luckier than that of the former ones. This means not only that it was completed and preserved as a whole. *If* the others actually did remain incomplete— clearly we have always left this an open question—that may be the reason that their explanation was written subsequently and at a distance— not only with respect to time but also psychically—from the *Song-poem.* *The Ascent* and *the Night* are far more pedantic than the interpretation of the *Flame of Love.* The thinker (in the former ones) stands before the poem, the result of his original experience, almost as though before something foreign; in any case, as though before something actually inherited. And the zeal with which he endeavors to make the fundamental ideas and leading images clearly intelligible carries him off so much that in *The Ascent* his original intention to interpret the poem stanza by stanza and line by line is quickly dropped. In *The Night* it is realized rather late in the work. In *The Living Flame of Love,* in contrast, poem and interpretation are a single entity. That a certain amount of time lapsed between the composition of the one and then the other has not damaged the unity—on the contrary, John had hesitated to attempt the exposition because, as a task for the natural intellect, it seemed to him to be impossible. He decided to go ahead with it when the flame of love blazed up within him anew and flooded him with heavenly light. That which he had written earlier now opened to deeper levels of itself. And so the close connection to the course of thought in the four stanzas resulted effortlessly. The unity of thought was interrupted only at one point by a passionate argument with clumsy spiritual directors.[4]

That interpolation aside, from beginning to end, as poetical and mystical flight of the imagination, it is a perfect whole. A very special characteristic style developed as a result of the overflow of light. The saint had always lived out of the sacred Scriptures. Images and comparisons out of holy Scripture effortlessly suggested themselves everywhere, and he was glad to make use of them in order to confirm and fortify by the word of Scripture what his own experience had taught him. But here the harmony of personal experience with the revealed Word of God [5] and the events of sacred history is especially urgent.[6] One feels how, for the saint, the veils are raised and everything becomes transparent for the enlightenment of the mysterious commerce between God and the soul. What appears to the unenlightened gaze of the ordinary reader as mere external occurrence, St. John *reads* as though it self-evidently is an expression of a mystical happening. Only *one* example: Mordecai, who saved the life of King Ahasuerus, is for John an image of the soul who serves the Lord faithfully without receiving anything for doing so. But suddenly, "like Mordecai, once long ago, she is rewarded for her trouble and services. Not only may she enter the interior of the palace and appear in regal garments before the face of the king, but she receives the royal crown, the scepter and the throne of the king as well as the royal ring, and may do anything she likes and omit anything she does not like in the kingdom of her Bridegroom."[7]

19

The Bridal Song

B. The Soul's Bridal Song

1) The *Spiritual Canticle* as it Relates to the other Writings

Wherever John spoke of the union of the soul with God, words of the *Song of Songs* rose to his lips with great ease. But during the time in which his own soul was most severely shaken by all the pain and delight of love—in the months of imprisonment in Toledo—there the ancient bridal *Song* was born anew in his heart. It has been handed down in two versions, and the difference between them is significant for us.[1]

GESANG ZWISCHEN DER SEELE UND DEM BRÄUTIGAM	SONG BETWEEN THE SOUL AND THE BRIDEGROOM
1.	1.
Wo Du geheim wohl weilest, Geliebter, der zurückließ mich in Klagen? Dem Hirsch gleich Du enteilest, Da Wunden Du geschlagen Ich lief und rief, doch konnt' Dich nicht erjagen.	Where may you tarry in secret, Beloved, and leave me behind in keening? Like the stag you rushed away Since wounds you struck in me. I ran and called, but you I could not flush from hiding.

2.

Ihr Hirten, die ihr gehet
Durch Hürden hin dort auf des
    Berges Höhe,
Wenn ihr vielleicht ihn sehet,
Nach dem ich liebend spähe,
Sagt ihm, daß ich in Pein und
    Qual vergehe.

2.

You shepherds, since you go
Through sheepfolds up to
    mountain's height
If, of him, there, you should
    catch sight
Whom, lovingly, I seek with
    great resolve
Tell him that I in pain and
    anguish near dissolve.

3.

Mein Lieb will suchen gehen
Ich über Berge und in
    Flußrevieren
Die Blumen laß ich stehen,
Leid' Schrecken nicht von
    Tieren,
Will Starke und will Grenzen
    kühn passieren.
Frage an die Geschöpfe:

3.

Seeking my love, I will away
O'er mountains and where
    rivers lay,
I shall let flowers go untouched
And beasts will wake in me no
    fright
Nor might and bound'ries,
    keenly passed, deflect my way.
Question for the Creatures:

4.

Ihr Dickichte und Wälder,
Die unter des Geliebten Hand
    entsprangen,
Ihr frisch begrünten Felder,
Wo bunte Blumen prangen,
Sagt mir, ob er durch euch ist
    hingegangen.

Antwort der Geschöpfe:

4.

You thickets and forests,
Which sprang from the
    Beloved's Hands,
You fields fresh clothed in green
Where brilliant, all-hued
    flowers are on show,
Tell me, through you did his
    path go?
Answer of the Creatures:

5.

Ausstreuend tausend Gaben,
Sah'n wir ihn schnell durch
    diese Busche eilen,

5.

Scattering a thousand gifts,
We saw him hurry swiftly
    through these bushes,

Im Flug den Blick zu laben;
Sein Antlitz, sonder Weilen,
Ließ sie an seiner Schönheit
    haben.

His eyes did feast upon their
    sight, in flight,
His countenance, a'glance,
    close lingering
His beauty with them freely
    sharing

6.

Die Braut:
Ach, wer kann Heilung
    spenden?
O komm Du selbst, denn Dich
    nur möcht ich fragen
Wollst nicht mehr Boten senden:
Was sie für Nachricht tragen,
Die ich verlange, kann mir
    keiner sagen.

6.

The Bride:
Ah, who can give me healing?
Oh, come Yourself, for only You
    I'd ask!
No messengers, more, send my
    way
The tidings they should have to
    bring
For which I long, not one of
    them can say.

7.

Sie all', die von Dir sagen,
Die mir von tausend
Gnadenwundern sprechen,
Nur neue Wunden schlagen;
Es macht das Herz mir brechen
Ich weiß nicht was, wovon sie
    stammelnd sprechen.

7.

All they, who tell of you
Recount for me a thousand
    grace-filled wonders
But, wounding me anew,
They bring my heart to breaking
I-know-not-what it is of which
    they're speaking—this that
    they stammer, speaking.

8.

Wie harrst Du aus, o Leben,
Da, wo Du lebst, kein Leben zu
    erlangen?
Den Tod die Pfeile geben,
Die tief ins Herz dir drangen,
Durch das, was vom Geliebten
    Du empfangen?

8.

How is it that you persevere,
    O Life,
Since, where you live, no life's
    attained?
It's death the arrows give
Which deep into your heart are
    forced

By that which from th' Beloved
you gained.

9.

Willst Du nicht heilen kommen
Das Herz, das Du verwundet
    hast verlassen?
Da Du es mir genommen,
Wie kannst Du's liegen lassen
Und nicht den Raub den Du
    geraubt, nun fassen?

9.

Will you not come with healing
For the heart you left 'pon
    wounding.
Now that you've taken it away
    from me,
How can you let it lie,
And not take hold of plunder
    you have stolen.

10.

Niemand kann dazu taugen,
Als Du allein—O ende meine
    Peinen!
Auf Dich wend' meine Augen,
Du als ihr Licht mußt scheinen,
Ich wahre sie für Dich nur, für
    den Einen.

10.

No one can serve to quell
My pain, but you alone, oh,
    end it!
To you I turn my eyes
You, as their light, must shine
I keep them but for you, the one
    and only.

11.

O zeige Dich enthüllet
Und töte mich durch Deiner
    Schönheit Strahlen
Der Liebe Schmerzen stillet,
Denk' es in ihren Qualen
Sein Anblick nur der einzig sie
    erfüllet.

11.[2]

Oh show yourself unveiled
And slay me by your beauty's
    rays
Which soothes love's deep pain.
Remember this, that in her
    torment
The sight of him alone can fill
    her need.

11 (12).

O Du kristallne Quelle,
Daß jäh in Dir die Augen mir
    erstrahlten,

11 (12).

O spring of crystal clearness
If suddenly in you, those eyes
    shone on me

Im Antlitz silberhelle,
Die mich in Sehnsucht halten,
Die in die tiefste Seele mir
    sich malten!

From face in silvered brightness
Which 'prisoned keep me by
    desire,
Engraved in me in deepest soul
    your image.

II.

12 (13).

O wend' sie ab, Geliebter—
Ich bin im Fluge!
Der Bräutigam:
O Täublein, wend' die Flügel,
Der Hirsch läßt sich erblicken
Verwundet auf dem Hügel,
Das Wehen Deines Flugs soll
    ihn erquicken.

Die Braut:

12 (13).

Oh turn them away, Beloved,
I am in flight!
The Bridegroom:
Small dove, reverse your flight,
The stag appears to sight.
Wounded, he stands upon the
    hill
The breeze from your wings
    shall refresh him.
The Bride:

13 (14).

Du bist wie Berge, hehre,
Geliebter, und wie Waldtals
    Einsamkeiten,
Wie Inseln ferner Meere,
Wie rauschend Stromesgleiten,
Und säuselnd linder Lüfte
    Lieblichkeiten.

13 (14).

You are like mountains, lofty,
Beloved, and like wooded
    valleys' solitudes
Like islands set in distant seas
Like the rush of flowing streams
And whispers of soft airs'
    pleasantness.

14 (15).

Gleich stiller Nacht, der
    schönen,
Die schon das neue Morgenlicht
    durchdringet,
Musik mit leisen Tönen
Und Einsamkeit, die Klinget

14 (15).

Like tranquil night, the lovely
    night,
Already pierced by new morn's
    light
Music of softest tones
And solitude that rings,

Erquickend Nachtmahl, das die
Lieb' beschwinget.

The supper that refreshes, lends
love wings.

Tekst B.

15.

Text B.

15 (24).

Bride

Ein Blütenbett uns ladet,
Von Löwenhöhlen ist es rings
umgangen,
In Purpurglanz gebadet,
Von Frieden ganz umfangen,
Goldschilde tausend dran als
Zierde hangen

A bed of blooms invites us,
Encircled as it is with lions'
dens,
Bathed in a purple glow,
And encompassed completely
in peace,
By a thousand shields of gold
adorned.

16.

16 (25).

Folgend der Schritte Spuren
Des Liebsten eilen junge
Mägdelein;
Da Funken sie durchfuhren,
Sie stärkte würz'ger Wein,
Strömt Balsamduft von ihnen
himmlisch rein.

Following the trace of footprints
Of the Beloved, young maidens
hurry
Since sparks passed through
them in a flash
And spiced wine gave them
strength
Fragrance of divine balsam they
emitted.

17.

17 (26).

Im innern Kellerraum
Trank ich von dem Geliebten
und trat vor:
An weiten Feldes Saum
All Wissen ich verlor,
Fand auch die Herd' nicht, der
ich folgt' zuvor.

In the inner wine cellar
I drank of the Beloved, and
then stepped out:
At the bound'ry of spacious
fields.
Of knowledge, lo, I had no more
Nor found the flock I'd earlier
followed.

18.

Dort reicht' er mir die Brust,
Wollt mir sein süßes Wissen
  nicht verhehlen;
Ich gab mich ihm mit Lust,
Ließ auch an mir nichts fehlen,
Und dort versprach ich, ihm
  mich zu vermählen.

18 (27).

There he gave his breast to me,
Wished not to hide from me the
  sweetness of his knowledge.
I gave myself to him with ardor
Nor let any lack from me
  deprive him.
And it was there I pledged to
  be his bride.

19.

Ihm dient die Seele immer,
All meinen Reichtum hab' ich
  ihm verschrieben.
Die Herde hüt' ich nimmer,
Kein Amt ist mir geblieben
Nur *eines* üb' ich noch, und das
  ist Lieben.

19 (28).

My soul serves him at every
  hour,
All my riches I have consigned
  to him.
No longer do I tend the flock,
No office more belongs to me —
One thing alone I do and that is
  love.

Tekst J.

16.

Die Füchse fangt, die losen,
Des Weinbergs Reben schon in
  Blüte stehen,
Und während wir die Rosen
Zu dichtem Strauß uns drehen,
Laß niemand auf dem Hügel
  mehr mich sehen.

Jaen Text.

16.

Catch the foxes, the strays,
The vineyards' tendrils are
  blossom laden.
And while we with the roses
Wind for ourselves dense bouquets,
None shall let himself be seen
  upon the hill.

17.

Halt ein Nordwind! Dein
  Hauchen
Bringt Tod. O Südwind, komm
  du Liebe wekken,

17.

Desist, North Wind! Your
  breathing
Brings death. Oh, South Wind,
  come awaken love,

In Duft den Garten tauchen
Der Blumen, die sich recken,
Um den Geliebten lieblich zu
    bedecken.

Immerse the garden in the scent
Of flowers that stretch
To cover up the Beloved in
    loveliness.

18.

Nymphen, Judäas Sprossen,
Da Blumen wir und Rosen-
    büsche sehen
Von Ambraduft umflossen,
Bleibt ihr im Vorraum stehen,
Wagt nich zu uns'rer Schwelle
    herzugehen.

18.

You dryads, young offspring of
    Judea
Since we see flowers and
    rosebushes
And amber's perfume floods
    around us
Stand off—stay in the vestibule
Dare not approach so near our
    threshold.

19.

Verbirg Dich, ist mein Wille,
Geliebter! Schau zum Berge,
    der sich breitet.
Kein Laut durchbrech' die
    Stille!
Hab Acht, wer sie begleitet,
Die dort durch fremde
    Inselreiche schreitet.

19.

Hide yourself, that is my will,
Beloved! Look to the mount
    which spreads above
No sound break through the
    silence!
Behold who 'tis who accompanies
    her
As she walks through foreign
    island kingdoms.

Der Bräutigam:
20.

Ihr Vögel auf luft'gem Pfade,
Hirsch, Löwen, Gemsen, die im
    Sprung sich sputen;
Ihr Berge, Tal', Gestade,
Ihr Wasser, Winde, Gluten,

The Bridegroom:
20.

You birds on airy lanes
Stags, lions, chamois gamboling
You mountains, vales, and
    beaches,
You waters, winds, and fires,

Ängste der Nacht, die sorgend
    niemals ruhten.
	Fears of night which, worried,
	    never rested.

. . . .

Text B.

20.	20 (29).

Nicht auf dem Dorfplatz findet
Man mich, die sich zu zeigen
    nicht gesonnen,
Verloren ging ich, kündet;
In Liebesglut entronnen,
Ging ich verloren frei und ward
    gewonnen.
	No more on village square
	    you'll find me—
	Who with no mind to show
	    herself has said
	I have gone—been lost;
	Dissolved in incandescent love
	In freedom lost, and so was
	    found.

21.	21 (30).

Smaragden, Blumen glänzen,
Die wir im frischen Morgentau
    gefunden;
Wir flechten sie zu Kränzen,
Von dir mit Lieb' durchwunden,
Mit einem meiner Haare
    festgebunden.
	Emeralds and flowers glisten
	Which we have found, in
	    freshest morning dew
	We fashion crowns from them,
	    and you
	Weave love throughout their
	    span
	Which with one hair of mine is
	    bound.

22.	22 (31).

An jenem Haar, dem einen,
Das Du an meinem Hals sahst
    wehend hangen;
Am Halse sahst Du's scheinen,
Du hast Dich drin gefangen,
Eins meiner Augen weckte Dein
    Verlangen.
	And with that hair, that sole one,
	Which you saw hang aflutter at
	    my neck
	You saw it shine against my neck
	And with it tied yourself a
	    captive.
	One eye of mine awakened your
	    desire.

23.

Du hast mich angesehen,
Mit Gnadenreizen mich Dein
    Auge schmückte.
Davon ist es geschehen,
Daß ich Dein Herz berückte,
Anbetend, was in Dir mein Aug'
    entzückte.

23 (31).

You looked at me
And grace's charms your eye
    bestowed.
And so it was it happened
That I captivated your heart,
Adoring in you what enchants
    my eye.

24.

Du mögst mich nicht verachten,
Hast Du auch dunkelfarbig
    mich gefunden;
Wohl kannst Du mich betrachten,
Dein Blick ließ mich gesunden,
Mit Gnadenschönheit hast Du
    mich umwunden.

24 (32).

Don't let yourself despise me
Though you have found me
    dark of shade
You can well regard me,
Your glance made me recover
    health
And grace's beauty you've
    wound round me.

. . . .

21.

Bei holden Leiertönen,
Bei der Sirenen Sang laßt euch
    beschwören:
Laßt euern Zorn versöhnen,
Laßt an der Wand nichts hören,
Daß der Geliebten Schlaf nichts
    möge stören.

21.

By pleasant tones of lyres
By siren's *song*, give word on
    oath!
Let your anger be appeased
Let no sound strike the wall,
That the Beloved's sleep be not
    disturbed.

III.

22.

Die Braut ist eingegangen
In des ersehnten Gartens
    Lieblichkeiten,

22.

The Bride has entered
In the desired garden's loveliness.

Sie ruht nun nach Verlangen,	She rests now, as she'd craved.
Den Nacken läßt sie gleiten	Her neck she has let glide
Auf des Geliebten Arme, die	The Beloved's arms receive her,
sich breiten.	opened wide.

23.

In Apfelbaumes Schatten,
Da hab' ich Dich zu meiner
   Braut erkoren,
Reicht Dir die Hand des Gatten,
Erhob Dich, wo verloren
Die Ehre sie einst, Die Dich hat
   geboren.

23.

In the shade of the apple tree
There I chose you as my Bride
Gave you my hand as husband,
Exalted you, where lost
her honor, once, the one who
   bore you.

Tekst B.J.

Text B. and J.

Der Bräutigam:

The Bridegroom:

33 (34)

Schon hat die weiße Taube
Zur Arche mit dem Ölzweig
   sich gewandt,
Die kleine Türteltaube
Schon dem Gefährten fand,
Den sie ersehnt, am grünen
   Stromestand.

33 (34).

Already has the white dove
Turned to the ark, with branch
   of olive.
The little turtle dove
Already found her mate
For whom she'd longed, at
   stream's green bank.

34 (35).

Sie lebt in Einsamkeiten,
In Einsamkeit hat sie ihr Nest
gebaut,
Sie führt zu Einsamkeiten
Er, der ihr lieb und traut,
Den Lieb' entflammt, da er sie
   einsam schaut.

34 (35).

She dwells in solitude,
In solitude her nest she's built.
To solitudes she leads
Him, whom she loves and
   trusts.
In love he's 'flamed, since all
   alone he finds her.

Die Braut:
35 (36).

Laß Freude uns umwehen!
Daß wir in Deiner Schönheit
    schauen gingen.
Wo Berg und Hügel stehen,
Wo Wasser rein entspringen
Laß tiefer uns hinein ins Dickicht
    dringen.

36 (37).

Laß uns die Schritte lenken,
Wo schroff sich in den Felsen
    tief hinein
Verborgne Höhlen senken,
Da laß uns treten ein
Und kosten der Granaten jungen
    Wein.

37 (38).

Dort wirst Du dann mich lehren,
Wonach verlanget meiner Seele
    Streben,
Sogleich wirst Du gewähren
Mir dort, o Du mein Leben
Was Du mir schon an jenem Tag
    gegeben.

38 (39).

Des Lufthauchs lindes Leben,
Wenn süßer Nachtigallen Sang
    man höret,
Der Hain mit seinen Gaben

The Bride:
35 (36).

Let joy now ring around us!
Since in your beauty we have
    gone to see ourselves
Where mount and hill do stand,
Where waters, pure, from
    springs arise
Let us go deeper into thicket's
    hide.

36 (37).

Let us turn our steps
Where deep within steep cliffs
    concealed
From sight are spacious caves.
There let us enter,
Young wine from pomegranates
    we will taste.

37 (38).

There, then, you will teach me
That for which my soul's aim
    yearns
At once will you then give me,
You who are life for me, will
    grant
What you already gave me on
    that day.

38 (39).

The lightest whisper of the air,
When nightingale's sweet song
    one hears,
The sylvan glade with its
    donations

In heit'rer Nacht gewähret,	In night serene imparting
Die Flamme, welche ohne	The flame, which without pain
Schmerz verzehret.	's consuming.

39 (40).

Nie durft's ein Wesen sehen,	Ne'er being was dared see it,
Aminadab läßt auch sich nicht	Nor is Aminadab longer in
mehr blicken,	sight,
Belagerungsheer mußt gehen,	Beleaguering troops must vanish
Die Reiter talwärts rücken,	And cavalry retreat to valley
Dort unten die Gewässer zu	Down there the flood to view.
erblicken.	

This *Song* from the prison is of overwhelming richness in images and thoughts. In this way it is essentially different from the stanzas of the *Dark Night* and *The Living Flame of Love*. In them, we had, each time, a simple picture that dominated the whole: flight into the night; glowing embers out of which burst towering flames. Here, in the *Spiritual Canticle* of course, we also have a volume giving us a unified whole— we shall come back to this idea—but within it, a continuous change of images. There, simplicity and silence, here the soul and the whole of creation are in movement. This is not simply a difference in the literary style: the difference in style arose out of a deep-seated difference of the experience behind the writing. *Night* and *Flame of Love* alike give a cross-section of the mystical life at a determined moment of the process and, in fact, both at a point in which the soul has just left all created things behind and is now occupied only with God. Her relationship to the things of the world is dealt with only in retrospect.

The *Spiritual Canticle* gives the whole mysterious process again— not only in the interpretation but in the stanzas themselves—and is written by a soul that is most intensely gripped by the visible charms of creation. With wonderful images and enchanting sounds the world outside, the world from which he is cut off, invades the cell of the prisoner, who is a poet and sculptor, one susceptible to the magic of music. Of course he does not pause at the picture and sounds. They are for him mysterious hieroglyphics that express—and in which he himself is able to express—what transpires concealed in a soul. The hieroglyphics are truly *mysterious*. They contain such a fullness of meaning that it seems impossible to the saint himself to find the right words in order to explain all that the Holy Spirit sang within him "in inexpressible groanings." [3]

Because of the Holy Spirit, we have these stanzas; we owe them to him. They are "inspirations of love and secret knowledge." The Holy Spirit has loaned them to the soul in which he has taken up his dwelling, and even the one thus graced cannot fully describe and make comprehensible anything similar to them. For that reason the author declines from the very start to explain everything. He proposes only "to give some general explanations" and "to leave the whole realm of meaning" to the stanzas "so that each one may derive profit from them according to the mode and capacity of one's own spirit." He is confident that "the mystical wisdom . . . need not be understood distinctly . . . in order to cause love and enthusiasm in the soul"[4] And so the Spirit who has poured his love into a soul will unlock a way of access for other loving souls to express that love mysteriously. The saint wishes to place no obstacle to this wind of the Spirit when it blows through the soul.

That is why he declares that his own explanations are non-binding. When we have read the explanations we are honestly grateful for them; for the opposition between the poetic mystical bent of the *Song* and the entirely other style of the explanation are more deeply felt here than in the *Ascent* and the *Night*. In it we have the most extreme opposite to the *Living Flame of Love*, although both writings have a great affinity chronologically and according to content. Not only is this so because the thinker and teacher stands before the poem as before something factual that has been given and is almost strange. (At all events, this is due in part to the difference in time: the greater part of the stanzas were written in Toledo in 1578; the first draft of the explanations was written in Granada in 1584.)

Beyond that, one has the impression that besides the primary intention of revealing the meaning and doctrine of the image language of the poem, an additional consideration is operative here. Behind his spiritual sons and daughters for whom he wrote in the first place, there appears to be another audience popping up, one less well disposed and less receptive. We have had a suspicion urged upon us even in the effort to understand the *Ascent* and the *Dark Night* that in the important questions of the boundary between the truly mystical and that of the *ordinary* life of grace, the exposition is not entirely impartial. Rather, we surmise it was influenced by the thought of the Inquisition's watchful eye and the suspicion of Illuminism, which cropped up from the first against everything that was mystical.[5] The *Spiritual Canticle* seems to be even more heavily influenced by this consideration. And the reconstruction of the second redaction seems to be largely determined by it. This reconstruction did not limit itself only to the explanations but cut deep into the *Song* itself.

Here we would like to call attention first of all to four facts which apparently have an inner connection:

1. The second redaction contains a stanza [11] that was not on hand originally. (This stanza did, to be sure, pop up in some printed editions which were, in other respects, in line with the first version, but had apparently taken it from a manuscript of the second version.[6])

2. The second version divides the *Song* into three sections: I, II, III.

3. It makes a change in the order of the stanzas and so disrupts the original construction.

4. It interjects as an appendix to the *Song*, before the explanation to the first stanza begins, an *argumentum*, a short statement regarding the leading thought patterns. According to this statement, the stanzas treat the journey of a soul from the moment at which she began to dedicate herself to God until [she reaches] the highest stage of perfection, spiritual marriage. This is why the three stages, or ways, that lead to this goal are touched upon: the way of purification, the way of illumination, and the way to union; or the states of beginners, proficients (as far as spiritual betrothal),

and the perfect (the state of spiritual marriage). The final stanzas treat of the state of the saints toward which the perfect strive.

The inserted argument with its stress on the usual differences of the three ways corresponds to the later partitioning of the *Song* into three sections. (Looking back on the way that was traversed, an allusion to the three ways is interwoven at the beginning of the second version.)[7] The inserted stanza 11 expressed the longing of the soul for the unveiled sight of God, in eternal life. It prepares for the change in interpretation of the stanzas 36-39 (35-38). These stanzas, in the first version, refer unmistakably to the state of mystical marriage while in the second version, through a few changes and additions in the explanations, they become an anticipatory description of eternal life.

All this points to a uniform intention in the second redaction: depicting the mystical development of the soul as much as possible in a traditional and unsuspected form and to differentiate the highest step, mystical marriage, penetratingly from the perfection of the soul in eternal life. We will soon have to determine whether the rearrangement of the stanzas serves the same purpose. Even though the rewording of the first interpretation obviously happened in the attempt to move all that was suspicious or could have been misconstrued as such into the correct light, that concern seems to have been operative even in the first version. The saint also gave the customary declaration at the introduction to the *Ascent* and the *Living Flame of Love* that he submitted everything to the judgment of the church, and beyond that, he based his doctrine on sacred Scripture. But here all this happens with greater emphasis. At the end of the prologue[8] he assures us that he does not intend to affirm anything of himself or in simple trust in his own experience or in whatever he learned from insight into other souls; much more, he plans to confirm and explain everything through passages of sacred Scripture, at least everything that was the more difficult to understand.

As a matter of fact, the Scripture quotations in *The Spiritual Canticle* are not in every case as spontaneous as in the *Living Flame of Love*, especially the numerous parallel passages out of the *Song of*

Songs. Often they give the impression of presenting evidence that certain expressions he ventured to make were based on the linguistic usage in the sacred Scriptures and were being used in the same sense as those in Scripture. In the long run, perhaps, the undeniable difference between the poem and its interpretation is made somewhat comprehensible through this external purpose, even though other circumstances also contributed. It has already been pointed out that through the fullness and variety of its images, this poem differs from the others that were explained in writing.

Now the interpretations are almost like a dictionary of the language of the images. In a certain sense this is suggested through the character of many of the images. The images and what they portray are not the same as far as their origin goes, contrary to a symbol in the proper and strictest sense of the term, for example, the symbol of night or flame. There is a certain similarity between the image and that which it designates and therefore there is an objective foundation for the sign's function. But this foundation is not sufficient to understand the meaning of the images without adding something.

Their language must be learned and, besides, it appears in the choice of its expressions to be far more arbitrary than any natural language of words, even though not as arbitrary as an artificial language or a system of symbols deliberately chosen according to one's opinion. From this freedom of choice and the loosely relevant connections it follows that the images do not have one meaning but allow for various interpretations. And turned around, that which they indicate can also be described in other ways because they are not inevitable expressions. All these traits add up to a description of that which we call an *allegory*. It was in vogue at the time, a distinguishing mark of baroque poetry. John was very familiar with the poetic artistry of his time and had allowed himself to be formed by it. Thus the application of this artistic medium was already naturally easy for him and he handled it in his poetry with mastery.[9] But when, in the interpretation, he lines up definition upon definition and sometime gives several totally different expressions for a single image—for example, in the second Stanza, the *shepherds* are interpreted as either the desires and inclinations of the soul or as angels—

then there is more than allegory in itself demands. This impairs the impression made by the poem through a dissolution of its unity into a fullness of details and underlining what is unusual and arbitrary about the images. Is there also behind this heaping up of explanations an intention of forestalling questionable and dangerous interpretations? The heart of the poet must sometimes have revolted against the procedure of the interpreter. His assurance that through his own interpretations he had no intention of inhibiting the breathing of the Spirit in the soul of the reader may, at all events, be taken as a request that one concentrate above all on the poem itself.

2) The Principal Progression of Thought in the Saint's Interpretation
When we allow the *Song* in its first version to have an impartial effect on us, it seems to us a faithful expression of the whole *mystical way.* We emphasize "mystical" because the saint himself says, in the already mentioned retrospect on Stanza 27 (22),[10] that the first five stanzas are devoted to the beginnings of the spiritual life, the time, in which the soul practices meditation and mortification; only with the sixth stanza, as the second version [Canticle B] directs, does a description of the contemplative life begin. But we already hear the cry of longing with which the *Song* begins: *A donde te escondiste?* (Where have you hidden yourself?), the plaint of a soul wounded in the depth of her heart by the love of God. She knows her Lord, and surely not only "from hearsay," but has personally met him, has experienced his touch in her inmost region. Her pain is the pain of the lover who was allowed to taste the happiness caused by her Beloved's presence and must now do without it. He has left her behind, moaning and sighing; "for the absence of her Beloved causes continual moaning in the lover ... especially when the soul, after the taste of some sweet and delightful communication of the Bridegroom, suffers his absence and is left alone and dry."[11]

Must we not think of high mystical graces when there is talk of "burning touches of love" "which pierce and wound the soul like fiery arrows, leaving her wholly cauterized by the fire of love?" The will is so inflamed that it seems to the soul "that it is consumed in that flame, and the fire makes it go out of itself, wholly renews it . . . as in the case of the Phoenix that is burned up in the fire and is born anew."[12]

Once more we recognize in this portrayal the union of love that according to the description of our holy Mother Teresa and of Father John himself prepares for the mystical betrothal and marriage. [13] This is a totally new condition for the soul that she herself does not yet understand. Therefore she seeks the one who has escaped by looking at creatures, but she finds no satisfaction in them. That clearly distinguishes her from those beginners in the spiritual life who find joy in the usual practices of piety because they have not yet entered the night of contemplation. The soul whom God has touched interiorly can no longer find rest in anything that is not God. "No medicine can be gotten for these wounds of love except from the One who causes them." That is why the wounded soul hurries outside and calls after the Beloved. "This departure . . . refers to a departure from all things . . . and the departure from oneself through self-forgetfulness and loving God."[14] The soul now can do nothing but love God and is consumed with longing to see him. And the Lord cannot resist this yearning for long. The love that he has enkindled moves him to show new unheard of signs of his love. He appears suddenly and raises the soul in sudden flight up to himself.[15]

This description of spiritual betrothal that, because of the torment she feels in these rapturous visits, draws her away from all the natural demands of her being, corresponds absolutely with what we found described by our holy Mother in the sixth dwelling place of the Interior Castle. Weak nature fears total dissolution and so she cries out "O turn them away, Beloved!" (those divine eyes she had so longed for). But this request is not made seriously. The soul is much more desirous of being freed from the bonds of this life in order to be capable of bearing the bliss of his nearness. But it is not yet time for all this. The *Vuélvete, paloma* ("Small dove, reverse your flight.") calls her back into her earthly existence. She must be satisfied temporarily with what can be given here. And that is superabundant.

Now the play of love begins between the divine Lover and the beloved soul. She no longer has need of creatures in order to find a way to the Beloved by means of them. He is looking for her himself and, time and again, he shows her more and more of his beauty. Still, all the charms of creatures must serve her now in order to sing the praise of the divine beauty. In her union with the heavenly Bridegroom she will be overwhelmed with gifts, adorned with wonderful charms and powers, totally immersed in love and peace. Because she experiences the life of God, she rejoices at the fire of love that he enkindles in other souls. She herself is now led internally into the "innermost wine cellar," the most hidden sanctuary of love where God communicates himself to her and transforms her into himself. Totally filled by the overpowering bliss of this new, divine life she forgets all the things of this world; all desire for them disappears. And as the Beloved surrounds her with incomparable tenderness, so she also gives herself unreservedly to him; she lives only for him and is dead to the world. In this loving union all the virtues blossom. The soul happily recognizes the heavenly beauty with which she herself is now adorned. But she knows that all of this wealth has been summoned by God's gracious glance and she wishes to use it for no other purpose than to give pleasure to the Giver himself. All disturbances are to remain far from the blissful life of love. The Lord himself takes care that everything that could stand in the way of a lasting union vanishes. And so he is able to lead her into the longed-for garden where she may remain with him in totally undisturbed rest. In deepest union, he will introduce her to the hidden secrets of his Wisdom, and let her be enkindled in the flames of love. And no created being will obtain a glimpse of that which God has prepared for the soul whom he keeps safe in himself forever.

This—in a brief overview—is how we believe we may understand the original development of the Canticle as an ascent from one step of the union of love to others, or as being drawn inward to an ever deeper level. First there is a fleeting encounter, then—after the yearning and pain of searching—a being drawn up into the most intimate bond, a time of preparation for the continuing entrance into this bond, and finally, the imperturbable peace of marriage. One can then hardly speak of a partitioning into three ways or stages of purification, enlightenment, and union. Rather, there are three effects that are connected with one another in the whole of the life of grace and on the whole mystical path,[16] even though at the various stages one or other is more prominent. In the description of the *Spiritual Canticle*, union is at the beginning and end and rules the whole. Purification is mentioned most of all at the transition from betrothal to marriage. Enlightenment is in step with union.

In the arrangement of the stanzas in the first redaction, it is to be noticed that the transition from betrothal to marriage is flowing and begins at an early stage. In Stanza 15 (24) the whole intimacy of union has been reached. In contrast to marriage, there is but this difference, that disturbances are still possible, which must disappear so that the union can become lasting. Through a rearrangement of the stanzas in the second redaction the boundary is more distinct. The exclusion of all disturbance is preliminary, the description of full union follows it, beginning with the entrance into the longed-for garden (Stanza 22). This is an essential advantage of the second redaction and makes up for the small blemish, namely, that after the marvelous 15th stanza with its magic of the night, there follows immediately the reference to the "foxes in the vineyard."

It is easily understood that when the stanzas were written down the first time, the sequence was not at once the most pertinent. After all, the stanzas did not come into being all at one time; and those which originated from the time of imprisonment had, in any case, accumulated, bit by bit, following upon the inner experiences. As was mentioned earlier, statements of various witnesses exist on the question of whether the poem could actually have been written down in the prison or only after the escape. The former is probable, but does not exclude the possibility that the prisoner had to conserve his *Song*s for a longer time in his heart, before he obtained writing materials. Perhaps he sang first one verse, then another, to himself, as they fit his mood. And, as soon as it was possible, he put them on paper without assessing the best sequence of stanzas as carefully as it was then done in the final redaction. These considerations make it seem advisable, after carefully weighing the thought content and the artistic form, to follow the second version.[17] We will not lose sight of what we learned was intended by the second redaction and so shall evaluate the original meaning of the stanzas accordingly.

3) The Dominant Image and its Meaning for the Value of the *Song*

The first synopsis was intended only to discover the meaning of the whole. It could give only a slight indication of the abundance of individual features. If one wishes to attempt that, one must seek to penetrate the metaphorical language of the poem. To do that the saint's *vocabulary* is the accepted guide, though one need not follow it slavishly.

The basic mood of the *Song* is marked by the tension experienced by the loving soul between painful desire and blissful discovery. This basic mood has found expression in the image which at the same time rules the whole, not considering the abundance of individual images which are included and subordinated in it: the image of the bride who longs for the beloved, who rouses herself to seek him and finally blissfully finds him. This is nothing new for us. In the *Night Song* the bride, after all, leaves her house in order to hurry to the beloved. In the *Flame of Love*, also, she turns to the Bridegroom.

But there the bridal relationship stands not at center stage, it is rather a background which is taken for granted. Here in the *Canticle*, it is the focal point for everything. This image is not an allegory. When the soul is called the Bride of God, there is not only a relationship of similarity between two things which permits one to be designated by the other. There is, much more, such an intimate union between the image and the reality that it is almost impossible to speak of them any longer as a duality. Turned around: the meaning of the expression, being engaged [to be married] has nowhere as fitting and perfect a fulfillment as in the love relationship of God with the soul. That is the hallmark of a symbol-relationship in the strict and actual sense. The relationship of the soul to God as God foresaw it from all eternity as the goal of her creation, simply cannot be more fittingly designated than as a nuptial bond. Once one has grasped that, then the image and the reality directly exchange their roles: the divine bridal relationship is recognized as the original and actual bridal relationship and all human nuptial relationships appear as imperfect copies of this archetype—

just as the Fatherhood of God is the archetype of all fatherhood on earth. By reason of this copy-relationship, the human bridal relationship becomes useful as a symbolic expression of the divine, and in view of this function that which is a purely human relationship in actual life takes second place. Its actual reality has its highest reason for existence in that it can give expression to a divine mystery.[18]

20

The Bridal Symbol

4) The Bridal Symbol and the Specific Images

What relationship has this principal image, the bridal image, to the colorful, manifold, allegorical representations? In order to answer this question we must return to one asked earlier: are these images to be considered as arbitrary poetic expressions or as inspirations of the Holy Spirit? This question was put to the saint himself by Sister Magdalen of the Holy Spirit. She writes in her testimony that John had left the copybook, containing the poems written in prison, in Beas, and she was given the task of making some copies. She was full of amazement at the liveliness of the language, the beauty and fine exactitude of the expressions. So, one day, she asked the poet whether God had inspired those words that contained so much in themselves and were such a treasure. He answered: "My daughter, God gave me some of them, and at other times, I sought them."[1]

We can glean the same information from the work itself. In the preface we are told with emphasis that the stanzas are inspired by the Spirit of Love for which reason it will be impossible to find the right words with which to explain them. This obviously points to the difficulty of the subsequent explanation of their meaning. The poetic expression and its contents seem to have been received from the Holy Spirit simultaneously. However, it is soon impressed on us that even when the expression seems to be immediately clear, it is not possible to impart adequately what the Spirit of God allowed the soul to feel and understand interiorly. For that reason, the explanation resorts to images and comparison in order to indicate some of that content. Therefore, it will be necessary to distinguish in the experience of the mystic what is purely spiritual and interior from the linguistic expression. And yet this formless and unmethodical abundance of the spirit will never permit itself to be fully captured in words.

The grasping for images and parables can indicate a specific searching for an apt expression. But it can also be the apprehension of what is being offered by the Holy Spirit. If John points to images from holy Scripture, which frequently sound strange and are open to misinterpretation, we are entitled to think of supernatural help even in the choice of linguistic expressions. Indeed, the concept of *inspiration* is not to be taken to mean that not only what the sacred authors say but all their images and words as well must be attributed to divine inspiration. In many instances, however, it is obvious that the external word is to be understood as the Word of God in a literal sense. This, in some instances, was the case with John of the Cross, as he himself stated. But even when he himself sought for the expression, the assistance of the Holy Spirit cannot be excluded.

The liveliness of his artistic power of imagination, stimulated through the unnatural deprivation of all that could satisfy the external senses, could conjure up an abundance of splendidly colored images before his soul. But when these images harmonize with what he experiences interiorly, this is no longer to be attributed to the imaginative power or deliberate interpretation: he *finds* in the images those expressions for the unspeakable realities that he sought. The Holy Spirit unlocks for him the spiritual meaning of the colorful sensory abundance and guides him in his selection. This is how the unity of the whole is to be understood as well as the power of conviction possessed by the images. Of course, this does not hold for all of them. Certainly, some were chosen in a purely natural way and in the awkward sense of the word, far-fetched. Perhaps that is the case even more frequently for the subsequent explanations than for the images.

The world into which the *Song* leads us is the world as it is described to herself by the soul who is filled with desire and inebriated by love. She only goes out in order to find the Beloved. Everywhere, she tries painstakingly to discover traces of him. Everything reminds her of him and has significance for her only insofar as it gives her news of him or can bring him messages from her.

Just as a stag fleetingly appears at the edge of a wood and swiftly vanishes as soon as a human eye perceives him, so did the Lord act in their first encounters. He showed himself to the soul, but he escaped before she could take hold of him. The crystal clear spring that refreshes the lost seeker is for her, faith. Pure is the truth it gives, unclouded by error, and from it streams, toward her, the water of life that bubbles on to eternal life (Jn.4:14). With longing she bends over it: could not the eyes of the Beloved beam at her from this clear mirror? His eyes—these are the divine rays that touched her in her inmost depths, enlightening and inflaming her. She feels his eyes always on her: that is how they have been impressed in the deepest part of her being. All this is clearly understandable in a general way. Over and above this, however, the description tells us that the articles of faith, which portray for us the divine truths (rays) in veiled and imperfect fashion, are the *face*; this face is to be called "silvered-over" because the pure gold of truth is offered to us covered by the silver of faith.[2] We can no longer follow the portrayal or find a connection, anymore, with the principal symbol. We are faced here with a purely rational, artificial interpretation that we can accept on the authority of the poet and commentator—or again, reject, since he has given us that liberty.

What the soul has long desired and begged for happens. Suddenly and unexpectedly the searcher meets the gaze of the divine eyes. Her passionate desire has moved the Beloved "to visit her sublimely, delicately, and intimately and with mighty force of love."[3] He has appeared anew, like the stag—on the hilltop, that is, on the watch-tower of contemplation. He allows only a glimpse of himself since "however sublime may be the knowledge God gives the soul in this life, it is but like a glimpse of him from a great distance."

And, also, he is wounded. "Among lovers, the wound of one is a wound for both, and the two have one and the same feeling."

The breeze of her flight brings him refreshment. He calls her *"Dove"* because she ascends in the high and easy flight of contemplation, and because she has simplicity of heart and is consumed by love. This breeze of her flight is the spirit of love, which she exhales in this exalted contemplation and sublime knowledge of God, just as the Father and Son breathe out the Holy Spirit.

Flight, we are to understand, is the infused knowledge of God; the *breeze of the flight*, however, is the love that it engenders. And it is this love that attracts the Bridegroom and refreshes him by the cool waters of its spring. "As a breeze cools and refreshes a person worn out by the heat, so this breeze of love refreshes and renews the one burning with the fire of love. For in the lover, love is a flame that burns with a desire to burn more." And because the love of the Bride fans the flame, it is a refreshing breeze.[4]

Since the soul now enjoys the presence of the Beloved, her cries of desire end; she begins, much more, to praise the grandeurs she experiences in this union with him. For in the flight of the spirit, as we have seen, the betrothal with the Son of God takes place. Here "God communicates to the soul great things about himself, beautifies her with grandeur and majesty, adorns her with gifts and virtues, and clothes her with the knowledge and glory of God, just as a betrothed is clothed on the day of her betrothal."[5]

She enters a "state of peace and delight and gentleness of love" and no longer knows how to do anything but: "count up and tell in *Song* her Beloved's grandeurs." She experiences in the ecstasies of love what St Francis wished to say with the words: "My God and my all."[6] God is now all things to the soul, the good of all spirits, and so she finds in creatures an image of his perfections. Each of these sublime attributes is God and all of them together are God. "And since the soul in this ecstasy is united with God, she has the feeling that all things are God" as St. John experienced when he said, "That which was made, in him was life."[7] This does not mean that the soul sees creatures by means of God "comparable to seeing things by light, but rather says only that in this possession of God, the soul has the feeling that all things are God." This, again, is not a clear and essential vision of God. To be sure, it is "a strong and overflowing communication," but only a "glimpse of what God is in himself."[8] Through this weak glimpse the perfections of creature are unveiled for the soul.

The mountains with their soaring heights and the loveliness of their fragrant flowers have something of the sublimity and beauty of the Beloved. In his peace, the soul rests as in a cool and quiet, lonely, wooded valley. In the knowledge of God a wonderful new world opens for her—like that which a mariner finds among strange islands. Like a river that overflows and sets all things under water, fills all depths, and with its thunder drowns out all other sound, the torrent of God's spirit seizes the soul mightily and so overpowers her that it seems that all the rivers of the world have flooded in upon her." But this causes her no suffering, for they are rivers of peace, and their inundation "fills her totally with peace and glory." With its waters, it fills the low places of her humility and the voids of her appetites, and in the rushing of the torrents she perceives "a spiritual voice that ... prevails against all other cries and exceeds all the sounds of the world . . . It is like an immense interior clamor and sound that clothes the soul in power and strength" just as occurred when the Holy Spirit descended upon the apostles. The mighty wind that the inhabitants of Jerusalem heard was but an indication of what the apostles experienced interiorly. This spiritual voice, despite its strength is delightful to hear. St. John heard it "like the voice of many waters and like the voice of a great thunder," and yet it was as gentle "as the sound of harpists playing on their harps" (Rv. 14:2).[9]

When soft breezes play, whistling against the cheek, it is like the delightful way the attributes and graces of the Beloved are infused in the soul: "a most sublime and delightful knowledge of God and his attributes, which overflows into the intellect from the touch produced in the substance of the soul by these attributes of God.

As the feeling of a breeze delights the sense of touch, and the whistling is perceived by the sense of hearing so is the feeling of the Beloved's attributes felt and enjoyed by the soul's power of touch, which is in its substance (mediated by the will); and the knowledge of these attributes is experienced in its hearing, which is the intellect." This communication is most pleasant and beneficial. "As the whistling of the breeze pierces deeply into the hearing organ, so this most subtle and delicate knowledge penetrates with wonderful savoriness into the innermost part of the substance of the soul, and the delight is greater than all

others . . . because the substance, understood and stripped of acci-
dents and phantasms, is bestowed on the soul." "This divine *whistling*
that enters through the soul's hearing is not only substantial knowledge, but rather an unveiling of truths about the divinity and a revelation of divine secrets. . . .

As often as a communication of God is mentioned in Sacred Scripture . . . as being received by hearing, one may usually assume . . . it is
a revelation of the naked truths to the intellect. These are pure spiritual revelations or visions that are given only to the spirit without the
service and help of the senses. For this reason the communications of
God . . . by means of the hearing . . . are very lofty and certain."

So one assumes that our father, St. Elijah, saw God "in the gentle
breeze (1 Kg. 19:12) and Paul also, when he "heard secret words that
people are not permitted to utter" (2 Cor.12:4). For the "hearing of the
soul is the vision of the intellect." Of course, it is not a perfect and
clear vision of God as in heaven, but is still a "ray of darkness."[10]

Because the soul receives such dark and unfathomable knowledge
and enjoys such refreshing rest in the bosom of the Beloved, she compares this knowledge to a tranquil night; but a night that is already
illumined by the light of dawn, because it is "a tranquillity and quietude in divine light, in the new knowledge of God, in which the spirit
. . . tastes the sweetest rest." It finds itself "quieted and put to rest in
God," then "is elevated from the darkness of natural knowledge to the
morning light of the supernatural knowledge of God. . . . When this
morning light breaks there is neither entirely night or entirely day, it is
much more . . . a twilight."[11]

In the tranquillity and silence of this illumined night "the soul is permitted to become aware of the wonderful harmony and sequence of divine
Wisdom in the variety of her creatures and works. Each of them and
all together they have a certain relationship with God. And every single
creature raises its voice in its own way to express how much God is in
it, so that it is for the soul a harmonious symphony of sublime music
surpassing by far all the serenades and melodies of the world." But it
is silent music since this peaceful and quiet knowledge is shared without the sound of words and "one enjoys in it the sweetness of music and

the quietude of silence."[12] This sonorous music is heard only in solitude and estrangement from all exterior things. That is why the solitude itself is called "sounding".

As the vision of God is the food of the angels and saints, so the tranquil knowledge of the peaceful night refreshes the soul as a supper. She enjoys it with the happy feeling that all the cares and sufferings of the day are past. The Beloved himself "takes supper with her" (Rev. 3:20). He gives her a share in the enjoyment of all his goods, and refreshes her and, in being bounteous, he deepens love in her.

Adorned by the virtues that God's overflowing mercy has lent her, the Bride appears to herself as a garden full of fragrant flowers or a blossoming vineyard. She feels the presence of the Beloved in her heart as though in his own bed. She offers herself together with all her wealth of flowers in order to give him the highest service, and to please him, and to ward off every disturbance. But the sensory appetites, which have been pretending to be asleep, suddenly burst forth, goaded by the evil spirits, to disturb the peaceful floral kingdom of the soul. The devil "considers it worth more to himself to hinder a small fraction of this soul's rich and glorious delight, than to make many others fall into numerous serious sins. The others namely have little or nothing to lose, but this soul has very much to lose because of all her precious gain."[13]

So the evil spirits stir the appetites to violent excitement in an effort to confuse the soul. If they are unsuccessful, they assail her with bodily torments and noises in order to distract her. But the suffering becomes frightful when they vigorously attack her with spiritual terrors and horrors. "If permission is given them they can do this very easily, for since the soul at this time enters into great nakedness of spirit for the sake of spiritual exercise, the devil can easily show himself to her because he also is spirit. At other times he attacks her with different horrors . . . and, in fact, just when God is beginning to withdraw her from the house of the senses in order that she ... might enter the garden of the Bridegroom. The devil knows that once the soul has entered into that recollection, she is so fortified that however much he may try he cannot do her harm. Frequently when he goes out to block the soul, she recollects herself very quickly in her deep interior hiding place where she finds intense delight and protection. Then the terrors she suffers seem so exterior and far away that the devils not only fail to frighten her but cause her happiness and joy."[14] If, however, she does become disturbed, she then begs the angels to "catch the foxes" for it is their task to scare away the evil spirits.

When all parasites have been removed, the soul can enjoy, in union with the beloved, all the flowers of the virtues that open under his gaze and emit their fragrances. She binds them into a bouquet "and offers each of them and all together with delightful acts of love to the Beloved. But she needs his help to do this; without his favor and help she would not be able to form a bouquet. Together they fashion the bouquet to resemble a pine cone, in which all the pieces are firmly fastened forming one perfect whole. So, too, is the perfection of the soul; it embodies a fullness of perfect and strong virtues incorporated in orderly fashion. While the bride is forming this bouquet through the practice of the virtues no one should appear on the *hill* to disturb her, that is, no particular knowledge or remembrances should come forward in any of the soul's faculties so she will not be diverted from her loving lingering with God.

But there is something else that can trouble her happiness. In the time of betrothal the Beloved is not yet continually united to her. And since her love is very intense and intimate, it is intense torment for her when he draws back. For this reason she fears dryness like the cold north wind, which kills all blossoms. She takes refuge in prayer and spiritual exercises in order to master her dryness. But at the high level of the spiritual life that she has attained, all communications of the spiritual life are so interior that they cannot be achieved through any activity of her own faculties. Therefore she calls upon the moist, warm south wind for help, for in it the flowers will open and give off their fragrance. This is the Holy Spirit "who awakens love in her." When he takes hold of her "he wholly enkindles and refreshes her, quickens and awakens the will and the appetites . . . to the love of God." She begs him to blow *through* her garden, not *into* her garden. "For there is a considerable difference between God's breathing *into* the soul and his breathing *through* the soul. Breathing into the soul means the infusion of grace, the gifts and virtues; to breathe through the soul, however, is a touch and activity of God by which the virtues and perfections that have already been given are renewed and put in motion, so that a wonderfully sweet fragrance is spread abroad.

It is just as when one shakes aromatic things," they then give forth a "fullness of fragrance as never before." So the soul does not always have actual experience and enjoyment of her virtues. In this life, they are much more like flowers that are still budding or like spices that are covered over. But sometimes, when the divine spirit breathes through the garden of the soul, he opens all the buds of the virtues and uncovers the spices of the gifts, perfections and riches of the soul. "So by disclosing her interior treasure and wealth, he reveals all the beauty of the soul." The fragrance of these blossoms of virtue is at times so abundant in the soul that she is wholly clothed with delight and bathed in inestimable glory. Some of it also has a habit of "spreading outside her, so that persons capable of recognizing it are aware of her experience. To them such a soul appears to be a pleasant garden filled with the delights and riches of God.

And even when the blossoms are not open . . . such holy souls have a certain mysterious greatness and dignity about them that causes awe and respect in others." In the breathing of the Holy Spirit, the Son of God communicates himself to the soul in a lofty manner. He it is who more than all others finds delight in her fully opened and fragrant adornment of flowers. She longs for this in order to delight him. He has nurtured her and transformed her into himself, and so, now, she is "ripened, prepared and seasoned with the flowers of virtues, gifts and perfections." At their fragrance and sweetness the lovers both rejoice. "For this is characteristic of the Bridegroom: to unite himself with the soul amid the fragrance of these flowers." [15]

In the midst of this happiness, the soul suffers because she still lacks full mastery over her lower faculties. There are still movements of the senses and appetites that impede the life of grace. The soul turns toward these lower movements and begs them not to overstep their boundaries. She calls them *nymphs* because by flattery and importunate demands they wish to seduce the will. She gives the name *Judea* to her sensory part "since by nature, it is weak, carnal, and blind like the Judean people."[16]

While the rose bushes of the higher faculties bring forth blossoms of virtue and give off the amber fragrance of the Holy Spirit, those nymphs are to remain in the *antechamber* or the *outskirts* of the inner senses and not touch the threshold of the inmost region, that is, the first movements of the higher part of the soul. (At this stage, it appears that not only its meaning but this stanza itself is artificial and influenced far too much by the popular taste of that time. The following stanza clearly fits once again into the frame of the whole.)

The longing of the soul is concentrated on seeing God face to face. In her inmost region she has found him and she would like to remain hidden with him there. When he reveals to her in the secret chamber of her heart the glory of his divinity, nothing of that should penetrate to the outside so that no disturbance will come from there. The soul knows that the weakness of her sensory nature would succumb under the sublimity of what occurs on the *mountains* and that would hinder the spirit from seeing the face of God. So, totally free from all the burdens of the body, she would wish to experience the touch of the divine being in her inmost depth, and to enjoy the wonderful jewelry with which he himself has adorned her: a knowledge of his divinity that greatly exceeds the ordinary ways of knowledge.

But the Bridegroom himself also longs for the marriage. He wishes to lend the Bride the singular fortitude of soul, purity, and sublime love she will need in order to bear the strong and intimate embrace of God. He produces perfect harmony in her soul. All useless wanderings of the phantasy, all the powerful demands of the passions, and all hesitant timidity find an end. All the mountains and valleys are leveled: all that is excessive and all that is less than adequate. The waters of affliction must depart, the winds of hope become silent, the fire of joy may no longer inflame the Bride; all horrors conjured up by the evil enemy to spread darkness in the soul and to darken the divine light are banished. So the Bride is able to rest totally undisturbed in the arms of the Beloved. She has reached such grandeur of spirit and stability that nothing can shake her any longer.

Although she possesses the most sensitive feeling about her own or others' sins, they no longer cause her sorrow. For in this state the soul has lost everything "that involves weakness in her practice of the virtues. Only what is strength, constancy and perfection in these virtues remains. For the soul in this transformation of love resembles the angels who judge perfectly the things that give sorrow without themselves feeling sorrow, and who exercise the works of mercy without any feeling of compassion."[17]

If the Lord permits the soul to feel things and suffer from them, it is so that she might gain more merit; such experience has nothing to do with mystical marriage. Her hope, too, inasmuch as possible in this life, is fully satisfied through the union with God. She expects nothing more from this world.

"Her joy is ordinarily so great that she resembles a sea; it neither decreases by the outflow of waters nor increases by the inflow." True, she may be granted accidental joys numerous times but "they add nothing to the substantial spiritual communication. She already possesses everything that could come to her anew. . . . Here, in some way, she seems to share in a divine attribute. For although God finds delight in all things, he does not delight in them as much as he does in himself, for he possesses within himself a good eminently above all others." So, too, all new joys serve the soul only as encouragement to give herself to the enjoyment of union. If she finds something that is satisfying, then simultaneously there awakens in her the remembrance of the far higher good present within her and she turns to him in order to seek her delight in him. In comparison, the gain that comes to her from what has been added is "something so insignificant that we can call it a nothing." In all this it seems to her that she receives new delights, because the good that she continually enjoys anew is for her something always new.

"Yet were we to desire to speak of the glorious illumination that God sometimes gives to the soul in this habitual embrace, we should fail to find words to explain anything about it. It is a certain turning toward her in which he bestows the vision and enjoyment of this whole abyss of riches and delight he has placed within her. As the sun shining brightly on the sea lights up great depths and caverns and reveals pearls and rich veins of gold and other minerals, so the divine Sun reveals . . . to the bride . . . all the riches of her soul. . . . Yet, despite this lofty enlightenment, the soul experiences no increase, the sun only brings to light what was previously possessed so she may enjoy it."

Thus enlightened, strong, and firmly rooted in God, she does not allow herself to be frightened by the horrors of the evil spirits. "Nothing can touch or confuse her anymore." She has entered into her God and there enjoys perfect peace, which surpasses all understanding and cannot be expressed in any human words.[18]

"The bride has entered the sweet garden of her desire." The whole way lies behind her, the preparation has ended, she has remained faithful in the time of betrothal. Now God calls her to consummate this marriage in his flowering garden: that is God himself, the desired One, in whom she is now fully transformed. "The union wrought between the two natures and the communication of the divine to the human in this state is such that even though neither changes its being, both appear to be God. Yet in this life the union cannot be perfect, although it is beyond words and thought."[19]

At the goal, here, the soul possesses a wonderful, divine fullness of grace, incomparable with that of the spiritual betrothal. Her peace is much deeper and more stable. She feels herself joined to God in a veritable, intimate, spiritual, embrace, and through this she lives the life of God. Her neck rests on the arms of the Beloved: he lends her his strength in order to transform her weakness into divine strength.

She has entered into a new paradise. The marriage is consummated under the apple tree. The faithful soul is introduced to the wonderful secrets of God, above all the sweet mysteries of the Incarnation and Redemption. Just as in paradise the enjoyment of the forbidden fruit of the tree destroyed human nature and gave it as prey to corruption, so has she been redeemed and restored by him under the tree of the cross. It was there on the height of the cross that the Bridegroom extended to her the hand of his grace and mercy and through the merits of his passion and death put an end to the enmity that separated humanity from God ever since the original sin. Under the tree of paradise, the mother (human nature) in the persons of the first parents was dishonored through sin. Under the tree of the cross, life is restored to the human soul. The betrothal under the cross is not simply to be put on an equal with the mystical betrothal: the former is consummated at baptism and at once, while the mystical betrothal is attached to personal perfection and is therefore attained little by little, depending on the generosity of the soul. Fundamentally, though, it is the same union.[20]

21
The Bridal Symbol
and the Cross

5) The Bridal Symbol and the Cross
(Mystical Marriage—Creation, Incarnation, and Redemption)

We are at an essential point and must try, in our understanding, to penetrate even deeper than the explicit words of the saint's own explanations take us. We have seen the cross as the emblem of the passion and death of Christ and of everything connected therewith either as a cause or as sharing significance. In this, we have to consider on the one hand the fruit of the death on the cross: the redemption. But here we are given an indication that in a most intimate connection the incarnation is a necessary condition for the redemptive passion and death, and the fall into sin is reason for both. Earlier on, the thought was expressed that the sufferings of the *Dark Night* are a share in the passion of Christ, above all in that most intense pain: abandonment by God. This received emphatic confirmation through the *Spiritual Canticle* since here the yearning for the hidden God is *the* suffering that rules the entire mystical way. It will not cease even in the bliss of the bridal union. Indeed, in a certain sense, it increases as the knowledge and love of God increase since it makes more and more perceptible the presentiment of all that the clear vision of God in glory will bring us. (This is astutely developed in the second redaction.)

But what painful human desire can compare itself with the suffering of the God-man who was in possession of the beatific vision his whole life long until by a free decision of his will he deprived himself of this delight during that night in the garden of olives? Impossible as it is for a human spirit or a human heart to imagine or to feel what eternal bliss is like, so impossible is it to penetrate the unfathomable mystery of being robbed of so much! He alone, the only one who experienced it, can give a taste of it to those he chooses, in the intimacy of the bridal union. The abandonment by God in its entire profundity was reserved for him exclusively. It was possible for him to endure it only because he was at the same time God and man. As God he could not suffer, as only man he could not have grasped what a good it was of which he robbed himself. So the incarnation is a condition for this suffering; human nature, capable of and actually suffering, is a tool for the redemption. Human nature as exposed to the danger of the Fall and actually fallen, is the motivation for the salvific passion and therefore also for the incarnation.[1]

Through sin human nature, represented by the first humans, lost its honor—its original perfection and graced elevation. It is raised up anew in every individual human soul that is reborn through the grace of baptism into the state of the children of God. It is crowned in the chosen souls who attain to bridal union with the Redeemer. This happens "under the tree of the cross," as the ripened fruit of the death of the cross and in co-suffering this death on the cross. But how are we to understand that the place of this elevation and that of the fall are one and the same place, the tree of the cross and the tree of paradise, one and the same? It seems to me the solution lies in the mystery of sin. The tree in paradise, the fruits of which were forbidden to human beings, was, after all, the tree of knowledge of good and evil. Human beings could only get an authentic experimental knowledge of evil and its radical opposition to good by doing evil. So we may see in the tree of paradise an emblem for human nature in its openness to sin and in the fruit of the tree, actual sin (the first as well as every succeeding one) with all its consequences. But the most terrible result of sin, and therefore the revelation of its terrifying effectiveness is the passion and death of Christ.

The redemption is also the fruit of the tree of paradise in a multiple sense: because sin moved Christ to accept the passion and death, because it was sin in all the forms in which it appears that crucified Christ, and because thereby sin became the instrument of redemption. The soul united to Christ, however, in her co-suffering with the Crucified (that is, in the *dark night of contemplation*) attains to "knowledge of good and evil" and experiences this as redemptive strength. After all, it is repeatedly stressed that the soul arrives at purification through the keen pain of self-knowledge (as recognition of one's own sinfulness).

Now it is necessary to note that the mystical union is to be interpreted as participation in the incarnation. This is already suggested by the close connection between the two mysteries. It is indicated further through the terminology in which the saint speaks of mystical marriage. When he speaks of "so intimate a union between the two natures and such a communication of the divine nature to the human" that the soul wedded to God appears to be God,[2] one is reminded of the relationship of the two natures of Christ in the hypostatic union. Theologians, after all, like to designate the acceptance of human nature by the divine Word as a marriage with humanity.[3] By means of it, the God-man has opened the way to individual souls. And every time that a soul surrenders so totally without reservation that God can raise her to mystical marriage, it is as though he becomes man anew. Naturally, the essential difference remains that in Jesus Christ both natures are one in one person, while in mystical marriage two persons enter into a union and their duality remains intact.

However, through the mutual surrender of the two, a union results that comes close to the hypostatic one. It opens the soul for the reception of divine life and makes it possible for the Lord, through the entire subjection of the individual's will to the divine will, to make disposition of these persons as of members of his body. They no longer live their life, but the life of Christ; they no longer suffer their own pain, but rather, the passion of Christ. Therefore they also rejoice in the life of grace that the Lord enkindles in other souls when the spark of divine love touches them and the wine of this love causes in them holy inebriation.[4]

The soul that has attained to mystical marriage finds herself in the Beloved's *inner wine cellar*, that is, on the highest step of love. The saint here distinguishes seven steps of love, which correspond to the seven gifts of the Holy Spirit. He sees the last and perfecting gift, that of fear: "When the soul attains to the perfect possession of the spirit of fear, she has the spirit of love in its perfection; for this fear, the final one of the seven gifts is totally filial and the perfect fear of the child arises from the perfect love for the Father."[5]

In this most interior union the soul *drinks* of the Beloved. Just as a drink "is diffused through all the members and veins of the body, so this communication is diffused substantially in the whole soul . . . as much as her being and her spiritual faculties permit. With the intellect she drinks wisdom and knowledge, with the will, sweetest love, and with the memory she drinks refreshment and delight in the remembrance and the feeling of glory."[6]

When she comes out of her deep absorption—this is not an interruption of the essential union, but only its effect on the faculties—she has "lost all knowledge." "In this union, she has had a drink of the highest wisdom, which makes her forget all worldly things. And it seems that her previous knowledge, and even all the knowledge of the world is pure ignorance in comparison with this knowledge. . . . Beyond that, the elevation and immersion of the mind in God in which the soul is as though carried away and absorbed in love, entirely transformed in God, does not allow attention to any worldly thing. The soul is not only annihilated with respect to all things and estranged from them, but undergoes the same even with respect to herself, as if she had vanished and been dissolved in love. . . . In a way, the soul in this state resembles Adam in the state of innocence, who did not know evil. For she is so innocent that she does not understand evil, nor does she judge anything in a bad light. And she will hear very evil things and see them with her own eyes and be unable to understand that they are so. . . . (There is no contradiction here to that which was said a short time ago: contemplation lends knowledge of good and evil; knowledge belongs to the beginning of the mystical way, the not-knowing about evil belongs to the restored innocence at the peak of perfection.)

Besides, about the not-knowing of the soul on this step, it "is not to be thought that because she remains in this unknowing she loses there her acquired knowledge of the sciences; rather, these habits are perfected by the more perfect habit of supernatural knowledge infused in her. Yet they do not reign in such a way that she must use them in order to know, although at times she may still make use of them. For in this union with divine wisdom these habits are joined to the superior wisdom of God . . . as when a faint light is mingled with a bright one, the bright light prevails and is what illumines. But the faint light is not lost, rather it is perfected.

"Yet when the soul is absorbed in that love, she loses all particular knowledge, forms of things . . . and no longer knows anything about them .... First, because in that drink of love she is so absorbed in God . . . that she cannot actually be occupied with any other thing; second— and this is the principle reason—transformation in God makes her so consonant with the simplicity and purity of God, in which there is no form or imaginative figure, that it leaves her clean, pure, and empty of all former forms and figures."[7] This unknowing, however, lasts only until the particular effect of that act of love has passed.

The *drinking in the cellar*, however, has another effect: in place of the old self an entirely new one emerges. Before the soul enters the state of perfection, there remains, no matter how spiritual she may be, a small *herd* of desires, joys, and imperfections. "She follows this herd and seeks to pasture and satisfy it." The intellect usually keeps a bit of its old appetite for knowing things, the will is still captivated by some personal desires and gratifications of its own. One still desires the possession of certain trivialities and fosters certain inclinations, likes to snatch at demonstrations of esteem and is easily offended, finds gratification in choices in eating and drinking according to one's taste, and is assailed by useless cares, joys, suffering and fears. This is that herd of imperfections that follows so many souls "until, having entered the interior wine cellar to drink, all transformed in love they lose it, entirely."[8]

In the bridal union God surrounds the soul with such love that the most tender love of a mother cannot compare with it. He "gave her his breast," that is, he reveals his secrets to her and gives her the *sweet knowledge* of mystical theology, the secret knowledge of God. In return, the soul surrenders herself unreservedly to him. "She has but the desire to be totally his forever, and never to possess in herself anything other than him."

And since God has removed from her everything to which her heart was attached, she can now give herself to God really and totally, not only according to her will but also in her works. The two wills are now perfectly one, forever united in fidelity and stability. Even in her first movements the soul will never again turn against what she recognizes to be the will of God. She no longer knows anything but love and walks always with the divine Bridegroom. She has attained to that degree of perfection "the form and nature of which is love." She is "so to say, all love. All her actions are inspired by love and she employs all her faculties and possessions only for love. . . . She is conscious that her Beloved values nothing but love and that he is served by nothing else. Because she wishes to serve him perfectly, she uses everything in pure love of God. . . . As a bee sucks honey out of all the flowers and seeks nothing else in them, so the soul, with amazing ease, extracts the sweetness of love out of all the things that happen to her in life."⁹

The reason why God finds satisfaction only in love and its expression is that all our works and trials are a pure nothing in his sight. We cannot give him anything, he needs nothing and asks for nothing. "He wants but one thing, the exaltation of the soul." The only thing that gives him pleasure is the enrichment of the soul. "Since there is no way by which he can exalt her more than by making her equal to himself, he is pleased only with her love. For the property of love is to make the lover equal to what he loves. And since the soul here possesses perfect love, she is called the bride of the Son of God, and that signifies equality with him. It is equality in friendship in which the possessions of both are held in common."¹⁰

The soul now stands with all she is and has at the service of God. She takes it so much for granted that she is to work for him and his honor that she does so often without thinking about it and without being conscious that she is working for God. Formerly she usually had some "unprofitable occupations. . . . For we can call all her habitual imperfections so many occupations . . . the inclination to speak about useless things, thinking about them, and also carrying them out, not making use of such actions in accord with the demands of perfecting the soul." She no longer knows any of these "works," for "all her thoughts, words, and works are now of God, and directed toward him."¹¹ She has now no other office than to love. All her faculties are now employed only through love and out of love. This holds true of her prayer life as much as for her occupation with temporal things. Before the union in love, she had to practice love in her active as well as her contemplative life.

In this state now she should no longer become involved in other works and exterior exercises that might be of the slightest hindrance to the attentiveness of her love toward God. This is so even when it concerns works that would be of great service to God. For "one spark of this pure love is more precious to God, more useful for the soul, and more beneficial to the Church than all other works put together—even though it seems one is doing nothing."[12]

If the world considers such a person who no longer wants to know anything about its business and distractions to be lost, the soul is happy to accept this reproach. Freely and courageously, she confesses: "yes, I have lost myself." After all, this being lost is for her synonymous with having been won: "she seeks neither gain nor reward, but has only one wish, to lose all and herself, in order to belong to God."

Interpreted spiritually, it can be said that in communing with God she has given up all natural means and ways and communes in faith and in love only with God. So she is won over to God, because "in reality she is lost to all that is not God."[13]

Now, everything is indeed a gain for the soul. She is adorned with choice virtues and graces as with *flowers and emeralds*. Woven into a garland, they form a perfectly beautiful bridal ornament. And all the holy souls together form on their part a garland, which the bride-Church weaves together with Christ the Bridegroom. All the blooms with which the soul is adorned are gifts from the Beloved. The *hair* that binds the virtues close together is the will and its love, the *bond of perfection* (Col 3:14). Without this thread the blossoms of virtue would fall apart and be destroyed.

Love must be strong to keep the garland of virtues together. When it is so, and faith is true and simple, then God looks on her with satisfaction and makes himself her captive. "Great is the power and the tenacity of love for it captures and wounds God himself. . . . Whoever possesses him with such unselfish love, achieves all he wants. But whoever does not know this love speaks to God uselessly and is not in a position to gain anything from him, not even through extraordinary works. . . . The soul recognizes this truth and she also perceives that, far beyond her merits, he has favored her with such great graces."[14]

She attributes nothing to herself, all to God. If she is lovable in his eyes, it is because his loving glance has made her so. Through his grace he has made her so beautiful that he can now love her intimately. After all, God cannot love anything outside himself. When he "so loves a soul, he puts her somehow in himself and makes her his equal, and so he loves the soul within himself, with himself, that is with the very love by which he loves himself. This is why the soul merits an increase in love with every work that she performs in God. Placed in this grace and dignity, she merits God himself in every work."

To work in God's grace means for the soul to behold God. Enlightened through grace, the eyes of her spirit deserve to see what previously was concealed by her blindness: "the sublime virtues, abundant sweetness, immense goodness, love and mercy, and the numberless benefits she has received from God. . . . " All of this she was formerly unable to behold or adore. " For great is the rudeness and the blindness of the soul without God's grace!" This soul does not consider the duty she has to recognize God's proofs of grace and to adore him; this does not even enter her mind. "Such is the misery of those who live in sin, or better said, are dead in sin."[15]

Once God has "blotted out this sin and ugliness, he no longer reproaches her for it or fails to impart greater favors." But the soul should not forget her former transgressions. Then she will not become presumptuous, will always remain grateful, and her confidence will grow to expect even greater things. The remembrance of her former disgraceful condition increases her happiness at the side of the divine Bridegroom. If of herself she had been *dark* because of sin, now she is arrayed in beauty because God looked at her graciously and thereby made her worthy of new graces. For he gives "grace for grace" [Jn.1:16].

"When God finds a soul made attractive through grace, he is impelled to grant her more grace, for he dwells within her well pleased with her. If prior to her being in grace, he loved her only on account of himself, now that she is in grace he loves her not only on account of himself but also on account of herself. Enamored by the beauty of the soul . . .

he ever shows her more love and gives her more graces, and as he continues to honor and exalt her, he becomes continually more captivated by and enamored of her. . . . Who can express how much God exalts the soul that pleases him? It is impossible to do so, nor can this even be imagined, for after all, he does this as God, to show who he is."[16]

For the sake of the Beloved, the soul had freely sought solitude, that is, she had renounced everything terrestrial. Still in this solitude she lived in trouble and anxiety. But now God has led her into a new, perfect solitude where she finds rest and refreshment. "In this solitude away from all created things, the soul is alone with God and he guides, moves, and raises her to divine things." And "it is he alone who works in her without using any kind of assistance. God works in her and communicates himself directly to her . . . through himself alone without using as means the angels or any natural ability. All the interior and exterior senses, all creatures, and even the soul herself do very little toward the reception of the remarkable supernatural favors that God grants in this state . . . he does not want to give her any other company, nor does he entrust her to anyone but himself."[17]

From the highest peak of this life the soul yearns for the beatific vision. She longs to reach the *mountain* of essential knowledge of God, in the eternal Word, and to the *hill* of "God's wisdom of the lower rank, which is in his creatures, works and wondrous decrees." This divine Wisdom, like clear water, washes away all the stains of her ignorance. The more love grows, the stronger will be her desire to know the divine truths with clear and pure understanding and to penetrate ever deeper into the abyss of the incomprehensible judgments and secrets of God. "To arrive at this knowledge, it would be a singular comfort and happiness for her to take upon herself all the afflictions and trials of the world, and to accept everything, no matter how difficult and painful it might be . . . The thicket and incomprehensibility of judgments and ways to which the soul wishes to penetrate, can . . . also be taken as a symbol . . . of the pain and trouble that the soul wishes to take upon herself. For in suffering she finds the greatest joy and her highest gain because it is a means to penetrate deeper into the thicket of the delectable wisdom of God. Suffering purifies and the more the purity increases, the deeper and clearer the knowledge and therefore the purer and more exalted the joy because it is a knowing from further within. Not being content therefore with just any kind of suffering, the soul wishes . . . to take upon herself even the agony of death . . . as a means . . . , to see God.

"Oh! When will we fully understand how a soul cannot reach the thicket and wisdom of the riches of God, which are of many kinds, without entering the thicket of many kinds of suffering, finding in this her delight and consolation? When will one be convinced that the soul with an authentic desire for divine wisdom wants suffering first in order to enter this wisdom by the thicket of the cross? . . . The gate entering these riches of the wisdom of God is the cross . . . and it is narrow."[18]

It leads to the *deep caves in the cliffs*, that is, "to the sublime, exalted and deep mysteries of God's wisdom in Christ, in the hypostatic union of the human nature with the divine Word and in the corresponding union of mankind with God. . . . Each of the mysteries that are united in Christ . . . is in itself an abyss of wisdom and contains countless recesses of secret judgments of predestination and foreknowledge concerning the children of the earth. . . . However numerous are the mysteries and marvels that the holy doctors have discovered and no matter how deeply saintly souls have understood in this earthly life, they have in reality explained and discovered almost nothing. Christ is and remains an impenetrable abyss . . . " filled with "all the treasures of wisdom and knowledge" (Col.2:3). The soul can attain to these treasures only if she "first passes through the straits of exterior and interior suffering to be purified according to the plans of divine wisdom. Even a limited knowledge of these mysteries can be attained in this life only through much suffering, and through having received numerous intellectual and sensible favors from God and through proven practice in the spiritual life; for all these favors are inferior to the wisdom of the mysteries of Christ. They are but preparations for coming to this wisdom."[19] The enjoyment of this divine Wisdom is the *young wine* that the lovers taste together.

"Above all, the soul desires a love equal to God's. She desires to love God as she is loved by him. But in this life she cannot attain this even on the highest level. It requires the transformation in glory. There she will love God with the will and strength of God himself, united with the very strength of love with which God loves her. This strength lies in the Holy Spirit in whom the soul is there transformed. The Holy Spirit is given to the soul so that she may come into possession of the strength of this love, and he supplies and completes all that is lacking in her for this powerful transformation in eternal glory."[20]

Together with the perfection of love, she awaits eternal glory, that is, the vision of the divine Being, which God has destined for her from eternity. She names this only in second place, because love, which has its seat in the will, is the first goal; for it is the property of love to give, not to receive while that of the intellect, which is the seat of essential glory, is to receive, not to give. "The soul in the inebriation of love does not put first the glory she will receive from God, but rather thinks only of how she can surrender herself to him through true love without concern for her own profit." Besides, the first petition includes the second within it "for it is impossible to reach the perfect love of God without the perfect vision of God." The vision of God—this it is that God has prepared for her from eternity. But it is that "which no eye has seen, no ear has heard, and what has not entered into the human heart" (1 Cor.2:9; Is.64:4). What the soul surmises about it is so overpowering that she can find no other word for it than *what*. It is impossible to give an explanation of this mysterious word. The Lord himself indicated this in the Book of Revelation through the mouth of St. John in seven different expressions, words and comparisons: "To him that overcomes I will give to eat of the tree of life, which is in the paradise of my God" [Rv.2:7];

"Be faithful unto death and I will give you the crown of life" [Rv. 2:10];

"To the one who overcomes I will give the hidden manna and a white stone, and on the stone a new name will be written, which no one knows save the one who received it" [Rv. 2:17];

"To the one who overcomes and keeps my commandments until the end will I give power over the nations. That one will rule them with a rod of iron, and as a vessel of clay they shall be smashed, as I also received power from my Father. And I will give that one the morning star" [Rv. 2:26-28];

"The one who overcomes will thus be clothed in white garments, and I will not cross the name of that one from the book of life. And I will confess this name before my Father" [Rv.3:5];

"And I will make the one who overcomes a pillar in the temple of my God, and this victor shall go out no more. And I will write upon this one the name of my God and the name of the city of my God, the new Jerusalem, which comes down out of heaven from my God, and also my new name" [Rv. 3:12];

"To the one who overcomes I will give to sit with me on my throne, as I also have conquered and sat with my Father on his throne. Let whoever has ears to hear, hear" [Rv.3:21-22].

"All these are the words of the Son of God, explaining the "what". They cast the "what" in very perfect terms, but they still do not explain it. For what is immense cannot be clothed in words."[21]

The soul in this state of spiritual marriage is not totally ignorant about this immense and inexpressible "what." The transformation in God has given her some pledges of it: the *light whisper of the air* that is given her by the Holy Spirit, an exhalation, precisely, of this Holy Spirit, the Spirit of love, whom the Father and the Son breathe out together. The Spirit "in that transformation of the soul, in the Father and the Son, breathes out to her in order to unite her to himself. For this transformation of the soul would not be true and total if the soul were not transformed in the three Persons of the Most Holy Trinity in an open and manifest degree. And this kind of spiration of the Holy Spirit in the soul, by which God transforms her into himself, is so sublime, delicate, and deep a delight that a mortal tongue finds it indescribable, nor can the human intellect, as such, in any way come near to grasping it.

When the soul is blessed with this transformation in this life, this mutual spiration between God and the soul takes place with notable frequency . . . with the most blissful love for the soul. But it never reaches the open and manifest degree proper to the next life. . . . One should not think it impossible that the soul be capable of so sublime an activity. When God has once favored her by union with the Most Blessed Trinity in which she becomes deiform and God through participation—who can then find it incredible that she also understand, know, and love in the Trinity, together with it as does the Trinity itself! . . . This means transformation in the three Persons in power and wisdom and love, and so the soul is like God through this transformation. He created her in his image and likeness that she might attain such an exalted resemblance."[22]

The result of the soul's *breathing the air* is that she hears the sweet voice of her Beloved and unites her own voice in delightful jubilation. As the nightingale sings in the springtime when wintry cold, rain, and inconstant weather has passed, so the *Song* of love sounds out a new spring of the soul when she "feels, after all the storms and changes in life, divested and purged of imperfections, penalties, and clouds in the senses and the spirit . . . in freedom, and breadth, and gladness of spirit . . . refreshed, protected and penetrated by joy. . . . She intones . . . in union with God, a new and jubilant *Song*. He gives his voice to her that so united with him she may join him in the praise of God, together." For it is God's aim and deep desire that "he perceive her voice in an expression of perfect jubilation." It belongs to the perfection of the *Song* of praise that it be rooted in the knowledge of the mysteries of the incarnation. The soul in the state of union performs very perfect works. Therefore, her *Song* of jubilation is sweet both to God and to herself, even if it does not yet attain to the perfection of the new *Song* of glory."[23]

God reveals himself to her as creator and preserver of all being (as *the glade* with its multitude of animals and plants) and she comes to know the grace, wisdom, and beauty of God to be found in each creature of heaven and earth as well as in their mutual relationships and their harmonious order. This happens now in the dark night of contemplation, in a secret manner of reception, of which she is unable to give any account. It happens in the "serene night" of the clear vision of God.[24]

Finally the flame of divine love will transform her into the perfection of love without causing her any pain. This is "possible only in the beatific state where this flame is delightful love. . . . The variety of greater or lesser intensity of the flame gives no pain, as it did before the soul reached the capacity for this perfect love." However, in this life the transformation is never free from pain, even in the highest degree of love, and nature still becomes agitated. "The pain arises from the vehement desire for the beatific transformation . . . nature becomes disturbed because the weak and corruptible senses are involved through the strength and height of so much love. Any excellent thing is a pain and detriment to natural weakness. Yet in that beatific life the soul will feel no detriment or pain, although her understanding will be very deep and her love immense. For God will equip her for one and strengthen her for the other, consummating her intellect with his wisdom and her will with his love."[25]

The soul awaits the glorious fulfillment in the deep peace of the certainty that she is fully prepared for it, and there is no danger for her to fear from any side. The evil enemy has been so thoroughly routed that he no longer dares to show himself. No creature has any idea of what she enjoys in her hiddenness in God. She is no longer besieged by passions and appetites which threaten her rest. Her sensory faculties are so purified and spiritualized that they are able to share in the grandeurs God communicates to her in the inmost region of the spirit. To be sure, they cannot taste *the flood* of these spiritual goods; they can only "see" it. "For the sensory part . . . has no capacity for the essential and proper taste of spiritual goods, whether in this life or the next. It can, though, through a certain spiritual overflow, receive sensible refreshment and delight from them. This delight attracts the corporeal senses and faculties to the inner recollection where the soul drinks the waters of spiritual goods." They *dismount*, as riders do from their horses, because they "discontinue their natural operations ... and give themselves over to spiritual recollection."[26]

In the colorful series of images the whole way of the soul has been uncovered for us. At the same time, with it we were allowed an insight in the secret designs of God that were set in place along this way from the very morning of creation. And we see how the hidden way of the soul is woven together with the mysteries of faith. From all eternity the soul has been chosen to share the triune life of the Godhead as bride of the Son of God.

In order to lead the bride home, the Eternal Word clothed himself with human nature. God and the soul are to be *two in one flesh*. But because the flesh of sinful human beings riots against the spirit, all life in the flesh is battle and suffering: for the Son of Man even more than for any other human being; for the others, more in proportion to the intimacy of their bond with him. Jesus Christ woos the soul, in that he substitutes his life for hers in the battle against his and her enemies. He chases away Satan and all evil spirits wherever he personally encounters them. He snatches souls from the tyranny of the evil ones. Relentlessly he uncovers human malice wherever it approaches him in delusion, disguise, and obduracy. To all who recognize their own sinfulness, remorsefully acknowledge it, and long to be liberated from it, he extends his hand. But he demands that they follow him unconditionally, and renounce everything that can oppose his Spirit within them.

Through all this he rouses the rage of hell and the hatred of human malice and weakness against himself until they break loose and prepare the death on the cross for him. Here, in the extreme torment of body and soul, above all in the night of abandonment by God, he pays divine Justice the ransom for the accumulated debt of sin of all times and opens the sluice of paternal Mercy for all who have the courage to embrace the cross and the crucified one. Into them he pours his divine light and life. But because this light unceasingly annihilates all that stands in his way, they experience it first as night and death. This is the dark night of contemplation, the death on the cross for the *old self*. The night is so much darker, the death so much more painful, the more forcefully this wooing by divine Love grips the soul, and the more unreservedly the soul surrenders herself to it. The progressive collapse of nature gives more and more room to the supernatural light and to divine life. It overpowers the natural faculties and transforms them into divinized and spiritualized ones. Thus a new incarnation of Christ takes place in christians, which is synonymous with a resurrection from the death on the cross. The *new self* carries the wounds of Christ on the body: the remembrance of the misery of sin out of which the soul was awakened to a blessed life, and a reminder of the price that had to be paid for that. The pain of yearning for the fullness of life persists until, through the door of actual physical death, entrance into the shadowless light is gained.

So the bridal union of the soul with God is the goal for which she was created, purchased through the cross, consummated on the cross and sealed for all eternity with the cross.

22

In the Image of Christ Crucified

III. [UNTITLED]

St. John's doctrine on the cross could not be spoken of as *a science of the cross* in our sense, were it based merely on an intellectual insight. But it bears the genuine stamp of the cross. It can be likened to the wide-spread branches of a tree that has sunk its roots in the greatest depth of a soul and which has been nourished by the heart's blood. Its fruits are seen in the life of the saint.

The love he bears in his heart for the Crucified is manifested by his love for the crucifix, which was characteristically expressed in the little house of Duruelo. It is well known what an impression it made on our holy Mother: "When I entered the little church, I was astonished to see the spirit the Lord had put there. And it wasn't only I, for the two merchants, my friends from Medina who had accompanied me there, did nothing else but weep. There were so many crosses, so many skulls! I never forget a little cross made for the holy water fount from sticks with a paper image of Christ attached to it; it inspired more devotion than if it had been something very expertly carved."[1]

The assumption is that the first Discalced Carmelite, who formerly studied carving and painting, personally fashioned these crosses as adornments for his small monastery. They correspond completely with what he later wrote about the veneration of images: that precious materials and artistic completion can become a danger because they can easily distract one from the essential—from the spirit of prayer and the way to union with God.[2] But, through the crucifix and through all other means, he wished to lead himself and others to union. For that reason,

275

too, he liked later to carve crosses to give away. He could think of no better way to express his gratitude to his friendly prison guard in Toledo, Padre Juan de Santa María than to give him a crucifix. This gift must have been exceptionally precious to both the donor and recipient for a very special reason: John had received it in Duruelo from our holy Mother. This was probably an additional reason for him to detach himself from it.

That Our Lord was greatly pleased by this love for the image of the cross and the zeal with which John fostered devotion to the cross is attested to by the visions of the cross that have been mentioned above.[3] In any case, they served to make an even deeper impression of this sacred sign on his heart. He held his crucifix in his hand during the last night of his life. Shortly before midnight, as the foreseen moment of death approached, he gave it to one of those present to hold while "he passed his arms underneath his tunic, and laid out his body with his own hands. He then took back *el santo Christo* and began to speak to it tenderly. . . . He kissed it for the last time before lightly and unnoticeably, he expired."

It is beneficial to honor the Crucified in images and to fashion such as will encourage devotion to him. But better than any image made of wood or stone are living images. To form souls to the image of Christ, to plant the cross in their hearts, this was the great task in the life of the reformer of the order and the director of souls. All of his writings are in the service of this task. His letters and the testimonials to his activities speak even more personally of his dedication.

In the Carmel of Granada he gave his spiritual daughter, María Machuca, the holy habit and the name María de la Cruz. She was brought to him in the speak room[5] and it was remarked that he would probably "love her greatly because she was called 'of the Cross.'" He replied: "Indeed I will love her greatly if she is a friend of the cross."[6] He used to urge the persons with whom he dealt to take the cross into their hearts. They should have "great predilection for suffering, purely for the sake of Christ alone, without seeking any earthly consolation." Often he would say, "My daughter, ask for nothing other than the cross, and that, in fact, without consolation; for that is perfection."[7]

To his penitent Juana de Pedraza in Granada he wrote in reply to her complaints about her suffering:[8] "All these are knocks and rappings at the door of your soul, which . . . increase love and cause one to pray with greater zeal and to raise one's spirit in petition to God. . . . O my Lord, great God of Love, with what treasures you enrich those who love nothing and seek pleasure in nothing but Yourself! You give yourself to them and unite yourself to them through love. And so you allow the soul to taste in love what there is in You she longs for most of all and what will be most useful for her. For this reason the cross—even until we die of love—cannot be wanting to us anymore than to our Beloved. He imposes suffering on us according to the measure of our love, in order that we may bring greater sacrifices and collect more merit. But all this is of short duration since it lasts only until the knife is raised; then Isaac remains alive and receives the promise of his reward."[9]

St. John was particularly close to the Carmelite nuns of Beas. As superior at Calvario (soon after his escape from imprisonment) and as Rector of the college of Baeza, he was in the vicinity and was able to be with them in person, and by giving sermons, spiritual talks, and admonitions in the confessional, he was able to influence them. Later, too, he was a guest of theirs. Correspondence supplemented the oral direction. In a letter of November 18, 1586, we read: "Whoever . . . seeks satisfaction in any thing is no longer an empty vessel, which God can fill with his inexpressible delight. In this way one turns away from God instead of approaching him, and your hands cannot receive what God wishes to give . . . Serve God, my beloved daughters in Christ, follow in his footsteps through self-denial, in all patience, through silence and true love in suffering. Proceed without mercy toward any self-satisfaction and mortify everything that should die in you and hinders the interior resurrection!"[10]

To Madre Leonor Bautista, prioress of Beas, John wrote on February 8, 1588: "It consoles me when I consider that God has called you to an apostolic life, that is, to a life of contempt, and has led you on this way. For according to God's will the attitude of truly religious persons must be such that they have renounced everything, and everything has lost its meaning for them. They want God alone for their treasure, their consolation, and their delightful glory. God has granted your Reverence a great grace that now, forgotten by all, you can find your joy in him alone. Do not care whatever happens to you because of what, for the love of God, others want to do to you. You no longer belong to yourself, but to God."[11]

To a postulant he gives the advice: "With regard to the Lord's passion: Treat your body with wise rigor, with self-contempt and self-denial, and seek never to follow your own will and tastes. For this self-will was the cause of his passion and death."[12]

To the prioress of the newly-founded monastery in Córdoba he wrote: "God arranged for you to acquire such poor houses in such burning heat; you are to give good example and show that through your profession you give witness to the poverty of Christ. Those who apply for acceptance will see by your attitude what kind of spirit they must have when they enter. . . . Keep, most conscientiously, the spirit of poverty and contempt for everything worldly and occupy yourself with God alone, or, as you know, a thousand spiritual and temporal needs will grow in you, while you should have and feel only those needs you desire to have in your heart. For the one who is poor in spirit is more satisfied and happier in need, because he has set his all on complete nothingness and so in everything keeps freedom of heart. O happy nothingness, and happy solitude of the hearts that possess such strength that they subject everything to themselves, but do not subject themselves to any thing and shed all cares, in order the better to be inflamed by love." The Sisters "as the first-born should make use of the spirit that the Lord gives in such new foundations, and thus with completely renewed spirit walk the way of perfection in all humility and detachment, interior and exterior, not in a childish sense, but rather with a vigorous will. They should take upon themselves mortification and penance in the attempt to allow Christ to cost them something, and not be like those who seek their own comfort and consolation, in God or without him, but rather suffer it for God, in God or without him, in silence and hope and loving remembrance."[13]

The darkest path is the most secure. This doctrine from *The Dark Night* is stressed with great emphasis in spiritual direction: "Since your soul finds herself in this darkness and void of spiritual poverty, you believe you are lacking everything, and that everyone has abandoned you. Of course, that is no wonder since you even think God has forsaken you. However, nothing is missing. . . . Whoever seeks God and nothing else is not wandering in darkness no matter how dark and poor you think you are. Whoever does not walk in presumption and does not follow her own tastes whether in what concerns God or creatures, and does not insist on her own will, whether internally or externally, will not stumble now. . . . You were never in a better position than now, for you were never so humble and submissive and never thought so little of yourself and of all the things of the world. Never did you recognize yourself to be so evil and God so good, never did you serve God as purely and so much without self-interest as now. . . . What more do you want? What do you think—is serving anything other than fleeing from evil, keeping God's commandments, and taking care of our affairs as best we can? If you are doing this, what other perceptions, enlightenment and pleasures do you need, since in these the soul ordinarily meets so many deceptions and dangers? . . . That is why it is a great grace when God leads the soul in darkness and detachment so that she will no longer be led astray through her faculties. . . . Let us live on earth like pilgrims and the poor, like the banished and orphans, in dryness, without a way, and without anything else, but always in hope."[14]

The saint writes to his spiritual daughters most lovingly but the love is nothing other than a heartfelt desire for their eternal salvation. "As long as God does not give us this in heaven, tarry in . . . self-denial and patience with the wish, through your suffering, to resemble somewhat this great God in his humility and love for the cross. If our life does not consist in imitating (the Crucified) it has no value"[15]

St. John, accordingly, could not believe in the authenticity of supposedly higher graces in prayer in a soul that lacked humility. When he was commissioned by the General Vicar of the Discalced Carmelite Fathers, Padre Nicolás Doria, to evaluate a nun who was considered highly favored he expressed his opinion with conviction: "The principal fault . . . lies in this, that in her behavior there is no indication of humility; for the favors of which she speaks, if indeed there are any, are usually given only to a soul who has first totally emptied and, as it were, annihilated herself in perfect inner humiliation." Even though the effects of humility "are not as noticeable in all the apprehensions of God, these graces with which one is favored in the state of union—and this is what she is speaking of—still bring with them an attitude of humility. . . . Let them try her in the practice of sheer virtue, especially in self-contempt, humility and obedience. In the echo of such an impact, one will perceive the resonance of quality of soul which such great graces should impart. But these tests must be thoroughgoing, for there is no devil who is unwilling to suffer something for the sake of his honor."[16]

The same spirit exudes from the special counsels for the behavior of religious that the saint wrote down on various occasions. Among the instructions presumably written for the Carmelite nuns of Beas, we find the following three *precautions against the flesh:*

"1. In the first place, you should remember that you came to the monastery only in order to have all fashion and train you. In order to be free of all imperfections and all confusion which might be caused you by the character of the religious, and by the way they act, and in order to draw benefit from everything that happens, you must consider all to be instruments (this is really what they are) found in Carmel in order to work on you. One will belabor you with words, the other through actions, the third through thoughts that are directed against you. Submit yourself to them all as would an image which would be carved by one, painted by another, and gold-plated by a third. If you do not observe this, you will be unable to conquer your sensuality and your sensitivity, nor will you be able to get along with the religious in the monastery. You will not enjoy holy peace, and you will be unable to escape making many a misstep.

2. Never omit a work that does not appeal to you and for which you have no taste, if it is a matter of serving God. Neither do something solely for the sake of taste and for the satisfaction it would bring you . . . but rather as though it inspires aversion, otherwise you will never attain constancy or conquer your weaknesses.

3. A spiritual soul should never be preoccupied at its practices by what is pleasant about them and carry them out for that reason; even

more, she should never boggle at doing them because they appear to be unpleasant. One should rather prefer what is burdensome. . . . In this way one reins in sensuality. You will be unable to remove self-love nor will you arrive at the love of God in any other way."[17]

God calls souls into the monastery, "in order to test them and to purify them as gold is tried by fire and the hammer. For this reason, trials and temptations from human beings and evil spirits must come upon one, as must the fire of anxiety and lack of consolation. The religious must take such things upon herself in patience and in conformity with the will of God, and not in such a manner that God would be forced to cast her aside because she was unwilling to carry the cross of Christ with patience."[18]

"Do not look for a cross that appears lighter to you for ... the heavier the burden, the lighter it is when one carries it out of love for God."[19]

"If you are burdened, then you live in union with God who is your strength; for God holds the grieving one upright. If you are relieved of the burden you will find your strength in yourself alone, you who are weakness itself. For the strength and fortitude of the soul grows and is confirmed in the patient bearing of trials."[20]

"God values in you the inclination to dryness and suffering out of love for him more than all the consolations, spiritual visions, and all the meditations you could possibly have."[21]

"One cannot attain perfection if one cannot manage to be satisfied with nothing, so that the natural and spiritual appetites are satisfied in emptiness. This is required in order to reach both the highest degree of rest and peace of soul; and in this way the love of God is continually effective in the pure and simple soul."[22]

A whole series of maxims has the *imitation of Christ* as its direct object. "Progress in the spiritual life is impossible without the imitation of Christ. He is the way, the truth and the life and the gate through which those who wish to be saved must enter."[23]

"Let your first care be to have a glowing desire ... to imitate Christ in all your works; endeavor to do everything as the Lord himself would do it."[24]

"Should some pleasure offer itself to your senses which does not purely serve the honor and glory of God, renounce it and keep yourself free of it out of love for Jesus Christ who in this life sought no other pleasure . . . than to fulfill the will of his Father. He called that his nourishment and food."[25]

"Allow yourself to be crucified interiorly and exteriorly with Christ, and you will live this life in the rest and peace of his Soul, and keep yourself in his patience."[26]

"The crucified Christ should be enough to satisfy you; suffer and rest with him; without him, have neither suffering nor rest; for that, free yourself from all exterior things and from interior peculiarities."[27]

"If you desire to possess Christ, never seek him without the cross."[28]

"Whoever seeks not the cross of Christ, also seeks not the glory of Christ."[29]

"What does he know, who does not know how to suffer for the sake of Christ? The greater and heavier the burdens are, the better is the lot of those who bear them."[30]

"Rejoice always in God, your salvation, and remember how sweet it is to suffer in every way possible for him who is veritably good."[31]

"If you desire to be perfect, sell your will, give it to the poor in spirit, come to Christ in meekness and humility, and follow him to Calvary and to the grave."[32]

"The troubles and sufferings one bears for love of God are like precious pearls: the larger they are, the more valuable they are, and the more love for the donor they call forth in the one who receives them. So are also the sufferings a creature causes if one accepts them for God's sake, worth the more the greater they are, and they call forth a greater love of God. And for enduring suffering for God's sake on earth, which lasts but a moment, His Majesty gives endless and eternal goods in heaven: himself, his beauty and glory."[33]

One day, in the presence of the saint, a sister spoke disparagingly about a layman who was inimically disposed toward the monastery. She received the warning: "Then you and the others should be all the more friendly toward him; that way you would be the disciples of Christ." He added "It is much easier to bear the slight bitterness of such an occasion when one commends the person to God, than to bear the double bitterness of giving in to our will with such feelings against the neighbor."[34]

In conversation with a male religious he spoke to him urgently: "Were any person to advise you, even were he a superior, to accept a doctrine that suggests mitigation, and should he even attest it through miracles, do not believe him and do not accept it, but rather embrace penance and the renunciation of all things and do not seek Christ without the cross. We are called, as the discalced friars of the ever Blessed Virgin, to follow him with the cross by the renunciation of everything, even ourselves, and not to pursue our comfort and give in to our softness. Take care not to forget to preach this as often as the opportunity presents itself for this has such great meaning for us."[35] The love of Christ, which urges the disciple of the cross to lead others on the way he himself has found, speaks forcefully in this exhortation.

"Did you not know I must be about my Father's business?" (Lk.2:49) John refers to these first words of the Savior recorded for us as the great lifework of the Lord and his faithful followers. "Nothing else can be meant by that which is the eternal Father's business than the salvation of the world, above all the salvation of souls, since Christ our Lord applied the means foreordained by the eternal Father. And the holy Dionysius the Areopagite to confirm this truth wrote the wonderful sentence: 'Of all divine works, the most divine is to cooperate with God for the salvation of souls.'[36] That means: the highest perfection of each being in its rank and on its level is to raise itself according to its capability and its faculties and to grow into an image of God.

But what is most wonderful and divine is to cooperate in the conversion of souls and in bringing them home; for in this God's own activity is reflected and this imitation is the greatest glory. That is why Christ, our Lord, called this the work of his Father, the business of his Father. It is also an evident truth that sympathy with the neighbor grows the more, the more the soul is united with God through love. For the more she loves God the more she desires that he be loved and worshipped by all. And the more she desires this the more trouble she takes to bring it about as well through prayer as through all other exercises that are necessary and useful toward achieving it. And so great is the ardor and strength of their love, that those who are in possession of God cannot content themselves with their own gain and be satisfied with it; it seems to them not enough to go to heaven alone. They take the trouble with great longing and heavenly desires and extraordinary carefulness to draw many to heaven with themselves.

This may well come from their great love for God; it is the proper fruit of perfect prayer and contemplation, and the inclination that arises from them."[37]

If the zeal of the soul is here seen as the fruit of union, then on the other hand, the love of neighbor is an important means on the way to union: "Two things . . . serve the soul as wings on which to rise to union with God: sincere compassion with the death of Jesus and with the neighbor. And if the soul is seized by compassion with the suffering and cross of the Lord, then she also takes to heart that he took all of this upon himself for our salvation."[38] That is to say that whoever, in deep recollection, enters into the attitude of the Savior on the cross, into the love that surrenders itself to the limit, will thereby become united to the divine will, for it is the Father's will-to-save that Jesus fulfills in his love and surrender as Savior. And one's being will be united with the divine Being, which is self-surrendering love: in the mutual surrender of the divine Persons in the inner-trinitarian life as well as its outward activity. For this reason, self-fulfillment, union with God, and laboring for the union of others with God and for their self-fulfillment belong inseparably together. It is the cross, however, that gives access to all this. And preaching about the cross will be in vain, when it is not an expression of a life united with the Crucified.

"My Beloved, all for you and nothing for me; nothing for You and all for me. All that is hard and difficult I demand for myself and nothing for You.

"Oh, how sweet your presence is for me, for you are the highest Good. I want to approach you in silence and seek to discover your footprints, that you may be pleased to unite me to yourself in marriage; and I will not come to rest until I am happily in your arms; and now I beg you, Lord, let me never take myself back, but rather surrender my entire soul."[39]

John of the Cross' whole way of life is mirrored in these ardent sighs of a loving heart. He followed in the footsteps of the beloved Master on the way of the cross. That is why as a child he already chose a rough resting-place. That is why, as a boy, he served the sick in untiring dedication—as a living image of the Savior who would not allow himself any respite when he was importuned by those in pain and others who sought his help. He retained this love for the sick, the suffering members of Jesus Christ, all his life. Later when, as superior and visitator, he came to a monastery, after the initial greeting his first care was for the sick. He personally prepared their food, emptied their utensils, would not permit them to be taken to a hospital because of a lack of money, and severely reproved any negligence.[40]

For love of the cross, as a young religious, he lived in the monastery of St. Anne in Medina del Campo and in the College of St. Andrew in Salamanca in so severe a penitential manner that at the beginning of the Reform our holy Mother St. Teresa said of him that (in contrast to his much older companion Padre Antonio de Heredia) he "had no need of testing; for although he lived among the Calced he had always led a life of great perfection and of strict observance."[41]

In Salamanca, every evening, he had taken the discipline until he drew blood, then spent a large part of the night in prayer and for his brief period of rest had used a kind of trough as a bed. Of the poor little house in Duruelo, the companion of the holy Mother said, when she saw it: "Surely, Mother, there isn't a soul, however good, that could put up with this."[42] But for the two friars it was a paradise. It has already been recounted how it was ornamented with crosses and skulls. "The choir was in the loft. In the middle of the loft the ceiling was high enough to allow for the recitation of the Hours, but one had to stoop low in order to enter and to hear Mass. There were in the two corners facing the church two little hermitages, where one could do no more than either lie down or sit. Both were filled with hay because the place was very cold, and the roof almost touched one's head. Each had a little window facing the altar and a stone for a pillow." After Matins at midnight the friars remained in choir until Prime " . . . so deep in prayer that when it came time to say Prime their habits were covered with snow without their having become aware of the fact."[43]

In order to instruct the poor, ignorant people of the neighboring towns, they often "went out to preach, barefooted despite the deep snow and the bitter cold . . . when finished with their preaching and confessing, they returned very late to their house, filled with inner happiness which made all seem light to them."[44]

During the time that John had his mother and brother with him in Duruelo, he often took Francisco along as companion on his pastoral rounds. When he had finished preaching, they quickly withdrew, never accepting the invitations to dinner at the rectories. Then by the roadside, they ate the bread and cheese which their mother, Catalina, had packed for them.[45]

In this way, the saint lived true to the principles he later wrote down for others: "Seek to arrive, for the love of Jesus Christ alone, at detachment, renunciation, and poverty regarding all the things of this world."[46]

"One who is poor in spirit is totally satisfied and cheerful in want; and whoever has his heart set on nothing, finds peace in everything."[47]

The penances practiced by the two first Discalced Carmelite friars were so extreme that the holy Mother begged them to moderate them. It had cost her "so many tears and prayers" to find religious qualified to begin the reform, and now she was afraid the devil was inciting them to exaggerated zeal, in order to "shorten their days" and so destroy the work in its very beginning. But the friars paid little attention to her words and continued their austere way of living.

"Some while later, when the two had already gathered a small monastic family, Father John of the Cross was so exhausted by fatigue and some days of illness that he asked his Prior, Padre Antonio for permission to take his collation a little earlier. But as soon as he had taken the small repast he was filled with bitter remorse. He hurried to Padre Antonio and asked permission to accuse himself before the community. Then he brought stones and broken tiles to the refectory. He knelt on these during the evening meal, bared his shoulders and scourged himself until he bled. He interrupted taking the discipline only in order to accuse himself of his fault in a loud voice and moving words. Then the blows fell again until he collapsed. The brothers watched in shock and wonder. Finally, Padre Antonio in the name of obedience, told the innocent penitent to retire and to pray to God to pardon them all for their wretched unworthiness."[48]

John did not know how to spare himself even later in life. His cell was the poorest in the house, even when he was the superior. Ill and weak, to carry out an assignment from his provincial, he traveled in all directions through Spain in the burning heat of summer, 1586, a 400-mile long journey in the heavy woolen tunic and habit which he wore during summer and winter. As prior in Segovia he began construction on a new monastery. He was not only overseer, he joined in the work with his own hands, bringing stones to the site from the nearby quarries. All year round he went barefoot except for the pair of *alpargatas* he wore.[49]

In the great conflict within the Order John stands between the inimical brothers, Nicolás Doria and Jerónimo Gracián. He saw the good and the faults of both sides and sought to mediate, but his words had no effect. So he again resorted to the severe discipline. His traveling companion, Brother Martín, unable to listen to the cruel blows any longer, came with a candle to try to intervene. The saint complained that he was old enough to take care of himself. This same Brother Martín nursed him during a severe illness and took away a chain John had been wearing for seven years, and would not let him replace it. Blood flowed when the chain was removed. But Padre Juan Evangelista was unsuccessful in his attempt, during another journey together, to convince him to remove a penitential garment. He discovered that the saint wore, beneath his habit, breeches made from esparto grass and full of knots, and protested that ill as John was, this was cruelty. "Be quiet, my son, it is enough relief that I ride. We must not be totally at rest."[50]

During his final illness, the good Brother Pedro de San José had an inspiration. He would create a bit of diversion for the saint who was in excruciating pain. He engaged the three best musicians in Ubeda to come to the sickroom. His biographer, Jerónimo de San José, recounts that after a few moments, John had a mind to dismiss them kindly: it seemed to him that it would not do to mix earthly pleasure with a divine one. But in order not to sadden his brethren, he allowed the musicians to keep playing. However, when they asked for his opinion about it, he had to admit: "I did not hear the music. Another, a thousand times more beautiful, brought me into ecstasy the whole time."[51]

We can readily understand Baruzi when he believes the version given by another witness is more credible. Here the saint is reported as having said to his caretaker: "My son, give them some refreshment and thank them for the kindness they had wished to do me, then let them go. It does not make sense to shorten the time for bearing pain that the Lord has given me."[52]

This is completely consonant with the spirit of our holy Father John, to wish to carry his cross to the end without any mitigation. And again, the second half of the first account also has much going for it. His consideration for the brethren is very indicative of the sensitivity of the saint; and one cannot simply dismiss the mention of heavenly music since this tremendous lover of the cross, throughout his life-time, was obviously overwhelmed with consolations of every kind by the prodigality of God. Perhaps he received so much sweetness to taste precisely because he sought nothing but bitterness.

As much as John practiced severe corporal penance, he never saw it as a goal. It was for him a naturally indispensable means.

For one thing, it would bring the body and its sensuality fully under control and so prevent being hindered by them in the much more important inner mortification. And again, the suffering of corporal pain could serve as entrance to union with the suffering Savior. It is already evident how much greater weight he put on inner mortification from the fact that his exhortations to practice it take in much more room in his writings and counsels, just as, generally speaking, what pertains to the body takes a strikingly low profile in comparison with what concerns the spirit. True, mention is made several times about the mutual influence, especially of the participation of the body in the life of grace and glory, but in the first line the saint considers the human being a *soul*. It is a hallmark of his that he hardly ever speaks about *people* [or human beings], sometimes about *persons*, but usually about *souls*. He has said himself in clear words how he thinks about the relationship between exterior and interior mortification: "Submission and obedience are a penance of the intellect and of the judgment, and so in the sight of God they are a more pleasing and satisfactory offering than all other corporal works of penance."[53]

"Corporal penance without obedience is very imperfect, because beginners are impelled to it through their desires and through the satisfaction they find in it; since they act only according to their own will, they will increase their faults rather than their virtues."[54]

More than all else he rejected the practice of superiors who imposed excessive rigor in penance on their subjects. He himself always acted with wise moderation and repeatedly had to make good what others had destroyed through excessive zeal. That is how he came to be sent to the Novitiate in Pastrana at the request of our Holy Mother, in 1572, in order to bring to an end the exaggerations of Padre Angel, the Novice Master. When, in the autumn of 1578, a few months after his flight from prison, he was sent as prior to the hermitage at El Calvario he found there, too, an unreasonably exaggerated asceticism and he brought about its mitigation. His keen perception made him recognize that an interior insecurity lay behind such violence. There, he foretold that Pedro de los Angeles (who could not do enough when it came to severe penances) would go to Rome as a Discalced Carmelite, but would return as a Calced. Actually, the overzealous ascetic could not remain firm in his austere ways in the lax Neapolitan court, while on the contrary, John never wavered.

Naturally, in the relationship of exterior and interior mortification also, what is finally decisive is not the doctrine but the life. If we think of the lifelong practice of penance by the saint, it may seem that the purely spiritual cross can hardly surpass it. Of course, an actual comparison in such a case is impossible. There is no numerically demonstrative measure for interior mortification, as there is none for what is purely spiritual, and least of all a measure to compare these with exterior works. All the same—when we think of the basic principles of the saint as he developed them in the *Ascent*[55]: to enjoy nothing, to know nothing, to possess nothing, to be nothing!—then we may surely say that such is the *non plus ultra* of renunciation and even the highest degree of exterior works cannot match it. For the exterior works alone will rather increase self-confidence and in no way lead to the nothing, to the death of the self.

23
Spiritual Renunciation

But how can we prove that John himself really attained to that perfect spiritual renunciation that he requires? Is there not for us a padlock on the interior of this silent saint? True, we are unable to read therein as we can in the heart of our holy Mother, and of so many others who were impelled to write the story of their soul. Meanwhile, however, his heart does betray itself involuntarily in the writings and especially in the poems. In addition there are a great number of testimonies from those who lived with him that give a strong and uniform picture of his personality. Among these latter there are also some that are based on confidential communications from St. John. There were, after all, some people who were so close to him and so united with him in God, before all others his brother Francisco and several Carmelite nuns,[1] that he disclosed for them some of the secrets of his interior.

The purest and least clouded impression is probably given by the poems. In them the heart itself speaks. And in a few of them it speaks in such clear tones that it seems nothing terrestrial clung to them any more. In a few—not in all of them. The *Song of the Dark Night* is full of deep peace. In the sacred silence of this night not a trace remains of the noise and haste of the day. In the *Living Flame of Love* the heart burns in the purest heavenly fire. The world has totally disappeared. With all her might, the soul embraces God alone. Only the *Wound* remains to show the rent between heaven and earth.

The perfect satisfaction of the soul, out of which these *Song*s arise, manifests itself not only in the thoughts they contain but also in their poetic form. Their calm and simplicity are the natural sound of a heart that opens itself in these pure tones, entirely without compulsion and without any arbitrary stress just as the nightingale sings, and as a blossom opens. They are complete masterpieces, because there is no trace of art in them.[2]

The same may probably be said only about two other poems: *The Song of the Shepherd* (*Pastorcico*) and the *Song of the Threefold Spring*.[3] But they differ in content and form from the other two *Song*s and also from one another. In the *Song* of the shepherd the movement of the soul is not expressed immediately. The poet has seen a picture and has given it artistic form. He sees Christ the Crucified, he hears his lament about the souls, "who have arrogantly spurned his love." He forms it into a shepherd's *Song*, as was beloved in his time, and as he did in grand style in his *Canticle*. If there, the *Song* of *Song*s gave the impetus—is there not here the remembrance of the Good Shepherd who gives his life for his sheep? (Jn. 10) And is the lament of the shepherd about the disdainful shepherdess not an echo of that sorrowful call, as the Savior wept over Jerusalem? (Mt. 23:37) The ever recurring words *El pecho del amor muy lastimado* (*his heart an open wound with love*) give the basic feeling. They come from a heart that has forgotten itself and has entered into the heart of the Savior. It is the pure suffering of a soul freed from herself and united with the crucified that expresses itself in this poem. (This is in full accord with the report that during one Holy Week in Segovia he was incapable of leaving the house because he "suffered so intensely from the sufferings and the Passion of Christ our Lord."[4])

In the *Song of the Spring* the soul sings again about something that moves her in her inmost region, as in the *Dark Night* and in the *Living Flame*. But what moves her is not, as it was in those two, her own doing, but rather the interior life of the Godhead, as this was revealed to her by faith: the ever flowing spring, from which all beings come, and who gives to everything all light and life; the flowing spring that conceives another like itself, and together with this second one, brings forth a third of equal fullness. The *Song* that sings of these truths is not in any way a *thought-poem*. It literally *sings*, in the purest musical tones. In it the doctrines of faith have become flowing life: an eternal ocean flows in the calm beat of waves in the soul and sings its *Song* within her. And each time it strikes the shore, there is a dull echo: *Aunque es de noche* ("Although it is night"). The soul has boundaries—she cannot grasp the endless ocean. Her spiritual eye is not accommodated to the divine light—it appears to her as darkness. And so, in the midst of union with the Trinity, and even while enjoying the bread of life by which He gives himself to her, she lives a life of longing desire: *Porque es de noche* ("*Because* it is night."). The substance of dark contemplation is expressed in these verses.

The poem *Vivo sin vivir en mi*[5] ("I live, but not in myself") expresses almost the same thought in its leitmotiv: *Que muero porque no muero.* ("I am dying because I do not die.") The leitmotiv here is not, as it is in the *Song* of the Spring and in that of the Shepherd, a melody that involuntarily rises repeatedly out of the depth of the heart. Here it is a *theme* that is *treated* in variations. The one who constructs these artistic stanzas is conscious of his skill. He plays with the theme: the agony of this life, which is not the true life, is not the vital pain that expresses itself in these verses—it is its mirror image in retrospective thought, in the *reflection* that the poet captures. His powers are still active. And because his soul is not yet united [to God] in total submission without reservation, fear continues to rule that soul—fear that she will lose God, and so she laments her sins and considers them as strong bonds which chain her to this life.

A similarity in form seems to lie in several other poems that have a leitmotiv which is repeated. It is impossible to go into all of them here. Only with regard to the *Spiritual Canticle* need we return once more in this connection. Padre Silverio[6] calls it the first and at the same time the most beautiful among the poems, and truly, some of the stanzas have an incomparable magic. We also made clear for ourselves that the fullness of images are brought into a unity through the dominant bridal symbol.[7] However, it cannot be asserted that this whole splendor of imagery rose out of the depth of the soul without any arbitrary creative intervention. Much of this has been consciously and artistically formed, many a comparison has been fetched from afar. And this pluriformity of images and thoughts corresponds to the content: the restlessness of a mobile inner process of development. If we put this

Canticle, with regard to its content and form, opposite the four poems first discussed, then all of them together give us the answer to the question of how the saint may have practiced interior mortification. His soul has attained to complete detachment from self, to the simplicity and silence in union with God. But this was the fruit of an interior purification in which the richly endowed nature took upon itself the cross and surrendered itself into God's hand to be crucified; a spirit of highest power and vitality had given itself into captivity, a heart full of passionate fire has come to rest in radical renunciation. The reports of witnesses corroborate this result.

Padre Eliseo de los Mártires writes[8] that John did everything "with wonderful equanimity and dignity." "He was engaging in manner and conversation, full of spirit and encouragement for the people who heard him and who spoke to him about themselves. At this, he was so unique and so fruitfully stimulating that those who had anything to do with him left him spiritually enriched, full of devotion and enthusiastic about virtue. He had a high regard for prayer and for keeping in the company of God, and he answered to any doubts that one laid before him concerning either of these subjects with such lofty wisdom that all who sought his advice were very satisfied and improved when he let them go. He was a friend of recollection and of habitual silence. He laughed seldom and with much moderation."

"He was constantly in prayer and in the presence of God, in raising up his spirit and offering fervent brief prayers."[9] He never raised his voice, he knew no crude or silly jokes, nor did he ever give anyone a nickname. He handled all people with equal respect. In his presence no one was allowed to talk about anyone else except in praise. Even at recreation he spoke only of spiritual matters, and as long as he was speaking it never occurred to anyone else to say something. At the end of meals, also, he appended a spiritual talk and held all spellbound in whatever position they had happened to take. Actually, his influence on others was astonishing.

Even when he was with the Calced, his appearance was a signal for silence. With a brief sentence he was able to silence fears and temptations forever.[10] He was also eminent for his discernment of spirits.

Sometimes he sent away postulants who asked for admission into the order, even though they seemed thoroughly qualified to others or accepted applicants when the others had reservations, because to him lay open what was concealed to ordinary human judgment.[11] To one Carmelite nun, in confession, he pointed out a serious fault committed a very long time ago which she had never seen through and so had never confessed.[12]

Here belongs the well known story of our holy Mother, that when he distributed holy Communion in the Monastery of the Incarnation he gave her half of a host, apparently to mortify her because he knew of her predilection for large hosts.[13] He showed himself even more strict toward Madre Catalina de San Alberto Beas. She had declared that she was certain she would be able to receive communion on a particular day on which reception of the Sacrament was customary. When the day came, John passed her by at the distribution, even when she returned a second and third time. When he was asked for the reason, he explained "Sister considered this a certainty; I so acted to make her understand that what we imagine is in no way certain."[14] In both of these cases the saint's procedure apparently rested on knowledge about what the soul needed in order to be freed of imperfections. This sharpened supernatural sight is combined with an uncompromising determination that is not to be seen as a merely natural characteristic.

We know with what reverence and love he looked up to our holy Mother—how would the humble young religious have dared to treat the senior foundress so, had not the power of the Holy Spirit given him the strength to do so? How would this kind and gentle saint have been able on his own to teach in such a sensitive and humbling way as he did in that case in Beas? Of course, this goodness and gentleness are not to be considered merely natural gifts. We know from the incisive statements he made in his *Living Flame of Love,* and at other places in his writings, about inexperienced and violent spiritual directors that John could not be termed "a dove without gall." His descriptions of certain devout types of people in the final chapters of the *Ascent* are of such irony that in personal encounter they could have been very wounding. If, as a superior, he never made use of such sarcasm when relating with those under him, nor in the hours of recreation, this is proof that he was complete master of his nature. He lived what he taught, faithfully. When we compare his sayings about the virtues and gifts with the testimony about his behavior, we find the most perfect correspondence.

He demanded a *faith* that holds simply to the teaching of Christ and of his Church and that seeks no support from extraordinary revelations. During the chapter at Lisbon, several fathers, otherwise serious ones, went to visit a nun about whose stigmata a great deal of fuss was being made. These fathers preserved small pieces of material that were stained with blood from the wounds as though they were relics. John would have nothing to do with such things and neither did he go to see her. When later, in Granada, he was asked at recreation whether he had seen the stigmatic nun, he answered, "I neither saw her nor wished to see her, for I would be very distressed about my faith if it were to grow in the least measure over the sight of such things. "[15] His faith won "from the wounds of Jesus Christ more than from all created things" and had no need of any other wounds.[16]

John wanted a *hope* that "is unceasingly directed to God, without turning one's eyes to any other matter," and he was convinced that such a soul "obtains as much as she hopes for."[17] Padre Juan Evangelista testified that in the eight or nine years during which he lived with the saint he had always seen that he lived totally in hope and that this sustained him. He was able to convince himself of this especially while he was procurator in Granada when John was prior there. One day they were without what was needed for the convent and he asked for permission to go out to find some means of procuring it. He was urged to trust in God, that nothing should be lacking to them. A while later he returned and urged that it was already late and that he had sick brethren for whom he had to provide. The saint sent him to his cell to beg from God what he needed. He obeyed once more, but after a while hurried for a third time to the prior's office and declared: "Father, this is tempting God. Your Reverence must give me permission to go . . . it is already very late." This time he was given the permission, but in this manner: "Go, and you will see how God wishes to shame your deficiency in faith and hope." And really, everything they needed was brought into the house just as he was prepared to set out on his way. He experienced similar things at other times as well.[18]

It is hardly necessary to speak again about love: the entire doctrine of the saint is a doctrine of love, an instruction how the soul will arrive at being transformed in God who is love. All depends on love since at the end we will be judged about love. And his whole life was a life of love: it was intimate union with the nearest relatives in the love of God; self-forgetful, self-sacrificing care for the sick; paternal goodness toward those under him; tireless patience with penitents of all kinds; reverence toward souls; a burning desire to free them for God; a most delicate ability to discern the manifold ways of divine providence, and therefore the most tender adaptation of the various stimuli. For instance, he led the novices out into the open, allowed each one to choose a place according to his own preference "to be solitaries, on the mountain, quite alone, weeping, singing, or praying, as God moves him."[19]

Nor had he any sharp words for his enemies. What they do to him, is for him only the work of God. We will speak of this again. All these various forms of the love of neighbor have their roots in the love of God and in the love for the Crucified. After all, we have continually seen that for him, love is essentially "the practice of perfect renunciation and suffering for the Beloved."[20] How he practiced this in life has already been shown in multiple ways and will become clear in what follows.

The correspondence of his doctrine with his life shall be shown in one more significant instance. John repeatedly stressed in his writings that one should renounce not only all natural knowledge and satisfaction but also all supernatural favors from God—visions, revelations, consolations, and the like—in order to go to meet in dark faith the incomprehensible God himself. The testimony of witnesses from the most varied times of his life point out that the saint was overwhelmed with extraordinary favors of grace. But they also make known that he sought to resist them with all his might. In Segovia, when he went through the house, even while talking with someone, he secretly made a fist and struck the wall with his knuckles to guard against going into ecstasy and losing the thread of the conversation.[21]

To Madre Ana de San Alberto he confided, "My daughter, I always carry my soul into the heart of the Most Holy Trinity. It is the will of my Lord Jesus Christ that I carry it there." But he received such immense consolation so frequently that he thought his weak nature could not support such extremes, and he did not dare to allow himself to become totally recollected. It has already been said that for some days he denied himself the celebration of the Holy Sacrifice of the Mass out of fear that during it something "irresistible would happen to him that would be widely spoken of."[22] Repeatedly he complained about this "weak nature"—too weak to sustain an excess of grace, but strong enough to seek and to desire the cross in every possible form. And the Lord did not fail to grant that as well.

More effective than the mortification one practices according to one's own choice is the cross that God lays upon one, exteriorly and interiorly. The way of his faithful servant was from beginning to end like that of the Savior, a way of the cross: crushing need and poverty in the first years of his childhood, useless straining to be of assistance to his mother in the bitter struggle to exist, then an occupation that demanded the extreme investment of his physical and spiritual stamina and constant subjugation of the self. Such were the beginnings of the school of the cross. Thereupon followed the disappointments regarding the spirit of the Order to which God's call had led him, and surely doubts and inner struggles with the resolution to change to the Carthusians, and after the successful beginning of the Reform in Duruelo a chain of most severe trials and sufferings in the battle over his ideal.

The happiest hours in the life of our Lord were surely those in the silence of night, in dialogue alone with the Father. But they were merely breathing spaces after activity that set him into the tumult of people, which gave him, daily and hourly, the mixture of human weakness, meanness, and malice as vinegar and gall for his drink. John, too, knew the bliss of silent hours in the night, of dialogue with God under the open heavens. As rector of the College in Baeza he bought a piece of land along the river. For days he was there with Juan de Santa Ana He spent the night alone in prayer, but sometimes "he sought out his companion, went with him to sit side by side in a verdant meadow on the bank of the flowing stream and spoke to him of the beauty of the heavens, the moon, and the stars.[23] As prior of Segovia he also had such an oasis: a hermitage that nature had hollowed out of the rock from where a very great stretch of land and sky could be viewed. There he often withdrew, as often as his duties would permit.[24]

To live for prayer in silence and solitude was what he desired from the years of his youth until the end. But for the most of his life he was overburdened by the duties of his offices. And just as he had followed the Savior in loving care for the sick (even with the *charisma* of miraculous healing) so he followed him in the self-sacrificing pastoral care for souls. As long as he was rector in Baeza, following his example, Confessions were heard from morning until night. He was at everyone's disposal. One time, Brother Martín, the porter, asked him for an "easy confessor" for a relative of his, a free-thinking military captain. John himself went down and converted this worldly fellow so thoroughly that he now came to the monastery "day and night" to take part in the community exercises.[25]

John had an inexhaustible patience with the scrupulous to whom no one else was willing to listen anymore. It caused his loving heart the greatest pain to see how souls were misled and tyrannized by ignorant and violent directors. Against these, the mild and kindly saint found as piercingly sharp words as the Savior used against the Pharisees. In the *Living Flame of Love* he interrupts the exposition on the anointings of the spirit, which are given as the most proximate preparation for union with God, to interject a long argument about spiritual directors: "The pity and sorrow of my heart at the sight of so many souls who sink again from the height they had achieved is so great that I cannot rest. . . . " The spiritual director "must be learned and discreet but he must also have experience. . . . If experience is lacking to him in purely spiritual things, then he will not succeed in leading the soul onward when God bestows the spirit on her . . . As a result, many spiritual masters cause great harm to a number of souls. . . . Knowing no more than what pertains to beginners—and please God they would even know this much—they do not wish to permit souls to pass beyond these discursive and imaginative ways of beginners when God wishes to lead the soul to higher levels."[26]

"Were a portrait of extremely delicate workmanship touched over with dull and harsh colors by an unpolished hand, the destruction would be worse, more noticeable, and a greater pity than if many other portraits of less artistry were effaced. The Holy Spirit painted with a delicate hand, and a coarse one spoiled his work. Who will succeed in restoring what has been undone? . . . How often is God anointing a contemplative soul with some very delicate unguent of loving knowledge, serene, peaceful, solitary, and far withdrawn from the senses and from what is imaginable . . . and then along comes a spiritual director who, like a blacksmith, knows no more than how to hammer and pound with the faculties . . . and he immediately directs: 'Come, lay aside all these things, they are all just idleness and a waste of time.'"[27] When such directors lack the necessary knowledge "they should not undertake to meddle rudely at a work they do not understand but should rather leave it to another who does have the necessary knowledge for it. It is no light matter or slight fault to cause a soul to lose inestimable good and sometimes leave it in ruin through presumptuous counsel.

Thus one who recklessly errs . . . will not escape having to give an account for the damage he has caused. The affairs of God must be handled with great tact and foresight, especially such in so vital and sublime a matter as the direction of souls where there is at stake almost an infinite gain in being right and almost an infinite loss in being wrong."[28]

Completely inexcusable is a director who "will not allow a soul he is guiding ever to leave his hands on account of vain considerations and intentions" when the soul has need of some more sublime doctrine than he has. "Not everyone capable of hewing a piece of wood knows how to carve a statue from it, nor does everyone able to carve know how to perfect and polish the work. And not every one who does know how to polish also knows how to paint it, no more than one who can paint it can know how to put the finishing touches on it and bring the work to completion. . . . Were you only a hewer who can lead the soul to contempt of the world and mortification of its appetites, or were you a good carver who could introduce the soul to holy meditations, and if you understood no more—how would you lead this soul to the ultimate perfection which . . . is the work that God must do. . . . God leads souls in varying ways. . . . Where can one find the man who like St. Paul can be all things to all so as to win them all (1Cor. 9:22)? In this way you tyrannize souls and deprive them of their freedom."[29] In the same way, John who was himself a superior who won all hearts through self-giving kindness, and who expressed a necessary reproof with mildness and paternal love, rejected decisively any brutal way of regimented leadership: "If . . . in an Order, Christian and monastic politeness . . . get lost and when instead, superiors are rude and behave brutally . . . one should bewail that Order as lost."[30]

24
Conflicts Within the Order and Final Days

John's hard sayings are inspired by the saint's passionate solicitude for souls. Christ ransomed souls by his passion and death, and every single one is endlessly precious to him and to his faithful disciple. The goal of the Reform was to establish living conditions in which God's perfecting hand could do its work on chosen souls without hindrance. We know what suffering John gladly took upon himself when this work was threatened from external enemies. Perhaps his soul suffered even more when within the reform of the order itself an authoritarian spirit arose which threatened God's working in souls. The danger arose from opposing sides. Padre Jerónimo Gracián was urging external activity in the missions. John was certainly not lacking in an appreciation of the apostolate in heathen lands. He took it very much to heart that in most parts of the world "our true God and Lord" was still unknown and that he was known only in one very small part.[1] But he did not want any external activity at the cost of recollection.

Nicolás Doria represented the opposite extreme, he wanted solitude and strict penance, but he went about mandating this ideal rigidly. This contradicted the spirit of our holy Mother and her first companions; it contradicted the Spirit of God himself, for he blows where he wills. Teresa herself had suffered much because of the defective understanding of her confessors. That is why she made certain in her constitutions that her daughters were to have the freedom of consulting with spiritual guides who earned their confidence. Nicolás Doria wanted to take this freedom from them. Provincial since 1585, vested with far-reaching authority from Rome, he instituted a centralized form of government, a *consulta*, which was to appoint the priors, preachers, and confessors. Together with Teresa's foremost daughters, Ana de Jesús and María de San José, and with the old friends of the Reform, Luis de León and Domingo Báñez, John fought to protect the legacy of the holy foundress. They were, after all, *his* daughters also whose spiritual life was involved. In Avila, in Beas, in Caravaca, Granada, and Segovia, in so many souls under his careful tending, his hand at once both gentle and firm, so many a gorgeous garden filled with blossoms had sprung up just as he had described in his bridal *Song*. Must it not have seemed to him that his life's work was being shattered when now the hailstorm of persecution fell on these gardens of paradise?

At the chapter in Madrid, he had confronted the provincial with full determination, true to his principle: "If no one dares to make the superiors aware or bring forth objections when superiors are at fault . . . and if those who have influence and are obliged by the law of love and justice lack the self-confidence to . . . intervene . . . then one can reckon the order as lost."

As a result of the confrontation, he was deprived of all offices and so of all authority to help others through intervention from outside. Those in authority even went so far as to attack his honor and maneuver to expel him from his order. He maintained the most perfect peace of soul. This shows now that it was a genuine plea when he begged to suffer and to be despised for the Lord's sake; that they were not empty words when he wrote that Christ had accomplished the most marvelous work of his whole life during the time he hung on the cross.[2]

According to the testimony of Padre Eliseo de los Mártires, he had once pointed out while commenting on the passage in Paul—"The signs of a true apostle were performed among you in all patience with signs and wonders and mighty works" (2. Cor. 12:12)—that the apostle ranked patience ahead of wonders. "Thereby he wanted to say that patience is a more certain sign of an apostolic man than would raising someone from the dead be. And I can certify that John of the Cross was an apostolic man because he bore the troubles that were heaped upon him with inimitable patience and resignation, and they were, after all, so severe that they could have toppled the Cedars of Lebanon."[3]

A clear insight into the condition of the soul of the saint is presented by his letters from the chapter in Madrid in which he was passed over in all the elections to an office. To Madre Ana de Jesús[4] he wrote on July 6, 1591: "If things did not turn out as you desired, you ought rather to be consoled and thank God profusely. Since His Majesty has so arranged matters, it is what most suits everyone. All that remains for us is to accept it willingly so that, since we believe he has arranged this, we may show it by our actions. Things that do not please us seem to be evil and harmful, however good and fitting they may be. And it is obvious that this is not evil or harmful, neither for me nor for anyone. It is in my favor since, being freed and relieved from the care of souls, I can, if I want and with God's help, enjoy peace, solitude, and the delightful fruit of forgetfulness of self and of all things. It is also good for others ... for thus they will be freed of the faults they would have committed on account of my misery."[5]

At the same time he asked of María de la Encarnación, who was prioress of Segovia at that time, "Do not let what is happening to me, daughter, cause you any grief for it does not cause me any. What greatly grieves me is that one who is not at fault is blamed. Men do not do these things, but God, who knows what is suitable for us and arranges things for our good. Think nothing else but that God ordains all, and where there is no love, put love, and you will draw out love."[6] The one able to speak thus had interiorly come to resemble the Crucified One.

Now the time had come for him to do so exteriorly as well and to be allowed to die the death on the cross of love. Now his final wishes were to be granted: "I desire only that death should find me in a remote place far from all traffic with people, without friars whom I should have to lead, without friends who could console me, and visited by all kinds of pain and suffering. I wish that God would prove me as a servant, after having tried the tenacity of my character so often in my work. I wish he would visit me with illness, as he has brought me into temptation through health and strength; I wish he would allow me to be tempted by shame as he has allowed me to be tempted by the good name I had even with my enemies. Lord, deign to crown the head of your unworthy servant with martyrdom."[7]

At the chapter in Madrid, the hermitage of La Peñuela was assigned as his residence. This was no punishment for him. He hoped to find there the solitude he so greatly desired. But, after all, one may not think that the arguments and the decisions of Madrid did not move and affect him interiorly. On the way from Madrid to La Peñuela he arrived at four o'clock one morning in Toledo with his companion Padre Elías de San Martín. Both said Mass. They then shut themselves up in a room to converse. Without taking any food, they remained together until far into the night. Then John declared to all that he was departing, completely consoled, and that in the strength of the grace God had given him on this day, he was ready to endure every kind of suffering.[8]

Was that not a Gethsemane-night in which the Lord sent him an angel to console him? All the severe works of penance he had practiced during his life, all the persecutions including the imprisonment in Toledo, and the hostile treatment by the prior of Ubeda, all of this—in the opinion of Padre Silverio[9]—was scarcely more than a shadow image of suffering in comparison with what was caused him by the establishment of the notorious *consulta.* To human view, his life's work lay in ruins behind him, as he set out on the way to Peñuela—just as it was with the Lord when he allowed himself to be bound and led from the Mount of Olives to Jerusalem.

The mountain solitude of la Peñuela afforded him a breathing spell of silent prayer before his ascent to calvary.[10] To be sure, he was not left completely to himself here. The friars were happy to have the father of the Reform with them. The prior bade him to take over the spiritual direction of the whole community. He was with them in recreation. But they were aware that until the hour of recreation he was constantly in prayer. Even before daybreak, he went out to the garden. Then, kneeling among the reeds by the banks of the stream, he remained in prayer until the warm sun reminded him it was time for the Holy Sacrifice. After he had celebrated, he withdrew to his cell and spent all his time in prayer when no duties of the common life called him away. Sometimes he went to a hermitage and remained there as though in ecstasy before God. The witness testifies that occasionally he also was occupied in writing spiritual books. (We are not certain what is meant here. The well known major tracts had all been composed in earlier times.)

The rocks were for him beloved companions. "Do not be surprised at my spending time with them, " he said, "because I then have less matter for confession than when I converse with people."[11] The news that invaded his solitude was well designed to destroy recollection and equanimity. Padre Juan Evangelista wrote to him about the attacks made by Padre Diego Evangelista in the Carmelite monasteries of the nuns in Andalusia, in order to blackmail the sisters into making accusations against the saint. (At that time Sr. Agustína de San José in Granada was given a large collection of the saint's letters—considered by the nuns to be so many "letters of St. Paul"—and note-books filled with quotations from his spiritual lectures and conversations, so that these might not fall into Diego's hands.) When complaints were made to him, Nicolás Doria declared that the visitator had no instructions to act in such a manner, but he did not punish him. He was his close friend and remained that.

John had at an earlier time severely reprimanded this Diego for having spent whole months away from his monastery in order to preach. Now Diego wanted to use the favorable opportunity to get his revenge. A few months later—after the saint's death—he declared: "If he were not dead, the habit would have been taken off his back, and he would have been driven out of the order." Several of the faithful sons of the father of the Reform had been afraid of that. Juan de Santa Ana wrote to the saint to tell him so. He received the reply: "My son, do not be distressed on that account. The habit can be taken away only from those who refuse to amend or obey. Now, as far as I am concerned, I am fully prepared to repair all my faults, and to obey, no matter what penance may be imposed on me." And to Juan Evangelista he wrote: "My soul does not suffer at all from what you tell me. It draws therefrom a lesson of the love of God and of one's neighbor."[12]

So he preserved his peace of heart, " very happy in this holy solitude" and when high fever compelled him to leave it, he did so "with the plan to return here immediately."[13] Just as he had not personally chosen his place of residence before moving to la Peñuela, rather letting himself be assigned somewhere in holy obedience, so now he wished to have a place assigned to him where he should seek healing. He was given a choice between Baeza and Ubeda. Baeza was the college he had founded, and whose first rector he had been. There one of his faithful sons, Padre Angel de la Presentación was prior and awaited him with fervent love. But at the head of the foundation of Ubeda there was Padre Francisco Crisóstomo of whom John had made an enemy in a similar manner as had happened with Diego Evangelista. So for him it was a foregone conclusion that he would choose Ubeda. Since the convent had been established but recently and was poor, and because he himself was unknown in that city, he hoped there to "bear the difficulties of illness with more effect and merit."[14]

So, on September 22, 1591, he mounted the little mule a friend had procured for him and began the last journey of his life. It was truly a most painful one. For several days he could not swallow even a morsel; and his weakness was such that he could scarcely remain on his mule. And the sore leg hurt him so much that it seemed as if it were being cut off. That was, after all the seat of the illness. The leg had at first been very swollen, then one after another five suppurating wounds had opened in it. They gave the saint occasion to pray: "I thank you many times, my Lord Jesus Christ, that Your Majesty has deigned to lend me on this one foot alone the five wounds you bore on your feet, hands and side. How have I merited so great a grace?"

And he never complained even when he had the most excruciating pain, rather he bore everything with the greatest patience.[15] Now in this condition he had to ride seven miles over mountain trails. They proceeded very, very slowly. He spoke of God to the brother who accompanied him. When they had gone three miles, his companion suggested a halt at the banks of the Guadalimar. "In the shade of this bridge your Reverence can rest a little, and the joy of seeing the water will give you an appetite for a mouthful." John consented, "I will gladly take a rest for I need one; but as for eating, I cannot, because I have no appetite for any of the things that God has created, except asparagus, and that is out of season." The brother helped him to dismount and sit down. Then they noticed, on a stone, a bundle of asparagus, bound with an osier twig, as in the market. The brother believed it to be a miracle, but John would not hear of it. He sent the brother to look for the owner and when nobody could be found he had to put a *cuarto* on the stone as payment.[16]

A few hours more—then they were at their destination. The prior received the traveler, sick unto death, and showed him into the poorest and smallest cell in the monastery. The doctor, Licentiate Ambrosio de Villareal, examined the wounds. He diagnosed erysipelas; many collections of pus had formed. A painful intervention had to be made. The surgeon wanted to find the seat of the infection and exposed the bones and nerves from the heel to the top of the calf of the leg. In the excruciating pain, the patient said, "What have you done, señor?" He looked at the wound and cried out, "Jesus, this is what you have done!" Later, the physician told Padre Juan Evangelista, "He suffered the most amazing pain imaginable with incomparable patience." To others he also expressed his wonderment that the sick man could suffer with such peace and so lightly; he declared that John of the Cross must be a great saint, for it seemed to him impossible to suffer such tremendous, continual pain without complaining unless one were very holy and had a great love of God and only if one could count on the support of heaven.[17]

All those around him had the very same impression. The friars considered it a grace to have such a model in their midst. Only the prior remained embittered for a long time. When he visited the patient it was in order to remind him that when John had been vicar provincial of Andalusia he had corrected him. He could not bear to see how the friars and outsiders vied with each other to lighten the suffering of the patient invalid.

(In this respect the precaution to go to a place where he was not know had been in vain: holiness nowhere remains so hidden that it will not find those who revere it.) Don Fernando Díaz of Ubeda had on a former occasion heard John sing the Gospel—at the foundation in la Mancha—and it had been enough for him to have full confidence in him. As soon as he heard of the arrival of the patient, he sought him out and came thereafter to see him daily, sometimes even three or four times a day. Once the prior met him as he was about to take out some of the saint's laundry and bandages to be washed. Several pious ladies considered themselves lucky to be allowed to perform that service of love for him; they were rewarded for it by the wonderful aroma that emanated from these pus-soaked linens. Father Prior now forbade Don Fernando to trouble himself about it, he would see to it himself. He was often heard to complain about the expense of the care of the saint, and how much his food cost.

Padre Diego de la Concepión, prior of La Peñuela, accordingly insulted him when he sent to Ubeda six bushels of wheat for the community and six chickens for the invalid. Padre Bernardo de la Virgen, the infirmarian, noted, day by day, the "very great aversion" that the prior had for the patient. He gave orders that visits were no longer permitted without a special permission, and finally he forbade Padre Bernardo to take further care of John, because he felt he was doing too much for him.

The infirmarian now promptly sent a report to the provincial of Andalusia, the elderly Padre Antonio de Jesús, who had been the saint's companion in the days of Duruelo.[18] The provincial hurried there at once in order to set things right and he remained four to six days in Ubeda. He sharply reprimanded the prior, and gave all the others the command to visit the patient and do for him everything possible, as much as they were able. Padre Bernardo was restored to his office as infirmarian with the injunction to care for him with the greatest love; if the prior were to refuse anything that was necessary, he should at once turn to the provincial and in the meantime, borrow money for whatever was necessary. In all this time not a word of accusation was heard from John against the hostile prior. He bore everything "with the patience of a saint."[19]

Padre Antonio was present at the first operation. As he was about to speak encouragement, John apologized for not being able to answer. He was being "devoured by pain." And still the peak of corporal suffering had not yet been reached. New abscesses formed on the hips and shoulders. The surgeon apologized before the second operation. "No matter, if it is the right thing to do," replied the new Job. He urged the doctor to operate at once. All pain and suffering were for him "benevolent thoughts of God." In the letters that he wrote from that sickbed— they have not been preserved, we know about them only through the testimony of witnesses—he wrote of what a joy it was to be allowed to suffer for the Lord. The corporal torment did not hinder his absorption in prayer. He sometimes bade his youthful nurse, Lucas del Espíritu Santo, to leave him alone—"not in order to sleep" continues the reporter, "but rather to give himself more ardently to the contemplation of heavenly things." Once the infirmarian recognized that, he not only became unobtrusive himself but sometimes sent visitors away. The physician shared the understanding, "Let us leave the saint to pray. When he . . . comes back to himself, we will tend to him."

This physician "had become a different person" at the bed of his patient. The saint gave him a copy of the *Living Flame of Love* written in his own hand. He often read it for his own consolation.[20] The veil that hid the glory of heaven from the soul kept growing more and more transparent. Ever more of the glory shown through it. The physician told the invalid about the near approach of death. A joyful cry is his response: *Laetatus sum in his quae dicta sunt mihi: in domum Domini ibimus.* " [I rejoiced at the things that were said to me: we shall go up to the house of the Lord] (Ps. 122:1). The Fathers wished to give him Viaticum, but he said that he would tell them when he was ready.

Ever since the vigil of the Feast of the Immaculate Conception he knew the day and hour of his death. He gave it away with the words: "Blessed be the Lady who intends me to quit this life this Saturday." Then he made an even more definite statement: "I know that God, our Lord, is about to do me the mercy and favor of allowing me to recite Matins in Heaven."

Two days before his death he used a candle to burn all his letters— a very large number of them—because "it was a sin to be a friend of his." On that Thursday evening, he asked for and received Viaticum. All of those who asked him for a remembrance, he referred to his superior: he was poor and owned nothing. He also had them summon this superior, the prior Francisco Crisóstomo, and begged for forgiveness for all his faults, adding the petition: "My Father, the habit of the Blessed Virgin that I have worn and used—I am a poor beggar and have nothing for my burial—I beg your Reverence for the love of God to give it to me out of love for neighbor." The prior blessed him and left the cell. It appears that in this instant his inner resistance had not yet broken down. But in the end he knelt weeping at the feet of the dying John and excused himself that the "poor convent" had not been able to offer him more to alleviate his suffering. John answered: "Father Prior, I am quite satisfied: I have had more than I deserve. Have confidence in our Lord, a time will come when this house will have all it needs."

On December 13, he asked in the morning what day it was and when he heard it was Friday, he inquired frequently what hour it was: after all, he was waiting to say Matins in heaven. On this last day of his life he was more silent and recollected than ever. Most of the time his eyes were closed. When he opened them, he fastened them, filled with love, on a copper cross.

About three o'clock he asked that Padre Sebastián de San Hilario be brought to him. This was a young friar to whom John had given the habit in Baeza. Now he was ill of a malignant fever some cells away. He was brought in and remained perhaps a half hour. John had an important message for him: "Padre Sebastián, your Reverence will be elected a prior of the order. Pay attention to what I tell you, and try to bring it to the notice of superiors, telling them that I mentioned it to you immediately before my death." It was something that was important for the growth of the Province.

At five o'clock the saint broke into an exultant cry: "I am happy that, without deserving it, I shall be in heaven tonight." Soon thereafter, he turned to the prior and Fernando Díaz: "Father, will your paternity send word to Señor Fernando's home that they should not wait for him, he must remain here tonight." Then he asked for the holy anointing and received it with deep devotion; he gave all the responses to the prayers of the priest. At his urgent request the Most Blessed Sacrament was brought once more for his adoration. He spoke tenderly to the hidden God. In farewell, he said, "Lord, now I shall see you no more, with eyes of flesh."

Padre Antonio de Jesús and several other elderly fathers wished to stay with him, but he would not permit it. He would have them called when it was time.

When it struck nine, he spoke with great longing: "Three hours more. *Incolatus meus prolongatus est*" [My sojourning is prolonged] (Ps. 119:5) Padre Sebastián heard him also say that God had granted him three petitions for his consolation: not to die a superior; to die in a place where he was unknown; and that, after having suffered much. Then he lay so still and peacefully engrossed in prayer that they thought he was already dead. But, coming to himself again he kissed the feet of "his Christ." At ten o'clock he heard a bell ringing. He asked what that was for. They told him that his brothers were going to Matins. "And I," he said, "by the mercy of my God am going to recite them with the Virgin, our Lady, in Heaven." At about eleven-thirty he had them call the fathers. About fourteen or fifteen friars came who were ready for Matins. They hung their lamps on the wall as they came in. They asked the saint how he was. He grasped a rope that hung from a beam in the ceiling and raised himself up in bed. "Fathers, shall we recite the *De profundis?* I feel quite well." He looked "very calm, beautiful and happy," according to the testimony of the subprior, Ferdinando de la Madre de Dios. He intoned the psalm himself, the others responded. In this way "I don't know how many" psalms were recited according to Francisco García. They were the penitential psalms, which precede the *recommendation of the soul.* The reports given do not correspond on whether that followed immediately after the psalms and at what point John interrupted the prayers. He had become tired and had to lie down again. And he had one more wish: that someone would read to him part of the *Song* of *Song*s; the prior did so. "What precious gems!"[21] It was, after all, the love *Song* that had accompanied him through life.

Again he asked what time it was. Midnight had not yet struck. "At midnight I shall stand before God to recite Matins." Padre Antonio reminded him of everything he had done for the Reform, at its beginnings and later as superior. The saint replied, "God knows what took place in those days." But he did not want to count on that. "Pater Noster,[22] this is not the time to be thinking of that. It is by the merits of the blood of Our Lord Jesus Christ that I hope to be saved."

His brothers asked for his blessing and, at the provincial's command, he gave it. He recommended that they be truly obedient and become perfect religious.

Shortly before midnight he handed "el santo Cristo," his crucifix, to one of the bystanders, probably Francisco Díaz. He wished to have both hands free to lay out his body for burial. He then took it back and now he took leave of it, speaking most tenderly of the Crucified as he had earlier of the Eucharistic Savior.

Twelve strokes sounded from the bell tower. The dying man said, "Brother Diego, give the signal to ring the bell for Matins, for it is now time." Francisco García, bell ringer of that week, went out. John heard the tone of the bell and said, with the crucifix in his hand "*In manus tuas, Domine, commendo spiritum meum* [Into your hands, Lord, I commend my spirit]."

A parting glance at all those present, a final kiss for the Crucified One—then he stood before the throne of God to pray Matins with the heavenly choirs.

In this dying is there not some of the divine freedom with which Jesus Christ bowed his head on the cross? And just as on that first Good Friday signs and wonders proclaimed that it was truly the Son of God who had died on the cross, so now, too, heaven gave witness that a good and faithful servant had entered into the joy of his Lord.

Between nine and ten o'clock that evening, when at the wish of the saint most had gone to rest, Brother Francisco García had come to the head end of the bed and had settled himself between the bed and the wall to pray his rosary. As he was praying, the thought occurred to him that perhaps he might be able to have the joy of seeing something of what the saint beheld. While the psalms were being recited by the fathers, he suddenly saw a globe of light begin to shine between the ceiling of the cell and the foot end of the bed. It was so brilliant that it dimmed the fourteen or fifteen lamps of the friars and the five candles on the altar. As the saint expired without anyone noticing it, Brother Diego was holding him up in his arms. And he suddenly saw a great brightness over the bed. "It shone like the sun and moon, the lights on the altar and the two wax candles in the cell were covered as by a cloud and seemed to give no more light." Only then did Diego notice that the saint in his arms was lifeless. "Our Father went to heaven with that light," he told those present. Then when he and P. Francisco and Brother Mateo prepared the saint's body for burial a most sweet perfume emanated from it.[23]

Notes

ICS INTRODUCTION

1. See *Self-Portrait In Letters: 1916-1942* in *The Collected Works of Edith Stein*, 5, trans. Josephine Koeppel (Washington, D.C.: ICS Publications, 1993). All other references to Edith Stein's letters will be found in this volume.
2. See Sister Teresia de Spiritu Sancto [Posselt], *Edith Stein*, trans. Cecily Hastings and Donald Nicholl (New York: Sheed and Ward, 1952), 118.
3. Cf. *The Hidden Life* in *The Collected Works of Edith Stein*, 4, trans. Waltraut Stein (Washington, D.C.: ICS Publications, 1992), 91-93.
4. For a complete portrait of John see Federico Ruiz, et al., *God Speaks in the Night*, trans. Kieran Kavanaugh (Washington, D.C.: ICS Publications, 1991).
5. Jean Baruzi, *Saint Jean De La Croix et le Problème de l'Expérience Mystique, édition revue et corrigée avec les deux préfaces de Jean Baruzi (1924 et 1931),* intro. by Emile Poulat (Paris: Editions Salvator, 1999), 7-23.
6. *Obras del Místico Doctor San Juan de la Cruz, edición crítica, 3 vols.* (Toledo, 1912-1914).
7. Cf. P. Silverio de Santa Teresa in *Obras de San Juan De La Cruz*, 1, ed., P. Silverio de Santa Teresa (Burgos: El Monte Carmelo, 1929), 203-262.
8. See *The Ascent of Mt. Carmel*, bk. 2. chap. 5 in *The Collected Works of St. John of the Cross*, trans. Kieran Kavanaugh and Otilio Rodriguez, O.C.D. (Washington, D.C.: ICS Publications, 1991), 162-166.

9. Stanza 23, no. 6, in *The Collected Works*, pp. 264-265.
10. Ibid., stanzas 14 &15, no. 2, pp 525-526.
11. For facts about the manuscript and the Dutch Carmel see Francisco Sancho Fermín, *Edith Stein Modelo y Maestra de Espiritualidad* (Burgos: Editorial Monte Carmelo, 1997), 265-270; 207-208.

PREFACE

1. [Edith Stein/Sr. Teresa Benedicta used the critical edition by Padre Gerardo de San Juan de la Cruz (Toledo, 1912), known as the Edición Crítica and cited hereafter as "E.Cr.". At the very beginning of her work, she identified her quotations from Fathers Ambrose/Aloysius, the 1927 German translation of Padre Gerardo's critical edition. But soon she changed to cite only from Gerardo's critical edition. The quotations from St. John of the Cross in this English translation are to be found in *The Collected Works of St. John of the Cross*, tr. Kieran Kavanaugh and Otilio Rodriguez, O.C.D. (Washington, D.C.: ICS Publications, 1991). Cited hereafter as "CWJC".]

CHAPTER 1

1. Père Bruno de Jésus-Marie, O.C.D., *St. Jean de la Croix*, Paris 1929. [The English edition is by Benedict Zimmerman, O.C.D., *St. John of the Cross* (New York: Sheed and Ward, 1932). Hereafter cited as "Bruno *St. John*".]
2. Ibid., 10.
3. See J[ean] Baruzi, *St. Jean de la Croix et le Problème de l'Expérience Mystique* (Paris, 1931), 77f. Hereafter cited as "Baruzi".
4. Ibid., 91.
5. See Bruno *St. John,* 261.
6. Mt 20:19; 26:2.
7. Mt 10:38.
8. Mt 16:24; see also Mk 8:34 and Lk 9:23; 14:27.

9. Lk 9:23.

10. Lk 9:24; see also Mt 10:39; Lk 17:33; Jn 12:25.

11. *Edición Crítica* (Toledo, 1914), vol. 3, 173f. The shepherd's song is the plaint of the spurned Savior's love. One must not assert that here John is thinking of the people of Israel as the bride. There is a close relation to the individual soul here. [See CWJC, 57.]

12. Ibid., 174ff. [Also CWJC, 60.]

13. *S. Propheta Dei Elias Ord. Carmelitarum Dux and Pater,* inscription on the saint's statue in the Vatican Basilica. [See also CWCJ, 175 note 4 for A.2.8.4.]

14. According to our chronicler the original was written in Greek. The Latin translation by Aymericus of Antioch has been handed down to us as published in Salamanca, 1599. A French translation was published in the periodical *La Voix de Notre Dame du Mont Carmel,* Edition des Carmes Déchaussés, I-II, 1932-1933. [Today experts agree the work was written in Latin by the Carmelite provincial from Catalonia, Philip Ribot (d.1391). See John Welch, O.Carm., *The Carmelite Way* (New York: Paulist Press, 1996), 49-62.]

15. 1 Kgs 17:3-4.

16. 1 Cor 1:17-18, 22-24.

17. Phil 2:7,8.

18. Gal 2:19-20.

19. Rom 6:3ff.

20. Gal 6:14.

21. Gal 6:17.

22. 2 Cor 12:9.

23. Gal 5:24.

24. See Bruno *St. John,* 53f; also the *Vida* of Gerardo de San Juan de la Cruz in E.Cr., I, 36f.

25. See Bruno *St. John,* 220.

26. We hope that in the most recent persecution of the Church it has remained intact. There is a good copy of the sketch in Bruno's book.

   [In her note Edith refers to events during the Spanish Civil war that began in 1936. Three Carmelite nuns killed at that time have been beatified. John of the Cross's drawing is the frontispiece of the I.C.S. edition of the saint's complete works and a full description is given in the general introduction to that volume.]

27. Bruno declares it was a painting on leather depicting Christ bearing the cross. (*Vie d'Amour de Saint Jean de la Croix* [Paris, 1936], 238) He published this picture in the book St. Jean. But would the saint really have used the term *crucifijo* for such a picture? [A colored photo of this painting may be found in *God Speaks in the Night,* Federico Ruiz et al. (Washington, DC: ICS Publications, 1991), 338].

28. Thomas Perez de Molina wrote down the statement as Francisco, who could not write, dictated it. As he recalled it, the words were: "Lord, that all may attack my honor and consider me as nothing, for your love's sake." (See *Vie d'Amour*, 239.)We have given the whole account as literally as possible in order not to detract from its touching simplicity and to allow the intimate relationship between the two brothers to become apparent through it. There was the most profound bond between them throughout their lives. When the Reform began, John called his mother, brother, and the latter's wife, to come to Duruelo to take care of the household. His mother did the cooking, the sister-in-law the washing, and his brother swept the cells. At first glance, this may be surprising in a saint who demanded such severe detachment from all creatures. But surely there is no contradiction here. If John acted in this manner, he did it advisedly: he did not find being together with his loved ones a hindrance in the contemplative life. From their childhood on, their relationship was presumably so much elevated to the supernatural sphere that it could no longer constitute a restriction. And where those closest according to blood are as well the closest in spirit there is such an ease of understanding that it is a foretaste of heavenly bliss. This also explains the intimacy of their communication.

29. See Bruno *St. Jean*, 329.

30. Letter 246 of August 1578, to Padre Jerónimo Gracián, in edition of his writings, Vol. V.2 (Regensburg, 1914), 294. [That information must have come in Bruno's book. Edith added her own marginal note here in her manuscript. Her reference is given as

letter 249, August 1578, taken from the *Neue Deutsche Ausgabe der Schriften* (Munich: Kossel-Pustet, 1939).]

31. Hieronymus de San José, *Historia del V.P. Fr. Juan de la Cruz* (Madrid, 1641), Vol. III, Chap. VII. ["Armen-Sünder"—poor sinner—is a colloquial expression for a condemned criminal so it was a very plain stool such as was used in a cell.]

32. [Edith here uses in German the word "Duckmäuser" as the epithet given John for bearing all "with patience and love". As this account is cited as coming from Jerónimo de San José, his Spanish word may be translatable as "hypocrite" but hers is definitely "coward". Cf. Bruno *St. John,* 169.]

33. For sources, see Bruno *Saint Jean,* 407.

34. Letter to Catalina de Jesús, Discalced Carmelite, Baeza, July 6, 1581 [In CWJC, Letter 1]. Holy Mother intervened for him with Gracián to effect his recall to Castile (her Letter 362 was written in Palencia on March 23 or 24, 1581 to Gracián).

35. He confided this to the venerable Sister Ana de San Alberto. See Bruno *St. John*, 170.

36. This was harshly refused, but Our Lady personally came to his assistance immediately thereafter. See Bruno *St. John*, 178ff.

37. See poem 8: *For I know well the spring (Que bien sé yo la fonte)* Gerardo (E.Cr., III, 142) assumes that, except for a few stanzas that were added later, this poem originated in prison. [CWJC, Poem 8. Poems hereafter cited as "P".]

38. Compare the introduction to *The Spiritual Canticle (Cántico Espiritual)* in E.Cr., II, 137f. and the stanzas of the Canticle in the same volume 161ff, and in III, 158ff. [In CWJC see C. Stanza 1, 12. In the translation of the entire poem, Edith uses "keening" but here she translated the line as " . . . left me behind in tears."]

39. Cf. CWJC, N. Stanza 5, 359.

40. See Bruno *St. John,* 175.

41. [That the "Dark Night" was written in prison is unlikely.]

42. [See CWJC, A.2.7.3.]

43. [CWJC A.2.7.5 "to seek God in oneself" expresses John's meaning. Instead, Ambrose translated the Spanish (E.Cr., I, 122) "buscar

a Dios en sí" in *Aufstieg zum Berge Karmel*, 100, ambiguously as "Gott in ihm suchen" i.e. "to seek God in him." Edith, choosing "him" with a capital "H" as a reference to God, wrote "Gott in Gott" ("God in God") here.]

44. [CWJC A.2.7.5 reads "all that is most distasteful in God or in the world; and this is what loving God means." Here, Edith did not copy from Ambrose the qualifier "most" nor his "joyfully ready to choose."]
45. See E.Cr., I, VI, 122-3. [CWJC, A.2.7.6.]
46. [CWJC, A.2.7.7.]
47. [CWJC, A.2.7.11.]
48. E. Cr., II, 282. [CWJC, C.Stanza 23.2.]

CHAPTER 2

1. *De divinis nominibus*, chap. II, no. 2, Migne P.G., III, 640.
2. Here we will not go into the disputed question whether they were never completed or were subsequently mutilated. [Whenever sources are mentioned in this book, it must be remembered that much research has taken place since 1942 and Edith's access to what was available in her circumstances was very limited.]
3. Other poems also stem from the time of his imprisonment but we are concerned for the time being only with those which serve as the starting-point for the treatises.
4. The bridal symbol is no less significant, but that is not pertinent at this point. When treating of the *Spiritual Canticle* it will be spoken of in detail.
5. [Here, in the German there is a juxtaposing of the words *Gegenspiel—Gegenstand* which it is impossible to duplicate in English. Counterpart and object give the meaning but miss the interesting wordplay.]
6. [Edith writes *"seelisch-geistige"* here, an awkward construction to point out a specific application of what might otherwise be an ambiguous use of *"Geist"*. She returns to this thought below.]
7. E.Cr., III, 160f. [CWJC, C.Stanza 15.]

CHAPTER 3

1. Text in E.Cr., III, 157 (CWJC, 50ff.) The translation [by Edith] is done with the help of various versions given in the German edition published by the Theatiner Publishing house, plus a literal Flemish translation by Cyriel Verschaeve, *Schoonheid en Christendom* (Brugge, 1938), 57f., in order to give the original text as nearly as possible.

2. [1) "Ventura" was translated into the German "Geschick" which connotes "skill" as well as "chance or fate".

   2) There are two connotations in the German *Liebessehnen*: love's yearning or love's tugging sinews. Two other versions Edith consulted used "love's woes" (Ambrose) and "love aglow with fervor" (Cardinal Diepenbrock). In the text below the soul is said to "strain with all one's might" and "tugging sinews" expresses that effort more accurately than would possibly languid "yearning".]

3. A.1.4.4.

4. This is treated in the first book of the *Ascent of Mount Carmel* [hereafter referenced as "A"] and in the first part of *The Dark Night* [hereafter referenced as "N"] which is entitled *The Dark Night of the Senses.*

5. This *obscurity*, grounded in sin, is totally different from the *darkness* that has its origin in God and that leads to the elimination of that obscurity.

6. [CWJC, A.1.5.2; A.2.6.4.]

7. [CWJC, A.1.13.2.]

8. [Ambrose uses "Eindrücke", i.e., impressions, for "experience satisfaction" in this context.]

9. [CWJC, A.1.13.6-8.]

10. [CWJC, N.1.3.3.]

11. [CWJC, N.1.3.1.]

12. [CWJC, N.1.8.3.]

13. [CWJC, N.1.8.2.]

14. [CWJC, N.1.9.3.]

15. [CWJC, N.1.9.4.]

16. [CWJC, N.1.9.8. The following quotations are from N.1.9.6-7.]
17. [CWJC, N.1.9.6.]
18. [CWJC, N.1.9.6-7.]
19. [CWJC: The quotations in this section are taken from N.1.10.1,3,4,6.]
20. [CWJC, N.1.12.6. In the remainder of this commentary excerpts are briefly quoted. They may be located in N.1.13,14.]
21. N.2.3.1.

CHAPTER 4

1. A.2.3.1.
2. A.2.3.2.
3. See A.2.3.2-4.
4. See A.2.4.2-4 for this and the following quotes.
5. See A.2.4.4.
6. See A.2.4.5ff.
7. A.2.4.6.
8. A.2.5.3.
9. The preceding excerpts will be found in A.2.5.3-4; this final one is from A.2.5.7.
10. See A.2.7.6,7. [Here Edith copied from the German translator the ambiguous terminology by which the Spanish: *"buscase a sí mismo en Dios"* (seeking self in God) is juxtaposed to *"buscar a Dios en sé."* Ambrose expressed the latter in German as *"Gott in ihm suchen"* which literally is: *"looking for God in him."* Edith capitalized the "I" in "ihm," thereby making the pronoun refer to God rather than to the person himself. However, by adding the qualifiers explaining what is sought, it is clear that John's teaching in A.2.7.5 is being expounded here. Edith continues to quote from A.2.7.6-7, in what follows here.]
11. A.2.7.5.
12. A.2.7.8. [The word *ramas* was translated as "water sprouts" by Ambrose.]

13. [This may well be the longest passage copied literally from Ambrose. It gives an insight into Edith's "understanding of the mystery of Christ." See A.2.7.11.]

CHAPTER 5

1. See A.2.8.3.
2. See A.2.8.4.
3. See Pseudo-Dionysius Areopagite, *De mystica theologia,* I, 1; A.2.8.6. [See also Edith Stein, "Ways to Know God" in *Knowledge and Faith* (Washington, D.C.: ICS Publications, 2000), 83-118.]
4. A.2.9.1.
5. Ex 19:9-16; 24:15-18. See A.2.9.3.
6. 1 Kgs 8:12; see also 2 Chr 5:13,14 and A.2.9.3.
7. Jgs 7:16-20. See A.2.9.3. [This is a symbol of the relationship between faith and divine light.]
8. Cf. A.2.11.6 for this and the preceding quotations.
9. [In this entire section, Edith has at times condensed John of the Cross's teaching, and at others quoted literally from A.2.10-11. She will continue to do this in what follows, and does not in every instance give the exact reference.]
10. This and the preceding quotes are taken from A.2.12.3-5.
11. These are given in the *Ascent* 2.13.2-4 in a somewhat different form. [The first sign given in the *Night* is the second in the *Ascent.* The second sign in the *Night* is the third in the *Ascent.* The third sign in the *Night* is the first in the *Ascent.* In the *Night* these signs denote the purifying action of God in the soul through the onset of infused contemplation.—Editors' note by Gelber/Leuven.]
12. The preceding quotations can be found in A.2.14.2.
13. A.2.14.11; see also Sir 35:17.
14. Cf. A.2.15.4-5.
15. A.2.16.9. See also Nm 12:6-8.
16. The excerpts in this section may be found in A.2.17.3,5,9.
17. For this and preceding quotations see A.2.22.3-8.

18. [This and the preceding quotations are taken verbatim from Ambrose's German translation. See A.2.22.7-11.]
19. Cf. A.2.23.1-4 for the teaching and the excerpts quoted here and immediately following.
20. [At this point, Ambrose's translation lists "God, angels, souls" as incorporeal beings. The Spanish (E.Cr., Lib. II, Cap. XXII) reads here *"como son el Ser Divino, Angeles y almas".* *Ser Divino* (the Divine Being) is not found in any of the manuscripts of the "Ascent". Cf. A.2.24.2-4 for this quotation and the two that follow.]
21. Cf. A.2.24.4.
22. A.2.24.5-9.
23. Cf. A.2.26.5-9 for this and the preceding notes.
24. Cf. A.2.26.3-10 for this and the preceding quotes. [The slight variations come from Ambrose's translation of St. John into German which was Edith's source here.]
25. [This should read "spirit of prophecy." Here Edith copies from Ambrose "Geist der Propheten," i.e., "spirit of the Prophets," whereas St. John [E.Cr., Libro II, Cap. XXIV] writes "al espíritu de profecía." Cf. A.2.26.11.]
26. For this quote and the foregoing doctrine see A.2.26.13-18.
27. These and the foregoing quotes are to be found in A.2.27.4-7.
28. This and foregoing quotations are from A.2.29.6-7.
29. This and foregoing quotations are from A.2.29.6-7.
30. A.2.29.12.
31. A.2.30.3.
32. See A.2.30.5.
33. A.2 31.2. For the quotations preceding this one see A.2.30 and 31.
34. [Here there is a discrepancy between the Archivum Carmelitanum *Kreuzeswissenschaft* and the autograph. "Wenn" (when) and "wem" (to whom) can easily be misread by a copyist. Both Ambrose and CWJC A.2.32.2 agree that "to whom" is correct for the Spanish "a quien"—cf. E.Cr., I, 265.]
35. A.2.32.4.
36. A.2.32. [This final chapter of Book Two of the Ascent contains the many quotations in the text here.]

CHAPTER 6

1. See A.3.2.3-6 to compare this quotation and the preceding ones.
2. A.3.2.14. [Cf. CWJC for a more exact rendering of St. John's teaching here. The German translation from which Edith copied the quotation follows a different version of the Spanish.]
3. For this and preceding quotations, see A.3.3.4. [In the German translation from which Edith copied literally, another quote is attributed to St. John of the Cross here: "In any case, that which solely refers to God and what contributes to that dark and general, pure and simple knowledge of God need not be renounced but only that which brings him near to us through a figurative presentation or through comparison with a creature." It does not appear in E.Cr. nor in A.3.4. Father Michael Linssen, O.C.D, Director of the Archivum Carmelitanum Edith Stein (b. Sep. 4, 1939-d. May 23, 2001), put it in an endnote in his Dutch translation of *Kreuzeswissenschaft*, adding the comment "The content is not consistent with the argumentation of St. John's doctrine."]
4. For these quotations see A.3.3.3-6.
5. A.3.4.1.
6. For the quotations in this section see A.3.5.2-3.
7. See A.3.6.2-3.
8. These quotations may be checked against A.3.7.2.
9. A.3.8.5.
10. A.3.9.1-4.
11. For this and the foregoing quotations see A.3.10.1-2.
12. Cf. A.3.12.1 for this and the following quotes.
13. Cf. A.3.13.3.
14. Cf. A.3.13.4.
15. [For the teaching and quotations found in the preceding paragraphs see A.3.13 in its entirety, especially par. 6-8.]
16. [For a Thomistic concept of *passio* see St. Thomas Aquinas' *Quaestiones Disputatae de veritate*. Edith Stein made a translation of this work into German in 1931-32.—Editors' Note by Gelber/Leuven.] [For the quotations here and above, see A.3.14 and 15.]

CHAPTER 7

1. With reference to this and preceding quotations see A.3.16.1-6.
2. See A.3.17.2.
3. [Cf. CWJC, Letter 13.]
4. [Edith's note here attributes these quotations to "a hitherto unpublished source in E.Cr., I, 402ff." The probable source: Letter 13, To a Discalced Carmelite Friar etc.]
5. [Edith again calls it a quote from an hitherto unpublished fragment, E.Cr., I, 406. See again L 13.]
6. A.3.18.3.
7. A.3.19.3-4.
8. A.3.19.5-6.
9. A.3.19.8.
10. A.3.19.11.
11. A.3.20.4.
12. Cf. A.3.20.1-4.
13. Quotations here and above are from A.3.21.1-2.
14. For this and preceding quotes cf. A.3.22.1-6.
15. For this and preceding quotations see A.3.23.1-6.
16. For this and preceding quotations see A.3.24.1-5.
17. [Note that the Spanish in E.Cr., I, 343 "enemistad a la servidumbre" is paraphrased by Edith as "reluctance to perform acts of service." In CWJC it is translated in 3.25.4 as "aversion to servants."]
18. For the other quotations in this section see A.3.25.1-6.
19. This and preceding quotations are from A.3.26.1-8.

CHAPTER 8

1. This and preceding quotations are taken from A.3.27.1-4.
2. This and preceding quotations may be found in A.3.28.1-9.
3. This quotation and preceding ones are from A.3.29.1-5.
4. For this and preceding quotations see A.3.30.1-5.

5. A.3.31.4.
6. For this and preceding quotations see A.3.31.2-10.
7. [The text of Ambrose's translation of John of the Cross has "will" in this instance. A question mark and a note of Edith's here suggest that perhaps another word was expected in place of "will", that is, the memory as the faculty which corresponds to hope. The editors of the German edition here appended their own note: "Satisfaction in the will" is correct according to the Thomistic viewpoint, as may be seen in *Sum. Theol.,* II, q 2 a 18 c "Spes est in appetitu superiori, qui dicitur voluntas, sicut in subjecto." But Edith was right in questioning the word since John of the Cross says "memory" here.]
8. The quotations here are from A.3.32.1-4.
9. See A.3.33.5 and notes thereto.
10. A.3.34.
11. See A.3.35.1-7 for this and preceding quotations.
12. For this and preceding quotations see A.3.36.1-3.
13. A.3.37.
14. A.3.38.5.
15. A.3.39.2.
16. Should be Gen 22:2. Edith copied Ambrose's reference to Exodus.
17. A.3.42.6.
18. A.3.43.3.
19. A.3.44.3.
20. For this and preceding quotations see A.3.44.4.
21. The quotations here and in preceding paragraphs may be found in A.3.45.1-5.

CHAPTER 9

1. In some of the manuscripts [of the Spanish of St. John of the Cross] the two fragments that were published in E.Cr., I as Chapters 45 and 46 follow. We have used their content at an earlier point in this book where they were relevant. (See the beginning of the preceding section on the Purgation of the Will.)

2. As a brief guide to mysticism (understood as a theological discipline) we may consider the *Treatise on the Dark Positive and Negative Knowledge of God*. Gerardo, for the first time, printed them in the works of the saint (E.Cr., III, 287ff.) In his introduction (page 271ff.) he mentions some reasons that may be adduced for and against the authenticity of this manuscript. In my estimation there are a series of *interior* reasons *against* the authenticity, which Gerardo does not mention. Therefore, I cannot assume that the work stems from the saint himself and must use a great deal of caution when making use of it. However the author, in any case, has an exact knowledge of the writings of our holy Father; there are sharp and clear compilations. On the whole, however, it appears to me, there is a certain displacement of the crucial point toward the purely natural and active. It may also be that there was no personal experience of the highest stages of passive prayer, which was what the saint was primarily considering.

3. *Living Flame of Love*.1.10. Explanation of the third line of the first stanza. [This work is hereafter cited as "F".]

4. *De Trinitate*, XII 4 and 7.

5. In actuality, *Thomas* connects the memory with sensuality because it recognizes the past *as* past, therefore distinguishing it from the present: this, he says, is a function of sensuality. Because the intellect recognizes not only the present, but also *that* it recognizes, so to say, that it possessed this knowledge before, the memory may be counted as belonging to the spiritual part of the soul. (*De Veritate* 9, 10a 2 corp.; *Investigations of Truth*, I, 266ff.)

6. [Here Edith used *entzogen* (taken from) and *erzogen* (educated) employing a mnemonic device in German which cannot be duplicated in translation.]

7. In explaining the manifold concepts covered by the word *faith* I am following here the distinctions that St. Thomas makes in the *Quaestiones disputatae de veritate,* q 14 a 7 ad 7. [This is the work of Aquinas which Edith translated from Latin into German.]

8. [See CWJC, A.2.29ff.]

9. Cf. A. 2.14.2 ff. *The Short Treatise on the Dark Affirming and Negating Knowledge of God*. E.Cr., III, 287ff.

10. See A.2.3 and A.2.5.4.

CHAPTER 10

1. A.2.7.11ff.
2. Pseudo-Dionysius the Areopagite, *Mystica Theologia*, I, 1.
3. John speaks about the relationship of faith and contemplation at different points in different expressions. We shall return to this topic at the end of this paragraph.
4. N.2.3.3.
5. N.2.4.1-2.
6. N.2.5.2.
7. This and the foregoing quotations are taken from N.2.5.1-5.
8. N.2.5.6-7.
9. This and the foregoing quotations are from N.2.6.1-6.
10. This and the preceding quotations are from N.2.7.4-7.
11. This and the preceding quotations are from N.2.8.1-5.
12. N.2.9.3.
13. N.2.9.5
14. N.2.9.6-7.
15. This and the foregoing quotations are from N.2.9.6-9.

CHAPTER 11

1. [In the German edition, the reference is given as "(5 Mos. 5,6)." The transposition was copied exactly from page 115 of Aloysius's translation of John of the Cross.]
2. The quotations in this section are from N.2.11.
3. This and the preceding quotations are from N.2.12.1-7.
4. Cf. N.2.12.7.
5. N.2.12.7.
6. [In German handwriting the *un* of "Trunkenheit" (inebriation) and the *oc* of "Trockenheit" (dryness) appear almost indistinguishable. In her Manuscript (page 221) Edith has clearly and correctly copied from Aloysius: "Trunkenheit" (page 125). In *Edith Stein's Werke* (Verlag Herder: Freiburg-im-Breisgau, 1953-1983) in all three editions of *Band 1*, page 121, the word is mistakenly given as "*Trockenheit*." Cf. N.2.13.5.]

7. [Here John of the Cross quotes from *Psalm 103* and immediately follows with a quote from Eph 4:24 in the same sentence. Aloysius did not include the second quote but gave a reference to the first, and Edith copied exactly.]
8. For this and preceding quotations see N.2.13.1-5;11.
9. N.2.16.4-5.
10. For this and preceding quotations see N.2.16.7,9,13,14.

CHAPTER 12

1. Cf. N.2.17.3.
2. This and the preceding quotations are from N.2.17.6-8.
3. Cf. N.2.18.4.
4. This and the preceding quotations are from N.2.18.1-5.
5. [In *Kreuzeswissenschaft* part of the phrase "persisting *yet unwearied* suffering" was omitted making the quotation incomplete; also, the source, St. Augustine, is not identified.—Editors' note.]
6. The exposition on the rungs of the ladder may be found in N.2.19.1-5. [The variations in expression can be explained in that the Spanish manuscript of the *Dark Night* translated into German and used by Edith is not the same one translated as CWJC.]
7. [A serious typographical error is to be found on page 128 of the 1983 Archivum Carmelitanum volume, *Kreuzeswissenschaft*. The incorrect word "Beschauung" (contemplation) when compared with the text of Edith's handwritten manuscript shows she clearly and correctly copied "Beschämung" (being shamed) from page 158 of Aloysius's translation. In script an abbreviated line is used over the *u* to distinguish it from an *n*; in Edith's handwriting, the two dots (umlaut) over the *a* are joined together, probably causing it to be taken as a line over the next letter, *u*. If this is overlooked St. John would erroneously be quoted as " . . . nor can she be restrained through *contemplation*."]
8. The quotations in this section may be found in N.2.20.1-6, although with slight variations in wording.

9. There are differences in expression but this and the preceding quotations are to be found in N.2.21.1-12.

10. N.2.22.1.

11. [Edith copied this rather unusual expression exactly from Aloysius's translation of the *Dark Night,* page 174.]

12. [Where Edith's literal translations and quotations from Aloysius vary from Kavanaugh/Rodriguez, though only in expression not in meaning, the text follows hers. Compare this and the preceding quotations with N.2.23.1-14.]

13. N.2.24.1-4.

14. N.2.25.1-4.

15. [According to *Kreuzeswissenschaft,* six *stanzas* are said to have been explained. This is clearly a mistake, according to the editors of the volume. Kieran Kavanaugh, in a commentary within his introduction to the *Dark Night* addresses the question, pointing out that only two stanzas were fully commented on, with six unexplained. If Edith was writing at speed it does not take much imagination to suppose she said six and meant two. See CWJC, 353.]

CHAPTER 13

1. Here one must recall that in these distinctions we are using a spatial image for something that is not spatial. Actually, the soul "has no parts, and there is no difference as to inward and outward." Cf. F.1.10.

2. What can here merely be indicated in a few words about spiritual being is explained in detail in *Finite and Eternal Being: An Attempt at an Ascent to the Meaning of Being.* [Vol. 9 of *The Collected Works of Edith Stein* (Washington, DC: ICS Publications, 2002).]

3. F.1.12. [The expression "point of rest" was copied literally by Edith from the translation by Aloysius, page 13. In a long footnote, the German translator pointed out that St. John of the Cross wrote at a time when science had not yet arrived at the designation "center of gravity." The concept St. John used did not come from physics, but

rather from the philosophy of his day which held that whatever was material was attracted by what was "more" material—a stone fell to the earth because it was the smaller of the two and it would have kept on "falling" until it reached the very center of the earth, where the earth's material weight was greatest.

Hereafter, "point of rest" will usually be translated as "deepest center," but it should be noted that it describes not merely a place but also an activity. The soul has not only arrived at a point, but it is "actively" resting there.]

4. A.2.26.14.

5. See *Disputed Questions on the Truth*, q. 8 a 11 c. [The reference here is to Edith's German translation of this work of Thomas Aquinas.]

6. See Ibid., q.8 a 8 ad 7.

7. Cf. F.2.32-3.

8. Our Mother St. Teresa of Jesus likens the soul to a castle with many dwelling places. In her principal mystical work, the *Interior Castle*, she tells of seven Dwelling Places (*The Interior Castle,* 1.1).

9. Our holy Mother calls the body the outer wall of the castle.

10. [The German word "Mensch," in the singular, means human being, whether masculine or feminine; the plural, "Menschen," means people or mankind. For the singular, the masculine pronoun "he" is consistently used. This translation will follow the German in the use of the masculine for "Mensch" as, for the same reason, "she" is used consistently when the soul is spoken of, and "he" when the Spirit ["Geist"] is discussed.]

11. *Disputed Questions on Truth*, q.9 a 4.

12. Cf. F.4.14-16.

13. *Interior Castle,* VII.1.3.

14. F.1.9.

15. F.3.78f.

CHAPTER 14

1. A.2.5ff. Here only this life is taken into consideration; the union in glory, which is again different, is not included.

2. *Spiritual Canticle*, 11.3.
3. *Interior Castle*, V.1.10.
4. Thomas Aquinas, *Truth*, q 19 a 2 c.
5. *Interior Castle*, V.3.
6. *Interior Castle*, V.1.12; V.2.9,12.
7. *Interior Castle*, V.1.6.
8. [This and the preceding quotations are from *Interior Castle*, V.1.9-11.]
9. [*Interior Castle,* VI.4.1.]
10. F.3.25.
11. We shall see later that also in the *Spiritual Canticle* the explanation is not completely uniform.
12. A.2.32.2.
13. Cf. on this Baruzi, Vol. 1: *Les Textes*, as well as the Introduction in the most recent critical edition by Silverio.
14. Letter to M. Ana de Jesús, October 1578.
15. *Spiritual Canticle*, 13.7.
16. When in one and the same created being the indwelling modifies itself, it is in fact a modification [a change of mode] and not a combination of one mode with another. When a soul receives sanctifying grace, God does not then dwell in her in two differing modes; rather, the indwelling of presence and that of grace are a single unit.
17. "Multi *crediderunt* in nomine eius. . . . Ipse autem Jesus non *credebat* semetipsum eis" (Jn 2:23-24). Cf. Augustine, *Tract. in Joan.* 11-12, Migne, P.L., XXXV, 1474ff.
18. *Interior Castle*, V.1.9; N.2.20.3; *Spiritual Canticle*, 13.2.
19. *Interior Castle*, VI.6.9; *Spiritual Canticle,* 14-15.2.
20. *Interior Castle*, VII.1.5; *Spiritual Canticle,* 22.2.
21. It is impossible here and now to examine how far this can be validly applied to human interpersonal relations.
22. F.3.78.
23. In the discussion of the *Living Flame* we will arrive at it at once. St. Teresa describes the Blessed Trinity's descending to the mystical marriage in *The Interior Castle,* VII.1.

CHAPTER 15

1. A.2.2.1.
2. Among others, A.2.5.3; A.2.7.3; A.2.8.6. Pseudo-Dionysius uses the expression "ray of darkness" in the first chapter of *Mystical Theology.*
3. A.2.9.3.
4. Here at the same time we have documentation for the description of faith as loving knowledge. For contemplation, cf. especially A.2.13 & 14.
5. A.2.10.4.
6. A.2.14.2.
7. *Spiritual Canticle,* 12.2.
8. This feeling herself in the depth is something other than the simple knowledge of self that the holy Mother already assigns to the first dwelling place. It is a becoming aware of oneself without stepping opposite oneself. In this, one's own being remains mysterious, just like the presence of God therein. Here, the inmost center is not restricted to the seventh dwelling place, where the marriage takes place, but rather comprises the entire sphere of the mystical event.
9. Night of the Spirit, 2.7.4.
10. *The Living Flame of Love.* It should be noted that this could also be read as *Flame of Living Love.*
11. F.Prologue addressed to Ana de Peñalosa.1.
12. Jn 7:38.
13. F.1.1.
14. This and the preceding quotations may be found in F.1.4-6.
15. F.1.8.
16. This and the preceding quotation are from F.1.9,14.
17. This and the preceding quotations are from F.1.15-17. The distinction made with regard to eternal glory and the taking up of the matter of doubts about the possibility of receiving such superabundant graces are additions from (B), the second redaction.
18. F.1.17-18.
19. This and preceding quotations are found in F.1.23-26.

20. F.1.27-28.
21. F.1.30-31.
22. F.1.35.
23. With this the explanation of Stanza 1 comes to a close. F.1.35-36.

CHAPTER 16

1. F.2.1.
2. F.2.2-4.
3. [St. Teresa's] *Life,* 29.13-14.
4. John wrote this about two years after the death of our holy Mother. He did not yet know that the transpiercing left visible traces on her heart.
5. F.2.12-13.
6. This and preceding quotations are taken from F.2.17-20.
7. F.2.21.
8. F.2.21-22.
9. F.2.27-28.
10. This and preceding quotations are from F.2.33-36.

CHAPTER 17

1. In F.3.2.
2. 2 Mac 1:19-23.
3. F.3.8.
4. Cf. F.1.8.
5. F.3.10.
6. F.3.17.
7. [Here there is a significant typographical error in the Archivum Carmelitanum editions (1-3) which may confuse scholars. The word *harm,* in German "Schaden," was misprinted as "Schatten." Edith's handwritten manuscript very definitely has "Schaden," i.e. harm, which is the correct term in the context. "Schatten," shadow, is incorrect and confusing especially since in the paragraphs preceding this there was a discussion of "shadows."]

8. This and preceding quotations are from F.3.14-18.
9. This and foregoing quotations are from F.3.21,22.
10. It was already stated earlier [note 269 above] that betrothal here is not used in the strict sense of mystical betrothal—in contrast to the *Spiritual Canticle,* Stanzas 14 and 15.30.
11. F.3.25-26.
12. This and preceding quotations are from F.3.68-69. See these especially, with their notes, to understand what is meant by "sense" and "feeling" in these paragraphs on the "caves."
13. F.3.76.
14. End of the explanation to F.3. This and the preceding quotations are found in F.3.79-84.

CHAPTER 18

1. These last quotations and the paraphrases of the doctrine of St. John are from F.4.1-14.
2. F.4.16.
3. End of the treatise on the *Living Flame of Love* and Stanza 4, F.4.17.
4. *Living Flame of Love*, explanation to Stanza 3, Paragraph 27. At that point we passed over that insertion in order not to break the thought process. It will find application in our Part III.
5. St. John availed himself of every opportunity to give an example of living by the Word and applying its lessons to his own life.
6. Our rendering of the content of the *Living Flame* gives but a very weak picture of this since we have used but a very few of the abundant scriptural examples. (This also applies in the other writings.) Anyone who wishes to get the correct impression must themselves take up the saint's writings.
7. F.2.31. [Est 6:10-11 and 8:1-2,15.]

CHAPTER 19

1. [The German is taken from the Archivum Carmelitanum volume of *Edith Stein's Werke*, Vol. 1, 3rd edition (Verlag Herder: Freiburg-

im-Breisgau, 1983). Following the German version is its *literal* translation into English, i.e., the translator concentrated on meaning without regard to rhyme or rhythm.]

2. This is the stanza which, as stated above, was inserted in the second redaction. [A short introduction to the *Spiritual Canticle* in the CWJC, pp. 461-68 gives more recent information on the two redactions.—Trans.]

3. Rom 8:26.

4. *Spiritual Canticle,* Prologue.3—foreword to Anne of Jesus who asked for an explanation of the stanzas.

5. Cf. the helpful and pertinent explanation of the Inquisition by J. Brouwer, *De achtergrond der Spaanse mystiek* (Zutphen, Netherlands, 1935).

6. Cf. Silverio in the appendix to the *Spiritual Canticle, Obras*, III, 456.

7. Compare the explanation of Stanza 27 (B version) with Stanza 22 (J version).

8. Cf. *Spiritual Canticle,* Prologue.4. [This work is herafter cited as "C".]

9. How much he is working here naturally as an artist, and how much under the special inspiration of the Holy Spirit, cannot be measured. We shall return to this question.

10. *Obras*, III, 131f.; 319f. [See in CWJC the Theme given immediately before Stanza 1 of the Canticle as well as the Commentary to Stanza 22.3. "Pouring out a thousand graces," quoted there, is the first line of the fifth stanza mentioned without a number in that commentary.]

11. C.1.14.

12. C.1.17.

13. Cf. above the explanation of the various forms of union.

14. C.1.20.

15. Explanation of C.13.2.

16. This corresponds also with the opinion of [Pseudo-Dionysius] the *Areopagite* with whom the tripartition originates.

17. Therefore in what follows the numbers given to stanzas will be from the second redaction, and the number assigned to that stanza

in the first redaction will be shown in parenthesis. (This is the reverse of what we have done so far.)

18. Cf. Eph 5:23ff.

CHAPTER 20

1. This is the Carmelite nun for whom he made the sketch of the Mountain. Cf. Letter 17, and *Obras I*, 133.

2. Commentary on Stanza 12(11).4.

3. Commentary to Stanza 13(12).2.

4. Commentary on the last line of Stanza 13(12).12.

5. Introduction to Stanza 14(13) and 15(14).2.

6. [The Spanish "Dios mio, y todas las cosas" was translated into German by Aloysius of the Immaculate Conception as "My God and my all." Edith took this quote literally from his translation.]

7. Jn 1:4, in a translation formerly in use.

8. Commentary on Stanzas 14 and 15.5.

9. Commentary on Stanzas 14 and 15.11.

10. Pseudo-Dionysius, *The Mystical Theology*, 1.1.

11. Commentary to Stanza 15(14).23.

12. St. 15(14), line 3.

13. Introduction to Stanza 16.2. (This stanza has been added in the second redaction.)

14. Commentary on Stanza 16.6.

15. Commentary on Stanza 17(26).10.

16. Commentary on Stanza 18(31).4. [This line seems a perfect example of a forced or far-fetched application of a scriptural reference. It should be noted that Edith herself makes a parenthetical comment on this in the next paragraph. It would be unfortunate to lose sight of the reality that every one of us has such a lower, sensory part of the soul that is weak, carnal, and blind.]

17. Commentary on Stanza 20(29).10.

18. Commentary on Stanza 21(30).15.

19. Commentary on Stanza 22.4.

20. This commentary to Stanza 23(28) is quite expanded in the second redaction. The comparison of the betrothal at baptism with the mystical betrothal is a new addition. It is due to the effort to bring union of grace and mystical union into close connection.

CHAPTER 21

1. We see that sin and its consequent necessity for redemption are not the only motivation for the incarnation. [Another reason] seems to us to be sufficiently inherent in the ordering of creation toward its perfection in Christ. John of the Cross also knows of a reason for the incarnation independent of the fall into sin. Cf. the *Romances*, P 9.
2. Commentary to Stanza 22.4.
3. John of the Cross treats of the incarnation as marriage with humanity when he writes of creation in the *Romances* (P 9). Here this marriage indeed appears to be the motive for creation. Remarkably, the fall into sin is totally ignored in the *Romances*. The redemption appears as liberation from the yoke of the law.
4. Cf. the Commentary to Stanza 25(16).2 and 7.
5. Commentary to Stanza 26(17).3.
6. Commentary to Stanza 26(17).5.
7. Commentary to Stanza 26(17).14-17.
8. Commentary on Stanza 26(17).18-19.
9. Commentary on Stanza 17.8.
10. Introduction to Stanza 28.1.
11. Commentary to Stanza 28.2-8.
12. Introduction to Stanza 29.2.
13. Commentary on Stanza 29.5-11.
14. Introduction to Stanza 32.1.
15. Commentary on Stanza 32.6-9.
16. Commentary on Stanza 33.1,7-8.
17. Commentary on Stanza 35.5-6.
18. Commentary on Stanza 36.6,11,13.
19. Commentary to Stanza 37.3-4.

20. Commentary to Stanza 38.3.
21. Commentary to Stanza 38.5-8.
22. Commentary on Stanza 39.3-4.
23. Commentary to Stanza 39.8-10.
24. Commentary on Stanza 39.10-12.
25. Commentary on Stanza 39.12-14.
26. Commentary on Stanza 40.5-7.

CHAPTER 22

1. Teresa of Jesus, *The Book of Her Foundations,* Chap.14.6. [Washington, D.C.: ICS Publications,1985.]
2. A.3.37.2, see also above Section II.#2.1(e).
3. See above I.#4.
4. Bruno *St. John,* 355.
5. [A room separated by double iron barriers into two sections where the sisters, singly or in community, met their visitors in Carmelite monasteries is often referred to as "the speak room."]
6. Bruno *St. John*, 297.
7. Cf. *Otros Dictamenes de Espíritu*, Dictamen decimo, E.Cr., III,70. [Not in CWJC.]
8. [These letters were copied exactly by Edith from the 1925 German translation of St. John's writings. Since then more research has been done on the letters. Compare, for significant differences in meaning, the letters Edith quotes and their translations in the ICS *Collected Works of St. John of the Cross.* N.B.: this letter and the six which follow are meant to show St. John's care of those under his spiritual direction.]
9. [Letter 11 in *The Collected Works of St. John of the Cross*. This was no. 10 in the German translation. Hereafter the numbers assigned in the German will be given in parentheses following the number in CWJC.]
10. Letter 7(6).
11. Letter 9(9).

12. Letter 12(11).
13. Letter 16(15).
14. Letter 19(19) to Juana de Pedraza.
15. Letter 25(21) to Madre Ana de Jesús, in Segovia, July 6, 1591.
16. [Cf. *Censure and Opinion*, CWJC.]
17. [Cf. *The Precautions*, Against Oneself etc. CWJC.]
18. [Four *Counsels to a Religious*. 4. CWJC.]
19. [Cf. *Counsels to a Religious*. 6. CWJC.]
20. [Cf. *Sayings of Light and Love*. 4. CWJC.]
21. [Cf. *Sayings*.14.]
22. [Cf. *Sayings*.54 (50 in E.Cr., III).]
23. [This and the eight quotations which follow are taken from *Otros Avisos y Sentencias*, E.Cr., III, 24ff. This is no. 76 of the sentences which are not included in CWJC.]
24. [Ibid., Sentence 77.]
25. [Ibid., Sentence 78.]
26. [Ibid., Sentence 80.]
27. Ibid., Sentence 81.
28. Ibid., Sentence 83.
29. Ibid., Sentence 84.
30. Ibid., Sentence 87. [Cf. also for the first half of the maxim, *Sayings*.175. CWJC.]
31. Ibid. Sentence 293.
32. Cf. S.165.
33. *Otros Dictamenes de Espíritu*, E.Cr. III, 67, first maxim.
34. Ibid., No. 2.
35. Ibid., No. 5. [This is nearly identical with the fragment of a letter to Padre Luis de San Angelo. Cf. L 24.]
36. *Heavenly Hierarchies*, 3.3. Migne, P.G., III, 165. The quotation is not exact in its wording.
37. *Dictamenes de Espíritu*, No. 10, E.Cr., III, 63.
38. Ibid., Sentence 11.
39. E. Cr., III, 57.
40. Bruno *St. John*, 223-4.
41. St. Teresa, *The Book of the Foundations,* 13.1.

42. Ibid., 13.3.
43. Ibid., 14.7.
44. Ibid., 14.8.
45. Cf. Bruno *St. John*, 86.
46. *Otros Avisos y Sentencias*, 355, E.Cr., III, 56.
47. Ibid., 356, E.Cr., III, 56.
48. Cf. Bruno *St. John*, 89.
49. These were hemp sandals made by hand; they were the usual foot-wear of the very poor.
50. Ibid., 303.
51. *Life and Works of St. John of the Cross*, Jeronimo de San José (Seville, 1702); in a French edition of the Carmelite Nuns (Paris, 1877).
52. Baruzi, 221. A whole series of accounts of this incident has been pre-served. Compare with the one of Brother Peter, another one given by Bruno in his *Saint John*, 347-8. "If God has sent me these great suffer-ings . . . why wish to soothe and lessen them by music? . . . I wish to endure, without any relief, the gracious gifts which God sends me."
53. *Avisos y Sentencias*, E.Cr., III, #286.
54. As above, #287.
55. As in II.1.C.2 (Active Entrance into the Night) above and in II.2.A (Divesting the Spiritual Faculties).

CHAPTER 23

1. Bruno and Baruzi used these sources, Bruno primarily from the acts of the Roman process for beatification and Baruzi out of Ms. 12738, among others from the National Library in Madrid. Silverio has included a portion of the testimonies in the latest Spanish edition of the works of St. John of the Cross: *Obras* IV, Appendix, 354ff.
2. There is nothing contradictory to this when John is found to be formally influenced by the poets of his time, occasionally even demonstrating linguistic leanings on them. For a literary evalua-tion of the poems, cf. the introduction by Silverio, Vol. 4 of the works, page LXXICff., and Baruzi, 107ff.

3. P 7 and 8.
4. Bruno *St. John,* 319.
5. P 5.
6. In *Obras* IV, page LXXIX.
7. Above in II.C.2) c. and d.
8. In *Obras* IV, 348.
9. 3rd Saying, *Obras* IV, 349.
10. Cf. Baruzi, as above, 290ff., and the testimony of Padre Martín de San José in *Obras* IV, 377.
11. Cf. the same testimony as above.
12. Baruzi, as above, 292.
13. St. Teresa, *Spiritual Testimonies*, no. 31.
14. Baruzi, as above, 293.
15. See the testimony of Martín de San José, *Obras* IV, 377.
16. Testimony of Juan Evangelista, as above, 390.
17. 119th Saying, E.Cr., III, 29.
18. Testimony of Juan Evangelista, *Obras* IV, 190f.
19. Bruno *St. John,* 308.
20. No. 123, *Avisos y Sentencias*, E.Cr., III, 30.
21. Bruno *St. John*, 317 as above.
22. Bruno *St. John*, 220.
23. Bruno *St. John*, 216.
24. Bruno *St. John*, 316ff., as above.
25. Bruno *St. John,* 222.
26. *Living Flame of Love*, Stanza 3.30-31ff.
27. F.3.42-43.
28. F.3.53-55.
29. F.3.57-59.
30. 15th Saying, E.Cr., III, 65.

CHAPTER 24

1. Bruno *St. John*, 291.
2. A.2.7.11.

3. Number 13, *Dictamenes de Espíritu*, E.Cr., III, 64.
4. This Ana de Jesús [Jimena] is not our holy Mother's renowned collaborator but rather the Foundress of the Carmel of Segovia.
5. Letter 25 to Madre Ana de Jesús (Jimena), in Segovia, July 6, 1591.
6. Letter 26 to María de la Encarnación (Jimena), July 6, 1591.
7. J. Brouwer, *De achtergrond der Spaanse mystiek* (Zutphen, 1935), 217.
8. Bruno *St. John*, 330.
9. *Obras* I, page 113, (Preliminares).
10. Bruno *St. John*, 332ff. and *Obras* V, 112ff. (Testimony of Padre Francisco de San Hilarión).
11. As above, Bruno *St. John*, 333.
12. Bruno *St. John*, 336 as above.
13. Letter 31 to *Dona Ana de Peñalosa,* September 21, 1591.
14. Testimony of Padre Pedro de San José, *Obras* V, 99.
15. Testimony of Padre Diego de la Concepción, *Obras* IV, 355.
16. Cf. Bruno *St. John*, as above, 342; testimony of Padre Bartolomé de San Basile, *Obras* IV, 394 and of Padre Francisco de S. Hilarión, *Obras* V, 114. One of the variations is that Bruno gives the distance in leagues which would double or triple the mileage to cover, depending on the Spanish units of measure. One version at least has the saint leave two *cuartos*.
17. Testimony of Padre Ferdinando de la Madre de Dios, *Obras* V, 114.
18. Padre Antonio, who had so generously made himself available as the first one to join in the Reform, was granted the great grace to support both our holy Mother and holy Father St. John at the hour of their death.
19. Bruno *St. John*, as above, 343ff.
20. Bruno *St. John*, as above, 348.
21. Bruno *St. John*, 355.
22. The Provincial was addressed that way in the Order [at that time].
23. The entire account of the death is given in Bruno *St. John,* chapter 21, 350ff. The notes thereto bring, in part, some literal statements from testimony by the witnesses.

Bibliography

I. WORKS USED BY EDITH STEIN IN WRITING
THE SCIENCE OF THE CROSS

This list is based on the bibliography prepared for the translation into Dutch (Carmelitana: Gent, 1987) by Fr. Michael Linssen, O.C.D., president of the Archivum Carmelitanum Edith Stein.

Areopagite. *See* Pseudo-Dionysius.

Augustine, St. *De Trinitate*. Migne, PL XLII.

_____. *Tractatus in Joannem*. Migne, PL XXXV.

Baruzi, Jean. *St. Jean de la Croix et le problème de l'expérience mystique*. Paris: Alcan, 1931.

Brouwer, J. *De Achtergrond der Spaansche Mystiek*. Zutphen, 1935.

Bruno of Jesus and Mary, O.C.D. *Saint Jean de la Croix*. Paris: Plon, 1929.

_____. *Vie d'Amour de Saint Jean de la Croix*. Paris, 1931.

Jerónimo de San José. *Historia del Venerable Padre Fr. Juan de la Cruz*. Madrid, 1641. See also below: Juan de la Cruz, *Vie et oeuvres*.

Juan de la Cruz (St. John of the Cross).

_____. *Des Heiligen Johannes vom Kreuz sämtliche Werke*. 5 vols. Trans. Aloysius of the Immaculate Conception and Ambrosius of St. Teresa, Discalced Carmelites, Munich, 1924-1929. [N.B. Although Edith took verbatim, so many quotations from them, inexplicably these volumes are not included in the bibliography that the editors of the *Edith Steins Werke,* Romaeus Leuven, O.C.D., and Dr. L.Gelber, prepared for *The Science of the Cross*. The citation is still missing in the third German edition of 1983, but is included in the bibliography for the Dutch translation (1987). For the first few footnotes in her manuscript, Edith gave the German translation as reference but then soon began to identify only the *E.Cr.*, volume and page numbers, since these would be universally applicable. This may account for the omission of these German volumes in the bibliography. Trans.]

_____. *Obras de San Juan de la Cruz Doctor de la Iglesia.* Editadas y anotadas por Silverio de Santa Teresa, O.C.D. 5 vols., Biblioteca Mística Carmelitana, 10-14. Burgos, 1929-1931. Abr.: *"Obras."*

_____. *Obras del Místico Doctor San Juan de la Cruz* Edición Crítica y la más correcta y completa de las publicadas hasta hoy, con introducciones y notas del Padre Gerardo de San Juan de la Cruz, Carmelita Descalzo. 3 vols. Toledo, 1912-1914. Abr.: *"E.Cr."*

_____. *Vie (par le Père Jerôme de Saint-Joseph) et oeuvres spirituelles de l'admirable docteur mystique le bienheureux P. Jean de la Croix.* Traduction nouvelle faite sur l'édition de Séville de 1702, publiée par les soins des Carmélites de Paris. Paris, 1877.

Migne, J.P. *Patrologia Graeca.* Paris, 1857-1866. Abr.: "Migne, PG."

_____. *Patrologia Latina.* Paris, 1844-1855. Abr.: "Migne, PL."

Pseudo-Dionysius. *De caelesti hierarchia.* Migne, PG III.

_____. *De divinis nominibus.* Migne, PG III.

_____. *De mystica theologia.* Migne, PG III.

Stein, Edith. *Des hl. Thomas von Aquino Untersuchungen über die Wahrheit (Quaestiones disputatae de veritate).* Her German translation, vols. I and II, Breslau: Otto Borgmeyer, 1931-1932; publ. as vols. 3 and 4 of *Edith Steins Werke,* Louvain, 1952, 1954.

_____. *Endliches und Ewiges Sein. Versuch eines Aufstiegs zum Sinn des Seins.* This work was not yet published in German, but still in manuscript form, when Edith Stein wrote *The Science of the Cross.*

Teresa de Jesús (of Avila). *Obras de Sta. Teresa de Jesús.* Editadas y anotadas por el P. Silverio de Sta. Teresa, O.C.D. Vols. 1-9. Biblioteca Mística Carmelitana. Burgos, 1915-1924.

_____. *Sämtliche Schriften der Hl. Theresia von Jesu.* Neue Deutsche Ausgabe übersetzt nach der Spanischen Ausgabe des P. Silverio de

S. Teresa, O.C.D. von P. Aloysius ab Immaculata Conceptione aus dem Orden der Unbeschuhten Karmeliten. 6 vols. Munich, 1933-1941.

Verschaeve, C. *Schoonheid en Christendom*. Brugge, 1938.

La Voix de Notre Dame du Mont Carmel. Edition des Carmes Déchaussés, I-II, 1932-1933.

II. WORKS USED IN THE TRANSLATION OF THIS BOOK

Bruno, of Jesus and Mary, O.C.D. *St. John of the Cross*. Introduction by Jacques Maritain, ed. and Postscript by Benedict Zimmerman, O.C.D. New York: Sheed & Ward, 1932.

The Collected Works of St. John of the Cross. Trans. Kieran Kavanaugh, O.C.D. and Otilio Rodriguez, O.C.D. Washington, D.C.: ICS Publications, 1991.

The Collected Works of St. Teresa of Avila. 3 vols. Trans. Kieran Kavanaugh, O.C.D. and Otilio Rodriguez, O.C.D. Washington, D.C.: ICS Publications, 1976-1985.

Stein, Edith (Sr. Teresa Benedicta of the Cross, O.C.D.). *Ways to Know God*. Trans. Rudolf Allers, Lebanon, PA., 1981 [appeared in later translation by Walter Redmond in *Knowledge and Faith*. Washington: ICS Publications, 2000. "The Collected Works of Edith Stein," 8.]

Index of Persons and Places

Alcalá, 27
Ana de San Alberto, Sr., 298
Ana María de Jesús, Sr., 24,
    175, 279, 305
Ambrosio de Villareal, 309
Andalusia, 29
Avila, 24, 27, 30
Antonio de Heredia, 285-6,
    310, 312-3

Baeza, 23, 277, 280, 295, 298,
    304
Baruzi, Jean, 5, 288
Bernard, St., 143
Bernardo, Padre, 310
Bridget, St., of Sweden, 11
Bruno of Jesus and Mary, O.C.D.,
    5, 285

Caravaca, 23, 304
Castile, 28-9
Catalina, John's mother, 7,
    286
Crisóstomo, Francisco, 26,
    308

David, 22
Díaz, Fernando, 309, 312-3
Diego Evangelista, 307, 314
Doria, Nicholas, 25, 279,
    287, 303
Duruelo, 9, 27, 285-6, 298,
    310

El Calvario, 277, 289
Elijah, 19, 25
Eliseo de los Mártires, 294,
    304

Fontiveros, 15
Francis St., 248
Francisco, John's brother, 16,
    25, 291;
    with his family, 22
Francisco Mateo, Brother,
    314

García, Francisco, 314
Germán, 26, 28
Gethsemane, 23, 30, 306
Golgotha, 22-3, 30

Goliath, 22
Gracián, Jerónimo, 25, 27,
 287, 303
Granada, 11, 296, 304

John, St., the Evangelist, 249
Juan Evangelista, 17, 287,
 296, 307
Juan, (Yepes) de la Cruz
 (John of the Cross), 9,
 confirmed in grace, 17;
 23-27
 de Santo Matías
 (of St. Matthias), 9
Juana de Pedraza, 279
Jerónimo de San José, 287

Leonor Bautista, Mother, 277
Lucas Del Espíritu Santo, 311

Madrid, 25, 304-5
Magdalen of the Holy Spirit,
 245
Maldonado, 27, 29
Mancera, 27
María de la Encarnación, 25,
 305

Mariano, Ambrosio, 27
Martín, Brother, 287, 299
Mary, the Blessed Virgin, 13,
 15, 22, 313
Medina del Campo, 13, 22,
 285
Moses, 72

Paradise, 32
Pastrana, 27, 289
Paul, St., 72
Pedro de San José, 287
Peñuela, La, 26, 306, 310

Salamanca, 16, 113, 285
Sebastián, de San Hilario,
 312
Segovia, 25, 297, 299, 304-5
Silverio de Santa Teresa, O.C.D.,
 6, 293

Teresa, of Avila, 24-27, 29,
 167-175, 196-7, 275, 285,
 303
Toledo, 27-28, 30-31, 306

Ubeda, 26, 308

Subject Index
of Edith Stein's Thought

Contemplation, 54, 58, 66,
   69, 136, 152, 176, 182-3,
   191, 239, 262

Denudation, threefold, 61
Detachment, process, 45

Ethics, 165
Emblem, 41-2, 259

Faith, vital role in reaching
   goal, 10, 21, 46, 53, 59,
   61, 65, 112
Feeling(s), 10, 114, 209
Freedom, fruits of spirit ripen
   in, 54, 86, 117, 136, 145,
   148, 153, 159-165, 178,
   237

God, soul's relationship with,
   116-117;
   plan in creating the soul,
   242
Goal, must be known to
   understand the way, 81

Grace, impossible to receive
   grace unless freely accepted,
   168

Human being, 5, 37, 41, 55,
   58, 115, 118, 142, 156,
   160, 162-8, 177, 260, 272

"I", The, that in soul by
   which she possesses herself,
   160; its movements, 162-3
Image, 10, 12-13, 15-16, 18,
   23, 26,36, 39, 41, 46, 58,
   71, 73, 116-119, 142, 154,
   158-9, 177, 182, 237, 242,
   246, 272, 283
Indwelling, new mode of,
   176

Love, divesting herself of all
   that is not God, 61

Night, 46-47, 49-50
   John's prevailing symbol,
   night not cross, 3;

dark night school of all
virtues, 53

Person, 10, 12, 47, 49, 58, 66,
74, 77-8, 115-6, 118, 154-5,
161-3, 165, 168-9, 177-9,
183, 195, 197, 205, 208, 210,
213, 257, 261, 265

Realism, 10-12, 18

Science, of cross, 10-1, 15, 17,
20-1, 23, 26, 31, 33, 38, 275
Self-knowledge, won
through experience of dark
night, 31
Spirit(s) , 153-7
duties, abilities,
communication, 160-61
Spiritual, in the inmost heart,
the life of the soul from
and in God, 157
Sin, 19, 21-2, 49-50, 91-2,
102, 143, 168, 184, 196,
209, 251, 255-7;

most terrible result of sin,
passion and death of
Christ, 260-1, 266, 272-3,
293
Symbol, 9, 12, 17, 26, 38-42,
146-7, 237, 242-3, 247,
267, 293

Union with God, 59, 63,
65-8, 73-5, 81, 83, 84, 86,
88-90, 103, 112, 129, 133,
140, 152, 167, 169, 171,
173;
knowing God in new way,
178; this kind of union,
John's goal, 179, 191,
201-3, 210, 255, 271,
281, 284

Vocation, of Discalced
Carmelite, participation in
Christ's cross, 9; name in
religion, mission, 9; of artist,
become an image of what he
portrays, 12

Index of Texts
from St. John of the Cross

In listings marked by an asterisk (*) a note explains a difference between the German translation which was Edith's main source and the writings of St. John as found in *The Collected Works of St. John of the Cross* (Washington, D.C.: ICS Publications, 1991). See the latter also for a subject index. (The references for the *Ascent* and the *Dark Night* are to chapters and paragraph numbers.)

Ascent of Mount Carmel

Book One		7.5,6	32;62	16.9	70	29.6-7,12	
1.4	45	7.7-11	64;	17.3,5,9			76-7
5.2	47		121;		71	30.3-5	78
13.2	48		304	22.3-11		31.2	79
13.6-8	49	7.8	63		70-1	32.2*	80;
		8.3,4	65	23.1-4	71		178
Book Two		8.6	66;181	24.2-4*		32.4	80;82
2.1	181	9.1-3	66;181		72		
3.1-5	58;	10.4	182	24.5-9	73	Book Three	
	119	11.1-6	67	26.1-10		2.3-6	82
4.2-4	59,60	12.3-5	68		73-4	2.14*	83
4.4-6	60	13.2-4	68;181	26.11*	74	3.3, 4*,6	
5.3-7	60-1;	14.2,8,11		26.13-18			83
	167;		69;		75;	4.1	83
	181		117;		155	5.2,3	84
6.4	47		181-2	27.4-7	76	6.2,3	84
7.3	181	15.4,5	69	29.1-3*	116	7.2*	84

8.5	85	20.1-4	93	29.1-5	100	36.1-3	105
9.1-4	85	21.1,2	94	30.1*	101	37.2	105;
10.1,2	85	22.1-6	94	30.1-5	101		275
12.1	86	23.1-6	95	31.2-10	102	38.5	106
13.3-8	86-8	24.1-5	95	32.1-3	103	39.2	106
14.2*	88	25.1-6	96	32.4*	103	42.5,6	107
14.15	88	25.4*	95	33.5	103	43.3	107
16.1-6	90	26.1-8	97	34	103	44.3,4	108
17	90	27.1-4	99	35.1-4	104	45.1-5	109
18.3	91	27.3	100	35.5*	104		
19.3-11	92;93	28.1-9	100	35.6,7	104		

Dark Night

Book One		3.3	123	13.11*	138	22.1	148
3.1-3	48;49	4.1,2	124	16.4-5	139	23.8	153
	50	5.1-7	124	16.7,9,13,14		23.1-14	
8.2,3	50	6.1-6	126		140		151
9.3,4	50;51	7.4-7	127;	17.1-8	141;	24.1-4	152
9.6,7,8	51		184		142	25.1-4*	
10.1,3,4,6		8.1-5	128	18.1-5	143		152
	52	9.3-9	129-31	19.1-5	144		
12.6;13;14		11	134	20.1-6	145;		
	53	11.4*	134		146		
		12.1-7	135-36	20.2*	147		
Book Two		13.5*	137	20.3	183		
3.1	54	13.1-10	138	21.1-12	148		

Living Flame of Love

Prologue		4-6	188	14	189	Stanza Two	
	187	8	205	15-17	190	1	195
		9	162;	18	190	2-4	196
Stanza One			189	23-26	190	12-1	198
1.1	187	10	115;	27- 28	191	17-22	200
1.10	114;		156	30-31	192	27-28	201
	153	12*	153	35-36	193	31	219

32-33   157
33-36   202

Stanza Three
2   203
8-10   205

14-22   206-7
25-26   173; 208
27   218
30-32   299
42-55   300

57-59   301
68-69   209
76   210
78-79   162; 179
79-84   212

Stanza Four
1-14   215
14-16   162
16   216
17   217

Spiritual Canticle

Prologue
3   234
4   236
Stanza
1   29
1.14   238
1.17   239
1.20   239
Stanza
6.4.1   172
Stanza
11.3   167
Stanza
12.2   182
12 (11).4   247
Stanza
13.2   177; 239
13 (12).4-12   247-8
13.7   175
Stanza
14(13)   248
14(13).2   183; 248

14(13).5   248
14(13).5-11   249
14(13).12-18   249
14(13).23, 24   250

Stanza
15(14)
2   248
50-51   250-1
Stanza
16.2   251
16.6   252
Stanza
17.5   262
17.8   264
17(26).10   253
Stanza
18(31).4   254
Stanza
20(29).10   255

Stanza
21(30).15   256
Stanza
22.2   177
22,4   256; 261
Stanza
23(28)   257
Stanza
25(16).2,7   261
Stanza
26(17).3,5   262
26.14-19   263
Stanza
27.8   264
Stanza
28.1   264
28.2-8   264
Stanza
29.2   265
29.5-11   265
32.1-9   266

33.1-8   267
35.5-6   267
36.6-13   268
37.3-4   268
38.3   269
38.5-8   270
39.3-4   270
39.8-12   271
39.12-14   272
40.5-7   272

Romances

9   272-3

*Letters &
Misc. Works*

Letter 7 (6)
    277
Letter 9 (8)
    278
Letter 11 (10)
    277
Letter 12 (11)
    278
Letter 13 (12)
    91
Letter 16 (15)
    278
Letter 17
    245
Letter 19 (19)
    279

Letter 24
    283
Letter 25 (21)
    279;
    305
Letter 26
    305
Letter 31
    307

Sentences

Avisos
76-78   281-2
80-81,
    83-84
        281-2
123   269
286, 287
        288-9
355-56 296
Otros Avisos (2)
7   294

Maxims

Dictamen
1,2   282
Dictamen
5   283
Dictamen
10-1   284
Dictamen
13   304

*Sayings
of Light
and Love*

Sayings
4, 14, 54
    281
Saying
165   281

*Censure
and Opinion*
    280

*Counsels to
a Religious*

4, 6   281

Precaution
    281

Index of Texts
from Other Authors

ST. TERESA OF AVILA

Book of the Foundations
Chap. 13.1,3   285
       14.7-8   285-6

Interior Castle
       I.1   159

Fifth Dwelling Place
       V.1.6   170
       V.1.9-11   167;170-1;177
       V.1.10   167
       V.1.12   170
       V.2.9,12   170-1
       V.3   170-1

Sixth Dwelling Place
       VI.4.1   172
       VI.6   177
       VI. 9-11   177
       VI. 12   175

Seventh Dwelling Place
       VII. 1.5   162;177;179

Letters
To M. Ana de Jesús,
Oct. 1578   175

Life
Chap. 29, 13-14 196-7

Spiritual Testimonies
No. 31   310

AQUINAS, ST. THOMAS

De Veritate
8, a 8 ad 7; a 11 c
                114;143
9, a 10, 2 corp. 114;160
14, a 7, ad 7   115
19, a 2 c   143

AUGUSTINE, ST.

De Trinitate, XII 4, 7
                114;176

Tract. in Joannem, 11-12
                176

BARUZI, JEAN

Les Textes, Vol. 1
                173

St. Jean   288

BRUNO, O.C.D.

St. John of the Cross
                285;290;301;
                303;321-331

EDICIÓN CRÍTICA. VOL. 3

Otros Dictamenes
                70;291;300

PSEUDO-DIONYSIUS

Mystica Theologia, I, 1
                35;66;121;241

De Caelesti Hierarchia, 3.3
                283

De Divinis Nominibus, II, 2
                35

Other Volumes in the
Collected Works of Edith Stein Series
Available from ICS Publications

Vol. 1: *Life in a Jewish Family.* Edited by L. Gelber and Romaeus Leuven. Translated by Josephine Koeppel (1986).

Vol. 2: *Essays on Woman.*Edited by L. Gelber and Romaeus Leuven. Translated by Freda Mary Oben. 2d edition, revised (1996).

Vol. 3: *On the Problem of Empathy.* Translated by Waltraut Stein. 3d revised edition (1989).

Vol. 4: *The Hidden Life.* Edited by L. Gelber and Michael Linssen. Translated by Waltraut Stein (1992).

Vol. 5: *Self-Portrait in Letters.* Edited by L. Gelber and Romaeus Leuven. Translated by Josephine Koeppel (1993).

Vol. 7: *Philosophy of Psychology and the Humanities.* Translated by Mary Catharine Baseheart and Marianne Sawicki (2000).

Vol. 8: *Knowledge and Faith.* Edited by L. Gelber and M. Linssen. Translated by Walter Redmond (2000).

Vol. 9: *Finite and Eternal Being.* Edited by L. Gelber and R. Leuven. Translated by Kurt F. Reinhardt (2002).

Other Works About Edith Stein
Available from ICS Publications

Herbstrith, Waltraud, ed. *Never Forget: Christian and Jewish Perspectives on Edith Stein.* Translated by Susanne Batzdorff. Carmelite Studies 7 (1998).

Neyer, Amata. *Edith Stein: Her Life in Photos and Documents.* Translated by Waltraut Stein (1999).

Sullivan, John, ed. *Holiness Befits Your House: Canonization of Edith Stein—A Documentation* (2000).

The Institue of Carmelite Studies promotes research and publication in the field of Carmelite spirituality. Its members are Discalced Carmelites, part of a Roman Catholic community—friars, nuns, and laity—who are heirs to the teaching and way of life of Teresa of Jesus and John of the Cross, men and women dedicated to contemplation and to ministry in the church and the world. Information concerning their way of life is available through local diocesan Vocation Offices, or from the Vocation Directors' offices:

2131 Lincoln Road, NE, Washington, DC 20002-1199

P.O. Box 3420, San Jose, CA 95156-3420

5151 Marylake Drive, Little Rock AR 72206-9436